FUTURES IN PUBLIC MANAGEMENT

What a fascinating read to anyone in and between the practice and policy of public services, especially in the contexts of health, care and welfare! This thought-provoking edited collection increases much-needed understanding on how relational approach can foster a public management paradigm shift to better address the complex societal challenges of our societies. Importantly, the relational approach provides insights into the complex, dynamic and interconnected systems of practice and policy of public services.

—***Paula Rossi*, Senior Researcher,**
School of Management, University of Vaasa

We are at an inflection point in the future of public services and public service reform. The Emerging Relational Approach to Public Services is required reading for anyone interested in how we may learn from the failures of the New Public Management era to shape a period characterised by innovative relational approaches to designing and delivering public services. Wilson and colleagues' work is at the bleeding edge of such thinking.

—***Michael J. Roy*, Professor of Social Innovation**
and Sustainable Organisations/Associate Dean (Research and Innovation),
Stirling Management School, University of Stirling, UK

This book presents new international evidence on the relational approach to public services. It offers a refreshing analysis of what it takes to create an alternative basis for public management, both in theory and in practice.

—***Taco Brandsen*, Chair of Public Administration,**
Radboud University

There is a growing consensus that radical change is needed in the purpose, form and function of public policy and governance. The authors suggest that New Public Governance perspectives have generated unintended consequences which have 'solidified NPM in practice, rather than supplanting it'. It brings together international evidence and new perspectives on relational approaches to public management. This book plants the relational 'standard' in both the theoretical and practice field.

—***Peter Murphy*, Director of the Public Policy and**
Management Research Group, Centre for Economics, Policy and
Public Management, Nottingham Trent University

The time for relational public services is now. This rich and ambitious book provides essential conceptual and practical guidance for public managers, practitioners, and academics to co-create public services in an interconnected world.

—***Dr Koen Bartels*, Associate Professor, University of Birmingham**

This book is essential reading for anyone who wants to understand how to improve public services in a context of complexity and a growing demand for more relational approaches.

—***Dr Rick Muir*, Director of the Police Foundation**

This book makes a refreshing and compelling case for the need to move beyond New Public Management and fully embrace a relational approach to public management. It highlights the limitations and shortfall of existing ways of working and proposes an alternative approach, one that privileges relationships above all else, and as key to achieving better, effective and meaningful social outcomes. The book serves as a call to action for policymakers, practitioners, and academics to engage in a serious collaborative effort to redefine public service delivery underpinned and grounded in relational principles. It will take us all to make this happen and I for one am grateful for the academic expertise so carefully represented here.

—***Kristy Docherty*, Director of Public Services and Sector Engagement Lead, Co-Director of the Scottish Prevention Hub, Edinburgh Futures Institute**

Futures in Public Management is a must-read for anyone grappling with the limitations of transactional governance and searching for more effective, human-centred alternatives. It makes a compelling case for relational approaches as a fundamentally different way of thinking about public services, policy, and outcomes. This book brings together critical insights and practical examples that challenge conventional wisdom and offer a way forward for those of us working to reshape public management in service of real, meaningful change. Essential reading for policymakers, practitioners, and anyone invested in the future of public services.

—***Dr Luke Craven*, Chief Executive Officer, Partnerships for Local Action and Community Empowerment (PLACE)**

Futures in Public Management: The Emerging Relational Approach to Public Services critically re-evaluates the role of public management in an era where public services are increasingly challenged by complex, interdependent issues. The authors engage in a timely and essential debate on the limitations of the New Public Management paradigm, advocating for a more relational approach that

The time for relational public services is now. This rich and ambitious book provides essential conceptual and practical guidance for public managers, practitioners, and academics to co-create public services in an interconnected world.

—***Dr Koen Bartels*, Associate Professor, University of Birmingham**

This book is essential reading for anyone who wants to understand how to improve public services in a context of complexity and a growing demand for more relational approaches.

—***Dr Rick Muir*, Director of the Police Foundation**

This book makes a refreshing and compelling case for the need to move beyond New Public Management and fully embrace a relational approach to public management. It highlights the limitations and shortfall of existing ways of working and proposes an alternative approach, one that privileges relationships above all else, and as key to achieving better, effective and meaningful social outcomes. The book serves as a call to action for policymakers, practitioners, and academics to engage in a serious collaborative effort to redefine public service delivery underpinned and grounded in relational principles. It will take us all to make this happen and I for one am grateful for the academic expertise so carefully represented here.

—***Kristy Docherty*, Director of Public Services and Sector Engagement Lead, Co-Director of the Scottish Prevention Hub, Edinburgh Futures Institute**

Futures in Public Management is a must-read for anyone grappling with the limitations of transactional governance and searching for more effective, human-centred alternatives. It makes a compelling case for relational approaches as a fundamentally different way of thinking about public services, policy, and outcomes. This book brings together critical insights and practical examples that challenge conventional wisdom and offer a way forward for those of us working to reshape public management in service of real, meaningful change. Essential reading for policymakers, practitioners, and anyone invested in the future of public services.

—***Dr Luke Craven*, Chief Executive Officer, Partnerships for Local Action and Community Empowerment (PLACE)**

Futures in Public Management: The Emerging Relational Approach to Public Services critically re-evaluates the role of public management in an era where public services are increasingly challenged by complex, interdependent issues. The authors engage in a timely and essential debate on the limitations of the New Public Management paradigm, advocating for a more relational approach that fosters transformative and effective public service delivery. Drawing on international empirical evidence, the editorial team have integrated contemporary public management theories, including Human Learning Systems and Complexity Theory of Outcome Creation, to offer fresh insights into navigating modern governance challenges. This book is a crucial resource for public management scholars, policymakers and practitioners seeking to advance service innovation, embrace complexity and enhance the impact of public services on citizens' lives.

—***Dr Katri-Liis Lepik*, Associate Professor,**
Tallinn University

CRITICAL PERSPECTIVES ON INTERNATIONAL PUBLIC SECTOR MANAGEMENT

Series Editors: John Diamond and Joyce Liddle

Recent Volumes:

- Volume 1: Emerging and Potential Trends in Public Management: An Age of Austerity
- Volume 2: Looking for Consensus?: Civil Society, Social Movements and Crises for Public Management
- Volume 3: European Public Leadership in Crisis?
- Volume 4: Multi-Level Governance: The Missing Linkages
- Volume 5: Developing Public Managers for a Changing World
- Volume 6: From Austerity to Abundance? Creative Approaches to Coordinating the Common Good
- Volume 7: Reimagining Public Sector Management: A New Age of Renewal and Renaissance?

EDITORIAL ADVISORY BOARD

CRITICAL PERSPECTIVES ON INTERNATIONAL PUBLIC SECTOR MANAGEMENT VOLUME 8

FUTURES IN PUBLIC MANAGEMENT: THE EMERGING RELATIONAL APPROACH TO PUBLIC SERVICES

EDITED BY

ROB WILSON
Manchester Metropolitan University, UK

HANNAH HESSELGREAVES
Manchester Metropolitan University, UK

MAX FRENCH
Northumbria University, UK

MELISSA HAWKINS
Northumbria University, UK

DAVID JAMIESON
Northumbria University, UK

MARTIN KING
Northumbria University, UK

AND

JONATHAN KIMMITT
Durham University, UK

emerald PUBLISHING

United Kingdom – North America – Japan
India – Malaysia – China

Emerald Publishing Limited
Emerald Publishing, Floor 5, Northspring, 21-23 Wellington Street, Leeds LS1 4DL

First edition 2025

British Library Cataloguing in Publication Data
A catalogue record for this book is available from the British Library

ISBN: 978-1-83608-195-1 (Print)
ISBN: 978-1-83608-194-4 (Online)
ISBN: 978-1-83608-196-8 (Epub)

ISSN: 2045-7944 (Series)

Printed and bound by CPI Group (UK) Ltd, Croydon, CR0 4YY

INVESTOR IN PEOPLE

To those who help us to be part of healthy, positive and supportive relationships.

We thank you

CONTENTS

ABOUT THE EDITORS

Rob Wilson is a Professor in the Policy Evaluation Research Unit (PERU) in the Sociology Department at Manchester Metropolitan University having served at Newcastle and Northumbria Universities as a researcher, a Faculty member and a director of a research centre. His interests and expertise are in relational public services and the role of digital systems and platforms to support social innovation.

Hannah Hesselgreaves is a Professor of Public Service Reform and Director of the Policy Evaluation and Research Unit (PERU) at Manchester Metropolitan University. She is an experienced evaluator and has interests in the development of new approaches to relational evaluation which are key to the sustainability of reforms in public sector.

Max French is an Assistant Professor at the Newcastle Business School, Northumbria University. His is expertise is in complexity and outcomes in public service management. He has published widely including a recent book for Policy Press on Complexity for Outcomes.

Melissa Hawkins is an Assistant Professor at the Newcastle Business School, Northumbria University. Her expertise is in learning and action research in public sector particularly the role of learning partners and partnering for reflection and improvement.

David Jamieson is an Assistant Professor at the Newcastle Business School, Northumbria University. His expertise is in information and data in public services including the role of digital platforms.

Martin King is a Lecturer at the Newcastle Business School, Northumbria University. His areas of expertise include deliberative democracy, particularly the challenges and opportunities of digital tools, and leadership in public sector.

Jonathan Kimmitt is a Professor of Entrepreneurship, Business School at Durham University. He is interested in social innovation and entrepreneurship including the tools and mechanisms for funding entrepreneurs and social action.

ABOUT THE CONTRIBUTORS

Emily Burn is a Research Fellow at the Centre for Care, an Economic and Social Research Council Centre which works to develop our understanding of care. She is based at the University of Birmingham. Currently, Emily is exploring what characteristics of local social care ecosystems lead to flourishing and improved outcomes for people drawing on care and support.

Lowis Charfe is a Senior Lecturer at the University of Central Lancashire within the School of Health, Social Work and Sport and a member of ThemPra. She teaches on a range of course within the department. She is passionate about using social pedagogy as a way of supporting organizational and cultural change. Her previous employment background has mainly been located within working with children and young people as a Social Worker. Lowis has an interest in supporting the development of social pedagogy in all areas of social work and social care. Previously, she worked as a qualified social worker in a Leaving Care Team, supporting young care leavers to live independently and Youth Offending Team Officer. She was the co-author of the first social work book to focus on the use of social pedagogical practice: *Social Pedagogy and Social Work* (2019) published by SAGE.

Ron Charlton is the Data and Information Lead for Changing Futures Northumbria creating innovative ways of using data, capturing person centric context informing relational practice. He created the 'burning platform' method articulated in this chapter and developed evaluation measures that provide agile responsive data to iterate relational practice. He is now involved in the development of a unique digital platform with Northumbria University that negates technical expertise to iterate and change with what is learnt. Ron has had a varied career, serving in the army as an aircraft engineer, a national maintenance manager for a well-known ophthalmic company and served 23 years as a police officer, gaining a sound understanding of multiple public services responses to peoples presenting issues that experience complex needs. Also being a main carer for a family member with complex needs, he has first-hand experience of system responses to trying to get needs met in complexity.

Mieke van der Bijl-Brouwer (she/her) is an independent researcher, a teacher and a speaker. Her expertise and interests include design theory and practices for complex societal challenges, systemic design and transdisciplinary practices and education. Mieke has worked in various research, design and education roles across the Netherlands and Australia. Mieke is an adjunct fellow at the Transdisciplinary School at the University of Technology Sydney. She holds a Master of Science in Industrial Design Engineering from Delft University of Technology and a PhD in User-Centred Design from the University of Twente, the Netherlands.

Dixon C. Dick is the Founder and CEO of Archethought Inc. a company formed to align technology solutions with municipal and community-based organizations. Dixon has over 40 years; experience delivering complex solutions from start-up to Enterprise scale, including hardware sensors, networked operating systems, cloud computing, Artificial Intelligence and HPC. Dixon has a Computer Science Engineering degree from the University of Illinois Urbana-Champaign and took graduate coursework from Florida Atlantic University and The University of Houston, including Operating Systems, Network Systems and Neural Networks. His enterprise career includes work with IBM and Compaq Computer on today's dominant PC and network platforms. As a start-up founder, Dixon developed a patent for assured delivery of data across public internet over multi-modal circuits using public key infrastructures. He is a Visiting Fellow in Computer Science and Environment with the University of Northumbria, collaborating on the development of trustworthy and governable platforms for human communication.

Peter Horsselenberg has been working as a researcher at the Professional Agency research group of the Amsterdam University of Applied Sciences since 2014. He is also affiliated with the consultancy firm BDSi and a number of MBA courses in the field of organizational behaviour, personal leadership, team coaching and thesis supervision. He has consultancy and research experience in organizational behaviour, team behaviour and professional behaviour. His research focuses on the collective agency of professional teams, with a focus on the role of professional dialogue in strengthening collective agency.

Gianni Jacucci has retired as a Professor of Organization and the former Chair of Information Engineering, at the University of Trento. He has had a long career in Organizational Intervention for the Adoption of Information Infrastructures, and he is still active in the field. His Laboratory for the Social Study of Information Systems has developed the Social Practice Design approach to support organizational change during technology innovation, applied to several dozen instances in organizations, institutions and companies.

Deborah James is a Professor of Educational Psychology. She is the Deputy Pro Vice Chancellor for Health and Social Care at Manchester Metropolitan University. She did her undergraduate degree in Speech Science at UCL in the 1990s, graduating with a first-class degree and a licence to practice as a speech and language therapist. Classified as 'non-standard entry' at UCL, with two shabby A levels in English Lit. and Theatre Studies and Grade D in Maths, interactions with four years of excellent teaching at UCL sparked a love of science and a belief in education as a leveller of equality. Her PhD in psychology at the Institute of Child Health explored the impact of sensorineural hearing impairment on language and reading in Deaf/deaf children. She has been working within a strengths-based paradigm, using video feedback with families and workforces around children with complex needs for nearly two decades across health, social care and education.

Marlieke Kieboom (she/her, MA, MSc) is an anthropologist with specializations in conflict studies and complex emergency management. Marlieke worked as a researcher, designer and social innovator across Europe and Canada, always fostering cross-organizational collaborations and transformative change. Her expertise includes systemic design, service design and building infrastructures that foster the well-being of communities, places and nature. She believes in the power of open, creative and community-led design to create equitable and regenerative futures. Marlieke is currently a Design Director with the Public Service of British Columbia, Canada | Turtle Island.

Roman Kislov is a Professor of Health Policy and Management in the Faculty of Business and Law at Manchester Metropolitan University and Deputy Theme Lead for Implementation Science in the NIHR Applied Research Collaboration Greater Manchester. He serves as Secretary of the Society for Studies in Organizing Healthcare (SHOC) and holds visiting positions at the University of Manchester and Queensland University of Technology. Roman conducts qualitative research into the processes and practices of knowledge mobilization, with a particular interest in boundary management, collective leadership and implementation of change. Prior to pursuing an academic career, he worked as a doctor for a gold mining company in Central Asia. Roman's work has appeared in *Human Relations, Organization Studies, Public Administration Review, Public Administration* and *Public Management Review.* He is a lead editor of *Managing Healthcare Organisations in Challenging Policy Contexts* and a co-author of a Cambridge Element on *Implementation Science.*

Michael Macaulay is a Professor of Public Administration at Victoria University of Wellington (NZ) and has previously held professorial positions in the United Kingdom and South Africa. He has held numerous editorial posts for international public administration journals and has worked with many government agencies and NGOs around the world, including the United Nations Office on Drugs and Crime (UNODC), the Council of Europe and Transparency International. Michael has developed online integrity training for the Australia Public Service Commission and has co-authored evaluations on NZ Police and the Public Services Commission. He advised the Public Service Commission on the Public Service Act 2020 and has helped craft the reforms to the Protected Disclosures Act 2022. Michael is currently the Chair of NZ Police's expert advisory panel on emergent technologies.

Joy MacKeith is the co-creator of Triangle's Outcomes Star suite of tools and co-founder of Triangle, the social enterprise that exists to support their use. Prior to founding Triangle, she was a Director at Compass Partnership providing consultancy services to the third sector and government and a researcher at the London School of Economics where she laid the foundations for their successful Masters in NGO Management. She began her working life at the Simon

Community, working in community with people who were previously street homeless. She is a songwriter, focusing practitioner and mindfulness teacher and has written and spoken widely about the Outcomes Star and relational approaches to measurement and public services. She is the author of 'Enabling Help: How social provision can work better for the people it services'. Joy stood down as the Director of Triangle in 2023 and now works freelance as a writer and researcher.

Mike Martin is a Professor of Enterprise Information Sciences at Newcastle Business School, Northumbria University. He has had a long career in Industrial Research in the European Computer and Telecommunications sectors. He has spent the last three decades trying to understand why the IT infrastructures to support care and well-being services, especially in multi-organizational settings, invariably fail to meet expectations and usually impede progress and cooperation.

Jennifer Eckford McCabe is a Strategic Support Lead at Pathfinder Birmingham. Her role involves fundraising, communications and operational work to ensure the Pathfinder team are supported in their work with families. Jenny's background is originally in environmental work: she's worked in areas ranging from environmental youth work at a city farm, to working in Birmingham City Council sustainability team gathering data on carbon emissions. More recently, she trained as a science teacher, and when she's not working for the Pathfinder, she is teaching at Elmfield Steiner school in Stourbridge. She is also in the final stages of study for a doctorate in education.

Rob McCabe is the Strategic Lead and CIC Director for Pathfinder Birmingham. He has 33 years' experience in social care. Following a Diploma in Social Work and BA (Hons) European Social Work Degree, Rob started out in residential care and support roles within schools and further education, subsequently working as an education social worker and manager in the Youth Offending Service, before beginning work on developing the Birmingham Pathfinder. His passion is centred on ensuring that Pathfinder involves listening, talking, thinking, rethinking, advice-taking, laughing and lots of appreciating the amazing people around him.

Giampaolo Montaletti holds a PhD from Bologna University and is a Visiting Research Fellow at the Northumbria University. He has extensive experience in policy implementation including working on a range of Italian Government and EU commission funded programmes for the Italian Chambers of Commerce and the Regional Government of Lombardy on Active Labour Market Programmes (ALMPs). He is highly experienced in strategic frameworks development and budget management, as well as design and construction of new policy instrument and has significant expertise in statistical analysis. His current interests are in theoretical and experimental public policy design and evaluation.

Donald E. Nease, Jr, is a Professor of Family Medicine at the University of Colorado – Anschutz Medical Campus, where he serves as the Director of Community Engagement and Health Equity for the Colorado Clinical and

Translational Sciences Institute. He completed his undergraduate degree and medical school at the University of Kansas, residency training in Family Medicine at the Medical University of South Carolina in Charleston and a Faculty Development Fellowship at the University of North Carolina – Chapel Hill. Dr. Nease's passion is to improve health in partnership with communities, patients, clinicians and healthcare. He works this territory from the level of individual interactions to community and population-based interventions. https://orcid.org/0000-0001-8323-3720.

Catherine Needham is a Professor of Public Policy and Public Management at the Health Services Management Centre, University of Birmingham. She is a Co-Investigator in the ESRC Centre for Care. Her research focuses on social care (including personalization, co-production, personal budgets, older people, care workforce, care markets). She has published a wide range of articles, chapters and books for academic and practitioner audiences. Her most recent book was published by Policy Press in 2023 and entitled *Social Care in the UK's Four Nations: Between two Paradigms*.

Christianne Ormston is a Visiting Fellow at Newcastle Business School at Northumbria University alongside working across involvement and commissioning roles at North East and North Cumbria Integrated Care Board (NENC ICB). Christianne is an experienced academic researcher, public involvement and policy professional, with significant experience in health commissioning, public participation, strategy development and engagement-based roles across a range of public sector organizations and within universities.

Bruno Sobral is a systems thinker with significant executive experience building and managing research institutes, scientific research strategy and implementation and execution of such strategies, in academic, corporate and non-profit research environments. Professor Sobral has over 30 years of experience building and managing research institutes and leading interactions between wet lab and computational scientists with the goals of scientific discovery and informatics infrastructure design, development, deployment and evolution. In the last 5 years, Professor Sobral has increasingly focused on social infrastructure co-design, development and implementation in increasingly participatory action research models, from a salutogenic perspective, leading with community ownership and motivated by equity and acting through curb-cutting co-design.

Daniel van Middelkoop is a Professor of Professional Agency at the Amsterdam University of Applied Sciences in the Netherlands. Together with his research group, he uses an action research approach to study and actively strengthen the agency of cooperating professionals and craftsmen. He relates the need for professional agency to the need for and capacity of professionals and craftsmen to deliver 'good work'. He also leads the Work Lab and is a leading Professor in the Centre for Economic Transformation, a research group in which the transformation of work is researched on the level of (cooperating) professionals and craftsmen, organizations and the labour market.

Kate Wicker is a Research Associate in the School of Education at Manchester Metropolitan University. Her interests are in evidence-based policy and practice, particularly in terms of understanding the mechanisms and impacts of social programmes. She is currently working across multiple large-scale and mixed-method evaluations of educational interventions in primary and secondary school settings in the United Kingdom. Kate did her PhD on the nature of expertise and its role in policy debates at the University of Leeds.

FOREWORD

Writing this foreword is a delight for me because after spending 20 years trying to work ever more relationally in public services as a consultant and local authority director, the people who bring you this collection of insights have been instrumental in helping me understand what relationality is and critically how to learn and iterate more effectively.

In recent years as Director of Public Service Reform at Gateshead Council and the lead for Changing Futures Northumbria, I've been leading the development of the 'Liberated Method'. It's a relational approach to supporting people who are struggling and to supporting public sector leaders/workers that are lost in or hiding from the understanding of complexity and emergence needed to be effective. This work has seen lives turned around from crisis after many years bouncing around the public service ecosystem at huge cost whilst things got worse. It's also seen demand reduce into critical services who can then be liberated to work more preventatively and proactively. Like many other relational approaches that innovators are doggedly developing, this stuff works.

For many years, I couldn't put my finger on why it worked and why public services weren't grabbing this work with both hands. So, I sought help from the good people across the river at my local university who I'd noticed were asking similar questions.

Through this enquiry, I came to know and befriend some of the authors of this book. Rob Wilson and Hannah Hesselgreaves have both, in their contrasting and complementary ways, helped me experience epiphany after epiphany without ever themselves professing to know any of the answers. I was quite prepared to be outthought and overawed by academics blessed with big brains and time to think but I was game to try to keep up and hang on, but I've instead learnt that there is a mutuality, indeed a relationality between practice and academia that can be beautiful. I think this book brings that to life.

Rob's focus on human and system interaction and Hannah's focus on learning as a leadership focus have transformed my thinking, my work and its prospects. They've learnt with me rather than instructed me, and in doing so, we've come to understand more about relationality in public service (and what it is up against).

There are two epiphanies that I think this book foregrounds, the first being the simple and profound truth that if you're not learning alongside somebody then you're not working relationally with them and the second is that a focus upon learning is more productive that a focus upon productivity.

That second one blows my mind. Think of all those transformation programs that are efficiency driven, focusing hard on structure and flow and often illusory predictability. For anything requiring context and nuance, which is to say anything that matters to anyone, this axiom is a public service reform game changer.

As is this book, which offers breadth and depth in the exploration of relational public service that speaks to both its innate and necessary complexity and its unifying coda, which is that transactions should be subordinate to or contextualized by relationships. This book is important and comes at an important time because the opposite is far more observable in public services, i.e. any relationality is often within the confines of the transaction or standardized process – relationality has been essentially relegated to being largely an issue of style or tone (customer charters are visible examples of this).

There is a growing cautious optimism, in the United Kingdom certainly and as this book shows far beyond, that the game could be up for this line of thinking. Austerity and a focus on efficiency and standardization has created a pattern of growing consumption and failure demand which is unignorable and has been exacerbated by disinvestment in community services and social care. Public services in their current form are running out of road. This book is important as it offers hope of a better alternative through credible practice and evidence.

My sense from this book and my experiences with several of its editors and authors is that the hope goes beyond the method and into the community of practice. Relational practice is weirdly rife, weird because it's intuitive and observable in so many places but remains largely the preserve of the project or prototype. The solidity of the work, the profundity of the learning and the generosity of the sharing make this book a valuable resource for the e mission to move from transactional to relationally oriented services.

The editors of this book have understood the importance of the alliance needed to move the dial and have skilfully reflected that in this broad view of relational practice. Their contribution to building this community through such means as the Human Learning Systems collaborative and their Relational Public Service conferences places them well to bring all of these terrific examples together.

My delight in writing this foreword stems from my growing confidence and understanding that anyone can locate and develop their practice in the pages of this book. A caseworker with a sample of one can meaningfully explore their experience of relationality and its role in their successes and frustrations as validly as me, any of the authors and anyone else. The entry requirement is to be human and curious.

This book shows well that relational public service is more effective and that the road to normalising it is paved with complexity and emergence. Yet it also shows that relational working is as old as time and anyone can do it. I'm often asked where to start, and this book only goes to confirm the answer to this: start anywhere and go everywhere.

Mark Smith,
Independent Public Service Consultant and
Visiting Professor at PERU in Manchester Metropolitan University

PREFACE

Public services are something that ought to extend far beyond mere administrative efficiency or routine service delivery. Yet this is something that has become overlooked in the rush to modernize, rationalize, streamline and channel shift service provision into predictable and straightforward linear delivery. At the heart of an effective public service lies one fundamental element: the possibility of relationships. Whether it's the interaction between citizens and their local governments, between organizations and their employees, between service providers and the communities they serve or between citizens and communities, the ability to build and maintain positive, trust-based relationships is crucial to progress and meaningful change.

This book seeks to explore the emerging international landscape of relational public service through a range of contexts from Colorado in the United States, the Lombardy region of Italy, to the cities of Manchester and Birmingham in the United Kingdom to British Columbia, Canada. It examines how public service agencies can shift from traditional, transactional models to more relational approaches – where understanding, empathy and collaboration drive decision-making, policy implementation and day-to-day operations. By recognizing the inherent value of relationships in public service, we open the door to more inclusive, responsive and sustainable systems that reflect the needs, voices and aspirations of all stakeholders.

Throughout this book, we explore key concepts and strategies that redefine how public servants and organizations can learn to foster deep, lasting interconnections between service providers and the public. Our chapter authors demonstrate through their work the successes and challenges of relational approaches in various public service sectors, from healthcare, welfare, and education to social services. They also highlight the challenges of sustaining and scaling relationality and the opportunities that this brings in rethinking how we can innovate the ecology and platforms we currently have. These examples serve as a testament and a provocation to cultivate a future of relationship-centred service delivery.

The journey through this book is not just about theory; it's about practical insights that can inspire public servants, policymakers, citizens and even academics to rethink how we engage with one another, with empathy, respect and a shared commitment to our common good.

As we move towards a future where collaboration, inclusion and trust are paramount, the principles outlined here offer inspiration for how public services can evolve to meet the challenges of the 21st century.

We invite you to explore these ideas with an open mind, a spirit of inquiry and a willingness to engage in the kind of relationships that can shape a more equitable, compassionate and responsive public service for all.

ACKNOWLEDGEMENTS

The Editorial Team would like to acknowledge our conversations with and wisdom of the scholars and practitioners who have supported the development of the Relational Public Services community including those who have attended the conferences in Newcastle-upon-Tyne in 2023 and 2024 and the IRSPM Stream on Relational Public Management and Social Complexity in Bologna, 2025.

INTRODUCTION: FUTURES IN PUBLIC MANAGEMENT: IS THERE AN EMERGING RELATIONAL APPROACH TO PUBLIC SERVICES?

Rob Wilson[a], Hannah Hesselgreaves[a], Max French[b], Melissa Hawkins[b], David Jamieson[b], Martin King[b] and Jonathan Kimmitt[c]

[a]*Manchester Metropolitan University, UK*
[b]*Northumbria University, UK*
[c]*Durham University, UK*

ABSTRACT

This introductory section aims to set the scene for this edited collection by situating the discussion of relational public management within a historical context alongside current discussions in policy and practice. The following assortment of chapters draws from the burgeoning academic and practice literature and draws on the experiences and insights provided by the contributing authors to provide a unique range of perspectives surrounding the emergence of relational thinking in public services. These are loosely collated into three areas: action learning approaches to public service development in practice, new approaches to understanding outcomes and the measures and forms of outcome measurement and academically framed debates that provide potential organizing frameworks as lens for thinking about relationality in public service.

Keywords: Public administration; public management; international public management; relational public services; relational public management; new public management; transactionality; action research; public service innovation; public service reform

Futures in Public Management
Critical Perspectives on International Public Sector Management, Volume 8, 1–11

Published under exclusive licence by Emerald Publishing Limited
ISSN: 2045-7944/doi:10.1108/S2045-794420250000008001

INTRODUCTION

Public management is facing a crisis both in terms of its legitimacy and its effectiveness. Social innovations that centre on relationships as both the sought outcome for social cohesion and the means of tackling societies big challenges are giving public management direction about how to change. Public services, funded and designed to achieve valued social outcomes ranging from educational attainment to public health to environmental sustainability, now require movement in delivery, management, policy, and scholarship to sustain the public outcomes that innovations in those services are creating (Bartels et al., 2024; Bartels & Turnbull, 2020; Wilson et al., 2024). Creating outcomes that matter to the public is becoming an increasingly complex task in an ever more trying climate. An underlying inertia resulting from the ongoing application of an orthodoxy of a rationalistic and transactional stance to public service reform which proliferated in the New Public Management (NPM) era risks an opportunity to be reformative across all the levers of social change. The gift of desperation felt by some social reformers has started to signal what can be changed *in spite* of necessary and responsive innovations in policy, commissioning, inspection, accountability, leadership and measurement. However, these reforms also demonstrate how public management can be evolved across the public sector and also how relationality can be absorbed into the leadership and management practices of public service. In this book, we bring together new evidence and perspectives from the worlds of relational public practice, data science and academia, with the aim of landing the case for a significant reappraisal of public management and public policy.

NPM offers a case study of how effective it is to develop a confluence of internally consistent public service practice, outcome measurement practices and academic debate in establishing a stronghold for social policy. NPM placed an emphasis on management, markets and measurements being applied to public service management and social interventions on the basis that they should be commissioned, contracted, managed and evaluated. It was believed that adoption of NPM would move public services away from a bureaucratic compliance model with poorly aligned incentives between stakeholders to one which aligned the divergent interests of policymakers, public managers, public servants and citizens thereby releasing the latent energy of innovation and entrepreneurship in the system towards shared goals at a stroke. NPM would use measurement to release information to enable market forces by managing performance, enabling citizen choice, improving competition between providers and driving out inefficiency in service offers. The language of government at all levels – international, national and local – is littered with ‘programmes’ aimed at the ‘modernisation’, ‘transformation’ or ‘improvement’ of services with limited effect on the services and lives of citizens or the social impact themes they purport to change, including reducing inequalities (for example health, pay, gender), economic growth and better institutional accountability.

Governments, philanthropic and non-profit organizations around the world have been increasingly adopting a transactional approach in the design of policy and the management of public services, the implications of which have been subjected to increasing scrutiny within public administration (Boyne & Law, 2005; Heinrich, 2002; Lowe, 2013; Lowe et al., 2020; Lowe & Wilson, 2017; Wimbush, 2011). Yet wherever such a transactional approach has been applied, be it within performance management, budgeting, commissioning or outcomes, its achievements have fallen short of expectation and need more importantly.

There is a growing consensus that radical change is needed in the purpose, form and function of public administration and governance. This rationalist approach (French et al., 2023) has manifestly failed to deliver on the promises made. Unsurprisingly, after over 40 years of these reforms being in place, there is a significant body of critique from academia and practice perspectives on issues created by marketization and performance management (Bevan & Hood, 2006; Lowe, 2013; Lowe & Wilson, 2017; Pell et al. 2016, 2020; Van Thiel & Leeuw, 2002), including problems of measurement and attribution (Bovaird, 2014; Jamieson et al., 2020; Lowe, 2013; Perrin, 2006; Wilson et al., 2011; Wimbush, 2011). Attempts to declare NPM deceased have been made before notably New Public Governance (Osborne, 2006) which attempts to bridge activities into a more collaborative stakeholder space; Public Value which sought to ascribe a wider set of values to organizations interventions and investment (Moore, 1995) and Digital Era Governance (Dunleavy et al., 2006) which emphasizes the use of information to simultaneously create horizontal agility, reduce bureaucratic load (including costs) and afford improvements in control of outsourced elements. These appear to have generated unintended consequences in that they have solidified NPM in practice rather than supplanting it (French et al. 2022, 2023). The persistence of NPM is indeed remarkable and the pervasiveness of its accounting methods have shaped the environment to be self-referential conditioning what can be set out both as policy objectives and their achievement in its own image (Lapsley & Miller, 2024). Such is the power of this conditioning that coherent alternative narrative to neoliberalism which seizes the imagination and binds together the lived experiences of practitioners, citizens and communities and the needs of those working in policy and politics have yet to meaningfully sustain (Clarke & Newman, 2024).

However, we have seen the emergence more recently of programmatic experiments in Public Service Innovation/Social Innovation. At the state level, the emergence of the relational approach to public management has been in development for approximately a decade. The spread of narratives surrounding relational practices are emergent in academia particularly in the United Kingdom and North America (Lamph et al., 2023) in what has been described as a relational 'turn' in public administration (Bartels & Turnbull, 2020) and sustainability science (West et al., 2020). This corresponds with a re-energized narrative of relational public service reform in the UK 'think tank' discourse drawing on innovations in practice to offer a range of future directions for government with many common recommendations of investing in local assets and community and citizen empowerment (Wilson et al., 2024). The initial framing of this discourse emanated from the UK-based policy think tank of the Institute of Public Policy Research (IPPR) in collaboration with Geoff Mulgan, which included the publication of two reports exploring the 'relational state' (Cooke & Muir, 2012; Muir & Parker, 2014). These reports and syntheses generated significant debate at that time about the direction of the state particularly in the strategy and investments required to make the state more 'relational'. The recommendations emphasized the need to work with communities to improve the relevance and impact of proposed programmes and build capacities of local assets. Since these initial explorations, significant policy trajectories have been proffered, demanding government and public service to be local and community-based rather than distant and centralized (Lent & Studdert, 2019), staffed in the main by generalists rather than specialists (Needham & Mangan, 2014), co-productive and co-creative with stakeholders instead of paternalistic and bureaucratic approaches (Bartels, 2020; Baines et al., 2024), capable of harnessing systems thinking and complexity rather than attempting to simplify matters (Hobbs, 2019; Lowe et al., 2022) and built around human rather than structural and transactional relationships (Cottam, 2018; Heimburg & Ness, 2021).

At the public management level, the relational public service design in the form of participatory design processes, relational leadership, and relational commissioning and contracting, has been necessarily bound not to policy directives from legislative or political work but to the work of public service innovation in practice. It indicates a refreshing shift towards policymaking and public management decisions being inherent in the service work enacted with the public and therefore is innately relational. Relational public service is intrinsically self-governable and accountable by its capacity and capability to be iterative and dynamic (French et al., 2023; Teece et al., 1997). Relational practice demonstrates how public servants adopt stewardship capability (creating permissive environments to stay on purpose and promote informed responsiveness within and across boundaries), coordinative capability (integrating and mobilizing resources for effective systemic responses) and adaptive capability (centring learning as the strategic core of management practice). These capabilities, enacted in public service, offer strong indications about what is required of policymakers, commissioners, regulators, evaluators and other players in the constellation of public sector functioning and, more notably, reform.

In this book, we provide new international evidence for reappraising public management in policy and practice by bringing together perspectives on relational approaches to public management. Building on current research, policy and practice in a range of applied settings and places, we present an alternative basis for enacting public management: that the objectives for and outcomes sought by institutions working with the public in contexts of health, care and welfare are inherently relational phenomena – they are always complex and cross-boundary, always co-produced by the individuals who experience them through interaction with those who are delivering them in relationship with those providing help and support. This is not enough, however, and for this geographically, professionally and disciplinary disparate body of work to come together, we seek to address the following questions for a burgeoning area of relational public service management:

- How do we now understand the potential trajectories, risks and opportunities in taking relational approaches?
- How can we address the new governance and management requirements of organizations and practice of relational public services?
- What requirements does relational management and public service reform have of new roles and responsibilities for stakeholders?
- What development and capacity building resources, including leadership, organizations and infrastructures, do we need to create to support relational management approaches?
- What is the new agenda for education, research and practice in the coming years?

We do this by considering the building the evidence for relationality across three domains, the intersections of which offer opportunities for an alternative public management paradigm: action learning approaches to public service development in practice; new approaches to understanding outcomes and the measures and forms of outcomes measurement; and three scholarly debates that provide organizing frameworks for viewing relationality in public service.

Action learning provides a framing for Section 1 (the first four chapters). Nease et al. outline learning from a community health initiative in Colorado and highlight the collective identity-forming quality of community-based participatory learning programmes of research whilst also highlighting the effort and labour necessary to establish and sustain relational work. This meaningful work is inherently problematic and unsustainable without those capabilities to build public management practice into the solutions McCabe & McCabe experience in Chapter 2. The McCabe's drive this home impactfully with a reflective account of how important relational working is in building place-based practice and identities, but how precarious these effortful outcomes become when investment is scarce. Sheer charisma, determination, altruism and passion are exemplary yet still unsustainable without corresponding methodological, political and policy shifts. In Chapter 3, Ormston and Macauley use social identity theory to map the ways in which Human Learning Systems (HLS) (an explicitly relational approach to public management) has helped foster a shared, common sense of identity and purpose in the context of a multi-agency leadership training programme. In Chapters 4 and 5, Middlekoop and Horseenlenberg and James et al. apply intentionally designed methods of professional dialogue to strengthening agency among public servants in the Netherlands and leadership development initiatives in Greater Manchester, respectively. All three of these chapters illustrate how highly specified initiatives for the design of work and development of public service capability can enable public service reform efforts and the experiences of those enacting them building capacity and confidence in those working in the sector.

The second section of this book is dedicated to new approaches to data, information, and measurement (Cornford et al., 2013; Wilson et al., 2024). Public services are funded and designed to achieve valued outcomes from educational attainment to public health to environmental sustainability. Outcome measurement has a history spanning more than 200 years, but only in comparatively recent history did these high-level goals – as aspirations, indicators of progress or performance targets – influence the operational delivery of public services. Alongside the NPM reforms, a raft of outcome-oriented performance systems, contracting relationships and investment vehicles have sought better outcomes through a transactional and rationalistic approach of disaggregation, incentivization and commodification. The hypothesized benefits of these reforms find little support in the empirical record, with real risks of perverse incentives, bureaucracy and diminished capabilities in public sector organizations. So, what role should high-level goals like outcomes play in a relational service context?

It is increasingly understood that performance targets always create perverse incentives in public services. Using outcomes as targets amplifies this problem because they lie beyond the ability of any individual agent to bring about independently or predictably. Those subject to performance management regimes, therefore, face a significant incentive to take shortcuts – by skewing, withholding and distorting data to make services accountable without corrupting the measurement and attribution processes on which they rely.

Relational alternatives to outcomes and outcome creation have been described by French et al. (2023), who consider the causes of social outcomes complex in their factorial variety and connectedness (compositional complexity), how variously those factors are experienced and manifest in lives (experiential complexity), the changing of these over time (dynamic complexity) and the deep and broad work involved across resources to tailor solutions to real world problems (governance complexity). This infinite variation renders rationalist approaches to understanding social outcomes inadequate at best and destructive at worst: undermining innovation by misusing data to set targets, incentivising the gaming of data to attempt demonstrable 'meeting' of targets and the skewing and tunnelling of real world understanding that results.

Key to a relational approach to public management are issues of the production, interpretation and consumption of data for the purposes of service design, management and governance. Since how we measure outcomes and use those data directly influences important decisions about what's on offer to the public, French et al. (2023) propose a Complexity Theory of Outcome Creation (CTOC), outlining the dynamic capabilities as enabling features of complex public service environments. Emergent outcomes are thus co-created products of relationships as complex systems. Considering outcomes in these ways, as an alternative to the product of a service, is a long-standing endeavour from a sociological perspective and has made its way into complexity sciences and population health circles as 'Complex Adaptive Systems'. However, empiricism lags in determining how measures and processes of measuring authentically reflect the messy nature of reality.

From the practice world, shining examples such as Buurtzorg (Monsen & De Blok, 2013), Outcomes Star (Mackeith, 2014, 2024) and Poverty Stoplight (Burt & Sanabria, 2019) have begun to show that tools built on a range of alternative relational perspectives are both possible and effective in addressing the question of what would a relational approach might look and feel like for managers, practitioners and citizens which seeks to engage with the diversity of people and places as opposed to the current framing of one size fits all or what works. Taking these ideas beyond the service contexts and seeking to address issues at the systemic, institutional and leadership levels are also crucial and work is emerging in these areas such as the HLS movement (French et al., 2023; Lowe et al., 2021) or from the local collaboration perspective 'bespoke by default' standpoint exemplified in the example of the 'Liberated Method' approach (Smith et al., 2025).

There is a perspective, still in its infancy, that considers a relational approach to the use of data and information with and by stakeholders as a key to more co-productive interpretative measurement processes such as learning. Questions also remain about the design or public service information and data systems, ownership of platforms and the implications this has for collaboration in policy and practice. This section's chapters address the emergence of new approaches to the production and interpretation of data and how these can be captured through alternative approaches to leadership, learning, performance management or evaluation. In Chapter 6, MacKeith shows how the outcomes produced by the efforts of action learning discussed in the first section can be harnessed with Outcomes Star, a holistic tool which seeks to reflect the complexity, humanity and emergence of what's meaningful in one's whole life as an interconnected system. Outcomes Star has built a strong reputation as an instrument for relational working in public service and the chapter tells the fascinating history of how this came to fruition.

But what of the swathes of traditionally captured, transactional and administrative data captured over decades by statutory bodies to 'demonstrate outcomes'? Montaletti, in Chapter 7, offers an innovative method for seeking hidden relational patterns in these data, using statistical-qualitative methodologies in labour market activation programmes in Italy. The resultant network diagrams show evolutions in relationships and act as graphical artefacts for use in discussions to co-produce new insights about employment programmes. Similarly, Charlton reports on a deep and longitudinal analysis of transactional citizen interactions with services in Chapter 8. These citizens have multiple and complex needs so their engagement with public services is extensive, prolonged, and detailed. However, the representation of these life stories has the potential to illustrate individuals' relationships with services over time, the service failure demand inherent in transactional approaches to complexity and the surprising sources of help.

The linked contributions from Martin followed by Martin and Jacucci adopt a cybernetics perspective in Chapters 9 and 10 to initially conceptualize relationality and then applying a conversation analytical modelling approach to outline the specification of a future information systems environment. They employ Krippendorff's (2009) systems determination, arguing that social systems require participation in them to be understood: they are not understood from outside its bounds because the conversations in them constitutively determine the nature of them, and our understanding of them. These ideas of participation and engagement in 'communicative action' (Habermas, 1984) go some way to explaining the requirement for relational public service as described in the work in the early chapters to be action-oriented.

These alternative practices of relational work conceived as action learning, and the ways in which data and measurement are understood, signal the diversity required from across sectors to generated public value. For instance, social enterprises hold an increasingly important role in the delivery of public services, particularly in the United Kingdom, and are generally characterized as aiding beneficiaries that have needs which are not being satisfied by a 'market'. Often regarded as a product of the neoliberal ethos of NPM, they are now a consistent feature of public service delivery and service relations.

Key to a relational approach to public services are the role of higher education and research institutions. Traditional roles for academics are in the role of policy expert or evaluator of public management and public services. Relational approaches to public service have increasing demands of a wider range of scholarly schools of thought typically contributory in the social sciences to support social innovation. For example, public management is an applied interdisciplinary area that can scaffold public innovation and draws on a range of perspectives, including sociology, politics, economics, psychology, social policy, public administration, management, information systems and education, and from different practice backgrounds, including from the worlds of design, health and social care, public leadership, social entrepreneurship and the civil service. Furthermore, relationality has contemporary resonance with public administration and opens scholarship out more fully utilize concepts central to policy, management and administrative practice – from co-creation to network governance to citizen participation to collaborative innovation. All recognise and explain how effective public services depend on the quality of relationships amongst the diverse actors involved.

In a wider vanguard of change including the adoption of social innovation approaches such as co-creation, a number of proposed roles to the potential relationships that higher education institutions and academics have to learning (including HLS) are emerging through innovative forms including partnerships with academics and consultants and the provision of services for research (Hesselgreaves et al., 2021). Part of this mix is the concept of engaged scholarship and academic informed practice, which seeks to build boundary spanning activity for an ongoing process of applied research and knowledge production for new models and approaches to change to occur (see for instance Lowe et al., 2021; Bartels, 2020; Smith et al., 2025). Section 3 explores the forms of scholarship that enable and sustain learning in public management and social innovation more broadly, from the fields of social pedagogy, ecosystem development, and design thinking.

Charfe surfaces the lurking issue of power when working relationally as a leader through the lens of social pedagogy in Chapter 11. She appraises HLS through the lens of Social Pedagogy as an approach that allows power to be explored given its central tenet of human freedom and flourishing and adopt HLS to consider how power is a relational element manifest in working reflexively across professional, personal and private selves. Charfe concludes that open and trusted dialogue in safe learning spaces supports the great responsibility brought with power and part of that work is critiquing the role of power structures in systems that are expressly trying to appreciate complexity. Burn and Needham pick up the notion of intersecting people and organizations trying to sense make in Chapter 12 using the ecological metaphor of ecosystems. They apply this to social care in the United Kingdom as a way to encourage conversations about whole systems, which are notoriously challenging to make discussable, such that these ecosystem conversations move beyond diagnosing composition complexity, and thus, paralysis, towards the production of relationships that foster human flourishing within the familiar framing of nature.

Kieboom and Van Der Bijl-Brouwer in our final contribution to the collection (Chapter 13) bring attention to the paradox of relational design: moving beyond the status quo when that is all that is available to do design with. They make the distinction between designing for relational services and service-designing as a form of relating as a way of overcoming the paradox and encourages reflexivity among public service designers to acknowledge the inherent neoliberal tendencies in the mindset, problematization and pursuit of relational public service design. Kieboom and Van Der Bijl-Brouwer demonstrate how viewing public designers as inherently complex and relational can move beyond relational public service design as merely the pursuit of building relationships, even if it's for other outcomes that matter. In this way, they explore how designers are part of the ecosystem, not just designers of it, which ought to challenge us to consider how potentially all roles in relational public service must adopt some insiderness, as Martin's chapter suggests, to enable complex public services to be 'constitutively determinable' (Krippendorff, 2009). By being prepared to participate, in whatever academic, design, innovation, management, service, leadership, commissioning, regulatory role one occupies, public management has a moment in time to align and make normal, forms of public service that enable human flourishing.

REFERENCES

Baines, S., Wilson, R., Fox, C., Aflaki, I. N., Bassi, A., Aramo-Immonen, H., & Prandini, R. (Eds.). (2024). *Co-creation in public services for innovation and social justice*. Policy Press.

Bartels, K. (2020). Transforming the relational dynamics of urban governance: How social innovation research can create a trajectory for learning and change. *Urban Studies*, *57*(14), 2868–2884.

Bartels, K., Heimburg, D. V., Jordan, G., & Ness, O. (2024). Debate: A relational agenda for changing public administration research and practice. *Public Money & Management*. https://doi.org/10.1080/09540962.2024.2402873

Bartels, K., & Turnbull, N. (2020). Relational public administration: A synthesis and heuristic classification of relational approaches. *Public Management Review*, *22*(9), 1324–1346.

Bevan, G., & Hood, C. (2006). What's measured is what matters: Targets and gaming in the English public health care system. *Public Administration*, *84*(3), 517–538.

Bovaird, T. (2014). Attributing outcomes to social policy interventions – "gold standard" or "fool's gold" in public policy and management? *Social Policy & Administration*, *48*(1), 1–23.

Boyne, G. A., & Law, J. (2005). Setting public service outcome targets: Lessons from local public service agreements. *Public Money & Management*, *25*(4), 253–260.

Burt, M., & Sanabria, L. F. (2019). The poverty stoplight and its psychosocial and multidimensional approach. In V. Ximenes, J. Moura Jr, E. Cidade, & B. Nepomuceno (Eds.), *Psychosocial implications of poverty*. Springer.

Clarke, J., & Newman, J. (2024). Debate: Beyond the new public management? *Public Money & Management*, *45*(1), 6–7.

Cornford, J., Wilson, R., Baines, S., & Richardson, R. (2013). Local governance in the new information ecology: The challenge of building interpretative communities. *Public Money and Management*, *33*(3), 201–208.

Cooke, G., & Muir, R. (2012). *The relational state: How recognising the importance of human relationships could revolutionise the role of the state*. Institute for Public Policy Research. https://ippr-org.files.svdcdn.com/production/Downloads/relational-state_Nov2012_9888.pdf

Cottam, H. (2018). *Radical help: How we can remake the relationships between us and revolutionise the welfare state*. Hachette.

Dunleavy, P., Margetts, H., Bastow, S., & Tinkler, J. (2006). New public management is dead—Long live digital-era governance. *Journal of Public Administration Research and Theory*, *16*(3), 467–494. https://doi.org/10.1093/jopart/mui057

French, M., Hesselgreaves, H., Wilson, R., Hawkins, M., & Lowe, T. (2023). *Harnessing complexity for better outcomes in public and non-profit services* (p. 144). Policy Press.

French, M., Kimmitt, J., Wilson, R., Jamieson, D., & Lowe, T. (2022). Social impact bonds and public service reform: Back to the future of new public management? *International Public Management Journal*. https://doi.org/10.1080/10967494.2022.2050859

Habermas, J. (1984). *Theory of communicative action* (T. McCarthy, Trans.). Beacon Press.

Heimburg, D., & Ness, O. (2021). Relational welfare: A socially just response to co-creating health and wellbeing for all. *Scandinavian Journal of Public Health*, *49*(6), 639–652.

Heinrich, C. J. (2002). Outcomes-based performance management in the public sector: Implications for government accountability and effectiveness. *Public Administration Review*, *62*(6), 712–725.

Hesselgreaves, H., French, M., Hawkins, M., Lowe, T., Wheatman, A., Martin, M., & Wilson, R. (2021). New development: The emerging role of a 'learning partner' relationship in supporting public service reform. *Public Money & Management*, *41*(8), 672–675.

Hobbs, C. (2019). *Systemic leadership for local governance: Tapping the resource within*. Palgrave Macmillan Cham.

Jamieson, D., Wilson, R., Martin, M., Lowe, T., Kimmitt, J., Gibbon, J., & French, M. (2020). Data for outcome payments or information for care? A sociotechnical analysis of the management information system in the implementation of a social impact bond. *Public Money & Management*, *40*(3), 213–224. https://doi.org/10.1080/09540962.2020.1714306

Krippendorff, K. (2009). Ross Ashby's information theory: A bit of history, some solutions to problems, and what we face today. *International Journal of General Systems*, *47*, 204.

Lamph, G., Nowland, R., Boland, P., Pearson, J., Connell, C., Jones, V., Wildbore, E., Christian, D. L., Harris, C., Ramsden, J., Gardner, K., Graham-Kevan, N., & McKeown, M. (2023). Relational practice in health, education, criminal justice, and social care: A scoping review. *Systematic Reviews*, *12*(194). https://doi.org/10.1186/s13643-023-02344-9

Lapsley, I., & Miller, P. (Eds.). (2024). *The resilience of new public management*. Oxford University Press.

Lent, A., & Studdert, J. (2019). *The community paradigm: Why public services need radical change and how it can be achieved*. New Local Government Network. https://www.newlocal.org.uk/wp-content/uploads/2019/03/The-Community-Paradigm_New-Local-2.pdf. Accessed on December 19, 2024.

Lowe, T. (2013). New development: The paradox of outcomes – The more we measure, the less we understand. *Public Money & Management*, *33*(3), 213–216.

Lowe, T., French, M., & Hawkins, M. (2020). Navigating complexity: The future of public service. In H. Sullivan, H. Dickinson, & H. Henderson (Eds.), *The Palgrave handbook of the public servant* (pp. 1–19). Springer International Publishing. https://doi.org/10.1007/978-3-030-03008-7_16-1

Lowe, T., French, M., Hawkins, M., Hesselgreaves, H., & Wilson, R. (2021). New development: Responding to complexity in public services—The human learning systems approach. *Public Money & Management*, *41*(7), 573–576.

Lowe, T., Padmanabhan, C., McCart, D., McNeill, K., Brogan, A., & Smith, M. (2022). *Human learning systems: A practical guide for the curious*. Centre for Public Impact. https://www.centreforpublicimpact.org/wp-content/uploads/2024/09/hls-practical-guide.pdf. Accessed on October 10, 2022.

Lowe, T., & Wilson, R. (2017). Playing the game of outcomes based performance management. Is gamesmanship inevitable? Evidence from theory and practice. *Social Policy & Administration*, *51*(7), 981–1001.

Mackeith, J. (2014). Assessing the reliability of the outcomes star in research and practice. *Housing, Care and Support*, *17*(4), 188–197.

MacKeith, J. (2024). Debate: The 'transactional gaze' and other lenses shaping and constraining the delivery of public services. *Public Money & Management*, *45*(1), 8–9.

Monsen, K. A., & De Blok, J. (2013). Buurtzorg: Nurse-led community care. *Creative Nursing*, *19*(3), 122–127. https://doi.org/10.1891/1078-4535.19.3.122

Moore, M. (1995). *Creating public value – Strategic management in government*. Harvard University Press.

Muir, R., & Parker, I. (2014). Many to many: How the relational state will transform public services institute for public policy reform. https://www.ippr.org/files/images/media/files/publication/2014/02/Many-to-many_Feb2014_11865.pdf

Needham, C., & Mangan, C. (2014). *The 21st century public servant*. University of Birmingham.

Osborne, S. (2006). The new public governance? *Public Management Review*, *8*(3), 377–387.

Pell, C., Wilson, R., & Lowe, T. (Eds.). (2016). *Kittens are evil: Heresies in public policy*. Triarchy Press.

Pell, C., Wilson, R., Lowe, T., & Myers, J. (Eds.). (2020). *Kittens are evil 2: Heresies in public policy*. Triarchy Press.

Smith, M., Hesselgreaves, H., Charlton, R., & Wilson, R. (2025). The 'liberated method'—A transcendent public service innovation in polycrisis. *Public Money and Management*. https://doi.org/10.1080/09540962.2025.2456120

Teece, D. J., Pisano, G., & Shuen, A. (1997). Dynamic capabilities and strategic management. *Strategic Management Journal*, *18*(7), 509–533.

Van Thiel, S., & Leeuw, F. L. (2002). The performance paradox in the public sector. *Public Performance & Management Review*, *25*(3), 267–281.

West, S., Haider, L. J., Stålhammar, S., & Woroniecki, S. (2020). A relational turn for sustainability science? Relational thinking, leverage points and transformations. *Ecosystems and People*, *16*(1), 304–325.

Wilson, R., Cornford, J., Baines, S., & Mawson, J. (2011). Information for localism? Policy sensemaking for local governance. *Public Money & Management*, *31*(4), 295–300.

Wilson, R., French, M., Hesselgreaves, H., Lowe, T., & Smith, M. (2024). New development: Relational public services—Reform and research agenda. *Public Money & Management*, *44*(6), 553–558.

Wimbush, E. (2011). Implementing an outcomes approach to public management and accountability in the UK – Are we learning the lessons? *Public Money & Management*, *31*(3), 211–218. https://doi.org/10.1080/09540962.2011.573237

CHALLENGES OF IMPLEMENTING SOCIOTECHNICAL INFRASTRUCTURE IN DATA-CENTRIC ORGANIZATIONS: LEARNINGS FROM A COMMUNITY INITIATIVE IN COLORADO, USA

Donald E. Nease, Jr[a], Dixon C. Dick[b] and Bruno Sobral[c]

[a]*University of Colorado, USA*
[b]*Archethought Inc., USA*
[c]*Colorado State University, USA*

ABSTRACT

In 2016, a partnership between the University of Colorado's Colorado Clinical & Translational Sciences Institute (CU-CCTSI) and local municipal leaders and the leadership of the local hospital was formed to tackle the siloed nature of social care services being delivered by over 90 community-based organizations (CBOs) and a set of local City departments. The City recognized that an inability to know who was receiving services from whom and a lack of communication among the entities resulted in large inefficiencies and difficulties in anticipating and fully meeting the needs of social care seekers. The CU-CCTSI team emphasized co-design of sociotechnical infrastructure based on Community-Based Participatory Research (CBPR) principles. CBPR emphasizes shifting the usual power relationships between academic researchers and communities using principles including: (1) Sees the community as a unit of identity. (2) Builds on strengths and resources in the community. (3) Facilitates collaborative, equitable partnerships. (4) Integrates and achieves a balance between research and action for the benefit of all partners. (5) Emphasizes local relevance of public health problems and ecological perspectives that recognize and attend to the multiple determinants of health and disease.

Futures in Public Management
Critical Perspectives on International Public Sector Management, Volume 8, 13–26

ISSN: 2045-7944/doi:10.1108/S2045-79442025000008002

Authentic partnerships require time in relationship development grounded in participatory, CBPR principles in order to promote authentic engagement. The importance of relationship building in CBPR parallels the emphasis in socio-technical approaches of designing infrastructure that supports relational engagement and mutual learning. Ultimately in our initial City engagement, their singular focus on data integration to the exclusion of these key elements led to the cessation of our work with that City.

Keywords: Sociotechnical infrastructure; middleware; community based participatory research; social determinants of health; human learning systems; communication platforms; codesign

INTRODUCTION

This chapter seeks to describe a case study of the nearly 8 year journey of the authors as they have worked to build sociotechnical infrastructure to support multi-agency social care in Colorado. In addition to describing the journey, we will identify key turning points and lessons learnt along the way while summarizing at the end our conclusions so far and recommendations for others who may be interested in following in our footsteps.

It is important to state up front our US frame of reference and additionally that none of our team comes from a public services background. We have entered this work as 'strangers in a strange land' bringing with us our training, experiences and biases from primary healthcare, information technology and public health. Further, in the United States, framing multi-agency social care as a complexity domain rather than a complicated clock, ala Hopper, that can be taken apart into ever smaller parts in order to 'fix' or 'solve' what's not working is relatively unknown among public services managers. New Public Management (NPM) approaches around reporting and measurement of outcomes as a path to improvement and cost containment are unstated but prevalent perspectives. Human Learning Systems (HLS)-based approaches have yet to reach a meaningful level of exposure or discourse in the United States.

Finally, our embrace of a sociotechnical approach is rooted in our belief that co-learning and co-creation of services and platforms to support care are essential. DN and BS come to this through their experiences conducting and teaching Community-Based Participatory Research (CBPR) while DD has reached this, while not having been exposed to the terminologies, through his decades of experience joining up IT systems and developing co-working spaces.

CONTEXT AND LITERATURE REVIEW

Over the past 15 years, there has been increasing recognition by the healthcare sector in the United States of the role of non-medical determinants of health, broadly categorized as Social Determinants of Health (SDOH). Within primary care, work was done to integrate SDOH concepts into the 'Community of

Solutions' framework developed by the Folsom Report in 1967, one of the foundational documents for the reorganization of primary care in the United States under the banner of Family Practice (Griswold et al., 2013; Group, 2012; Walker, 1967). In 2014, the National Academy of Medicine recommended standardizing the collection of SDOH measures in electronic health records (EHRs) (Institute of Medicine, 2014), and additionally since that time, direct and indirect incentives have arisen to push healthcare into the space of screening and in some fashion addressing SDOH in patients. In response to this new push from healthcare, a cottage industry developed around community resource referral platforms (Carter et al., 2019), which has now become a burgeoning market funded by private equity. Large EHR vendors such as Epic have formed alliances with some of these vendors, providing access to directories of social care organizations and referrals via integrated, clickable portals. These efforts are reminiscent of social prescribing programs that have been implemented in the United Kingdom and fail to recognize the lack of evidence for these programs' success (Bertotti et al., 2018; Bickerdike et al., 2017; Chris et al., 2022).

Against this backdrop, research has begun to address the pitfalls and promise of applying the usual medical model of 'screen and refer' to this space. Patients are often unclear about the purpose of such screening and may perceive this as an intrusion of healthcare into a space that is private (Broaddus-Shea et al., 2022; Nederveld et al., 2022). Healthcare administrators themselves recognize the challenges of maintaining lists of ever-changing resources and tracking the outcomes of referrals (Beidler et al., 2022). The work of explaining screening and making connections to resources often falls on already overworked staff as well (Page-Reeves et al., 2016). Little research to date has addressed the other side of the referral equation from the US perspective, community-based organizations engaged in social care. However, lack of capacity and of established relationships with healthcare practices and organizations and complexity of individuals' needs are certainly issues. Similar critiques are emerging in the United Kingdom, recognizing the need to engage with community actors to co-create systems of care involving health and social needs (Morris et al., 2022).

It is important to note that we approached all aspects of this work with a grounding in the principles of CBPR (Israel et al., 2001). Developed at the School of Public Health at the University of Michigan, CBPR emphasizes the importance of allowing communities to drive the direction of research in their communities, balancing power relationships between academic investigators and community members and ensuring that benefits accrue to communities equitably. For this work, a CBPR grounded co-design approach meant that our community partners were key in identifying the nature of the problems we hoped to address collectively, bringing to light and utilizing strengths and resources in the community whenever possible and that the expertise of all parties was recognized and valued. In many ways, there are commonalities between the principles of CBPR, co-design of relational public services and HLS work although the latter two were unfamiliar to us at the start.

METHODOLOGY

This chapter presents a case study of our team's efforts to address the challenges of complexity within the social care system and its relationship to healthcare by attempting to develop and implement a sociotechnical infrastructure in a medium sized community in Colorado. We will detail this in a narrative format, describing our team's journey and the learnings we have gleaned by diving headfirst into this work. While our team's initial engagement with the municipality has ended, the journey continues. We hope this case study and the lessons learnt will be illustrative and helpful for others seeking to implement information platforms to support relational public services.

FINDINGS/NARRATIVE OF THE JOURNEY

Beginnings: Travel to Newcastle and Exposure to Professors Martin, Booth and Wilson

In November 2015, DN was invited to spend a week in Newcastle with another US colleague to learn about joining up health and social care work being done by Professors Martin, Booth and Wilson, who were at that time located at Newcastle University. DN returned to Colorado much impressed by the conceptual framing around conversations of care and the necessity for middleware based sociotechnical infrastructure based on middleware needed to support these. However, it was initially challenging to find a community where there might be fertile ground to test out these approaches.

Invitation and Beginnings of the Work in Longmont, Colorado

In December 2016, an invitation came to meet with City of Longmont officials and the incoming CEO of the new UCHealth hospital, and this provided the first opportunity to explore bringing the 'coal' from Newcastle to fuel the fires of a new initiative in Colorado. In the meeting, Longmont's leaders spontaneously described the challenges of coordinating care across numerous capable social care organizations, (which in the United States are typically organized as charitable entities), healthcare and the City's own modest but active social care efforts in ageing, housing, etc. The leaders defined three priority areas of vulnerable older residents who were living independently, 'troubled' youth who were at risk, and individuals experiencing substance use disorders and housing issues. At this initial meeting, DN described the middleware approaches being promoted in Newcastle, whereupon the leaders asked whether such an approach might work in Longmont? This led to the subsequent 6–7 years of work.

After presenting the middleware, sociotechnical infrastructure approach to a subsequent meeting of more key individuals from City of Longmont departments and charitable organizations, DN assembled a team working from the platform of the University of Colorado's Clinical and Translational Sciences Institute (CU-CCTSI) and Department of Family Medicine, where DN held dual roles of Director of Community Engagement and Vice Chair for Research, respectively.

The team initially included a Masters of Public Health trained project coordinator, a Masters of Hospital Administration student and DN. Additionally, BS joined the work, operating from his platform of the One Health Institute, where he served as Director at Colorado State University.

Our initial work proceeded along two tracks: (1) conducting snowball interviews of leaders and staff at social care and healthcare organizations in Longmont in order to map and better understand the care landscape and (2) holding periodic convenings of these organizations to define a prototypical use case that could drive the sociotechnical infrastructure design work. During this initial work, we were fortunate to host Professors Martin and Booth for several visits that coincided with our convenings. The interviews resulted in engagement with over 90 different organizations that shared varying levels of knowledge of and connections with their peers. The web of organizations and the relationships among them are shown in the kumu.io map in Fig. 1.

Our convenings resulted in the definition and refinement of a Longmont version of Amy's story.

Amy's story: Amy lives by herself and has been fairly independent up until now with the assistance of the City's Senior Services division and Meals on Wheels. In this story, Amy begins falling at home, and the Fire Department answers several 911 calls over a short period to provide 'lift assists.' Neither Senior Services nor Meals on Wheels or her primary care provider are aware of

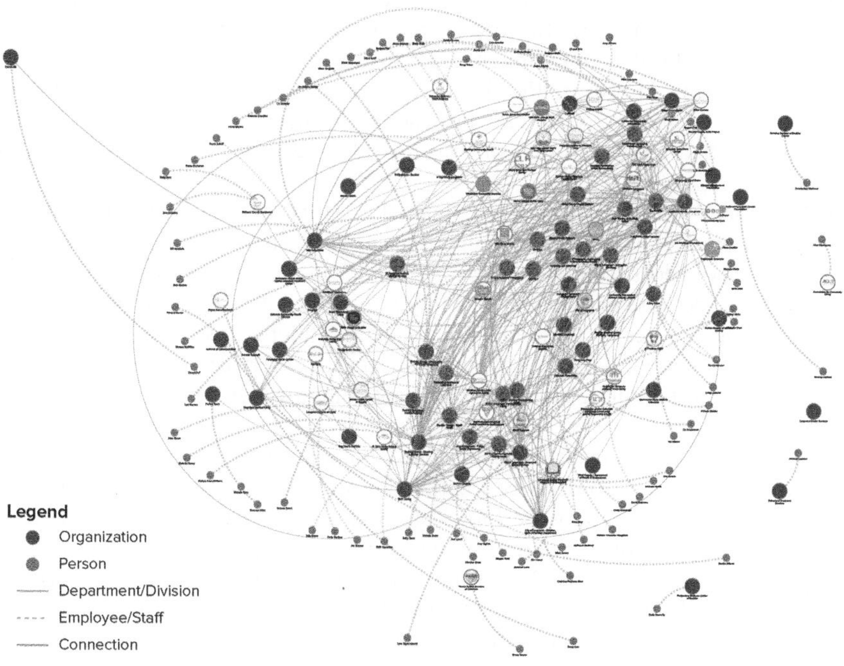

Fig. 1. Kumu.io Map of Longmont Organizations.

these 'lift assists' because there is no infrastructure in place to signal these events to the organizations caring for Amy. Because of this lack of infrastructure, early intervention does not occur, and Amy ultimately breaks her hip due to the repeated falls from an underlying urinary tract infection.

Key pieces of Amy's story that are relevant to the problem we proposed to address:

- A vulnerable individual receiving services from multiple organizations that span the City and community-based organizations (CBOs) in Longmont.
- Indicator events that signal that this vulnerable individual is either in impending or imminent crisis.
- A lack of infrastructure that links the City and CBOs that are already engaged in providing care services to the vulnerable individual.
- As a result of the lack of infrastructure, preventive measures are not taken, and a significant health event occurs.

During our convenings, we have heard repeated stories from our social care and City partners about how their efforts to meet individuals' needs are currently impaired by the lack of communication and coordination infrastructure. Two examples came from a local Federally Qualified Health Centre, which provides care irrespective of ability to pay, and the City's Public Safety Department.

- The care manager related a story of attempting to coordinate the care of a patient with mental health needs. The patient shared that they are receiving care at the local community mental health centre and gave permission to contact them. However, the Salud care manager neither had a way to get contact information for the care provider at the mental health centre nor a way to signal that individual that she was providing services on the physical health side.
- The City's Public Safety Chief related a story at one convening of the continuous high volume of incoming calls to 911 dispatch. These calls represent a variety of needs from vulnerable individuals in addition to 'emergency' calls. However, because of a lack of visibility into what other organizations might be providing services to these individuals, public safety must attempt to handle each call themselves. This resulted in a mismatch of services, as well as repeated calls due to the Public Safety Department being overwhelmed.

During our engagement and convening with organizations, we coined the term 'human middleware' to describe the function that many frontline individuals in these service organizations perform. In social capital terms, individuals functioning as 'human middleware' at times serve in bonding, bridging and linking capacities (Claridge, 2018). Specifically, we came to view individuals functioning as human middleware as a critical part of coordination among CBOs as they fostered a rich, synchronous informational exchange while building the human connections that were the lifeblood of the community. This term resonated with our CBO partners as well. That said, human middleware has its constraints: it is a very limited resource that is not sufficiently systematic to adequately coordinate among CBOs. By adding a sociotechnical middleware infrastructure to the existing human middleware we sought to (1) automatize and thus systematize certain forms of coordination among CBOs (e.g. notifications), and by so doing (2) free up limited human middleware capacity to do things only it can/must do (e.g. develop and sustain relationships, coordinate care and develop, test, redesign and innovate programmatic coordination activities).

In the Summer of 2018, the Longmont City Manager connected us with DD, who at the time had done contracting with the City around noise abatement using 'smart city' technology. DD rapidly came up to speed on the work, joining our convenings and beginning to develop ideas about the sociotechnical infrastructure platform. As DD joined the conversations, we began to develop important concepts such as 'information finding you.' This referred to the need for information to reach both seekers and carers in an automated fashion.

Funding Arrives and With It the Opportunity to Bring in Lived Experience of Care Seekers

In February 2020, just as the COVID-19 pandemic was beginning, Longmont's City Council approved one year of funding for the development of the platform to connect four City Departments along with 1–2 external CBO's. Due to COVID-19, actual contracting and funding was delayed, with a formal start date being pushed back to 1 November 2020. Our project management team included the academic team, Archethought, Inc., a Longmont technology start-up with experience in smart cities development and middleware and the City's Director of Community Services and a Community Programs Manager.

As we moved into a period of funded technical development, we were aware of the need to engage a smaller group of community members with lived experience seeking and receiving care became more important. Starting a Community Steering Board (CSB), made up of these individuals, was a part of our funding proposals, including the one ultimately funded by the City; however, it seemed initially unclear to our City partners what role the CSB would play. Several iterations of an invitational document were exchanged between the University, technical team and City partners, finally yielding an invitation that was used to recruit seven community members to the CSB. Because of the pandemic, our meetings were virtual over Zoom.

The CSB meetings in Longmont highlighted several key areas for enhancing the development of sociotechnical infrastructure to support a more relational public service system. Here is a synthesis of the findings from the meetings. This synthesis aims to provide actionable recommendations for developing a community-focused service platform that prioritizes relational, inclusive and effective public service management.

- *Alignment with sociotechnical infrastructure to support human middleware:* The CSB emphasized the importance of technology in facilitating engagement with social care providers, particularly through platforms that allow residents to manage their interactions and access services effectively.

- *Configuration of care:* A concept developed of allowing care seekers to configure their care emerged during the discussions. This meant that care seekers should have the ability to determine which organizations and individuals (friends, family or neighbours) should be invited to be part of their network of care such that the system is always an opt-in rather than opt-out proposal.
- *Accessibility and inclusion:* The 'digital divide' was discussed by CSB members. Discussions highlighted significant disparities in technology access, with some community members lacking basic digital tools. *The platform must accommodate these differences through alternative access methods or support.*
- *User-centric design and feedback:* The importance of feedback mechanisms within the system to acknowledge user interactions was noted as crucial for reducing uncertainty and improving user satisfaction.
- *Terminology and Communication:* The need for consistent and understandable terminology was a recurring theme, with suggestions to adopt a more relational and community-centred language, leading to the proposal of a glossary to ensure all users have a clear understanding of the terms used within the system.
- *Data privacy and security:* The CSB expressed concerns over data confidentiality. The security of personal and sensitive information remains a paramount concern, with discussions on ensuring that data within the system is protected from unauthorized access.

Development of the Sociotechnical Infrastructure

With the co-design input of our CSB, our team completed two sequential development efforts using standard web and database development tools. In the process, we discovered data-centric walled garden solutions were not a fit for the strongly relational approach we intended. In collaboration with our Newcastle colleagues and with co-design input from our CSB, a new approach was taken emphasizing a person-centric approach compared to our previous data-centric approach. In the most important decision of the project, a graph data approach was taken. A graph data approach emphasizes the connections or relationships as they evolve among individuals, roles, and organizations. 'Graph data' is inherently about relationships and means leaving the behind a standard database approach wherein a strict pre-definition of data and fields arises from a set of requirements specified in the procurement process. This database approach effectively freezes key elements in time, limiting the ability to reflect the complexity of ever-evolving relationships and communication among individuals. This proved controversial for City IT management as they had no experience with graph data and approaches that could capture evolving human relationships. This foreshadowed their ultimate selection of a Customer Relationship Management approach.

At the end of our initial funding period, we assembled City stakeholders for a demonstration of our prototype system. The system had the capabilities of creating a community, with the option to federate with other communities, creating 'branches' representing organizations serving individuals and roles both within those organizations (carers and administrators) and outside (care seekers) who could create conversations throughout the system. With recognition that more development was needed to reach the level of a deployable system, the Longmont City Council approved follow on funding for a Phase 2 implementation from the US federal American Rescue Plan Act (ARPA).

Contract Negotiations Stall

Thus began a long period of working to establish a contract with the City, during which a key champion of our work within the City retired. The champion was in the role of Director of Community Services and had served in that role for 32 years. The importance of her behind the scenes championing of our work became clear as our contracting became increasingly mired in red tape, with repeated requests for updated scopes of work and justifications.

The contracting exposed the nature of the data-centricity of the existing systems. During contract development, meetings were taken by the City as 'an Information Technology Project to be implemented.' This IT systems stance implied a known, specific structure, meant for systems with known parameters, expertise, expectations for service levels and so on. This approach is similar to that identified by Jamieson et al. in their social impact bond case study (Jamieson et al., 2020). We sought instead to describe the project as a learning project set up for discovery and to demonstrate the feasibility of a sociotechnical middleware infrastructure based on those learnings. Most importantly our team attempted to communicate the nature of change that was coming by including concepts of learning stewardship and management among the City Departments and CBOs implementing the platform. We communicated the key principles that this wasn't a project to develop software and implement IT. Rather, the key idea was to onboard and support the relationships among the key organizations and care seekers.

Through these discussions, it became clear that City management was operating from an epistemic perspective of solving 'complicated' problems by breaking them apart into their functional pieces, defining the data and measures around these, and using these data to solve the problems related to multi-agency care. All of this was consistent with NPM principles with all of the limitations associated with that approach (Jamieson et al., 2020; Lowe & Wilson, 2015). In contrast, we were coming from an epistemic perspective of complexity, seeking to build a platform to support a HLS approach (Lowe et al., 2020; Ormston & Macaulay, 2024).

During these protracted contract negotiations, our development went forward with the Newcastle team to fully embrace the human relational concepts discovered and prototyped during the what we now called Phase 1.

A key learning discovery was the importance and difficulty of implementing privacy and security. This was not from a technical point of view but a responsibility and ownership point of view. Our initial architecture was based on open-source technology from the Netherlands. When it turned out that the City would have to implement its own PIV (Personal Identity Verification) solution, we had to change our architecture. This strongly impacted our thinking going forward, and the concept of building the platform in a different way altogether was developed. These learnings led the team to a complete breakthrough in communications systems design. We were therefore very motivated to engage with Phase 2.

Taking a Step Back: A Clash of Understandings

Unfortunately, tensions within the City and between the City and our team ultimately slowed our team's engagement with the City to a halt. The feeling among the City team was that significant changes were in motion and further change would be necessary in order to capture, understand and make use of the findings and new architectures developed by the Project. A contributing factor to the project slowdown was a divergence in understanding due to the loss of the internal project champion. The imminent retirement of the champion was withheld knowledge, leading to a near full loss of the benefits gained from the co-learning journey. Looking back at our earliest meetings, the signs of misaligned understanding were present.

First, we were presented by the data integration vision called 'Slaying the Data Dragon' by the IT team. This data integration vision emerged as the guiding management principle to unite functions across differing departments. The impetus for data integration was rooted in the siloed nature of services in the City and the failure to effectively provide coordination and programme support across the local network of care. As we came to understand it, 'Slaying the Data Dragon' came about because each application delivered internally was typically developed or deployed as a walled garden, focused in an inward fashion towards solving a specific problem. This is not unusual, as many corporate projects are never funded unless they can clearly identify and solve a clear, cost or outcome driven problem.

This process led our team to reflect on the development imperatives in the data systems industry which are centred on a procurement model where the funder sets out a scope of work or request for proposals around a defined problem. Software vendors typically either solve the problems identified or acquire companies who have solved the point problems. By its very nature, the IT systems industry encourages and traps IT teams into data-centric walled gardens and the approach by the City reflected this. Upon this reflection, we learnt that walled gardens were antithetical to our sociotechnical middleware approach.

Walled garden IT systems also turned out to be heavily focused on compliance. Compliance addresses risk issues which command higher fees due to the visibility and higher potential costs of failure. Higher costs for failure led City IT to lean into compliance as a primary activity. New initiatives address compliance first to filter which change efforts to undertake. The benefits for a changed approach using human-centric principles and new databases were very different from known risk profiles provided by the Microsoft and other vendor driven solutions.

Finally, IT teams are not typically equipped to champion the end beneficiaries of services. These roles are held throughout the organization and must be championed separately. In an IT organization focused on vendor management, including deep engagement with end user benefits is hard to afford. Success for IT is therefore set up as a focus on data, vendor provided technology, walled gardens of data to solve point problems, compliance assurance and the reduction of most issues to known patters of integration among the standalone walled gardens.

The City IT infrastructure is thus an inwardly focused infrastructure based on walled gardens of compliance. This is almost the opposite of our learning where the need is for an infrastructure to support communication and coordination across agencies and CBOs.

LESSONS FOR POLICY AND PRACTICE

The key understandings from our learning journey:

- Interactions with our CSB continually reinforced the importance of relationships and the need to put humans at the centre of all aspects of our work. The CSB helped us maintain a 'north star' focus on these principles.
- If we recommend a human relational instead of a vendor supplied data centric commercial system, then we must change from offering database systems to human communication systems.
- If privacy and security are requirements intended to create trust and governance, then trust and governance must be intrinsic properties of the human communications systems.
- If trust and governance are to be intrinsic properties of a platform to support a complexity-focused HLS approach, then NPM approaches of surveillance and key performance metrics are ruled out.
- If surveillance-based economics are ruled out, then nearly all IT vendor systems are also ruled out as being incompatible with trust and governance.
- If no IT vendors systems are available, the development effort has to be made from the ground up, with the express understanding there are no passwords that permit management to 'see' all data and enable use of the platform in an NPM surveillance-based metrics approach.
- If there are no 'all seeing' superusers in management, yet local data stores had to be integrated and maintained, then the system would have to crystallize around the lowest level of data storage and management, remembering that existing systems must not only be maintained but be allowed to flourish by capturing, integration and presenting human signals to existing systems.
- In effect, we see the need to create infrastructures around the Walled Gardens that nurture and empower them in new ways, to help those who are most vulnerable engage in communication in familiar and accessible ways.

As a result of our meetings with CSB, we can summarize their recommendations for policy and practice in terms of relational public services:

- *Develop a Clear Glossary:* Implement a glossary of terms used within the platform to ensure clarity and consistency.
- *Ensure Broad Accessibility:* Design the system to be accessible to individuals with varying levels of digital access and literacy.
- *Incorporate Effective Feedback Mechanisms:* Integrate user-friendly feedback mechanisms to confirm actions and reduce follow-up inquiries.
- *Adopt Relational Terminology:* Use terminology that fosters a sense of community and support, moving away from transactional language.
- *Prioritize Data Security:* Implement stringent security measures to protect user data and ensure privacy.

CONCLUSIONS

As our team moves beyond work with the City of Longmont, our experiences and learnings have strengthened our resolve and appreciation of the need for the approach we are pursuing. This has been further strengthened by a final meeting with our CSB, who in their own humble and resilient way have encouraged us to continue along our path.

However, we ourselves are humbled by the recognition that for municipalities, data-centric approaches are beyond bread and butter; they have become institutionalized to the point where thinking differently amounts to heresy. As has been pointed out, data-centric approaches are reinforced by the constant pressure to minimize the risks on the municipal organization and by the approaches to City planning and management based on applying private sector management principles and practices to improve the efficiency and effectiveness of public sector organizations (Hood, 1991). While these pressures are not unique to municipalities and governmental organizations, smaller, charitable social care organizations have more flexibility. Even with these entities, if they receive public or other funding, funders may impose data reporting requirements that limit their flexibility.

Our approach has validated the importance of involving community in co-design and co-creation of infrastructures to support their well-being and health. This continues to be a growing theme in the literature (Haldane et al., 2019). Social media type approaches to this space have limitations of data security, misinformation spread and accessibility (Anawade et al., 2024; Chou et al., 2009; Dang et al., 2024). These issues were all echoed by our CSB members.

Our work fits into the context of this volume in its reinforcement of person-centric, relational approaches to care seekers. Our experience suggests that significant culture change may be required to realize success in larger organizations. Work with smaller, more nimble entities that can more easily appropriate these approaches may bear more fruit in the short term. Successes with networks of these smaller organizations may provide the evidence needed by policy makers and funders to unshackle larger organizations from data-centric approaches. As pointed out by Kuhn (Kuhn, 1996), revolutionary thinking often starts at the margins when and where it becomes apparent that the tried-and-true approaches are failing. We hope to be part of that kind of revolution.

REFERENCES

Anawade, P. A., Sharma, D., & Gahane, S. (2024). Connecting health and technology: A comprehensive review of social media and online communities in healthcare. *Cureus*, *16*(3), e55361. https://doi.org/10.7759/cureus.55361

Beidler, L. B., Razon, N., Lang, H., & Fraze, T. K. (2022). "More than just giving them a piece of paper": Interviews with primary care on social needs referrals to community-based organizations. *Journal of General Internal Medicine*, *37*(16), 4160–4167. https://doi.org/10.1007/s11606-022-07531-3

Bertotti, M., Frostick, C., Hutt, P., Sohanpal, R., & Carnes, D. (2018). A realist evaluation of social prescribing: An exploration into the context and mechanisms underpinning a pathway linking primary care with the voluntary sector. *Primary Health Care Research & Development*, *19*(3), 232–245. https://doi.org/10.1017/s1463423617000706

Bickerdike, L., Booth, A., Wilson, P. M., Farley, K., & Wright, K. (2017). Social prescribing: Less rhetoric and more reality. A systematic review of the evidence. *BMJ Open*, *7*(4), e013384. https://doi.org/10.1136/bmjopen-2016-013384

Broaddus-Shea, E. T., Duarte, K. F., Jantz, K., Reno, J., Connelly, L., & Nederveld, A. (2022). Implementing health-related social needs screening in western Colorado primary care practices: Qualitative research to inform improved communication with patients. *Health & Social Care in the Community*, *30*(5), e3075–e3085. https://doi.org/10.1111/hsc.13752

Carter, Y., Fichtenberg, C., & Gottlieb, L. (2019). *Community resource referral platforms: A guide for health care organizations* (pp. 1–98). SIREN (Social Interventions Research & Evaluation Network), University of California.

Chou, W. S., Hunt, Y. M., Beckjord, E. B., Moser, R. P., & Hesse, B. W. (2009). Social media use in the United States: Implications for health communication. *Journal of Medical Internet Research*, *11*(4), e48. https://doi.org/10.2196/jmir.1249

Chris, G., Farah, H., & Harmony, J. (2022). Social prescribing through primary care: A systematic review of the evidence. *Open Journal of Preventive Medicine*, *12*(02), 31–58.

Claridge, T. (2018). Functions of social capital – Bonding, bridging, linking. *Social Capital Research*. https://doi.org/10.5281/zenodo.7993853

Dang, J. H. T., Gori, A., Rios, L., Rolon, A. M., Zhang, J., & Chen, M. S. (2024). "You Don't Know If It's the Truth or a Lie": Exploring human papillomavirus (HPV) vaccine hesitancy among communities with low HPV vaccine uptake in Northern California. *Vaccines*, *12*(4), 372. https://doi.org/10.3390/vaccines12040372

Griswold, K. S., Lesko, S. E., & Westfall, J. M. (2013). Communities of solution: Partnerships for population health. *Journal of the American Board of Family Medicine: JABFM*, *26*(3), 232–238.

Group, F. (2012). Communities of solution: The Folsom report revisited. *The Annals of Family Medicine*, *10*(3), 250–260.

Haldane, V., Chuah, F. L. H., Srivastava, A., Singh, S. R., Koh, G. C. H., Seng, C. K., & Legido-Quigley, H. (2019). Community participation in health services development, implementation, and evaluation: A systematic review of empowerment, health, community, and process outcomes. *PLoS One*, *14*(5), e0216112. https://doi.org/10.1371/journal.pone.0216112

Hood, C. (1991). A public management for all seasons? *Public Administration*, *69*(1), 3–19. https://doi.org/10.1111/j.1467-9299.1991.tb00779.x

Institute of Medicine. (2014). Capturing social and behavioral domains and measures in electronic health records: Phase 2. https://doi.org/10.17226/18951

Israel, B. A., Schulz, A. J., Parker, E. A., Becker, A. B., & Community-Campus Partnerships for Health (2001). Community-based participatory research: Policy recommendations for promoting a partnership approach in health research. *Education for Health (Abingdon, England)*, *14*(2), 182–197. https://doi.org/10.1080/13576280110051055

Jamieson, D., Wilson, R., Martin, M., Lowe, T., Kimmitt, J., Gibbon, J., & French, M. (2020). Data for outcome payments or information for care? A sociotechnical analysis of the management information system in the implementation of a social impact bond. *Public Money & Management*, *40*(3), 213–224. https://doi.org/10.1080/09540962.2020.1714306

Kuhn, T. S. (1996). The structure of scientific revolutions. https://doi.org/10.7208/chicago/9780226458106.001.0001

Lowe, T., French, M., Hawkins, M., Hesselgreaves, H., & Wilson, R. (2020). New development: Responding to complexity in public services—The human learning systems approach. *Public Money & Management*, *41*(7), 1–4. https://doi.org/10.1080/09540962.2020.1832738

Lowe, T., & Wilson, R. (2015). Playing the game of outcomes-based performance management. Is gamesmanship inevitable? Evidence from theory and practice. *Social Policy & Administration*. https://doi.org/10.1111/spol.12205

Morris, D., Thomas, P., Ridley, J., & Webber, M. (2022). Community-enhanced social prescribing: Integrating community in policy and practice. *International Journal of Community Well-Being*, *5*(1), 179–195. https://doi.org/10.1007/s42413-020-00080-9

Nederveld, A. L., Duarte, K. F., Rice, J. D., Richie, A., & Broaddus-Shea, E. T. (2022). IMAGINE: A trial of messaging strategies for social needs screening and referral. *American Journal of Preventive Medicine*, *63*(3), S164–S172. https://doi.org/10.1016/j.amepre.2022.04.025

Ormston, C., & Macaulay, M. (2024). Developing a human learning systems approach for inter-agency collaboration: Lessons from the UK NHS. *Australian Journal of Public Administration*. https://doi.org/10.1111/1467-8500.12649

Page-Reeves, J., Kaufman, W., Bleecker, M., Norris, J., McCalmont, K., Ianakieva, V., Dessislava, I., & Kaufman, A. (2016). Addressing social determinants of health in a clinic setting: The WellRx pilot in Albuquerque, New Mexico. *The Journal of the American Board of Family Medicine*, *29*(3), 414–418.

Walker, J. E. C. (1967). Health is a community affair. *JAMA*, *199*(11), 864. https://doi.org/10.1001/jama.1967.03120110136043

THE BIRMINGHAM SEMH PATHFINDER'S LONG-TERM, HOLISTIC SUPPORT FOR FAMILIES: REFLECTIONS ON THE DEVELOPMENT OF THE MODEL

Jennifer Eckford McCabe and Rob McCabe

Birmingham SEMH Pathfinder, UK

ABSTRACT

This chapter discusses the development of Birmingham SEMH Pathfinder, an innovative family support approach, as the 'early help' offer in a deprived district of Birmingham, United Kingdom. Alongside its practice innovations, the Pathfinder is notable for being initiated from the 'bottom up' within the local authority, by a frontline social worker, Rob McCabe; and for maintaining a 'stake' within the authority despite operating on different protocols as an alternative model to 'mainstream' early help services. The Birmingham SEMH Pathfinder is so named as it was developed as a response to the needs of the cohort of school children designated by the term 'social, emotional and mental health needs' (SEMH). It has been operating in the Northfield district of Birmingham since 2016, offering sustained, relational support to families who are facing complex adversity. The Pathfinder works mostly through schools and also through a further education college and a children's centre. They have developed 'the Northfield approach', a model of family support which has three core features: open cases, building capacity in collaboration with the places children are and a partnership approach to core provision. Based on reflective interviews with the team, this chapter offers an overview of the challenges that they have faced in establishing, building and maintaining the work and the attributes, practices, strategies and tactics that they have found effective in enabling them to achieve this.

Futures in Public Management
Critical Perspectives on International Public Sector Management, Volume 8, 27–47

ISSN: 2045-7944/doi:10.1108/S2045-79442025000008003

Keywords: Service innovation; social emotional mental health (SEMH); schools; children; families; pathfinder; partnership; relational public services; reflection

INTRODUCTION

The Birmingham SEMH Pathfinder ('the Pathfinder') is an innovative 'early help' family support programme operating across the Northfield District of Birmingham since 2016. Its practice model is unique in the early help space in that it provides 'support on-tap' for as long as families need it and that it operates in partnership with, and out of, schools. It is also unusual in its positioning with one foot in the public sector (its strategic lead is a Children's Services head of service, and the local authority holds posts for the Pathfinder) and one foot in the third sector (the Pathfinder is a CIC). It is also unusual in that it has been designed and developed from the bottom up by its strategic lead, who was a front-line Youth Offending Service social worker when he began building the model. These things – which make the approach special – have also presented challenges in developing and maintaining it.

Based on the Pathfinder's experience, it is possible to suggest some ideas about tactics and strategies that might be helpful for those looking to establish similar work in new localities; the kind of people that they might wish to look for in workers and the conditions, circumstances and opportunities that can help or hinder their efforts (see Appendix 1). Beyond continuing to grow and deepen the Pathfinder's work in Northfield, the team's longer-term strategic goal is to see other Pathfinders, established in other places, finding their own ways to embed the Northfield approach or similar in their own context. It is unlikely that the team's learning will be unique, and it will be interesting to see which aspects of the Pathfinder's experience will prove to be common and which ones idiosyncratic and particular to its own particular journey.

This chapter will first set out the Pathfinder's approach in more detail, then locate it in the literature and finally offer reflections from the Pathfinder team on the qualities, tactics and strategies that have made this possible.

THE BIRMINGHAM SEMH PATHFINDER'S 'NORTHFIELD APPROACH'

This chapter discusses the development of Birmingham SEMH Pathfinder, an innovative family support approach as the 'early help' offer in a deprived district of Birmingham, United Kingdom. Alongside its practice innovations, the work is notable for being initiated from the 'bottom up' within the local authority, by a frontline social worker, Rob McCabe; and for maintaining a 'stake' within the authority despite operating on different protocols as an alternative model to 'mainstream' early help services. The SEMH Pathfinder is so named as it was developed as a response to the needs of the cohort of school children designated by the term 'social, emotional and mental health needs' (SEMH). It has been operating in the Northfield district of Birmingham since 2016, offering sustained, relational support to families facing complex adversity. The Pathfinder works mostly through schools and also through a further education college and a children's centre. In the Pathfinder's model of family support, they have developed 'the Northfield approach', which has three core features: open cases, building capacity in collaboration with the places children are and a partnership approach to core provision. For a timeline of the development of the approach, see Appendix 1.

The first and most important of these features is that they provide support 'on-tap' for as long as families need it something which is as innovative as it is controversial in the early help space. The Pathfinder believes that, far from creating dependency, the provision of un-time-limited support is crucial in establishing and maintaining the kind of deep trust that is required to make long-term, meaningful change. The second feature is utilizing school employed/based-pastoral workers, match-funded by the schools, who are well placed in terms of knowledge of school and the wider community. The Pathfinder core team offers co-working, training, supervision and support to develop them into Pathfinder family support workers. The third is the collective approach to staffing of the Pathfinder core team this was true at the time of writing....but not now...what to do: for example, one is employed by Aquarius, a substance misuse organization; another seconded in from a pupil referral unit; a senior assistant psychologist for the Pathfinder is employed by St Basil's, a homeless charity; but all posts in the core team are funded by the Pathfinder. In addition to these posts in common, the Pathfinder also has a number of co-located multi-agency professionals who are a part of its core team, such as workers from Birmingham Citizens Advice Bureau. Underpinning all the Pathfinder's work are its three key values: Shared authority, nurture and commitment to social justice.

Families who find their way to the Pathfinder – either by referral from their child's school, or by word of mouth from one of their existing families, or even by self-referral – are often experiencing poverty, marginalization and disadvantage, along with trauma that is often intergenerational. Many of their families are headed by a single-parent and facing the various pressures of debt, poor housing, SEND, substance misuse and domestic abuse. A net of intermeshed problems affects their mental and physical health and reinforce one another. There are agencies available to support them with specific problems, but no one trusted person that they can lean on who 'gets them' who knows their story and can be reliably there by their side to support them through the messy process of unpicking this net of problems.

The agencies each require you to turn up, and tell your story, to keep appointments and to manage your relationship with them. A substance misuse worker may understand how your damp, mouldy bedsit with extortionate rent and aggressive neighbours may be contributing to your addiction; they might even refer you to an organization that provides housing support, but at the doors of this new agency, you are usually alone again. At the Pathfinder, they offer that person, who is always there, and 'gets' all of it. Your Pathfinder worker can attend appointments with you or act as the 'conduit' to other professionals and organizations. They check in to see how things are going. They won't discharge you for non-attendance or tell you that time is up, but they will come round to see if you are okay. When you can't unravel a confusing form or labyrinthine piece of bureaucracy, they know who to call.

LOCATING THE NORTHFIELD APPROACH WITHIN THE LITERATURE

The Pathfinder's 'Northfield approach' was designed by frontline workers using practice-based wisdom and such basic first principles as the ethical 'golden rule' and by values of compassion, human dignity etc. Theorization of their model and connection with the academic literature has taken place subsequent to the design process in order to locate the approach within the current constellation of sectoral reform. There may be something indicated by the fact that a model as unusual as the Pathfinder has emerged from a design process focused on human perceptions of 'the Real' unpersuaded by idealized models or ideologically grounded theories.

The Pathfinder's Northfield approach can be understood as a response to the failings of the existing systems of social support: in particular, the tendency for outcomes and targets to take precedence over the real-life improvement in families' lives that they were originally designed to act as proxies for. As a result of this tendency, systems give preference to projects which most cost-effectively produce pre-determined metrics even when there is evidence that these metrics may be counter-productive. As such, the Northfield approach is part of a wider constellation of critiques of and responses to the existing paradigms underlying public management and business-as-usual practice. It is argued that the current business-as-usual approach to public service management in the United Kingdom (as well as in many similar nations) is a continuation of the model which emerged in the 1980s and became known as 'New Public Management' (NPM), a term coined in the early 1990s by scholars from the United Kingdom and Australia (Hood, 1991; Hood & Jackson, 1991). Prior to NPM, the public sector operated according to a system of top down, laws-based, bureaucratic Weberian administration. Whilst it has been described as ambiguous and multi-faceted and varying in its application (Dunleavy & Hood, 1994; Christensen & Laegreid, 2022), it is nevertheless distinct from traditional Weberian public administration in a number of key ways. It is typically driven by a move towards more efficiency and the adoption of practices from the private sector to achieve a more business-like operation: an emphasis on financial control and value for money and the setting of targets and ongoing monitoring of performance against these.

It is possible to recognize some of the more positive impulses that may have initially spurred the development of NPM as a response to the failings of the centralized, Weberian model. However, the Pathfinder strategic team do not believe that market forces, outsourcing, competition and standardized measurement systems are appropriate for many aspects of public management and perhaps least of all the societal duty towards and care of the most vulnerable. Their impacts range from unintentionally counter-productive consequences to the promotion of self-interested competition between different agencies vying for commissions or agencies massaging figures over a real genuine concern for truly meaningful outcomes for the humans involved. NPM has been described as a 'Shopping basket', and yet we believe this apparently agnostic approach to choice of mechanism and superficial impression of an approach which is adaptable to different countries and cultures belies the real effect of the underlying principles:

the rigorous enforcement of an ideology of the primacy of numbers (and specifically as they relate to money and its 'efficient' expenditure) over human lives. Hood and Dixon (2015) discuss that – despite the rhetoric of 'evidence-based policy' – there is considerable difficulty in evaluating NPM. This not only has implications for those who wish to support their criticisms with evaluation data, but – perhaps more concerningly for those offering alternative approaches – it makes it difficult to evidence the superiority of these over NPM. However, despite the difficulties, Hood and Dixon's evaluation finds that the evidence points to a range of outcomes 'from government costing about the same (but not less) and working about as well (but not better), to a darker picture of government costing substantially more and working decidedly worse' (Hood & Dixon, 2015, p. 178).

More recently, some theorists have noted that NPM has become 'middle aged', and led to paradoxical effects (Hood & Peters, 2004), and even asked whether it is 'dead in the water' (Dunleavy et al., 2006)? Certainly, there is evidence that amongst theorists at least, confidence in its ability to deliver improvements is waning or lost and the many strands of criticism leading into various new strands of 'post-NPM' (Çolak, 2019). Among these, we see aspects of the Pathfinder's approach echoed several of the principles of 'New Public Service' (NPS), particularly 'serve, rather than steer'; 'value people, not just productivity'; and 'value citizenship and public service above entrepreneurship' (Denhardt & Denhardt, 2000, pp. 553–557); and also in the 'New Public Governance' (NPG) approach – positioned as a 'third way' between NPM, and a return to Weberian management – which focuses on participation, partnerships, networks, unified services, and new ways of co-producing, and emphasises a more active citizen model (Çolak, 2019, p. 529).

However, Pollitt (2016, p. 429) argues that far from being 'dead', NPM, as a manifestation of a wider managerialism, is 'still very much with us', and this assessment aligns more closely to the experience of the Pathfinder team. The ideological and emotional conviction that the public sector has become too large and inefficient (Lapuente & Van der Walle, 2020, p. 463) seems to underpin a deep acceptance of many of the efficiency-oriented aspects of NPM in public sector management. Furthermore, despite the considerable academic literature engaged in defining, critiquing and tracking the development of this model, in our experience, discussion of or even awareness of this term is not generally widespread within practitioners or even managers within the public sector: an exacerbating factor in the difficulties of trying to challenge assumptions and practices which are embedded in it. Although the Northfield approach was developed by frontline practitioners, initially without reference to the wider world of 'post-NPM' alternative models of practice, their partnership with Lankelly Chase Foundation (LKC) introduced them to a number of other models and frameworks, which were addressing similar problems and proposing alternatives that shared features or an underlying ethos with their own. These include Human Learning systems (Centre for public impact, 2021), the Wigan Deal (The Relationships Project, 2024), the Liberated method (Smith et al., 2025) and 'Our Future Grimsby' (Our Future Grimsby, 2024). It has been reassuring and inspiring for the Pathfinder team to meet others attempting similar pieces of work at the level of practice.

METHODOLOGY

This analysis is based on reflective interviews with the strategic lead of the Pathfinder and reflections of other members of the team from their perspective as actors in the programme. We have used the analysis of these interviews to describe the journey of the design and development of the Pathfinder's model (see Appendix 1); the challenges faced in establishing and maintaining the model and the strategies and tactics employed in order to overcome these, or at least to continue to survive in the face of them. Presented below is a summary of the tactics and strategies employed/learnt by the team's leadership and the wider group to meet the challenges of establishing and maintaining the model.

REFLECTIONS ON THE QUALITIES, TACTICS AND STRATEGIES THAT HAVE BEEN USEFUL IN DEVELOPING THE 'NORTHFIELD APPROACH'

Understanding the True Value of Proper Care

The relational, contextual nature of the Northfield approach and the nature of its development cannot easily be separated: it evolved out of the lived and professional experience of its now strategic lead, Rob McCabe ('Rob') and those who subsequently joined the team. The human origins of the approach are therefore an important aspect of the journey to consider, insofar as they may have elements that are common to many considering similar innovations in their work, and also many elements which illustrate the uniqueness and specificity of such an organic, place-based development of practice.

Rob traces the earliest origins of the Pathfinder to the care and support roles of his early career before he began his social work training. These jobs – first in residential care homes and then, later, in special schools and one mainstream school – had certain features in common: they involved taking a key-worker role, really 'up close and personal' with those he cared for and supported; they involved all aspects of personal care but also building relationships and to advocate. Rob felt deeply privileged to build close relationships with people with disabilities and was impressed by many of the people he worked with: exceptional care workers with whom he has remained life-long friends. He remembers this time as an apprenticeship in deep relational work but also that this was not really valued: care workers are often seen as expendable commodities – there's high turnover and low salary and status. For him, the seeds of the Pathfinder were born there, in this conviction about the true value of proper care and the undervalued potential of those providing it. Other members of the team bring similar stories: from the lived experience of receiving or not receiving proper care at difficult points in their lives and also from the experience of being thwarted in their attempts to deliver proper care as professionals due to the restrictions of systems that had worked in.

Anger as Motivation

There wasn't one particular moment when Rob shifted from a focus on his own practice to an orientation towards system change. He says that instead there was a growing swell: waves of anger, incredulity and despair, over days and weeks and years. The swelling anger grew alongside the cumulation of stories of the young people he worked with:

> It's traumatic– kids taking their own lives, perpetrators - many of whom were also victims - committing horrific criminal acts; and I was there as an agent of the state, reading through CPS [crown prosecution service] records and writing pre-sentence reports that would determine their fate. When you are interacting with kids and families whose lives were dominated by adversity, it's not your trauma, but it feels like it is. It's sickening, but you normalise it on a daily basis...It's the wrong way around, the process dominates, and what's really not at the centre of it, actually, is the child. All through my criminal justice experience it was like that..."make sure you cover your back, make sure you do that paperwork, make sure you tick the box"...It was about the process and being seen to uphold those statutory duties because if there's a failure, you'd better have your backside covered. And what was being missed was the kids. (McCabe, 2024)

The Pathfinder's Northfield approach is the outcome of transmuting that anger into motivation to make positive change. Describing Rodsett House SEMH School when he began his work there, Rob says,

> It was just like a containment situation for the poorest kids who were in and out of custody, hurting people and creating victims. It was hellish, but also, as a problem, super-fascinating. It was as if all of my life experiences came together and also were reflected in that place, and I was destined to be there...right in the middle of some of our most systemic, oppressive failure. (McCabe, 2024)

As people have joined the Pathfinder team, this sense of anger is a common theme in their stories too. The ongoing process of transmuting anger into motivation for the work drives a shared sense of mission and a process of healing for the team themselves.

Asking Questions and Calling Out 'The Real'

Rob started to ask questions:

> ...to be the surly social worker in the team meeting, and say, 'well, this is bullshit': starting to ask why more. 'Why are we doing that', or, actually, more importantly – and I think that's the seeds of the Pathfinder – 'why aren't we doing this?' If resources are tight – if we've got Rodsett House SEMH School, and it's full of kids who are coming in and out of the system, why am I one of 30 social workers, from all across the city, going in and out of that school every day. Why would that be? (McCabe, 2024)

The reports (see Appendix 1) that Rob wrote were an exercise in using the starkness of the numbers to draw attention to the reality of a situation and demonstrates the power of data to communicate a message.

'Dancing in the Cracks'

Finding 'cracks' is often discussed as a tactic in systems change work. Roles which straddle more than one hierarchy or department can offer an opportunity to do this by leveraging the overlap and disjunction between mandates and jurisdictions to create a more authorizing environment than full membership of either might offer. For example, there was a lot of freedom within the mandate of Rob's role at this time: his position 'in between' the school and youth offending service (YOS) meant that the YOS didn't really 'own him'. The school was already under a lot of pressure, and so Rodsett House SEMH School's head-teacher felt that Rob had brought a really timely lens onto the problem and was just keen that he should come and help. All of which created a bit of space and freedom to be creative and entrepreneurial in setting up new initiatives. This arrangement meant that Rob was able to remain employed by the YOS but was authorized to focus full time on this work. This hybrid role created a 'crack' in which Rob was able to create more and more space for a new model of supporting these children and families.

'Stone Soup': Leveraging Each Opportunity to Create More Space

Rob went quickly from being a frontline social worker to having created something that meant he was in a central position in the cross-multi-agency meetings at the school, meeting with really senior officers. This led to him being invited to things like a city-level meeting to design an SEMH policy. Here, he found himself – still a grade 4 front line officer – advising senior officers about strategic considerations such as the profiling of children's backgrounds and risk levels.

With hindsight, Rob sees this as the start of the Pathfinder: that is, the creation of something alternative. He was learning what can happen if the system doesn't give you permission to do something, but you just go ahead and do it anyway. He was also learning that it's always about what else can you leverage in: he started with the reports, and suddenly, he had got the attention of people. He used this to leverage in support and interest and funding from the school and a freer hand with the YOS. These things gave him more strength in terms of negotiating terms of what he could do in his role. He kept building on this, creating more and more space.

The Pathfinder team have come to think of this in terms of the old story of 'stone soup'. The approach has been to 'make hay while the sun shines', to beg, borrow and steal and use each contribution as capital to win more. For example, it was through the multi-agency meetings that Rob had made an initial connection to the lead of the school nurse service, which he then built upon after connecting with Sarah, the school nurse at Rodsett House SEMH School by 'begging' a little of her time. He has also made a connection with the drugs support agency, Aquarius, and used the school nurse service contribution to leverage a contribution from them. He then had the beginning of a team to use in pitching that back to head teachers, now asking for school-based workers to be released into the project. Rob describes this as a typically 'working class entrepreneurial approach', which is an interesting contrast to the strategic approach generally promoted and expected by public management culture, which we discuss further below.

Finding the Right People

As important as Rob's leadership has been, the Pathfinder is the creation of all the workers, allies and supporters who have been drawn around and into the work. Finding the right people has been a vital element of building the work. There is something about the Northfield approach and the culture of the Pathfinder team which seems to attract people who share common characteristics. They are often already working within the system and struggling with the disconnect between it and their values; and the cognitive dissonance that their current roles provoke. They have a strong sense of how support work should be and may share aspects of lived experience with pathfinder families. They are courageous and value-led.

There is a set of 'working class manners' which are hard to define but which Rob had described as being something that people with this shared background recognize in each other. Rob even feels that it has a particular Birmingham flavour to it. It involves a kind of non-nonsense honesty, humour, recognition of something shared and a certain unaffected conviviality. This is a factor in what drew people to the work in the early days and which shapes the values that were modelled and later defined. Workers joke about the 'tea and biscuits' culture in the Pathfinder office, the tendency of the team to personalize and beautify each space they occupy with trinkets and fairy lights, the cosy sofa-filled nooks that they like to create 'for the families' wherever there is spare space, but these are only surface signifiers of this deep culture at work.

There is something about these people that they seem to find the Pathfinder, another reason for the importance of persistent, visible existence. Once they have found it, they are often deeply loyal, and as testament to this, during times of funding uncertainty, many of Pathfinder workers have chosen to remain in temporary Pathfinder contracts rather than take up the offer of a return to permanent ones within Birmingham Children's Trust (BCT). Earlier in the Pathfinder's story, one of the initial participating special schools was closing down at the same time that the Pathfinder was creating new posts within the Lumen Cristi schools that had just joined the model. All of these new posts ended up being filled by Pathfinder workers from the closing special school, demonstrating the value of Pathfinder training and also how much the workers had valued being part of the approach. For the Pathfinder, its work is only as good as the human beings delivering it, which is why it places so much importance on investing in, caring for and retaining good people when it finds them. The Pathfinder's retention figures speak for themselves: in the context of a national recruitment and retention crisis across children's services, the Pathfinder had a staff turnover rate of 4.6% over the last 8 years.

Nurturing Keystone Allies

Along the way the Pathfinder has been patronized by individuals or organizations who have been absolutely essential to them. Lankelly Chase Foundation was a rare organization among funders, who understood systems change and what it really looks like on the ground, in all its messy, precarious, beleaguered reality.

They stood by the Pathfinder and held them up through some really difficult times, feeling more like family or fellow members of a resistance than funders. Over the life of the relationship, Lankelly Chase have given the Pathfinder over £1m, paying for their rapid research evaluation and supporting the work of the strategic team, as well as supporting their more developmental work and staff wellbeing. Furthermore, in October 2022, Cathy Stancer, who had originally been Pathfinder's grant manager at Lankelly Chase, was seconded over to work for the Pathfinder and she remains with the Pathfinder one day per week.

In addition, leaders of partner charities, particularly those working in substance abuse, homelessness and domestic violence, have instinctively seen the sense in the Northfield approach and taken the Pathfinder under their wing or opened doors for them. Finding these influential, powerful and value-led allies whose mission overlaps with theirs and who understand the real work on the ground has provided the Pathfinder with lifelines when they have needed it most.

The Importance of Being Rooted in Place

The value of having a physical home in the community where you work is hardly a new revelation: the example of the Sure Start centres and the loss that was felt when they were closed is a powerful example in the minds of many in the care and support sector. Even so, the team were surprised by what a game changer it was for both families and staff when they got their first physical space at Kings Norton Fire Station. Making the space homely, human and welcoming was an important rite of passage for the Pathfinder and allowed them to create a space that manifested their values in a physical space that they could visit and participate in. From the point of view of the development of the project, they were surprised how a physical space could come to embody what they do and also how important it was for a sense of becoming a 'proper project'. The Pathfinder has since moved to St Nicholas Place, and the staff and families have 'Pathfindered' the new premises in exactly the same way, but the fire station was a key milestone for them, and staff still talk about it fondly. In an increasingly digitized world, where even the support and care sector is increasingly operating in the virtual sphere, they are convinced that creating a physical space within the community and making sure it feels welcoming and human is not a nice-to-have but essential.

Authorizing Environments

There has been the presence or absence at different times of an authorizing environment. As a bottom-up initiative, The Pathfinder has mostly responded tactically to this – noticing opportunities and leveraging relationships with those in more powerful positions to try and influence this. To this extent it can be possible to nudge and nurture one's own authorizing environment from below. Awareness of what an authorizing environment looks like (and doesn't look like) has been important to make good tactical decisions about where to invest time and effort and where not to.

Using Disruption to Seed the Good

The COVID-19 pandemic was a terrible time for so many Pathfinder families, and the team are still seeing the after-effects in children coming up through secondary school. However, the suspension of business as usual, the accelerated implementation of the locality partnerships model of early help, and Rob being drafted into the emergency response all created a space of possibility, wherein the principles and practices that were being developed in the Pathfinder's work became influential in setting up the locality teams.

The Blessings and Curses of Statutory Funding

The Pathfinder and its 'Northfield approach' have always been rooted in the local authority by virtue of Rob's continued employment by them; and trying to bring forth a new model of practice from within the existing one has involved real challenges. At times, they have been strongly advised to cut themselves loose, set up as a voluntary sector body and seek a commissioning relationship with the Authority, as this would allow them the freedom to operate exactly as they wished. However, they have always believed in the value of their position with one foot inside and one foot outside the system and that the friction and tensions that arise are but one side of a coin, the flipside of which is traction. Furthermore, there are indications that their presence has the potential to catalyze change within in a deeper way. They notice, for example, that the language they introduce in internal reports sometimes appears elsewhere shortly afterwards. Whilst they can't ever be sure that their work was the sole influence or even an influence at all (after all, principles such as relationality and sustained support are out there gaining ground in the zeitgeist), there is a cumulative sense that their existence exerts influence.

Recognize and Celebrate Success

The quality of restlessness that pushes Rob to keep moving things forward can have downsides. It can take other members of the team to point out our successes and remind him to join them in celebrating them. The drive to realize the vision can mean that successes are quickly eclipsed by the next task. Also, they rarely look exactly like the vision. The team remind each other that continued survival and existence is itself a great success and perhaps the greatest they can hope for at certain times. Furthermore, they remind ourselves that they are operating in a way that is not aligned with the metrics of the existing system, and under these circumstances, good work may feel unappreciated or even persecuted. This may even sometimes be a sign of success. Letting go of conventional rewards and markers of success can also be important. Instead, Pathfinder staff share nothing more proudly than a heartfelt thank you email from a family or from a head teacher who sees changes in the lives of the children in their school. In addition, they remind themselves that the Pathfinder is a movement not an institution. Everyone who comes into contact with the Northfield approach and witnesses its value goes away a little bit changed. The team remind themselves that they have no way of knowing what future projects, innovations and initiatives might be encouraged or prompted by those changes.

LESSONS FOR POLICY AND PRACTICE

Rob, the Pathfinder's strategic lead, could be considered a kind of model for a type of person or set of characteristics which have made him well-placed to do this work: undertaking the praxis of bottom-up systems change from within. First, his personal background and upbringing gave him key insights and understandings:

- Personal insight into the reality of intergenerational disadvantage and trauma: sympathetic but not romanticized.
- Personal experience of the protective factors that can enable a child to survive and even thrive in spite of these.
- A deep, genuine appreciation of and respect for the strength, resilience and tenacity of people in disadvantaged communities – particularly single parents – and the values that still remain within parts of working-class communities exemplified by the ethos of support and solidarity he knew in the pubs that his mother and father ran.
- Early career insight into the untapped potential of care workers and those in support roles in organizations but also a strong vision of what this looks like done right (as well as done wrong).

Second, whether informed by his own personal journey, or an innate personal characteristic, he has an approach to the work which has been useful in leading the organization through this journey. There is a piratic quality to these characteristics and attributes:

- A nomadic restlessness and willingness and drive to keep moving, not to rest on one's laurels but to be always ready to keep moving.
- Not looking for a position within the establishment in which to rest – having seen through the rewards that it offers – rather resting in a loyalty to a set of values, which means that one can't easily be 'bought'.
- Pragmatism rather than idealism in how one serves one's values.
- A preference for human relationships over systems.
- A lack of deference to the existing establishment and a lack of indebtedness to it, having grown up not a beneficiary of it. Rather a tendency to build human relationships one by one with individual people. A strong social and emotional intelligence that allows these connections to be made with the right people quickly.
- Following one's moral compass and being led by an unswerving commitment to doing what's right for the work. Following this as a guide rather than automatically asking for permission from the next rung up in the hierarchy.
- An entrepreneurial ability to see cracks and opportunities and to exploit these in service to one's values, also willingness to pitch endlessly, putting out fishing lines and leveraging each good contact to gain more ground and make new contacts.

Third, he happened to find himself presented with not only an unavoidable awareness of what was not working but a vision of how things could be better and an opportunity to make change. The Pathfinder team often wonder how many other potential 'strategic leads' are out there; what might they share with Rob; how might they differ and what they might they need to get started in their own locality.

CONCLUSION

At the time of writing, there were 25 schools and 1 further education college working with the Pathfinder; another 3 schools have recently requested to join and the Pathfinder currently has 30 (FTE) members of staff. The approach has spread largely through word-of-mouth, among head teachers who have been impressed by its impact and those who face similar challenges in supporting their children and families. The project has brought £2 million of match-funded resources, £2 million of external grant funding over the last 8 years and has £750,000 of match-funding per year in the form of school-based pathfinder workers. They have just secured a partnership with Centrepoint, a national homelessness charity. However, as a project that was entirely initiated and generated from the bottom up, within the largest local authority in Europe, that began with no mandate from above and that operates in the fertile, but uneasy space between public sector and third sector, getting to this point has not been easy, and their ongoing survival is by no means assured. They believe that not only is their approach to family support the best and most rational for their current families but that it represents a model of practice that could, and should be transplanted to other localities. The longer they are able to survive, the more chance that the example of the Northfield approach can seed other Pathfinders in other areas.

In the beginning, Rob faced the challenge of how to initiate change from a relatively non-senior position in the organization: how to find cracks and levers to open up a space in which it was possible to make a start and also to leverage more space. Once he had made a start, there was the problem of operating from within the system, bottom up: having conceived and developed the Pathfinder at a relatively junior level of local authority hierarchy, it has been difficult to convince and recruit the sponsors at more senior level necessary to create an authorizing environment to continue and maintain the work. Achieving a mandate to operate at district level was a huge achievement, but this came with expectations that the approach operate according to the same reporting and measurement protocols of the other delivery mechanism, which closed cases.

Sitting as the Pathfinder does with one foot in the public sector (as the Pathfinder's strategic lead, Rob is still a local authority employee), and one in the third sector (they have established a community interest company (CIC) and all of its funding is from sources external to the local authority) is in many ways a fertile and powerful place to be. For example, retaining that foot in the statutory sector enabled them to negotiate the data sharing agreement that means Pathfinder staff have access to vital information about their families held by the system that they wouldn't otherwise have access to. Furthermore, maintaining a foot in the system enables the Pathfinder to leverage far more potential change and accountability within the system than if they were located completely outside of it, for example as independent operators within the commissioning model.

However, the hybrid nature of the Pathfinder does mean that many funders have a hard time fitting them into their criteria, especially since the work can be seen as crossing over between the statutory and non-statutory sectors. Furthermore, existing partially within the system also means they are subject to many of the constraints it imposes. Regardless of how much a colleague or manager within the service may appreciate the value of the Northfield approach, they are often themselves constrained within the system. In the experience of the Pathfinder team, it also seems that although more senior officers might theoretically have more power to make changes, they are also often paradoxically more heavily constrained by the system itself. It can seem that in an organization as large, hierarchical and siloed as the city council and a sector such as children's services which is furthermore heavily prescribed at a national level, there is so much momentum behind business as usual that the system itself can seem to actively resist change. In discussing these challenges, Pathfinder staff use metaphors such as that of the Northfield approach as a virus, and the system seeming to stage an immune response, and of feeling like a 'thorn in the system's side'.

A key example is that the Pathfinder's holistic and long-term approach is difficult to fit into the measurement-oriented evaluation systems of 'NPM'. This leads to the approach being called 'expensive' even though the Pathfinder argues that it utilizes existing resources more effectively. It also means that they have been accused of 'creating dependency' even though they find that many of their families drift away naturally within 2–3 years and those who stay or return do so for good reason. The fact that the Pathfinder imposes no clearly defined endpoint on their families means that they are in tension with a system that counts 'cases closed' as positive outcomes. Furthermore, staying with a family for the long-haul means that as well as trajectories of improvement, they may also present with relapses and even aggravation of the presenting issues while they are with the Pathfinder. The team explain this by arguing that in many cases, the relationship is well-past the closure point of a mainstream case before they have built the deeper trust that then leads to disclosures of more serious problems. While the Pathfinder team see this as vindication of the long-term approach, the NPM system can only see that following Pathfinder intervention, things have 'got worse'.

The Pathfinder team discuss this at length in a forthcoming publication where they employ a comparison of the practices of regenerative land management to industrial farming, as a rich analogy for the differences between the type of management that would enable approaches like the Northfield approach and current norms of NPM, both in terms of front-line practices with families that honour each families own trajectory towards healing and change, and also the kind of authorizing environment that allows things like the Northfield approach itself to develop. Trying to bring forth a different model of practice as frontline practitioners, trained and experienced in various aspects of health and social care and community work, meant that they were developing their approach from first principles, initially without the benefit of theory such as the body of research describing business-as-usual as 'NPM', for example.

Another challenge is the tendency of systems to adopt new language in a superficial way. The adoption of 'buzzwords', which can give the impression of a change in practice, can even hinder real change by improving superficial appearances to the extent that the impetus for deeper change is defused. It can also mean that the words themselves become devalued and leached of meaning: as people become aware of the desirability of a particular quality, they adopt that language reflexively, meaning that it can become difficult for projects making actual changes to their practice to distinguish themselves and their key difference. Key examples are words such as 'holistic', 'sustainable' and particularly 'relational'. This is why in communicating the Northfield approach, the Pathfinder team emphasize the key aspect of their actual practice which is concrete and distinctive: 'not closing cases' and defend this as a core of their work.

Whilst there are examples of long-term relational support in other sectors, we know of few other examples of either truly sustained family support or of systems change projects that straddle the public and third sectors in the way that the Pathfinder's Northfield approach does. This means that the description of the Pathfinder's tactical and strategic approaches to meeting the challenges facing them can only be offered as 'their experience'. The Pathfinder team are keen to connect with others currently doing similar work and also those who would like to begin. They look forward to being able to compare notes, share ideas, tactics and strategies and learn what of their journey is common and what is particular in working within the system to reimagine children's services.

REFERENCES

Centre for Public Impact. (2021). Human learning systems – public service for the real world. https://www.centreforpublicimpact.org/assets/documents/hls-real-world.pdf

Christensen, T., & Laegreid, P. (2022). Chapter 4: Taking stock: New Public Management (NPM) and post-NPM reforms – trends and challenges. In A. Ladner & F. Sager (Eds.), *Handbook on the politics of public administration* (pp. 38–49). Edward Elgar Publishing.

Çolak, Ç. (2019). Why the new public management is obsolete: An analysis in the context of the post-new public management. *HKJU-CCPA*, *19*, 517–536.

Denhardt, R. B., & Denhardt, J. V. (2000). The new public service: Serving rather than steering. *Public Administration Review*, *60*(6), 549–559.

Dunleavy, P., & Hood, C. (1994). From old public administration to new public management. *Public Money & Management*, *14*(3), 9–16.

Dunleavy, P., Margetts, H., Bastow, S., & Tinkler, J. (2006). New public management is dead—Long live digital-era governance. *Journal of Public Administration Research and Theory*, *16*(3), 467–494.

Hood, C. C. (1991). A public management for all seasons? *Public Administration*, *69*, 3–19.

Hood, C., & Dixon, R. (2015). *A government that worked better and cost less?: Evaluating three decades of reform and change in UK central Government*. Oxford University Press.

Hood, C., & Jackson, M. (1991, September). Is there a new public management? Keys and locks in administrative argument. In *Paper presented at American Political Science Association*, Washington D.C.

Hood, C., & Peters, B. G. (2004). The middle ageing of new public management: Into the age of paradox? *Journal of Public Administration Research and Theory*, *14*(3), 267–282.

Lapuente, V., & Van de Walle, S. (2020). The effects of new public management on the quality of public services. *Governance*, *33*(3), 461–475.

McCabe, R. M. (2024). Interview with Jennifer McCabe. Accessed on 10 May, 2024.

Our Future Grimsby. (2024). https://www.our-future.io/our-work

Pollitt, C. (2016). Managerialism redux? *Financial Accountability and Management*, *32*(4), 429–447. https://doi.org/10.1111/faam.12094

Smith, M., Hesselgreaves, H., Charlton, R., Wilson, R. (2025). The 'liberated method' – A transcendent public service innovation in polycrisis. *Public Money and Management*. https://doi.org/10.1080/09540962.2025.2456120

The Relationships Project. (2024). Case study: The Wigan deal. https://relationshipsproject.org/project/the-wigan-deal/

APPENDIX 1: THE TIMELINE OF DEVELOPMENT OF THE PATHFINDER'S NORTHFIELD APPROACH

ORIGINS IN 'PROPER CARE AND SUPPORT'

The Pathfinder's Northfield approach grew out of the concerns and convictions of its now strategic lead which originated in his early career in care and support roles and then were compounded by his experiences as a social worker, first in the Education Welfare Service, then the Youth Offending Service. He was deeply concerned about the 'carousel affect' of repeated re-referrals and high levels of recidivism. But he also became convinced of the value of proper relational care and of the under-utilized and under-valued nature of support workers, particularly in schools.

TIMELINE OF DEVELOPMENT

Rodsett House SEMH School

From the beginning of his work in the YOS, Rob was spending a lot of time visiting Rodsett House SEMH school. The pupil cohort represented a concentration of children from some of the poorest and most deprived backgrounds of all. They would be placed there when their behaviour had got them excluded from all other options within the city. Despite this, Rodsett House was resourced as a special school: to provide additional support to meet children's physical or learning disabilities and conditions. Already extremely disadvantaged and troubled children with extreme social, emotional and mental health problems were being placed into a really disadvantaged set of circumstances – the school building was crumbling, there was high staff turnover and educational outcomes for the children were non-existent.

Starting With the Numbers: The Numbers, and the Stories Behind the Numbers

Around 2009, Rob started working more closely with the school to try and understand the extremely high levels of need and began cross referencing the

(Continued)

children on school roll against the YOS database. On a school roll of 172 kids, 75 were known to the Criminal Justice System: 45% of the school population. They had committed a total of 599 offences, and Rob calculated that the overall total cost using the National Audit Office unit cost was £3.1m, and this was conservative as not all details could be included. Rob subsequently tracked the children from that school year for a further 2 years. The number known to the criminal justice system in that cohort had increased from 75 to 96, and there was now a murder conviction. The costs had increased from £3.1m to £7.1m. These data were proof of what was obvious to those working with the children – not only was the level of need grossly underestimated when they arrived at the school but their trajectory was getting worse over their time at the school. What was funded as a special school was dealing with children many of whom already were or would become involved in criminality.

Redeployment Into Rodsett House School

In early 2012, Rob shared the report with senior officers and the Director for children's services. He was called to an executive City Council meeting, where his head of service presented the report. Ultimately, there were two outcomes: first, an emergency cross-multi-agency meeting was established at the school, which ran for 3 years, looking at the 50 most at-risk young people and trying to keep them out of prison; second, in April 2013, Rob got relocated to work full time in the school and tasked to coordinate the multi-agency work, lever in resources and act as a conduit between the school and the 5 YOS teams across the city. Ultimately, the actual impact of the multi-agency panel was limited. However, Rob's position in this group gave him 3 years of concentrated networking around bringing a mission together, and it also placed him visibly in the middle of the response to this problem.

Building Solutions Centred on Support Workers

In 2014, Rob released a second Rodsett House School report, focusing on children's services data related to the school cohort and included case studies which told the human stories behind the criminal involvement of the children and emphasized the importance of the family around the child. This report also included recommendations around use of support workers: building on Rob's experiences of these roles he argued that their relational expertise, shared social context and pastoral focus meant that they could be much better utilized than they were being. He argued for a model which enabled them to provide more sustained, holistic support to families upstream of statutory involvement becoming necessary.

For a year, Rob pitched the recommendations around the city, with little success. In Autumn 2015, he gathered head teachers from the City's four SEMH schools, its' Pupil Referral Unit (for permanently excluded children) and the Virtual School (for looked after children) for a meeting. He pitched his vision to them, and they agreed to collectively fund his salary so that he

(Continued)

could begin work on bringing forward the 'SEMH Pathfinder', which would utilize school-based workers to support the most at-risk children and their families at these schools.

The Beginnings of a Core Team: The Value of a Running Mate

Rob got permission from Rodsett House to do lateral checks and home visits for all the incoming year 7s at the school. In the next-door office was Sarah, the school nurse, who was doing medical checks on the incoming students. She had heard about Rob 'doing something different', and like most people in the school, she was aware of the Rodsett House Reports. Rob and Sarah compared their respective NHS and YOS databases and found shocking and relevant data on both sides that the other was unaware of. Both keen to deepen this collaboration, Rob pitched the idea of joint home visits to the head of the school nurse service, who agreed that Sarah could work in the Pathfinder four days per week.

Home Visits

They used this time to meet with the most fearful, mistrustful families. These meetings – mostly with mums – were a chance to trial a different, holistic approach, asking open questions about what the family needed. They found the 'full spectrum of ACES ["adverse childhood experiences"], trauma and disadvantage': many truly harrowing stories; and many families expressing a deep mistrust of statutory agencies. It was utterly compelling in terms of the deep support needs in these children's families, the level of issues unknown to the school and the value of open, relational listening; and they used the information gathered from these meetings to put the case for a new model of enhanced and sustained family support.

Rob shared the information gathered with the Heads of the City's special schools, arguing for a model of enhanced, sustained family support.

The Beginning of a School's Partnership

The six schools gave the go ahead for limited release of worker's time to work on this model, but budgets were tight, and so they couldn't contribute more than half a day to one day per week for each worker. This did, however, mean that Rob had the beginnings of a project and something to leverage, but they needed funding to consolidate what had been achieved and develop it into something more sustainable.

Lankelly Chase: The Systems Change Funder

In Dec 2015, Rob booked out three days just to call round funders, and conversations led him to a call with Cathy from LKC. Rob spoke for an hour, in a long, heartfelt pitch that led to a follow up meeting in London. Despite Rob's fears that he lacked the kind of business plan that such a significant foundation would require, the grants officers Cathy and Jess understood what

(Continued)

he was trying to do, and a long-term relationship began. Even before LKC made their first grant, their support was central in securing additional funding from the six schools and the project's first external funding from the 'Violence Reduction Unit'. By April 2016, they had funding for Sarah and an additional nurse to be seconded full time onto the project, and Claire had been released from Aquarius. They now had external funding and a core team.

April 2016: Launching the Pathfinder

Rob launched the 'Birmingham SEMH Pathfinder' at Rodsett House school and to the new team of workers from this and two other SEMH schools. They started to identify families, and the project rolled from there, with the first few months spent visiting families. These early meetings involved lots of disclosures: sometimes harrowing stories of traumatic experiences and of repeated failed attempts at support. The team was still based at Rodsett House school, with very little space in a very small office, 'alongside stored furniture and cobwebs'. Most of the work was done out on home visits – or seeing parents wherever they could. For the first year, this was the work, and there was a sense of things falling into place: the strong relationships that were being formed on the ground with the workers and also with the families felt significant. They were gathering reams of information from the families, and there was a sense of doing important research in the richness and significance of the information they were gathering.

2017–2019: Building the Work

The next 3 years were a fertile time. New posts were created at the Lumen Christi multi-academy, and other primary and secondary schools, as well as South and City FE College, joined the model at this time. They also secured premises in a disused community building at a local fire station; this was a significant breakthrough for the project, to have a neutral space to work in and for families to visit, which was important to help shape the identity of the Pathfinder.

Through links with the police, the team were also able to secure funding to develop the 'shared authority' aspect of the work. They created a family room out of the old station commander's office at the fire station, ran parents' engagement days and paid for Newman University lecturers to facilitate the development of a parents' manifesto for this aspect of the work. By 2018, the project expanded to 17 schools, and a real sense of momentum developed. The Pathfinder had been successful in 2 large bids, securing £450k. There was a sense of moving up the levels very quickly. Everything was building really well, and then in March 2020, the pandemic hit.

March 2020: Pandemic

At this time, although BCT were funding Rob's salary, and holding his contract, they weren't funding any other aspect of the project.

(Continued)

At the start of the pandemic, the Local Authority brought forward the planned roll-out of the new 'early help locality partnerships' as part of their emergency response. These are a new approach to Early Help, utilizing a network of commissioned third sector organizations to deliver support in the various localities. Rob was asked to join the emergency response, working as part of the central Authority team to establish the locality partnerships as well as assisting with the general 'war effort' of getting urgent support to families thrown into crisis.

Significantly, the Central team were interested in the Pathfinder's learning and assistance in establishing the locality partnerships. So, the Pathfinder moved 12 of its staff (Pathfinder coordinators working in Pathfinder schools) into the partnerships team. It was an incredibly busy and demanding time, but it was ultimately useful for the Pathfinder because the locality model comprised voluntary sector workers as well as children's trust workers and health colleagues. There was a shared sense of the importance of relational working, and they made valuable links with people who would become important future partners and allies in our work.

2021: Coming Out of Pandemic/Lockdown: Getting Core Funded

During the early stages of the pandemic, there hadn't been much conflict between the Pathfinder's Northfield approach and the work we were doing through the localities: it was just about getting the aid out there rather than following case management processes. However, as the work progressed, there began to be pressure to resolve cases as quickly as possible, and at least within the locality framework's deadline of 6 months, in order to enable the Authority to claim payment by results based on this. This was directly in conflict with the Pathfinder's core principle of not closing cases.

As the country emerged from the pandemic, the Authority agreed to provide core funding for the Pathfinder. However, Pathfinder workers – who had returned to Northfield from the other locality teams after the end of the first lockdown – were still holding up the Northfield locality work (which is one of the busiest and most complex in the City) in addition to picking back up the Pathfinder schools' caseloads. This meant that the Pathfinder had two hats but one pot of funding. In addition, the locality cases came with different criteria: they weren't following the Pathfinder's Northfield approach as it was core Authority Early Help work, which counted case closures towards their payment by results criteria.

That period from the pandemic through the next 3 years was probably the toughest for the Pathfinder because although they had the security of funding, they were caught in a maelstrom of corporate demands and – most importantly – they weren't really funded for what they were supposed to be doing. The team ended up in the strange position of doing work following protocols that they had literally been set up with the intention of changing.

(Continued)

2022: Statutory Funding: Blessings and Curses

Children's services funding for the Pathfinder fully covered their core costs in 2021 and 2022. This financial support brought some temporary stability but also the continued challenges of navigating ongoing tension between the Pathfinder's Northfield approach and authority operating protocols in early help. Then funding was cut to 50% in 2023 and – against the backdrop of the Council's section 114 bankruptcy notice – to zero (bar Rob's salary) by 2024. In addition, Lankelly Chase, who had been our main long term funding partner, was in the process of closing as a funding organization. With the loss of both sources of core funding, the Pathfinder suddenly faced a double cliff edge, and furthermore, they were concerned that the loss of statutory funding might affect their ability to attract external funding. The Pathfinder received the Authority's final decision to zero-fund just before Christmas in 2023, and things were looking very bleak.

11th Hour Rescue

Fortunately, early in the new year, they had a breakthrough: they were able to find funding from Centrepoint, a national homelessness charity. Rob met their CEO on the 29th of January and following that meeting, their board approved £250k funding for the year, with interest in another 2 years. Despite the chaos of funding uncertainty, in fact the model now is starting to take hold. The model is continuing to attract interest from new schools, not just from Northfield, but from other districts: with both secondaries and primaries wanting to join the model and interest is spreading between head teachers by word of mouth. The Pathfinder is now building a new relationship with Centrepoint, who are particularly interested in supporting the work to bring about a rigorous evaluation of the impacts of the Northfield approach. Furthermore, we now have two other major funders interested, and their involvement has the potential to be transformative, potentially allowing us to raise the profile of the work nationally.

REVERSION TO THE MEAN? EXPLORING THE BARRIERS TO EMBEDDING HUMAN LEARNING SYSTEMS

Christianne Ormston[a] and Michael Macaulay[b]

[a]*Northumbria University, UK*
[b]*Victoria University of Wellington, New Zealand*

ABSTRACT

This chapter explores the potential and some limitations of Human Learning Systems (HLS) thinking through the development of a case study of Collaborative Newcastle, a UK-based multi-agency health body (2020–2024). Based in the North East of England, Collaborative Newcastle was a non-statutory partnership made up of institutions in Newcastle including Hospitals Trust, the local Integrated Care Board (NENC ICB), Newcastle City Council and the voluntary sector. The aim was to reduce health inequalities using HLS principles and practices. HLS is one approach that can loosely be termed relational perspectives on public policy and management. HLS enables tailored, collaborative solutions to be created to help practitioners navigate effectively through complexity. It moves beyond linear thinking, focusing not simply on cause and effect in the context of public services as trying to deliver change with reduced resources, competing value sets and overworked practitioners.

The chapter reports on the successes that adopting HLS brought but also the barriers to implementation. Some of these barriers are exogenous and point to structural issues, such as funding restrictions, central–local and regional–local government relations. Others are endogenous: leadership churn, failure of continuous learning, perverse incentives and a propensity to fall back into more comfortable and familiar ways of working. The chapter shows that where barriers of either type are embedded, there is a tendency to revert back

Futures in Public Management
Critical Perspectives on International Public Sector Management, Volume 8, 49–67

Published under exclusive licence by Emerald Publishing Limited
ISSN: 2045-7944/doi:10.1108/S2045-794420250000008004

to the certainties of new public management (NPM) practice, which we suggest serves as a caution for all relational policy initiatives.

Keywords: Human learning systems; relational; health; new public management; leadership; local government

INTRODUCTION

Human Learning Systems (HLS) is one of a number of emerging concepts that can be mapped into the ever burgeoning literature on relational approaches to public management. It focuses on an approach to public management that enables practitioners to navigate effectively through complexity, acknowledging that many problems that public management looks to 'solve' are within environments where 'causes and effects are indistinguishable' and involve variety, change and lack of control (Lowe, Hesselgreaves, & Wilson, 2022; Lowe, Padmanabhan, et al., 2022; Lowe & Wilson, 2017). It is promoted as a response grounded in the reality of public service delivery, which understands public services as complex organizations who are trying to deliver change with reduced resources, 'stretched workers, and competing priorities' (Lowe, Hesselgreaves, & Wilson, 2022; Lowe, Padmanabhan, et al., 2022, p. 1). In so doing, HLS intersects with the dimensions of Bartels and Turnbull's (2020) classification of relational approaches, especially in the way it approaches dynamic systems.

HLS is attractive to both policy and management practitioners for a number of reasons. The inherent flexibility of HLS enables each initiative to be co-created and adapted for its specific context; each HLS project is unique; it already has a demonstrable track record of success, with no shortage of case studies available from around the world.[1] Perhaps most tantalizingly, it seems to be a genuine challenge to old ways of working. As the authors of this chapter have argued previously (Ormston & Macaulay, 2024), HLS is both a response and challenge to the paradigm of new public management (NPM), and as such takes its place among a range of approaches which include public value (Moore, 1997); new public governance (Osborne et al., 2022); outcomes-based management (Service Dominant Logic (Osborne et al., 2013); public service logic (Osborne, 2018); public service ecosystems (Petrescu, 2019); trust-based management (Bringselius, 2023) and even the new public bureaucracy (Lofgren et al., 2022). HLS focuses on continuous learning within organizations to enhance their effectiveness and achieve desired outcomes, recognizing that public sector organizations operate in complex and dynamic environments and therefore need to adapt and evolve.

This chapter provides a small warning about the development of relational approaches to public management, centring on a single-case study initiative. It will look at the barriers to implementation that are found in an ongoing HLS project, *Collaborative Newcastle*, which focuses on health outcomes in the North East of England. Despite a number of very positive developments, barriers around implementation of HLS still exist, and these have had a detrimental impact on it being embedded among stakeholders. Some of these barriers are exogenous and point to structural issues, such as central–local and regional–local government relations. Others are endogenous: leadership churn, for example, inhibits continuous learning and can encourage perverse incentives and a propensity to fall back into more comfortable and familiar ways of working. This chapter will explore these ideas and others, including issues around monitoring, funding restrictions and short-term funding. It will suggest that unless such barriers are overcome, there is a tendency to revert to the mean of NPM no matter how well-intentioned a project may be.

The chapter will begin with a brief literature review of HLS and then explore methods, with an overview of the case study, Collaborative Newcastle, and a brief discussion on its goals as an HLS initiative, including identifying where positive progress has been made. It will then discuss each of the barriers to implementation in turn. We apologize in advance for not leaning too heavily into theory but hope that this empirical case provides valuable insights to the HLS community, both scholarly and in the policy and management domains.

LITERATURE REVIEW

The HLS model explicitly unpacks the three distinct elements of its name: (1) human, (2) learning and (3) systems (Lowe et al., 2020). The 'Human' element of the model is characterized by a relational approach focused on a change in relationships and identities, whereby there is collective responsibility for creating the conditions needed for reaching better outcomes, becoming 'stewards of a system of care and support' (Lowe & Plimmer, 2019, p. 6).

The 'learning' aspect of HLS is a fundamental process that occurs at multiple levels within an organization (Lowe et al., 2020; Lowe, Hesselgreaves, & Wilson, 2022; Lowe, Padmanabhan, et al., 2022; Lowe & Wilson, 2017). HLS models in public management thus promote a culture of continuous learning and improvement within organizations. It recognizes the importance of individual, team and organizational learning to enhance performance and adaptability in complex and dynamic environments. By embracing this model, public sector organizations can enhance their effectiveness, responsiveness and ability to meet the evolving needs of society.

The final element of HLS is the 'system' component, which intends to be an approach that works within complex systems and relates to the perspective, power and participation in each HLS project rather than looking to be a systematic approach. One of the core tenets behind this work are that the issues that public sector and voluntary sector organizations are trying to address are complex and therefore the system response to such issues will need to be as well.

HLS case studies identify a number of barriers that can prevent HLS thinking from bedding into an initiative. The first is the difficulties inherent in changing established mindsets. For example, the Innovation Centre of the Finnish National Agency for Education (EDUFI) was an HLS project that sought to build capacity of those working in local and national education programmes to learn and improve. Here, the HLS approach to public management was 'in tension' with the evaluation approach of the national government (Rautiainen &

Tyrvainen, 2021, p. 18). This made it harder for experimental approaches to be implemented. It also identified that as public sector professional identities were linked to the requirement of specialist knowledge and being experts in their field, this led to resistance to shifting those identities towards a learning mindset (Lowe et al., 2021).

The EDUFI case study acknowledged that further barriers to HLS included mindsets that were resistant to change, a fear of taking risks, a lack of knowledge on the benefits of experimentation as a learning tool, a lack of time and space for creativity and a need to manage the expectations of all actors (Rautiainen & Tyrvainen, 2021, p. 18). These barriers, along with some others, are all prevalent in *Collaborative Newcastle*. Before we identify these, however, it is important to show the great strides that have been made in implementing an HLS approach.

Lowe et al. (2021, p. 69) note that 'shifting to a learning strategy rather than a control strategy may be the most difficult aspect of the shift to an alternative public management approach'. This is attributed to the fact that the focus on targets as a measure of performance and accountability is so 'ingrained' in the way public sector organizations operate that it takes a 'concerted' effort to change (Lowe et al., 2021). The challenge of local commissioners having to report to central bodies is also recognized, and organizations who have chosen to adopt an HLS approach still report to national bodies or central government using national performance measures.

The Plymouth Alliance for Complex Needs case study is an example of where a system has experienced challenges adjusting to a new way of working, where the principles of NPM were dominant and where there was scepticism towards HLS (Wallace, 2021, p. 7). For Plymouth Alliance for Complex Needs, this has involved a substantial period of adjustment whereby colleagues across the local authority services have had to develop 'bigger affiliations to systemic working', and whereby performance data for central government reporting has continued to be collected and submitted, but not used for local performance management (Lowe et al., 2021; Wallace, 2021). The Plymouth Case study also noted a further barrier included the wider structural challenge of diminishing funding within the system, which meant that in spite of positive improvements made through new ways of working, commissioners felt they were 'managing decline' (Wallace, 2021, p. 7).

These noted elements are very much understood within the literature as being a part of the trademarks of NPM as espoused by Hood (1991) and others. Simonet (2015) notes that NPM has been applied to healthcare because funding for healthcare is a growing expenditure in developed states like the United Kingdom due to technological progress and an ageing population (Simonet, 2015, p. 802). While NPM was encouraged to ensure good governance as part of the move to balance government budgets in the late 1990s and related to the resurgence of neoconservatism (Cribb, 2008), it has historically has been used to control critical elements of healthcare systems such as cost, quality and patient outcomes (Simonet, 2015, p. 803). NPM tenets to promote competition in healthcare to improve performance have led to the development of multiple, separate NHS organizations, with their own agendas, and limited obligations to comply with each other (George, 2017; Simonet, 2015). George (2017) comments that the introduction of non-clinical managers within the NHS, 'brought a controlling leadership style' not appropriate for caring services and that legacy of NPM brings the 'greatest hurdle' to the NHS (George, 2017, p. 30). Further to this, inefficiencies in the NHS have been widely reported (Joumard et al., 2010). Notably, the Francis Review (2013) of NHS failings in the Mid Staffordshire Foundation Trust attributed patient deaths to poor leadership, whereby staff were encouraged to give priority to organizational targets over patient care (Cunnane & Warwick, 2013). The findings from this review highlight the need for relational approaches and compassionate leadership in healthcare (Francis, 2013).

METHODOLOGY

The chapter is based on a live case study of a single organization and has utilized a mixture of methods including multiple key respondent interviews, documentary analysis and a degree of participant observation as one of the authors of this chapter is enmeshed in Collaborative Newcastle and has taken part in a number of its initiatives.

We are aware of the limitations of a single-organization case study but note that there is a tradition in public administration research tradition of single-case studies that have contributed to theory and practice going back to the 1950s (Jensen & Rodgers, 2001). Thomas (2011, p. 513) argued that for single case studies to be valid they must contain two components:

(1) A 'practical, historical unity', which I shall call the subject of the case study.
(2) An analytical or theoretical frame, which I shall call the object of the study.

Our single case studies embody both of these traits. We are also conscious of Eisenhardt's (1989) typology for case study research that encourages the use of 'opportunistic methods' as a means to interrogate emergent data. As Collaborative Newcastle is still very much up and running, this is precisely the type of emergence that the authors are exploring. In addition, we hope that in reflecting on an ongoing collaboration, we will avoid the pitfalls of historicity and 'retroactive sensemaking' (Eisenhardt & Graebner, 2007; Lawton & Macaulay, 2017) to enable us to look to the future of Collaborative Newcastle rather than the past. In terms of validity, Flyvbjerg (2006, p. 219) identifies five 'common misunderstandings' around case study research, the second of which is that 'one cannot generalize from a single case, therefore, the single-case study cannot contribute to scientific development'. Flyberg promotes for the notion of the 'critical case' from which a number of general ideas can be extended, which is an argument itself expanded upon by Ruddin (2006) and others, who further suggest that the notion of generalizability itself has evolved far past concerns around a single case.

Collaborative Newcastle is a UK-based multi-agency health body, established prior to the pandemic in 2020. It is a non-statutory partnership made up of key anchor institutions in Newcastle including Newcastle Hospitals Trust, North East and North Cumbria Integrated Care Board (NENC ICB) and Newcastle City Council as well as the voluntary sector. A key focus of its work is to reduce and address the health inequalities across Newcastle, and it was created to allow health system partners to work together in Newcastle to improve outcomes (Collaborative Newcastle, 2023). Its work grew from a focus of joint work around key areas of social health and social care provision and has expanded to include projects such as the Children and Families Newcastle initiative focused on early years and Special Educational Needs (SEND) support and duplication to personalization, which aims to improve the design and delivery of services for people with complex needs.

Collaborative Newcastle has attempted to use HLS thinking to shape and guide its development from the start, with a clear steer from the Newcastle upon Tyne Hospitals Foundation Trust Chief Operating Officer, who led the introduction of this initiative. *Collaborative Newcastle* partners recognized that a single, joint leadership programme for middle to senior managerial staff level across health and care organizations in the City would help to build stronger working relationships, embed trust and promote closer cooperation and collaboration. The staff included in this programme include healthcare practitioners such as nurses, doctors, psychologists and social workers as well as commissioners and senior voluntary sector leads. The aim being to embed HLS ways of working across various levels within the Newcastle health system. *Collaborative Newcastle* key priorities include:

- strengthening relationships and partnership working;
- attracting more people in leadership positions;
- supporting a more consistent and system-wide approach to leadership development;
- supporting and improving the well-being of staff;
- continuous improvement by making use of the lessons learnt through the pandemic.

(Collaborative Newcastle, 2022)

Collaborative Newcastle has been governed by a Chief Executives' Group which meets quarterly, and its main business conducted by a joint directors group which began to meet weekly from the start of the pandemic. This group predated the passing of the Health and Social Care Act in 2022, which formally established regional Integrated Care Systems (ICSs) by the UK Government. As part of the introduction of ICSs, Integrated Care Boards (ICBs) were created, which are statutory organizations with the responsibility for setting a plan for meeting their respective regional population health needs, commissioning health services and managing the NHS budget in those areas (Health and Care Act, 2022).

The introduction of the NENC ICB, of which the Newcastle healthcare system is part of and within which *Collaborative Newcastle* now operates, has seen the ICB formally delegate powers to place. The implication for *Collaborative Newcastle* governance is that an additional ICB subcommittee has been recently introduced to lead on the Newcastle Health System, which has commissioning powers, which is beyond the initial function of *Collaborative Newcastle*. In practice, it contains the same group of directors joined with ICB executive members in order to fit with nationally agreed ICB governance arrangements and to allow it to make commissioning decisions.

We conducted interviews using a key respondent strategy, from a range of actors in Newcastle Health Care System anchor organizations, including individuals who have been heavily involved in the Collaborative Newcastle Joint Directors Board or have participated in the leadership programme. This includes senior representatives from the NENC ICB, Newcastle Hospitals NHS Foundation Trust (NUTH), Newcastle Primary Care and Voluntary and Community Sector (see Appendix 1).

The interviews were supported by participant observation undertaken by the author as a practitioner already working within one of the Collaborative Newcastle organizations (NENC ICB). Participant observation included observation of key Collaborative Newcastle meetings, participation within the Collaborative Newcastle leadership programme and observation of broader Newcastle health system-based meetings where Collaborative Newcastle actors took part, including those exploring urgent care and primary care issues.

The questions asked in the interviews were shaped from the key driver of wanting to identify to what extent there had been a shift in approaches to public service delivery from NPM to HLS within the Newcastle Healthcare system.

The questions were then influenced from key documents and participant observation, including asking participants' understanding of the Collaborative Newcastle initiative, its aims and what had been achieved so far. It explored the leadership programme and whether participants who had taken part in the programme felt it had or would lead to changes of ways of working and views and understanding of the HLS approach. Participants were also asked to define how they understood complexity within the Newcastle Healthcare system, how relationships and trust had been fostered through Collaborative Newcastle and what learning points have been made through this approach. Finally, we explored how participants felt that the HLS approach may impact on how services are delivered by Collaborative Newcastle, including impacts on learning, monitoring and performance management, and outcomes. These questions were being asked to understand to what extent participants understood and recognized HLS principles within the ways of working espoused by Collaborative Newcastle and by the leadership programme.

We utilized thematic analysis to disaggregate the key findings from our participant interviews and participant observation and then collated them into two umbrella categories that reflect the HLS literature: (1) positive impacts and (2) barriers to implementation. Within each category, we identified further sub-themes: under 'positive impacts', we identify (a) forging strong relationships and (b) increased collaboration, and under 'barriers', we identify (a) structural change, (b) central/regional relations; (c) leadership churn and (d) funding issues.

FINDINGS

Positive Impacts From the HLS Approach

Collaborative Newcastle has gained numerous positives from its HLS approach, and these can be categorized into two interconnected but distinct components: the programme identified many positive elements that respondents saw as either being essential for this approach to work or as a positive benefit. Both sets of factors could, we suggest, be potentially transferable to other partnerships and if prioritized, be successful.

Relationship Building

Strong relationships were highlighted as a positive outcome of the HLS approach. It's no surprise that across the people that we spoke to, all noted the importance of putting the time in to develop and maintain strong relationships across the individuals within the Collaborative Newcastle director meetings and more broadly, across organizations at various levels.

> Compassion and empathy are a real tone in the meeting and that group doesn't have to make really difficult decisions, which means it's a different conversation. (R6)

Within this context, the value of the Collaborative Newcastle Leadership Programme was recognized as having a key role in encouraging the development of relationships and relational approaches across organizations at all levels:

> The biggest takeaway has been the relationships, the names I've put to faces and the contacts. (R1)

Respondents also started to talk about the importance of the strength of the relationships and acknowledged that if they weren't strong, it could pose difficulties:

> It's easy when you are patting each other on the back, but it's when you have to challenge each other, that tests the relationships. (R8)

It was important that these relationships had trust in place in order to be open to challenge and have difficult conversations. This was needed to have any success in meeting the complexities of the challenges faced:

> There has been a huge amount of trust built up between our leaders.........Urgent Treatment Centres is a key example, very difficult decisions to be made around resource. We are talking through it and keeping everyone around the table whereas 5 years ago it would have been a battle. (R3)

The importance was cited of greater freedom given to organizations, along with reduced monitoring. Once trust was effectively established, it allowed or should allow greater freedoms for organizations to act to meet challenges. It was felt that in this kind of environment, less monitoring of funding should be required because the trust is in place whereby all organizations feel they are working to meet the same outcomes and that those outcomes would be worked towards in an effective way.

> There has been some good examples of it happening – as the Clinical Commissioning Group was finishing, before it became part of the ICB, (they) managed to get £300,000 funding, and (said) I know that VCS providers are struggling with cost of living costs, and things like keeping community centres open, and (the Newcastle Place Director) managed to get some money to the VCS to allow them to fund Newcastle-based small VCS organisations. This was given without expectation or requests to prove how the funding was used, and was given in the spirit of trust that it would be used towards running costs. (R9)

Alongside this was the need to progress beyond transactional relationships and allow organizations the freedom to use funding the best way they know how without excessive monitoring, based on those trust relationships.

> Transactional funding is always an issue and I guess that's something we're trying to get past. (R1)

This then brings us on to the next stage in the trust continuum, whereby freedom and reduced monitoring had the potential to develop into pooled budgets and increased financial flexibility for organizations working with a partnership, which is strongly dependent on relationships and trust developed over time. In the case of Collaborative Newcastle, they hadn't reached a complete pooling of budgets.

> Have we got to a point where we are thinking about we can think about a true joint use of that money? No. We're working on it. (R2)

However, respondents talked about this being a potential aspiration and noted that progress was being made as the benefits of such an approach were recognized in terms of improving patient pathways:

> There's more freedom around the new money for discharge – we've seen that – there's more opportunity and we've been able to use that more creatively. We used some of that money for social work posts to enhance the pathway. (R3)

Increased Collaboration

In terms of practical examples, there have been areas of work whereby different organizations within the Newcastle Healthcare System have pooled resources, if not quite yet at the stage of pooling budgets. One example was the Acute Respiratory Hub, which was set up during Winter 23/24, to treat patients from Newcastle practices with minor respiratory infections. This intended to relieve pressure in the system, both in General Practice and in inappropriate attendances at the Emergency Department. It's operationalization required collaboration between matrons at an Urgent Treatment Centre in Newcastle, ICB commissioners, Newcastle Hospitals Trust staff and Newcastle General Practice Services, who were contracted to deliver the service. This involved pooling of access to clinical rooms, equipment, administrative support, prescribing and clinical staff. Issues arising were worked through in a collaborative way and built upon relationships that had been established through the Collaborative Newcastle Leadership programme. This was a positive example of HLS in action, but it's important to note that old ways of working did creep in, for example one matron who still wanted to 'charge back' for administrative resource costs. There were also requests for regular monitoring information made by the central ICB team who devolved the funding for the hubs.

More broadly, there was recognition of the benefits of taking on HLS working cultures across the Collaborative Newcastle organizations, even if they didn't explicitly acknowledge them as coming from HLS. Respondents recognized that the opportunity to take risks, potentially fail and experiment through different ways of doing things was important to the success of the approach, even if there are no clear examples of the opportunity to fail emerging through Collaborative Newcastle as yet:

> We have to create the cultures for people to learn and to experiment and take it on. (R4)

Respondents also embraced the need for a whole system approach. This idea is encompassed in the following respondent's comment:

> You can have the senior leaders in a room agreeing things but what happens to everyone else? Does the system, the people working from top to bottom, how well are they bought into working together and learning together? I think the system leadership programme has been excellent at that. (R8)

There was an emphasis on collaboration across organizations, including joint posts held across the system:

> ... (we) brought leaders working with children and families across partner agencies in Newcastle (such as community matrons etc) and said "your job as leaders at a matron level is to seek opportunities to collaborate". (R3)

Barriers to Embedding HLS

As the authors have previously argued (Ormston & Macaulay, 2024), there are lots of positives from the Collaborative Newcastle experience, and in particular our interviewees were generally supportive of the initiative. However, we also found some critical voices, raising concerns over the limitations of the project and moreover the sheer complexity of the problem with which it is tasked with addressing.

Structural Changes

The structural changes, which took place across the Health System across England during the time of and following our work, meant that there was very little structural stability in the system. This impacted on leadership churn, trust and relationships. It could be argued that in such a time of uncertainty, where relational bonds were being lessened, there could be a reversion to tried and tested ways of working. For HLS to work, there is a level of structural stability required which allows for flexibility and self-determinism for the organizational actors working within and for relational working to flourish.

As some interviewees told us, one of the biggest challenges to working in a relational way had been the impact of the introduction of the NENC ICB , which is the largest ICB in the country, and the additional governance and administrative complexity that has been brought with it. One of the most resonant observations was that this structural change had been accompanied by (small-p) political pressure, alongside the feeling that the ICB had been imposed externally rather than bringing organizations and communities along with it:

> The problem with Collaborative Newcastle is that you have lots of people from different worlds and when one of those worlds enforces a structure, and invites everyone into that, which is really what's happening with the ICB, then it can almost feel meaningless for the people that weren't part of it or don't really understand what's happening. (R6)

Respondents commented that the structural change had a negative impact on operational issues such as uncertainty around commissioning and contract renewal. Respondents talked about contract renewals being delayed, causing tension in relationships across the system. Concern was expressed about less agency or freedom to influence change within their area due to having to work within an externally imposed bureaucratic structure. Participant observation of meetings revealed that practitioners from various Collaborative Newcastle organizations were uncertain about how decisions were made around funding following the structural changes, including which committees held that responsibility or who they needed to speak to within the ICB.

Subsequent to the interviews taking place in early to mid-2023, there have been multiple structural disruptions to the Newcastle healthcare system, which has further intensified the complexity of the environment within which *Collaborative Newcastle* is attempting to operate. Within 6 months of the ICB being formed, NHS England asked all ICBs to reduce their running costs by 30% by 2025/2026, with at least 20% delivered by 2024/2025 (NENC ICB, 2024). NENC ICB has been required to save £17.6 million by April 2024 and consequently has had to consolidate estates, staffing, structures and operational focus (NENC ICB, 2024).

The ICB restructure has led to a wholescale repositioning of staff at all levels. This has included savings made through voluntary redundancies, compulsory redundancies and employee churn. This change has led to Newcastle becoming merged with its neighbour Gateshead, as part of a new, smaller, combined Newcastle Gateshead ICB team. ICB resources and key commissioner roles have been stretched to cover a broader geographical area, along with key actors changing within the system, contributing to leadership churn (discussed below).

Second, Newcastle Hospitals Trust, a driving partner within Collaborative Newcastle, has been the subject of a Care Quality Commission (CQC) inspection which has seen their status downgraded from 'Outstanding' to 'Requires Improvement' (CQC, 2024). This has led to huge leadership change, with a new Chief Executive and leadership team being introduced. The full impact of this has yet to be understood, but it is expected to have some impact on the leadership of Collaborative Newcastle.

Third, a further structural barrier mentioned by participants was the worsening of levels of need and increased health challenges experienced by communities post-COVID-19, making the environment faced by Collaborative Newcastle more complex.

These barriers have made the development and sustenance of key relationships more difficult to establish and maintain, decision-making more difficult for participants to navigate, with less resources in the system to support change (ICB cost savings), and participants' viewing increased governance and administration as a potential barrier to getting things done.

Central–Local and Regional–Local Relations

The second barrier, closely linked to structural change, is around who holds the primacy of decision-making and how those relationships influence the flexibility to which organizations can set their own agenda. Collaborative Newcastle is a perfect example of how local partnerships can have very limited scope to set their own priorities, as their direction is significantly influenced by the regional ICB, who in turn have to deliver centrally mandated NHS England targets. In addition, as previously noted, the Central Government cuts to ICB funding requiring them to save 30% across the country by 2025/2026, which has led to significant structural change and cost savings across healthcare systems in England. Under this cost-saving regime, ICBs have been asked by NHS England to more closely prioritize their work and focus on essential duties first. It is too early to say what this impact of this may be within North East and North Cumbria, but it is likely to impact on the resources available to support Collaborative Newcastle's work programme going forward.

Respondents talked about the central–local relationship between NHS at place level and national level and the primacy of the national priorities and targets, which challenges the HLS ethos:

> If you've got a large ICB that then has to go the Department of health it's got to justify a lot of stuff to very senior people in the system, and therefore it needs each place to provide assurance that national and regional priorities are being met. (R8)

Respondents also talked about how *Collaborative Newcastle* still needs to be able to respond to NHS England in terms of how it is using their short term funding to meet targets and monitoring. We explore this below in Section 4 about restrictions in spending funding and short-termism, which is inextricably linked to central–local and regional–local relations.

In addition, there are aspects of the *Collaborative Newcastle* work programme such as the review of urgent care services, which will be strongly influenced by national policy and regional priorities around urgent care. One example is the national drive to move to co-locate Urgent Treatment Centre services with Emergency Departments. This is an example where national and regional policy drivers may be prioritized over local preferences and need. This was acknowledged by respondents as a barrier to the HLS approach of autonomy, co-production and decisions made as close as possible to the people living and working in an area (Lowe, Hesselgreaves, & Wilson, 2022; Lowe, Padmanabhan, et al., 2022).

Leadership Churn

We have already mentioned the significant leadership churn that has taken place both within the NENC ICB, and specifically within the Collaborative Newcastle Directors group as a result of multiple structural changes impacting on leadership roles and staffing within organizations.

However, it was also recognized by the participants as a potentially significant barrier.

> There was leadership changes and so then we had to take a few steps back to start that journey again and we've had to do that a few times with finance as new people have come into post. (R2)

Collaborative Newcastle is now at a stage where key directors have moved on yet again, experiencing multiple rounds of leadership churn. This has been an acknowledged barrier by participants to the progression of the initiative and the projects that it wants to deliver.

> In terms of overall momentum, it's at a tricky phase now, because a lot of the original people in the founding anchor institutions have moved on. (R9)

A key example has been the review of urgent care whereby it has to pause while the incoming new Chief Executive of Newcastle Hospitals Foundation Trust comes into post.

Restrictions Around Accessing and Spending Funding for Projects

Respondents reported that ICB ways of working have also increased constraints on accessing funds and use of funding for projects, whereby even relatively small amounts of funding to boost known projects already endorsed by the ICB required official approaches to senior directors for approval. This was cited as a barrier to creative and relational working and reduced the opportunity for experimentation to take risks and to fail, which is part of the HLS approach.

The introduction of the regional structures was felt to be a challenge to the primacy of place and therefore respondents commented that they weren't always free to put the needs of place as a priority, as expressed through funding restrictions. This was acting as a barrier to act freely:

> ICB is saying place has primacy but you are only getting delegated certain amounts of money to do certain things and being told "well you can do that but you need to focus on delivering this" ….. "It feels like tokenism. (R2)

VCS respondents also talked about the contracting arrangements to their organizations being a barrier to acting freely due to the levels of reporting and monitoring required. In response to a discussion around whether the freedom was in place to spend funding in a way that they know would best support the healthcare system, a respondent commented:

> ...more broadly (freedom to spend allocated funding) isn't happening across the system and there's loads that needs to change in order to be truly working within a Human Learning System's ethos/way of working. (R9)

Respondents also talked about how Collaborative Newcastle still needs to be able to respond to NHS England as a priority in terms of how it is using their short-term funding to meet targets and monitoring. This meant that it still operates within the traditional NPM style of operation and also links to the barrier posed by central–local relations mentioned above. It was also felt to be restrictive in meeting the longer term issues that Collaborative Newcastle was trying to address.

LESSONS FOR POLICY AND PRACTICE: REVERSION TO THE NPM MEAN

There are, of course, many reasons why these driver and barriers have emerged, and we cannot speculate too much here. But perhaps, it has been significant that there was a conscious choice not to explicitly refer to HLS but to weave its core ideas throughout the leadership programme so that these served as a platform for learning, rather than touchstones to refer back to.

One interviewee acknowledged that leadership political pressure was even more far-reaching and directed nationally from NHS England so that *Collaborative* Newcastle had to ensure targets were met and monitoring put in place to '*keep the dogs off*' (R7). Additionally there are problems connected to the short-term nature of trying to approach complex problems:

> ...every target I get has to be delivered by March 31 of the following year ... when we are talking about multi-generational problems and issues ... how do you make a short term contribution to a long term solution that's helpful rather than cost shifting a problem to another organisation. (R4)

The reason we think these observations are so important is because they are redolent of typical concerns that were evinced for many years about NPM processes and practices. Even more interestingly, they were not the only echoes of NPM identified by our interviewees either.

The final key finding of this research, therefore, is that despite numerous jumping off points and an ostensible opposition to NPM ideas and practices, many of them are still being reflected in the work of *Collaborative Newcastle*. These echoes of NPM were frequently connected to the NHS more broadly rather than *Collaborative Newcastle* itself:

> ...it's great that we are trying to work like that but are still working within an NHS payment system which relies on meeting contracts or we still work in a local authority best value framework which tries to do this other thing. (R4)

It was also associated with the notion that much of the collaborative work is being undertaken by organizations that had previously been in competition for economic resources or political support. One practitioner example was offered by a matron who asked for the Acute Respiratory Hub administrative resource costs to be charged back, in requests for performance data from ICB teams and short-term funding. Perhaps more tellingly, certain organizations especially those in the voluntary and community sector, are still being held accountable by traditional targets and performance management:

> For me, it's [HLS] a really good model if the world was perfect. However, the problem is, how do you put that in place when everyone is still doing old models and other models. (R5)

The explicit reference here by a voluntary practitioner to 'old models' are traditional NPM practices, which were felt to be restrictive and limiting, and undermining creativity, due to the need to ensure that any funding received was spent in a way that the benefits could be easily measured. It was felt that this style of contract management did not always reflect an awareness of, or was able to accurately capture, the additional value or benefits that voluntary sector interventions can bring to communities. The impact of this is to limit risk and reduce creativity, learning and opportunities to 'fail', which is needed if HLS is to be introduced to its full realization.

We were also told that targets and goal-setting were perhaps being replicated under new terminology around the development of Objectives, Goals, Initiatives and Measurement milestones (OGIMs), which forms the detail of the newly published Newcastle Place Plan. The Newcastle Place Plan for 23/24 sets out *Collaborative Newcastle's* immediate priorities for the year, along with longer-term transformation and development plans for 2023/24–2028/29, which focus on addressing health and well-being inequalities (Collaborative Newcastle, 2023). This document, which will define and directs the work of *Collaborative Newcastle* contains a number of priorities, objectives, goals, targets and timeframes for completion, which doesn't appear to deviate significantly from a traditional NPM approach on measurement, monitoring and targets. It would be helpful to revisit the progression of this work in future to understand its progress, how it has been delivered in practice, how HLS relates to its delivery and explore to what extent this plan was influenced by the need to meet external targets set by wider organizations outside of the Newcastle system.

CONCLUSION

In any organizational change, or new innovation, there is frequently a desire to stay within comfort zones and use tried and true processes. The cases alluded to earlier demonstrate that HLS projects are also vulnerable to this process, and

Collaborative Newcastle, while obviously still an emergent initiative, also demonstrates these characteristics. It is interesting that many of the barriers identified are not those often associated with implementation problems. There was a notable lack of opposition from different stakeholders, which has traditionally been the leading barrier in other projects, particularly collaborative ones (McTigue et al., 2020). Even still, it is clear that there are key areas where *Collaborative Newcastle* is reverting back to the NPM mean.

The spectre of NPM may bring concerns, especially to practitioners, who have lived through enough policy change cycles to note a tendency to fall back into what you know. But in keeping with both the HLS literature, empirical cases, and our own case much of this may require an adjustment of mindset than anything else. We suggest that as far as possible, people keep pushing at points of difference away from NPM and embrace the HLS approach further. Our case suggests, this would be a beneficial approach, and we thought it would be helpful, therefore, to conclude by showing the green shoots of this approach in *Collaborative Newcastle*.

Our indicative findings suggest that there is a shared understanding of HLS principles and values (complexity, empathy, trust) among our respondents even if they were not identified explicitly as such. It was also apparent that despite numerous challenges there was enthusiasm for the way that *Collaborative Newcastle* was approaching its myriad workstreams and that these were being run in a way that enabled experimentation. Respondents were also quick to tell us stories about how *Collaborative Newcastle* responded to the COVID-19 pandemic and a number of interviewees also spoke of how new stories need to be created, to give a better sense of purpose and future development. As one interviewee suggested: *'people absolutely get it, people say that "HLS sounds like the Newcastle Way"'* (R4).

While we are cautious we suggest that this embracing of HLS principles and the desire to construct narratives, whilst always not explicitly identified, are classic symptoms of a new comfort zone being created. The adoption of an HLS approach was not given huge fanfare but was instead built into the leadership development programme so that most respondents spoke of its key features without directly referencing the HLS model. It is also worth noting that the leadership development programme has already been undertaken by around 300 people, all of which is focused on creating new mindsets to traditional problems. The identification of HLS principles and values, and the enabling of experimentation in a successful way, indicates that HLS is beginning to have some traction in shaping new ways of working. In terms of being able to sustain and grow HLS ways of working, there would be some benefit in giving actors in the system space to allow reflection on the benefits and positive impacts that they have experienced as a result of these new ways of working and to explicitly recognize that they working in a HLS way.

The Collaborative Newcastle Leadership Programme is a mechanism through which system-wide based practitioner reflection and appreciation of the benefits of HLS ways of working could happen. It is this embedding of practitioner reflection which will allow the sustainability and growth of HLS values and principles and help avoid retrenching into old mindsets. Where HLS initiatives seem to work is in securing their own, new comfort zone, one which enables people to work through complexity in their own way.

NOTE

1. See https://www.humanlearning.systems/case-studies/ for a number of HLS case studies.

REFERENCES

Bartels, K., & Turnbull, N. (2020). Relational public administration: A synthesis and heuristic classification of relational approaches. *Public Management Review*, *22*(9), 1324–1346. https://doi.org/10.1080/14719037.2019.1632921

Bringselius, L. (2023). Trust-based public management: Conceptualization and lessons from the Swedish trust reform. In C. Greve & T. Ysa (Eds.), *Handbook on strategic public management*. Edward Elgar.

Care Quality Commission. (2024). The Newcastle upon Tyne hospitals trust inspection report. https://api.cqc.org.uk/public/v1/reports/87a09ba4-e168-41ea-bcff-58d444105d71?20240124122737

Collaborative Newcastle. (2022). Learning to lead together – Newcastle system stewardship. *Key Pillars*. http://www.collaborativenewcastle,org.uk

Collaborative Newcastle. (2023) *Newcastle place plan*. https://democracy.newcastle.gov.uk/documents/s201640/4.1%20Collaborative%20Newcastle.pdf

Cribb, A. (2008). Organisational reform and health-care goods: Concerns about the marketisation in the UK NHS. *Journal of Medical Philosophy*, *33*(3), 221–240.

Cunnane, D., & Warwick, R. (2013, February 14). Francis report: What went wrong with NHS leadership? *The Guardian*. https://www.theguardian.com/healthcare-network/2013/feb/14/francis-report-nhs-leadership#:~:text=The%20Francis%20report%20points,of%20leaders%20in%20the%20NHS. Accessed on November 09, 2024.

Eisenhardt, K. M. (1989). Building theories from case study research. *Academy of Management Review*, *14*(4), 532–550.

Eisenhardt, K. M., & Graebner, M. E. (2007). Theory building from cases: Opportunities and challenges. *Academy of Management Journal*, *50*(1), 25–32.

Flyvbjerg, B. (2006). Five misunderstandings about case-study research. *Qualitative Inquiry*, *12*(2), 219–245.

Francis, R. (2013). *Report of the mid Staffordshire NHS foundation trust public inquiry*. Bit.ly/FrancisPublicInquiry.

George, M. (2017). The effect of introducing new public management practices on compassion within the NHS. *Nursing Times*, *113*(7), 30–34.

Health and Care Act 2022.C.31. https://www.legislation.gov.uk/ukpga/2022/31/contents

Hood, C. (1991). A public management for all seasons. *Public Administration*, *69*(1), 3–19.

Jensen, J. L., & Rodgers, R. (2001). Cumulating the intellectual gold of case study research. *Public Administration Review*, *61*(2), 235–246.

Joumard, I., André, C., & Nicq, C. (2010). *Health care systems: Efficiency and institutions*. OECD Economics Department Working Papers 769. OECD Publishing.

Lawton, A., & Macaulay, M. (2017). From birth to death: The life of the standards board for England. *Public Administration Review*, *77*(5), 720–729.

Lowe, T., French, M., & Hawkins, M. (2020). The human, learning, systems approach to commissioning in complexity. In A. Bonner (Ed.), *Local authorities and the social determinants of health* (pp. 241–262). Policy Press. https://doi.org/10.1332/policypress/9781447356233.003.0014

Lowe, T., French, M., Hawkins, M., Hesselgreaves, H., & Wilson, R. (2021). New development: Responding to complexity in public services-the human learning systems approach. *Public Money & Management*, *41*(7), 573–576.

Lowe, T., Hesselgreaves, H., & Wilson, R. (2022). Learning as meta strategy in public service. In T. Lowe, G. Eichsteller, H. Hesselgreaves, M. French, R. Wilson, M. Hawkins, D. Plimmer, A. Brogan, & T. Vita (Eds.), *Human learning systems: Public service for the real world* (pp. 54–74). Centre for Public Impact.

Lowe, T., Padmanabhan, C., McCart, D., & McNeill, K. (2022). *Human learning systems: A practical guide for the curious*. Centre for Public Impact, Healthcare Improvement Scotland and Iriss.

Lowe, T., & Plimmer, D. (2019). *Exploring the new world: Practical insights for funding, commissioning and managing in complexity, collaborate for social change and Northumbria business school.* https://collaboratecic.com/wp-content/uploads/2023/09/1.-Exploring-the-New-World-Report-MAIN-FINAL.pdf

Lowe, T., & Wilson, R. (2017, December). Playing the game of outcomes-based performance management. Is gamesmanship inevitable? Evidence from theory and practice. *Social Policy and Administration*, *51*(7), 981–1001.

McTigue, C., Rye, T., & Monios, J. (2020). Identifying barriers to implementation of local transport policy – Lessons learned from case studies on bus policy implementation in Great Britain. *Transport Policy*, *91*, 16–25.

Moore, M. H. (1997). *Creating public value*. Harvard University Press.

NENC ICB. (2024). *End of consultation report*. NENC ICB. Pemberton House.

Ormston, C., & Macaulay, M. (2024) Developing a human learning systems approach for inter-agency collaboration: Lessons from the UK NHS. *Australian Journal of Public Administration*. https://doi.org/10.1111/1467-8500.12649. Accessed on November 09, 2024.

Osborne, S. P. (2018). From public service-dominant logic to public service logic: Are public service organizations capable of co-production and value co-creation? *Public Management Review*, *20*(2), 225–231.

Osborne, S. P., Powell, M., Cui, T., & Strokosch, K., (2022), Value creation in the public service ecosystem: An integrative framework. *Public Administration Review*, *82*(4), 634–645.

Osborne, S. P., Radnor, Z., & Nasi, G. (2013). A new theory for public service management? Toward a (public) service-dominant approach. *American Review of Public Administration*, *43*(2), 135–158.

Petrescu, M. (2019). From marketing to public value: Towards a theory of public service ecosystems. *Public Management Review*, *21*(11), 1733–1752.

Rautiainen, A., & Tyrvainen, P. (2021). Enhancing learning systems through experimentation (human learning systems case studies). *Finnish National Education Agency (EDUFI)*. https://www.humanlearning. systems/uploads/7549%20CPI%20%E2%80%93%20Finnish%20Innovation%20Centre%20Case%20 v2.pdf

Ruddin, L. P. (2006). You can generalize stupid! Social scientists, Bent Flyvbjerg, and case study methodology. *Qualitative Inquiry*, *12*(4), 797–812.

Simonet, D. (2015). The new public management theory in the British health care system: A critical review. *Administration & Society*, *47*(7), 802–826.

Thomas, G. (2011). A typology for the case study in social science following a review of definition, discourse, and structure. *Qualitative Inquiry*, *17*(6), 511–521.

Wallace, G. (2021). Plymouth alliance for complex needs (human learning systems case studies). *The Plymouth Alliance*. https://www.humanlearning. systems/uploads/Plymouth%20 Alliance.pdf

APPENDIX 1: LIST OF INTERVIEWEES

Respondent	Job title/Sector
R1	NIHR clinical research representative
R2	Collaborative Newcastle representative
R3	Newcastle upon Tyne hospitals foundation trust representative
R4	Newcastle upon Tyne hospitals foundation trust representative
R5	VCS representative
R6	Primary care representative
R7	NENC ICB commissioning lead
R8	Primary care representative
R9	VCS representative

INITIATING RELATIONAL PUBLIC SECTOR REFORM THROUGH MICRO- AND MACRO-INITIATIVES IN THE EARLY YEARS SYSTEM IN GREATER MANCHESTER

Deborah James, Kate Wicker and Roman Kislov

Manchester Metropolitan University, UK

ABSTRACT

In this chapter, we outline how we worked as embedded collaborators through academic membership of Greater Manchester Combined Authority's (GMCA) School Readiness Board, as evaluators and leaders in a large UK Government-funded project on early outcomes and as consultants, delivering a strengths-based coaching programme for early years leaders across GM's 10 local authorities. As such, we were able to become embedded academic collaborators working with the system leadership rather than on it. Our coaching programme was delivered to leaders in the early years field where these strategies feed through into the Early Years Delivery Model and the GM School Readiness Programme. The findings show how a reflective approach to the challenges of leadership helped embed personal development through real-world relational encounters that maintained motivation and then created advocacy for the leadership programme across the lengthy timespan of its implementation. The participants eventually stopped asking for expert models and manuals of leadership development when they realized that they were engaged in an experiential leadership programme.

Keywords: Relational; leadership; soft power; workforce development; goals; narrative; early years

Futures in Public Management
Critical Perspectives on International Public Sector Management, Volume 8, 69–82

ISSN: 2045-7944/doi:10.1108/S2045-794420250000008005

INTRODUCTION

The Greater Manchester Model of Unified Public Services, known as the GM Model, articulates a vision for reformed public services in Greater Manchester (GMCA, 2019). The Model is organized around a core value of designing services around people and communities, working with strengths as well as needs. It is based on a systemic view of public services delivered through integrated place-based teams. It is underpinned by a network of relationships; between services and communities, between public, private and voluntary sectors, between organizations working in places and between place-based teams and specialist teams. The leadership required is integrated and shaped around place and people rather than institutions and is mirrored in a workforce that collaborates across institutional boundaries.

Commitment to reformed public services is well embedded in Greater Manchester. The GM Model can be traced through the Greater Manchester Strategy 2021–2031. The Strategy was published in the wake of the pandemic, which 'necessitated a collaborative approach to working at a scale not seen before across sectors and agencies across Greater Manchester' (GMCA, n.d., p. 7). This suggestion of a reinvigorated relational working approach in GM is substantiated in the details of 'how we work together' in the strategy, which focus on acknowledging the complexity of relationships in the region, the basis of trust on which they are formed and asserting a model of distributive leadership.

In this chapter, we outline how we worked as embedded collaborators through academic membership of GMCA's School Readiness Board, as evaluators and leaders in a large Department for Education funded project on early outcomes and as consultants, delivering a strengths-based coaching programme for early years leaders across GM's 10 local authorities. As such, we were able to become embedded academic collaborators working with the system leadership rather than on it (Wilson et al., 2024). Our coaching programme was delivered to leaders in the early years field, where these strategies feed through into the Early Years Delivery Model and the GM School Readiness Programme.

Our commitments to relational public sector came through our learning from clinical academic experience with families and workforces where focusing on strengths-based approaches has accelerated outcomes that were important for families (Pilnick & James, 2013) and supported change towards more person-centred design and delivery in charity and public sector organizations (James, Hall, et al., 2016; James, Pilnick, et al., 2016; James, Vincent, & Fisher, 2021). Within GM, we were able to support a more 'other' focused agenda, which was enacted in meetings between parents and professionals (i.e., where parents were given the first slot on the agenda) and in meetings between local authority leaders where the sending of messages from individuals was relinquished in favour of listening deeply to others and creating shared understanding across the combined authority (James, Wicker, et al., 2021). In this chapter, our aim is to describe and explore the outcomes of the leadership coaching programme from the participant's perspectives and discuss the design of the programme, addressing the 'how' of developing the 'relational capabilities of public service systems' (see Wilson et al., 2024).

LITERATURE AND CONTEXT

Relationality is a core element in theories of contemporary leadership in public services. In a review for the Leadership College for Government, which trains senior civil servants and public service leaders in the United Kingdom, King and Wilson (2020) found a general trend in leadership studies away from a focus on individual leaders' qualities towards the relational foundations of leadership and its impact on others in terms of empowerment and building trust. The review found that common to contemporary conceptualizations of leadership, including network or collaborative leadership, was a focus on social behaviours for the joined-up governance of public services. This represents a departure from the idea that leaders can act alone; in a pluralistic governance model, the role of leaders is to manage collaboration in an inclusive way, building relationships between actors in the system and mobilizing actors for change (King et al., 2020). An understanding of complexity in social issues, outcome creation and the delivery of public services is central to many discussions of relational leadership and prompts a requirement for collaboration and an understanding of the importance of workplace relationships (Clark et al., 2014; Ford, 2020; French et al., 2023). Overall then, this perspective has a focus on relationships rather than individuals as enabling effective leadership for public services.

In a context of relational public services, there is plenty of discussion on how leadership ought to operate in practice. Leaders must work across systems, collaborating on outcomes outside their own organizations, building trust and coordinating resources (French et al., 2023; Masters, 2021). As Clark et al. (2014, p. 8) state, 'relational leadership addresses the need for leaders to hold at the forefront of their thinking and actions a concern with modelling and fostering relations across all aspects of the system within which they work'. To this end, leaders should foster relationships among workers and between organisations (Bartels et al., 2024), engaging empathetically with others and 'creat[ing] space' for their participation in decision-making (Ford, 2020). This suggests the importance of social skills or soft skills to public service leadership (Dickinson, 2020), including sharing, listening, being responsive to and supporting others (Clark et al., 2014). For Lowe et al. (2024, pp. 2–4), this involves creating relationships that are more than transactional; instead, they are based on recognizing the value of the other person.

The implications of this understanding of effective leadership have created some impetus to consider how to design leadership development opportunities that focus on the relational practices that underpin the enactment of relational leadership (Ford, 2020; Tourish, 2020). In the context of UK local government, Iles and Macaulay (2007) report that historically most development efforts focused on individual leaders. Instead, they proposed an action learning approach that involves 'working on "real" problems whilst also paying attention to learning and relational processes' (p. 23). Similar themes have been taken up in more recent discussions on relational approaches to leadership development. Experiential learning in context is one aspect of this approach where leaders are supported to try new behaviours in the workplace (Dickinson, 2020). There is an aspect of challenge where new ideas are introduced to support systems transformation, alongside a commitment to strengths-based learning and confidence building (Hill et al., 2021). Relational practices are encouraged through creating interactional opportunities and developing empathy and regard for others. In this approach to leadership development, there is often a group learning process, with the facilitation of interactional processes that enables peers to learn together and develops peer trust and support (Iles & Macauley, 2007; Hill et al., 2021; Lowe et al., 2024, pp. 19–20). A recent case study of such a dialogic approach in Sweden that sought to develop how leaders conceptualized their identities, roles and relationships suggested its potential for supporting a move towards relational leadership in the workplace (Narbutaitė Aflaki & Bassi, 2024). Overall, these accounts suggest that through attention to social awareness and social skills, relational leadership development focuses not only on individual leaders but on their collective ability to work together and so focuses on the relational dynamics of leadership practices in context (Day, 2000).

A rich framework of collective leadership development comes from Eva et al. (2021). It describes how leadership development can be delivered to develop collectives rather than individuals. Their framework is designed as a quadrant chart, with leadership development programmes along two dimensions: context-centric/consultant-centric and normative/critical. The first dimension describes the extent to which the development is standardized or context-specific while the second describes the extent to which the development seeks to improve existing behaviours or fundamentally change ways of working.

The case study that is the focus of this chapter was one part of a wider programme of work that sought to adapt the coaching model developed by the first author (James, Wicker, et al., 2021) through co-design with locality leaders in the early years system in Greater Manchester. The coaching model invites participants to develop personal goals for change around aspects of relational practice, for example *really listening* or *making more time for reflection during conversations*. Video recordings of authentic conversations between the participants enable the supervisor to find moments when participants are practising their desired change (i.e., really listening and pausing to think). The moments of interactional strength, which are personalized to each participant's goal, are reviewed in a group session. All participants experience the impact of seeing themselves and their co-learners from a strengths-based perspective. Mapping the design of our programme to Eva et al.'s (2021) framework, the approach is balanced on the first dimension. The consultant's centricity is on the embodiment and adherence to principles and processes of strengths-based video review. The authenticity of conversations and personal goals ensures the programme is grounded in the situated context of the participants (their personal development and the development of their services). Mapping the programme along the second of Eva et al.'s dimensions surfaces the fundamental relational proposition of the video review method. Put simply, the objective is to enhance relational competency in work. The proposition is that enabling relationships to flourish will lead to better decisions because they are informed and shaped by the 'other'. Adapting behaviour is not an aim. Changing the priority of relational working is. However, participants become more attentive to their positive ways of relating through micro-analysis of video clips and behavioural change is observed because of the fundamental re-framing of work as relational. On both dimensions, our programme maps to the centre of Eva's quadrant.

In this chapter, we report a case study from one of the three localities that took part in the coaching programme. The research was approved by the Health and Education Research Ethics and Governance Committee at Manchester Metropolitan University (reference number 45901).

METHODOLOGY

In the case study area reported below, four participants who were all service managers in the early years started the programme, but only one completed it due to structural change in the locality. The locality had a strategic lead who worked closely to support implementation of the leadership coaching programme in their area.

We draw on short reflective online interviews that were conducted with the coaching programme participant (Sharon), the strategic lead of the locality (Hannah) and a partner member of the study team whose remit was to support implementation of the programme across GMCA (Jane).[1] Our findings draw on the process notes taken by the first author (consultant and supervisor of the video coaching programme). The interviews were conducted by the second author after programme delivery had finished.

The work took place over two years, from 2021 to 2023. The first phase of the leadership coaching project was consultant-led, with the first author delivering three full days of in-person training in relational-based coaching and co-design to participants over a period of 10 months. This core training was delivered alongside monthly locality group supervisions with the aim of participants both learning key concepts and experiencing coaching for themselves. The beginning of Phase 2, which lasted eight months, marked a move to peer-led delivery. The participants developed their own ways of talking about the key concepts of video coaching – safe space, encounter, creating space in dialogue through silence and pausing. They developed their ability to capture and review video from a strengths-based perspective and then made local plans on where and how to implement the video coaching method in their services. They continued to experience video review through group supervision from the first author while writing locality-specific coaching guides and protocols for relational leadership and arranged governance for video coaching in their localities. The final phase was delivered across 8 months and involved place-based implementation of the coaching programme. In the case study area, the participant co-led a series of workshops with their new team which was taking on the lead responsibility for implementing early identification of speech and language delay across health and early years.

[1]These names and the name of the locality have been changed to protect the identities of those involved in the research.

FINDINGS

The Case Study

In Berksley, the leadership coaching programme was initiated with senior leaders in the Start Well service. The programme was intended to support a locality focus on the implementation of a new cross-agency method of assessing communication and language at 18 months that was being delivered against a background of a move towards integrated working in the early years across Greater Manchester. The programme took place within these shifts to new ways of working, as well as in the context of a major review of early years' services in the area. Two participants left the programme as a result of the review and one left the organization, leaving one participant and the strategic lead in post to complete the programme. In the final phase, where the participant led coaching workshops with a group of leaders, there was a recognized need for sensitivity to this context of organizational change, as well as a desire to bring a newly-formed team of colleagues together. The involvement of the strategic lead in articulating a vision for the work, embedding it in local strategy through the Children and Young People's Plan and supporting the trainee, was a major strength, ensuring the continuation of the commitment of the Berksley team to the leadership coaching programme.

The Starting Points

The leadership coaching programme was commissioned through the School Readiness Programme Board to support the implementation of early identification for children with speech and language delays. It was aligned to the vision for reformed public services in Greater Manchester as articulated through the GM Model. All three research participants talked about the need for relationship development to support the place-based integrated working core to the GM Model. The GMCA consultant who was part of the design team for the leadership coaching, said:

> ...the relational coaching fits very much with that place-based team leader role because it's around not just your own leadership learning, but it's how your leadership learning impacts or drives or motivates those others around you. (Jane)

Jane went on to say that while there are various leadership programmes available for local government, few focus on the relational basis of effective public services, strengthening team relationships and supporting colleagues to learn from each other and work across professional silos.

The strategic lead in Berksley described the expected contribution of the coaching in terms of a service focus on partnership working and, in particular, an early years' delivery model to which muti-agency working is central. She said:

> I just really value the, I suppose I think of it as the idea of coaching. I know that it can make such a difference. And I think particularly in local government and the way that we're wanting to work in a more integrated way, across different organizations, we don't offer a great wealth of training courses. You know, we often stumble around, how do we develop not just motivated leaders, but leaders that can really tune into their teams. (Hannah)

Within Berksley, the leadership coaching was also conceived as a way to support team members working across the system in the context of organizational change. The strategic lead in the locality was keen on running the coaching to support her leadership team through a service review, cognizant of the implications of the review on the workforce. In addition, the participant on the programme described how the coaching could support a team as they implemented a new programme of work.

> ...one of the biggest changes for my team is we're gonna be starting implementing the assessment [to assess communication and language at 18 months]. And that is a huge shift in what they've been doing. And I knew, I anticipated, that it might cause a bit of unease amongst the team and thought we could use the leadership coaching as a way of sort of bringing the team together. (Sharon)

The support for the leadership coaching programme in Berksley was achieved through alignment with a strategic driver for integrated working, a valuing of the approach to leadership development – relational, 'tuned-in' – and the specific context of organizational transformation.

Sharon's Turning Points

Sharon was the coaching programme participant. We now consider her reflections on the leadership coaching and how it worked in Berksley. The participant's goals were like the North Star, helping set the course for the work on the ground. Sharon described her goal as 'sitting back and listening and thinking before I respond and react,' describing her motivation to move away from task-based working and the historically reactive professional culture which she had encountered through video review in the initial three training days. All the locality teams that took part in the programme were asked to discuss their implementation plans for the 18-month communication and language assessment in that initial training. They were videoed, and a strength from each locality team was played back to the whole group session. The two interviewees in Berksley recount the story of the video review, describing how their locality group focused on completing the task at the expense of conversation and reflection. The strategic lead, Hannah, said:

> ...they all laughed when they looked back at the video because there was very little talk. It was just like, 'right, let's get on with it. You do that. I do this, this, this, this, this' and they were all hands-on kind of action. And actually it was only really by seeing the video that they could reflect on that *[laughing]*, and they weren't actually actively engaging with each other, but they were doing the doing while they were trying to engage. And actually that wasn't a good use of their time. And I think that helped them to shift, to know that actually when you're given a task or we're given a task as a group, let's explore that. Let's listen to each other and actually let's identify what somebody else is saying. [...] And I think we need that because there are situations that arise where people are making decisions in isolation or they're making contrary decisions after things have been agreed, and I think we would benefit from some of that. So I think we have to use video camera because I think people need to see it, don't they, they actually need to see themselves, it's very strong. (Hannah)

Hannah here summarizes the power of the video in enabling the reflection of the group and how that in turn scaffolded reflections on practice. Sharon explains the powerful realization that she had during video feedback of their group interaction:

> When I first saw our video feedback, it was really, really clear that we were very task driven and very reactive. And we didn't think we were until we saw that video [. . .] When we had that first video feedback, everybody saw it, it didn't sit comfortably for us initially, but do you know what, that might have been the defining moment actually when I thought, I need to, my goal is different now. [..] I laughed actually because I thought, 'Oh my God, that's just, that's us, we are very reactive and task driven, and I know there's a place for that cause there's gotta be aren't there, but for me it was like, it was like an eye opener really. It was like, wow'. (Sharon)

The video footage that was fed back was a strength because it did contain a moment where one of the team members paused to listen to another. The responses from the participants show that using strengths (which are situationally and contextually defined, not behaviourally defined) can create moments of dilemma. Sharon went on to explain that this realization directly motivated the changes in her leadership practices.

Sharon talked about the benefits of putting her goal into practice:

> I'm sort of sitting back now and thinking about it, because I wanted to do that for myself, really, but also for the team. Because these changes [i.e. implementation of the communication and language assessment] have absolutely been quite big for the team. And I suppose I'm a bit of a solver. I wanna solve everybody's problems, which you can't do, and I suppose for me, it was sitting back and listening, and then just asking those tiny questions and putting it back to the person that's asking me. [. . .] And there isn't always a solution to everything. And really they're an experienced team, my team. They should be able to solve their own problems. And I wanted to be able to let them do that as well, rather than coming to me all the time and I'm saying, well, let's do this, this and this. [. . .] So I'm sort of trying to practice that really in in everyday working and even within our leadership team. [. . .] And I think all together, I think that has really influenced my leadership style now. (Sharon)

The initial framing of her goal was linked to the objective to implement the new early identification programme. Over time, her goal was framed in a more personal way because it was rooted in the situated practices of her interactions. She then began to reconsider the meaning and distribution of leadership. Sharon began to use her goal in a multi-agency setting, describing how the micro practices she had evolved through the coaching programme had helped her to respond rather than react, the deeper listening to other perspectives had helped her to overcome initial 'anxieties' and build trusting working relationships across the early years system.

The Power of Co-design

Co-creation was a key aspect of programme design. It was important that the programme was shaped by and responsive to local priorities and the needs of the group. This was a particularly important feature of the programme to the strategic lead:

> I think what was also very exciting was this idea of the leaders, established leaders, coming together to develop this programme together, that felt very exciting and I hadn't experienced or seen anything with the same kind of involvement from leaders. (Hannah)

Hannah described the initial hesitation of participants to take responsibility for leading on the direction of the programme, given expectations that it would be directed by the facilitator. While completing specific tasks including writing a locality-specific guide to video feedback, Hannah describes a process of collective learning emerging:

> I think that was sort of their turnkey moment when they could see that they could influence the shape of what they were wanting to do and they were using their own experience to be able to do that rather than somebody else telling them, 'this is best practice, this is what the research says, so this is why you're doing it'. They were actually being much more reflective, using others' ideas, as we all do, but actually demonstrating that they could put the structure in. And I think there was a greater pride in that, you know, they felt, when we were able to share that document with the wider, the wider coaching group. But then also we shared it with our own leadership team. It was that acknowledgement that this was something that they were doing. (Hannah)

Sharon in turn reflected on how the micro listening practices that had been central to her goal were put into practice in the programme of sessions that she led with the first author in the final phase of the project:

> I think in particular for me it was it was the listening to them, really listening to what they were saying and then changing what we were doing totally to reflect what they needed. So for example, obviously the implementation of the 18-month communication and language assessment is the big thing for us. And so we did a bit of work on change and how they felt, a lot of group work, a lot of feedback, but then some of the feedback that came back then changed our thinking of what we would do the next week. Because it reflected what they were saying, rather than just have that as a question and answer, it was about making that meaningful the week, the week after, if you will, at the next session. (Sharon)

The design of the programme, with its commitment to locality co-design of how the coaching programme was implemented, meant the priority of relational development was designed in through the principle of co-design. Sharon's reflections show how her personal goal helped her achieve the design commitment and it all made sense to her.

Outcomes

Sharon took part in the leadership coaching intervention during a period of complex change in her locality. She led a team that was implementing a new cross-agency method for assessing pre-school speech and language development. She described the coaching programme as 'inspirational' and 'transformational'. Her story of change echoes themes that we found in the wider programme of work in Greater Manchester around the impact of the programme on professional interactions and team relationships, particularly for new or integrated teams.

In a context of intense change and uncertainty, maintaining motivation amongst her team, which included new team members and members whose job roles had changed, was a particular challenge for Sharon, and she used the leadership coaching programme to guide her in supporting her team. Her goal was to move from what she perceived as a task-oriented and reactive leadership style towards a practice of 'sitting back and listening and thinking before I respond and react'. Sharon identified that the outcomes she particularly valued from the coaching were being able to listen to the concerns of her team, to support them to be actively involved in decision making, and to build strong team relationships. She explains:

> We've gone through a change and the change, even though we're a lot busier, we're a smaller leadership team than we were [. . .] So we have a lot of stuff that we need to get done, but I still think there's time to sit back and reflect and that's what I try to do now [. . .] speaking to the team about how we're gonna do it rather than 'this is what we're doing and this is how we're gonna do it'. Now I'm sort of turning that around a bit. So it's like, 'we've been asked to think about this, how would you think we want to do it?' and going forward, I've really tried to involve them in aspects of this communication and language assessment implementation. (Sharon)

Sharon's leadership, combined with her team themselves participating in the coaching, have contributed to team development: 'So I think probably the two things together really have created a bit of a more harmonious team [. . .] So I think that's been a real benefit for our team, a real benefit.' The strategic lead in Berksley spoke of the potential benefits of leadership coaching to integrated teams going forwards particularly around their priority work area of the communication and language assessment:

> . . .the [early years] practitioners that [my colleague] manages will be using the [health] trust systems. And so there's a lot of language of us and you and yours and ours and it's gonna take ages to stop that. But behind that comes some. . .unfortunate attitude, I suppose. I'm not trying to say that it's all negative, but I think we're all so developed in our own services that actually I think if we can work with the team leaders in the leadership coaching, it'll help them to be more self-aware and aware of others, which I think, it would be a really, a great strength when different systems and approaches are having to come together. (Hannah)

She went on to say:

> I think sometimes people are so used to leading that they're pushing forward, aren't they, and they're not necessarily bringing people along with them and that's what I really like about the leadership coaching is it, it does make you sit back and it does make you listen and tune in, and you can't, we've all got those regimented statutory things we've all got to face. And sometimes they become blockers and so I hope this will help people be more in tuned with each other. (Hannah)

Reflecting on the barriers that can be created by heroic leaders, a style which is perhaps inevitable in a system driven by the need to get things done, Hannah is recognizing leadership in the everyday practices that will enable a new model of working on the ground.

This case suggests the contribution that the leadership coaching programme can make to creating leaders for new or integrated teams in building professional trust, creating inclusive spaces and developing team identity. The design of the programme enfolded Eva et al.'s quadrant chart; the consultant-led elements of the programme (dialogic, video feedback) were place-based and co-designed, and while the work sought improvements in relational safety, it created space for disruptive safe encounters which provided opportunity for new ways of being and new ways of seeing leadership. The programme delivered learning that was itself relational and situated in practice to equip public service leadership to resonate with the principles of relational public services.

DISCUSSION

Reflecting on the wider programme of work in GM and the responses of participants within the leadership coaching sessions, it was the personal development activated by the articulation of goals, which were evidenced through real-world relational encounters, that maintained motivation and then created advocacy for the leadership programme across the lengthy timespan of its implementation. The participants eventually stopped asking for expert models and manuals of leadership development when they realized that they were engaged in an experiential leadership programme. The expertise of the facilitator was in the creation of a generative and safe space for relational development. This approach has the power to renew professional vision and engender relationships that are more than interactional sites for influence and leverage (James, Vincent, & Fisher, 2021; James, Wicker, et al., 2021).

One of the surprising findings from our wider programme of work was the theme of management efficiency. Participants of the programme spoke about improvements in efficiency that arose from changes in supervision, decision-making and team management. These concepts were not explicitly discussed during the leadership coaching sessions. On reflection, the commitment to situating the programme within and with the work on the ground may have inadvertently drawn up the management concepts that were a tacit but ever-present framing of practice in the participants' minds. This design factor created balance between consultant centric and context centric development.

Martin Buber (2023), a 20th century Austrian–Israeli philosopher, said that human existence is characterized by two fundamental modes of relating: the *I-Thou* relationship and the *I-It* relationship. An *I-It* relationship involves objectification where we experience the world and others as objects to be analyzed, used or categorized. In contrast, the *I-Thou* relationship is a reciprocal encounter in which individuals meet as whole beings, free from instrumental purposes. Buber states that we oscillate between the two modes (*I-Thou, I-It*), but if we approach in the subject-object mode (*I-It*) our learning from the observation is encapsulated in that mode, remaining an 'it' fixed for use in the purpose of the subject's endeavour. According to Buber, 'the improvement of the ability to experience and use generally involves a decrease in a man's power to relate' (2023, p. 92). The *I-It* mode is dominated by causality where 'every event that is either perceivable by the senses and physical or discovered or found in introspection and psychological is considered to be of necessity caused and a cause' (Buber, 2023). Conversely, the world through the *I-Thou* lens (Subject-Subject) is a world of relation in which 'I' and 'You' confront each other freely in reciprocity that is not involved in or tainted by causality. In the relational world, community is built by people standing in a living, reciprocal relationship to the 'You' – which Buber describes as the single living entre which is the 'I' for none. This leadership coaching programme prioritized the creation of relationships that were more than transactional because the value of the other person was seen and felt in the development of oneself and their work (Lowe et al., 2024).

Policy and Practice Recommendations for Relational Public Management

The participants framed their outcomes and impacts from the leadership coaching programme with reference to values, effectiveness and efficiency. The organizational drive for effectiveness and efficiency were not in the frame during the leadership coaching programme. The concept of encounter, which was introduced through the philosophy of Buber (2023), was a concept that was drawn on from the outset. The participants constantly referred to this concept; it was ever-present. It became normalized in their conceptualization of the programme, and *they* found a way of showing how relational encounters made them more efficient and effective.

Our recommendation relates to the design of programmes for relational leadership development. Programmes that reframe leadership from individual to relational can be facilitated by maintaining a learning dynamic between the knowledge that is context-specific and the expertise of the consultant. Creating fundamental change in ways of working is made possible by recognizing strengths in the existing ways of being. Leadership programmes that enable experiential learning where the interdependent nature of learning is both felt and understood by the individuals gives credibility and creates advocacy for relational leadership.

CONCLUSION

The leadership coaching programme was rooted in the *I-Thou* mode of existence. Commitment to co-design was an epistemological outflow from this philosophical starting position. Relational practice was framed in strengths – a praxis aimed at maintaining a subject–subject relationship. We exist by oscillating between the *I-It* existence and the *I-Thou* existence but greater appreciation to the *I-Thou* as the mode for delivering learning and development might create more effective relational practice in statutory systems more quickly. This programme of work was made possible by the political and strategic commitments for relational reform in Greater Manchester.

Our programme did not dichotomize collective/individual leadership – we cannot easily map our design on a quadrant, yet we see the value of articulating the design elements. Our programme was built on a philosophy of relatedness and the academic expertise that underpinned it was rooted in the alignment between the philosophical paradigm, the design choices and praxis. The movement towards a relational public sector needs courage to break with tradition and create radical new ways of seeing leadership, choices that can resist the waves of causal undercurrents that have saturated public sector management.

REFERENCES

Bartels, K. P. R., von Heimburg, D., Jordan, G., & Ness, O. (2024). Debate: A relational agenda for changing public administration research and practice. *Public Money & Management*, 1–3. https://doi.org/10.1080/09540962.2024.2402873

Buber, M. (2023). *I and thou* [Walter Kaufmann, Trans.]. Paperback reissue. Free Press.

Clark, M., Denham-Vaughan, S., & Chidiac, M.-A. (2014). A relational perspective on public sector leadership and management. *International Journal of Leadership in Public Services*, *10*(1), 4–16. https://doi.org/10.1108/IJLPS-03-2013-0006

Day, D. V. (2000). Leadership development: A review in context. *The Leadership Quarterly*, *11*(4), 581–613. https://doi.org/10.1016/S1048-9843(00)00061-8

Dickinson, H. (2020). Engaging and developing public sector leaders. https://assets.publishing.service.gov.uk/media/5f881f5c8fa8f50418473d02/NLC-thinkpiece-Developing-Leaders-DICKINSON.pdf. Accessed on December 10, 2024.

Eva, N., Wolfram Cox, J., Tse, H. H. M., & Lowe, K. B. (2021). From competency to conversation: A multi-perspective approach to collective leadership development. *The Leadership Quarterly*, *32*(5), 1–14. https://doi.org/10.1016/j.leaqua.2019.101346

Ford, J. (2020). Relational leadership: Public sector leaders into the next decade. https://assets.publishing.service.gov.uk/media/5f881ee28fa8f5042c3f2ad7/NLC-thinkpiece-Effective-Leadership-FORD.pdf. Accessed on December 10, 2024.

French, M., Hesselgreaves, H., Wilson, R., Hawkins, M., & Lowe, T. (2023). *Harnessing complexity for better outcomes in public and non-profit services*. Policy Press.

GMCA. (2019). The greater Manchester model. https://www.greatermanchester-ca.gov.uk/media/2302/gtr_mcr_model1_web.pdf. Accessed on December 10, 2024.

GMCA. (n.d.). Greater Manchester strategy 2021-2031. https://aboutgreatermanchester.com/the-greater-manchester-strategy-2021-2031. Accessed on December 10, 2024.

Hill, B., Sanderson, H., & Eichsteller, G. (2021). Human learning systems – Implications for workforce development. In Lowe, T., Brogan, A., Eichsteller, G., Hawkins, M., Hesselgreaves, H., Jennions, B. N., Plimmer, D., Terry, V., & Williams, G. (Eds.), *Human learning systems: Public service for the real world* (pp. 271–286). https://centreforpublicimpact.org/wp-content/uploads/2024/09/hls-real-world.pdf. Accessed on December 9, 2024.

Iles, P., & Macaulay, M. (2007). Putting principles into practice: Developing ethical leadership in local government. *International Journal of Leadership in Public Services*, *3*(3), 15–28. https://doi.org/10.1108/17479886200700018

James, D. M., Hall, A., Lombardo, C., & McGovern, W. (2016). A video feedback intervention for workforce development: Exploring staff perspective using longitudinal qualitative methodology. *Journal of Applied Research in Intellectual Disabilities*, *29*(2), 111–123. https://doi.org/10.1111/jar.12161

James, D. M., Pilnick, A., Hall, A., & Collins, L. (2016). Participants' use of enacted scenes in research interviews: A method for reflexive analysis in health and social care. *Social Science and Medicine*, *151*, 38–45. https://doi.org/10.1016/j.socscimed.2015.12.040

James, D. M., Vincent, S., & Fisher, S. (2021). Challenging behaviour around challenging behaviour. *Journal of Applied Research in Intellectual Disability*, *34*(4), 1166–1179. https://doi.org/10.1111/jar.12879

James, D. M., Wicker, K., Street, M., Bibby, R. J., & Robinson, J. (2021). Systems leadership in the early years. *Management in Education*, *38*(3), 99–106. https://doi.org/10.1177/08920206211031913

King, M., & Wilson, R. (2020). A literature review on effective leadership qualities for the NLC. https://assets.publishing.service.gov.uk/media/5fdb3940d3bf7f40d489eb07/A_literature_review_on_effective_leadership_qualities_for_the_NLC.pdf. Accessed on December 10, 2024.

King, M., Wilson, R., & Wilson, S. (2020). Organisational effectiveness and collaboration across the system: Literature review summary. https://assets.publishing.service.gov.uk/media/5fdb38b28fa8f54d58640dc5/Organisational_Effectiveness_and_Collaboration_Across__the_System__Literature_Review_Summary.pdf. Accessed on December 10, 2024.

Lowe, T., Hesselgreaves, H., Wilson, R., & Smith, M. (2024). Relational public service, human learning systems insights. https://www.humanlearning.systems/hls-insights-findings-from-our-research-2024/. Accessed on December 10, 2024.

Masters, J. (2021). Systems leadership in human learning systems. In Lowe, T., Brogan, A., Eichsteller, G., Hawkins, M., Hesselgreaves, H., Jennions, B. N., Plimmer, D., Terry, V., & Williams, G. (Eds.), *Human learning systems: Public service for the real world* (pp. 363–373). https://centreforpublicimpact.org/wp-content/uploads/2024/09/hls-real-world.pdf. Accessed on December 9, 2024.

Narbutaité Aflaki, I., & Bassi, A. (2024). Co- creating capacity? Empowerment and learning for front-line workers and organisations. In S. Baines, R. Wilson, C. Fox, I. Narbutaité Aflaki, A. Bassi, H. Aramo-Immonen, & R. Prandini (Eds.), *Co-creation in public services for innovation and social justice* (pp. 53–69). Policy Press.

Pilnick, A., & James, D. (2013). "I'm thrilled that you see that": Guiding parents to see success in interactions with children with deafness and autistic spectrum disorder. *Social Science & Medicine*, *99*, 89–101.

Tourish, D. (2020). Beyond heroic leadership. https://assets.publishing.service.gov.uk/media/5f881e578fa8f50429658794/NLC-thinkpiece-Effective-Leadership-TOURISH.pdf. Accessed on December 10, 2024.

Wilson, R., French, M., Hesselgreaves, H., Lowe, T., & Smith, M. (2024). New development: Relational public services—Reform and research agenda. *Public Money & Management*, 553–558. https://doi.org/10.1080/09540962.2024.2344902

STRENGTHENING PROFESSIONAL AGENCY THROUGH PROFESSIONAL DIALOGUE: RESULTS FROM A BOTTOM-UP ACTION RESEARCH APPROACH FROM THE NETHERLANDS

Daniel van Middelkoop and Peter Horsselenberg

Amsterdam University of Applied Sciences, The Netherlands

ABSTRACT

In order to deliver good work, professionals need agency – the ability to act and decide on the course of one's actions. The agency of professionals in the public sector is however increasingly under pressure. Research suggests that these limitations on the agency of public professionals in turn limit their ability to create and sustain positive outcomes for the people and populations they serve.

In this chapter, we discuss findings resulting from a longitudinal bottom-up action research approach in the Dutch education sector. The approach is aimed at strengthening the agency of public professionals, using professional dialogue as a central concept. We present and discuss both the methodology used and the results of that methodology in strengthening the agency of public professionals in 11 teams in 3 educational institutions.

The results suggest that there are clear benefits of a tailor-made support for teams of professionals, such as employed in the action research. In varying degrees and dependent on context, this started or accelerated reflection on and improvement in setting goals, cooperation in the team and quality of work, thus at least partly increasing the agency of public professionals in the teams. In varying degrees, the lack of sufficient team and organizational conditions were found to often hinder the development of agency of public professionals.

Futures in Public Management
Critical Perspectives on International Public Sector Management, Volume 8, 83–97

ISSN: 2045-7944/doi:10.1108/S2045-794420250000008006

Revaluing of the professional logic in the way work in public organizations is organised is needed in order to structurally improve the agency of public professionals.

Keywords: Professional agency; public professionals; good work; team conditions; organizational conditions; action research

INTRODUCTION[1]

Professionals in the public sector are hugely valuable to society; this is something almost everyone seems to agree on. We count on these professionals to deliver good work – meaningful, high-quality work (Gardner et al., 2002). Their work is often specific, context dependent and complex and cannot – or only to a limited amount – be codified in protocols or regulations. We trust upon these public professionals to help face and tackle an increasing array of social and economic challenges. The climate crisis for instance demands an energy transition while an ageing population and shortages in the job market demand different ways of working in healthcare, engineering and many other sectors. And in our search for answers and a way to approach these huge social and economic problems, those in public professions are seen as essential.

In order to live up to this promise, public professionals need agency – the ability to act and decide on the course of one's actions (Priestley et al., 2015). Professionals in the public sector, and their agency, are however increasingly under pressure since the 1970s (Freidson, 1973; van Middelkoop, 2022). Research in the Netherlands shows that the experienced agency of many professionals in the public sector in the Netherlands is limited – for instance in primary and secondary education (Evers & Kneyber, 2013; van Vroonhoven, 2024), vocational education and universities (van Middelkoop et al., 2018, 2023), youth care (Hunkar et al., 2021) or central government (Tonkens, 2008). Reasons stem from characteristics of the profession, for instance a view of teaching as a solo profession, but also from a managerial and financial focus that prevails above the 'logic' of public professionals as well as a perceived lack of institutional support for those professionals. Findings suggest that the limitations on the agency of public professionals limit their ability to create and sustain positive outcomes for the people and populations they serve.

Since 2015, the research group Professional Agency has used action research and a bottom-up-oriented approach aimed at professionals.[2] We specifically focus on professionals in the public sector – those employees with complex work that can or should not be 'codified' or structured, and whose jobs require, among other things, a fair degree of agency and cooperation. With our approach, we strive to increase that agency by strengthening cooperation and the relational ties between public professionals in the teams that participate. Over 40 teams of professionals participated in this research, using a guided and structured dialogue to strengthen their agency and improve the outcomes of their work. In this chapter, we will reflect on this granular approach to strengthen the practice of public professionals. In order to do so, we present the results of three sub-projects of this longitudinal research approach within 11 teams. By providing a discursive description of our findings, we will discuss benefits and drawbacks of the approach and explore next steps to further strengthen the agency of public professionals. We start however with discussing the literature on professionals and professional agency, after which we present the methodology used.

LITERATURE REVIEW

Before we go into details about the methodology of our action research approach and its' results, we will clarify several key concepts in that approach. We look subsequently at professionals and the way these professionals work together in teams and at the concept of professional agency.

The Agency of Public Professionals

The origins of the term professional go back a long time and are used widely. In the simplest sense, we are referring to someone who practices a profession. But the idea of a professional also includes the notion of delivering high-quality work. Public professionals do work that is important and complex, and they possess the knowledge and skills to produce good work with a high degree of competence (van der Krogt, 2015). Good work can be defined as work that is of high quality – or technically excellent – which is performed according to professional ethical standards and which is meaningful to the person doing the job (Gardner et al., 2002; Ruijters, 2018). They increasingly work together, most notably in teams, in order to be able to tackle the complexity of their work. The work of professionals is also always in service of someone: a client, customer or student; a professional is intrinsically motivated to help that person (van Middelkoop, 2022).

It is up to public professionals, within the unique and complex environment within which they operate, to determine what is necessary in any given situation to achieve high-quality work. Professionals therefore requires a certain measure of agency in order to achieve that quality. In line with the definition given by Priestley et al. (2015, p. 19), we define agency here as the capability to act on one's will, based on one's own free judgements and decisions. An important aspect of this definition is deciding on the direction of the action oneself. In essence, it's about the freedom of professionals to decide on the direction, intention and meaning of their own actions in their work, given the desired result of that work. This includes thinking on and deciding on what 'good work' is in a certain situation – what do teachers for instance consider to be good education, and how do they translate it into their educational practice? There is no universal approach to good work for public professionals; they have to adjust their actions, often on the basis of moment-to-moment internal deliberations, to the specific context in order to achieve the desired result.

But what determines agency? The degree to which professionals possess agency is determined partly by the individual (the agent) and partly by the culture and structure they act in (Archer, 1995; Eteläpelto et al., 2013; Giddens, 1979). On the individual level, it's about the competences, characteristics, values and professional background and experience of the professional. Culture and structure are about the way in which work, the organization and society have been set up, i.e. the way an organization is structured, the standards set within a professional field or profession or demands and expectations of public professionals within a society. It is important to realize that agency, structure and culture constantly influence each other. Existing structures and cultures restrict and/or strengthen the agency of an individual, who can never act independently of those forces. But vice versa, individuals through their actions also influence these structures and cultures. They can – often gradually and indirectly – change them or perpetuate them (Archer, 1995).

This continual mutual influence means that the agency of professionals is not a constant or absolute and therefore cannot be exactly pinned down. The degree to which agency is present depends on the professionals who act and the context in which they act (Hinostroza, 2020); it is always in flux. Agency is a capacity that only becomes real in particular situations that configure a certain space within which it is possible to act (Priestley et al., 2015, p. 19). A public professional may for instance, together with colleagues, have a great deal of agency in an environment where there's a lot of trust and where a lot of space is given to improve certain work procedures. In a similar situation but with different colleagues or in a situation where work has been 'regulated to death', and colleagues do not work together well, he or she will only have very limited agency.

The Agency of Cooperating Public Professionals

For the vast majority of organizations, working together has become the norm. This is most commonly organized in teams (Decuyper et al., 2010; Derksen, 2021). The importance and the benefits of teamwork are broadly endorsed in both popular management literature and in academic studies on professionals (i.e. Hargreaves & O'Connor, 2018). Cooperation between professionals can lead to an increase in their agency. As stated above, the agency of professionals depends on their knowledge, skills, background and values. Everyone is unique in this, and in that diversity lies the added value of cooperation. In cooperation, the expertise and roles of professionals can come together such that high-quality work can be achieved, and the agency of professionals can be strengthened. If this is the case, it empowers professionals to contribute to good work more effectively and to come up with solutions for complex problems they face in their work.

But of course, this added value is far from being something automatic. Research shows that cooperation between professionals remains limited to coordinating practical issues in many workplaces (Vangrieken et al., 2016). If cooperation does surpass this level of practical coordination, it is not always effective because of a number of team-related factors, such as a lack of psychological safety (Edmondson, 2013) or phenomena like 'groupthink' and 'social loafing' (Derksen, 2021; Vangrieken et al., 2015). When the goal of cooperation is unclear in the team or group or when the basic conditions for 'good teamwork', such as a limited size and interdependency, are lacking, cooperation can feel like a distraction for professionals, which contributes nothing at all to good work (Derksen et al., 2020).

But factors in the structure and culture of an organization can also limit the agency of cooperating professionals. In many workplaces, professional cooperation is promoted, but at the same time, the systems and processes are set up with a focus on individuals rather than teams or groups (Glastra & van Middelkoop, 2018). Moreover, the space and preconditions for professional cooperation have increasingly come under pressure due to the desire and a perceived need for control and efficiency on an organizational level. Moreover, when the aim of cooperation in an organization is imposed from the top down, it can also curtail agency of the professionals, because of increased control of professionals, or standardization of the work they perform (Watson, 2007, in Vangrieken et al., 2015, p. 29; see also Zinsmeister et al., 2022). When cooperation is introduced into organizations on the wrong grounds, for example as a disguised cost-cutting measure, it can also undermine professionalism (Derksen et al., 2020; Hackman, 2002; West & Hirst, 2005).

Through our action research methodology, we aim to increase the benefits of cooperation and increase the agency of the public professionals that take part in the research. We see cooperation not as an end in itself but as something that is deployed in the service of achieving good work together.

METHODOLOGY

In order to both understand and strengthen the agency of public professionals, a longitudinal bottom-up action research approach has been employed by our research group in over 40 teams between 2015 and 2023, with a total of over 400 individual interviews and well beyond a 100 dialogue sessions in teams. We follow the definition of Coghlan and Shani (2014, p. 535), who define action research as 'an emergent inquiry process in which applied behavioural science knowledge is integrated with existing organizational knowledge and applied to address real organizational issues. It is simultaneously concerned with bringing about change in organizations, in developing self-help competencies in organizational members, and in adding to scientific knowledge. Finally, it is an evolving process that is undertaken in a spirit of collaboration and co-inquiry.

The central concept in our methodology is professional dialogue. A professional dialogue is a conversation between professionals about their work, focused on strengthening the actions of those professionals and the quality of their work (Deglau et al., 2006). A professional dialogue can be both reflective and generative in nature (Isaacs, 1999). This means a professional dialogue for public professionals can be aimed at reflections on (the quality of) work and the way this work is conducted but also to generate new ideas and insights and translate these insights to actions for practice.

We applied this action research within teams in organizations in different levels of education (i.e. higher and vocational education, youth care) as well as in the private sector (i.e. energy sector). In these and earlier projects, we developed and refined a method called 'experimental learning lab for professional teams', which explicitly creates space for a structured and guided professional dialogue within a team. Through this dialogue, we aim to increase the agency of the professionals in the team and improve the team outcomes. With the Experimental Learning Labs (ELLs) methodology, teams work on defining their common goal and purpose as well as their performance.

A meaningful professional dialogue in teams is not something that is easily achieved – it requires practice, guidance and clear roles. Time and other constraints (see above) limit the possibilities for dialogue in many teams. In the ELL methodology, the two action researchers that guide the team have a role to provide structure and guidance, enabling team members to conduct a more meaningful and fruitful professional dialogue and to help the team formulate actions that result from that dialogue. This does however ask of the action researchers who facilitate the team to constantly navigate the tension between steering and supporting the team in the different phases of the ELL methodology. The action researchers have a spectrum of roles, ranging from directive approaches, such as setting conversational guidelines and making sure every team member has an equal 'voice' in the dialogue, to more facilitative strategies, such as listening, summarizing and asking questions (van Middelkoop & van den Berg, 2020). In order to strike a balance between these roles, the action researchers always have to keep in mind that the 'end goal' of the action research is strengthening the agency of the team. This means that any actions taken by the researcher is always in service of the development of the team's agency, and the team members are always ultimately in the 'steering seat' when it comes to the focus, form and sequence of the dialogue and consequent actions that come from that dialogue.

For this chapter, we draw specifically upon three more recent research projects (from 2020 until 2023) focused on strengthening the agency of professionals in higher and intermediate vocational education. Although there were some differences in the focus of and reason for doing these three projects, the ELL methodology was used in a comparable fashion. A total of 11 teams participated in these three projects. With the professionals in these teams, a total of 130 individual interviews and 35 dialogue sessions were held.

To maximize the chances to successfully carry out the process and increase the agency of the public professionals in the team, the following prerequisites had to be met in order to start with an ELL trajectory:

- Teams consist of at least 5 and a maximum of 15 public professionals who are jointly responsible for achieving (part of their) goals in their work. The team members must actively commit to participate in the project.
- Time and space in the task portfolios of professionals participating in the ELL must be realized by management, as well as financial means if necessary to realize interventions designed by the team (see Phases 3 and 4).

The ELLs Methodology

The ELLs methodology consists of four phases:

(1) Establishing commitment and social contract.
(2) Team diagnosis.

(3) Intervention design and implementation.
(4) Team evaluation.

Each phase has specific activities and steps to ensure the success of the ELL methodology. The details of each phase are provided below. All individual interviews and group sessions were recorded and transcribed and all dialogue sessions were guided by two action researchers.

Phase 1: Establishing Commitment and Social Contract

In the first phase, talks (non-recorded) are held with all stakeholders – team members as well as managers and supporting staff 'around the team' – to get a first view of the situation and needs of the team, the role of the action researchers and practical matters such as duration of the ELL and time investment. The prerequisites as mentioned above both from management and the team are discussed and established in as social contract.

Phase 2: Team Diagnosis

In this phase, both individual team members and stakeholders around the team (management, supporting staff such as HR) are interviewed, after which two dialogue sessions with the team are held.

In the individual interviews, views of the professionals on what constitutes good work (in this case good education and study success), functioning of the team and organizational factors that influence both individual and collective agency are addressed. Besides providing us with rich data, these interviews also form the basis for joint dialogue sessions in the team, which are guided by the action researchers. The goal of the first dialogue session is to establish a joint vision on good work (good education) and the joint objectives that the professionals strive towards in their work. The team members also discuss what helps and what hinders in realizing that vision and those objectives. In the second session, we address the collaboration within the team and the strengths and weaknesses of the team (see also Horsselenberg et al., 2022; van Middelkoop et al., 2018).

Phase 3: Intervention Design and Implementation

Building on the second phase, the team formulates a number of topics to work on with the aim of formulating and deciding about concrete interventions and actions. These interventions can either be focused on improving the team's outcomes (i.e. better quality of their educational programme) or at improving the functioning of the team. This is done in either one or two dialogue sessions, depending on the size and number of interventions chosen by the team, and guided by the action researchers. It is worth noting that the direction and design of the interventions are always decided upon by the team members and never by the action researchers. If the team feels there is a need, external experts can be deployed to assist the team members in further developing the intervention.

After the dialogue session(s), the team members work independently from the action researchers on implementing the interventions. If needed, the team members can actively ask either the action researchers or external experts for extra guidance.

Phase 4: Team Evaluation

In this phase, individual interviews are again conducted, following the same topical structure as in Phase 2, supplemented with a few questions evaluating the ELL trajectory. Through this final measurement, we are able to compare the team members' professional agency as it emerges from the interviews in this final stage with the agency that emerged from the interviews in the second phase. Based on these interviews, we map changes in the team conditions (i.e. psychological safety, use of expertise in the teams) and organizational conditions (i.e. leadership) that influence the team's agency, as well as the agency as experienced by the team members. This can be seen as a form of self-reporting of the agency as experienced by the team. We create a qualitative picture through questions in the interviews on the experienced ability to, for instance, determine the direction and approach of the educational design and pedagogical approach used in the classroom or the ability of the team to work together as a team on improvements in either education or the functioning of the team. In our analysis, we make a distinction between the experienced agency on the team's direct educational practice, the agency experienced in achieving improvements in the own practice as a team and the agency experienced by team members in influencing organizational conditions (van Middelkoop et al., 2023).

Additionally, a concluding, evaluative dialogue session is held with the team, based on the individual interviews from this phase. In this final session, the team also looks ahead and discusses how to continue working on strengthening their agency without the support of the action researchers.

Of the 11 teams that participated in the projects that form the basis for the findings below, 8 teams 'went through' all 5 phases, although the amount of time and energy spent on the intervention phase differed. One team decided beforehand to participate only in Phases 1 and 2 of the ELL, while two teams decided to stop participation in the ELL either at the end of the diagnostic phase or during the intervention phase.

FINDINGS AND REFLECTIONS[3]

Rather than presenting detailed findings of a limited amount of ELL trajectories in teams, we use a discursive approach to analyze and present the results of our action research conducted in the 11 teams. This allows us a more in-depth reflection and discussion of the methodological approach and the degree to which the agency of the teams in these projects was actually strengthened.

If we look at the ELL trajectories conducted with the 11 teams, we feel we can conclude that the professional dialogue – embedded in an action-oriented research approach like the ELLs – is a rich and worthwhile way to increase the agency of public professionals. Through the professional dialogue, we found that the agency of the teams that participated can be strengthened in a meaningful way although, in various degrees and with a considerable amount of tailor-made guidance from the action researchers. We also found that all participating teams were not used to or experienced in using a professional dialogue as a means of discussing their goals, the functioning of their teams and their agency. The main reason the professionals in the 11 teams distinguish for not being able to use a dialogue on their own is a severe lack of time and space, with the 'daily noise' of work taking up most or all of their attention. This resonates with what we encountered in the approximately 30 earlier ELL trajectories between 2015 and 2020. It strengthens our resolve and belief that support for the professional dialogue, both in providing time and space and in providing guidance through approaches such like the ELLs are needed to support public professionals to deliver good work in their daily practice. Below, we will highlight a few findings in more detail: the added value of professional dialogue in the ELL approach, team and organizational conditions we encountered that influenced the agency of the 11 teams and the actual experienced agency of those teams.

Agency of Cooperation Professionals

As stated in the literature, the agency of public professionals is not something static, but it varies depending on the context in which these professionals operate and in the case of this research, the characteristics of the team and the individual professionals in that team. We make a distinction in agency we encountered in realizing educational practice, in making improvements in either the educational practice or in the functioning of the team and in influencing the organizational context and stakeholders within that context.

If we look at the professionals in the 11 teams, most experienced a fairly high amount of agency on the level of educational practice. There were large differences among teams, with some teams reporting low levels of agency on this aspect. Agency seemed predominantly dependent on team conditions on this level, with notably expertise and engagement contributing positively to this aspect. Also, a clear and shared understanding of a common goal, and interdependence to reach this goal, significantly influenced the combined agency of the professionals in these teams.

When we look at achieving improvements, many teams experienced a lower collective agency, with some teams showing moderate but many teams showing limited agency. We found that professionals in the 11 teams were more motivated to realize improvement goals when those directly impacted the main goal in their work – in this case, high-quality education for students. They were less motivated for improvements aimed at internal team functioning or professional development, in which the teams also seemed to feel more dependent on either management or supporting staff.

The influence on organizational conditions shows low agency across the board of the 11 teams. We encountered a large perceived gap between the teams on the one hand and management and support departments on the other hand, with many teams displaying a perceived lack of access to and connection with both. Most professionals in the 11 teams do not see themselves as an actor that is able to influence conditions on the organizational level.

The Added Value of the Professional Dialogue for Strengthening Agency

Having given a broad overview of the agency experienced in the teams, the question remains whether or not the professional dialogue as employed in the ELL methodology serves to strengthen that agency. Again, due to the dynamic nature of agency, the answers differ across teams and contexts.

We found that the team dialogues help professionals to gain insight into both the goals they work on and the functioning of their team, through the combination of individual interviews and team dialogues in Phase 2 of the ELL methodology. Most importantly, most teams managed to create team goals that were more strongly 'shared' among its' members. They were also able to translate these goals into more concrete terms as a result of the dialogues. We encountered, for instance, that many professionals in the participating teams mentioned 'high-quality education' as a goal, but that answers on what high-quality education actually entails, could differ significantly. Through the dialogue, these images of high-quality education became part of the conversation and functioned as a starting point to create a shared goal or norm. Additionally, the dialogue sessions in ELL methodology helped most teams to get a clearer picture of the functioning of the team, gaining a shared image of strengths and weaknesses of the team as well as insights into the array of skills and talents of the team members.

We found that in many of the participating teams, there was a tension between a short-term performance orientation and a long-term orientation focused on shared meaning and desired impact of the work the team members strive towards. The performance (or management) orientation is goal-oriented, focusing on the short term and efficient solutions and results. The shared meaning-generating (or professional) orientation, on the other hand, is aimed at the long term and more deliberate, exploring diverse perspectives, asking questions, and investigating. Through the dialogue sessions in the second phase, the team members are able to explore and reflect on both elements and its' inherent tensions, which helps to construct shared understanding and meaning, while also taking into account the – sometimes pressing – needs from the performance orientation. Through the dialogue sessions, most participating teams became more effective in handling these two perspectives and bringing them into balance. The action researchers helped with this balancing act by guiding the group discussions and making sure that participating teams investigate, improve and evaluate their own educational practice as 'reflective practitioners' (Schön, 1983).

Even if almost all teams gained more insight into their goals and the functioning of the team and managed to gain a more concrete and shared understanding of their goals, the results are much more varied when we look at the intervention phase of the ELL methodology. Even though all teams were able to formulate interventions through the professional dialogue, both on improving the educational outcomes of their work and the functioning of the team, about half the teams reported not being able to fully or partly implement these interventions, painting a picture were a sizeable number of teams felt unable to structurally improve either their educational performance or their team functioning. This seemed due to both team and organizational conditions which the professionals in the teams experienced.

Although all teams report that there are 'team plans' in place, which are often drawn up and pursued annually, we saw that prioritization and a clear image of what needed to be done to achieve these goals were often not in place. Most teams lacked concrete plans and steps to achieve the objectives, and existing team plans often felt like something that 'just had to be done', part of a cycle of improvement from management. Through the dialogue and the guidance of the action researchers, most teams were able to formulate interventions that would contribute to the goals they themselves formulated. Implementation of these interventions however was made difficult by the fact that the team conditions – such as team size, interdependence, psychological safety, stability, diversity and skills in the team – were perceived very differently over the teams, with some team conditions being perceived as negative. In fact, in none of the teams we could describe all team conditions as positive, with stability being the most negatively perceived condition. Teams which experienced a lack of psychological safety, encountered the most problems in realizing interventions aimed at increasing both educational quality and team performance. Most strikingly, all teams in our research report an experienced lack of time and space, with 'daily noise' being experienced as hindering reflection and dialogue. The ELL dialogue sessions, and the guidance of the action researchers in it, seem to countermand this, with team members stating they appreciate the reflection and slower pace these discussions brought compared to the daily grind. The ELL sessions can therefore be seen as an intervention in itself. Nevertheless, the daily noise and lack of time makes itself felt again in many teams when they try and bring into practice the interventions they designed in the dialogue sessions.

The perceived lack of time and space is something that is caused by factors on the team level, but certainly also finds it origins on the organizational level. All teams experience an organizational context that is – in varying degrees of intensity – in constant flux. Almost all teams had to 'deal with' organizational changes such as fusions between departments or organizations or educational changes, such as a new educational programme, which influenced both the team goals and the way the team was organized. Many of the changes initiated at the organizational level are designed to come into effect on the team level. But it seems the impact of these changes on the professionals and the time and effort needed to realize those changes are structurally underestimated in the three large educational organizations in which our research took place. Most professionals reported a very low knowledge of and connection with supporting staff in either realizing those changes or on more practical matters regarding for instance assistance in team functioning. The impact of leadership varied more widely among the teams, with a positive effect in some teams, but a notable absence of guidance and support in many other teams. There seems to be a catch 22 situation, in which professionals in the teams do not see themselves as an actor to change organizational conditions. This in turn prevents them from addressing these conditions when those hinder bringing the desired change into effect in their daily practice. There were some positive exemptions to this in two teams, in which team members did manage to actively address and influence organizational conditions, growing their sense of agency through the dialogue sessions. It must be noted though, that in both teams, the drive of the team members to address these organizational conditions led to an above average active role for the action researchers, putting the issue back on the agenda of the teams when it threatened to disappear from the radar in the daily noise experienced by the team members.

LESSONS FOR POLICY AND PRACTICE

The role of public professionals in providing answers to contemporary challenges cannot be overstated. These professionals need agency to fulfil this role and deliver good work. It is therefore worrying that the position of many public professionals and their agency is under pressure in many contexts and sectors. Through our action research approach, we aim to contribute to strengthening the agency of public professionals in teams.

In our research, we found that public professionals work hard on a daily basis to realize good work – in the case of the research presented here: high-quality education for students in higher and intermediate vocational education in the Netherlands. We found that both team conditions and organizational conditions influence the agency of public professionals in teams and both require attention in public organizations if the agency of professionals is to be meaningfully strengthened. It is worrying that the perceived constant organizational change combined with the 'daily noise' many professionals experience, makes it hard for professionals to find the time and space needed for structural reflection on improvement of their practice and paradoxically seems to hinder effective and durable change.

Improving agency of public professionals requires thinking through both team and organizational conditions. Enough time for working together is quintessential but is also frequently underestimated; all too often organizations believe they have allotted sufficient time for cooperation, but in practice, the cooperating professionals experience it as insufficient or completely lacking in a context of near constant change and demands. Allotting time for professionals for reflection and dialogue entails more than providing hours in an excel sheet; it also involves the ability to come together and requires a context in which reflection and dialogue are encouraged and facilitated.

Strengthening professional agency and effective cooperation is not simple, and professionals themselves need to be able to understand what enhances and what undermines it in order to realize this. In addition, good support is an important condition at the organizational level for encouraging and improving that cooperation. Depending on the situation, such support may be offered by managers, HR professionals or specialised team and organizational coaches. Good support requires people who are knowledgeable and have an understanding of cooperation, as well as requiring that such support be tailored to that particular group of cooperating professionals. Through our ELL approach, we saw clear benefits of a tailor-made support for teams of professionals – starting or accelerating reflection on and improvement in setting goals, cooperation in the team and quality of work.

CONCLUSION

We'd like to conclude with a more fundamental reflection on what is needed to strengthen the agency of professionals in public organizations. Besides the more practical measures that can be taken which are described above, we feel it requires a fundamentally different view on how we organize work and who we give voice in determining that view. Bringing about the changes needed in organizations is in the end fundamentally about the logic governing the way our work is organized. There is a tension in public organizations between the logic of the professionals, who from the norms and standards of their profession strive to achieve good work, and the financial and organizational logic, which is dominated by process management and control, and conceptualized in terms of returns and cost efficiency (Freidson, 1973; van Middelkoop, 2022). In most public organizations, the value of and need for the professional logic is often formally acclaimed as the logic that should take central stage in work. But in reality, the system by which the work is organized is ultimately not controlled by those professionals but by administrators and managers. And with the increasing dominance of the New Public Management paradigm, the organizational and financial logics have become dominant in the public sector, with professionals increasingly feeling powerless to bring into effect changes they feel are needed when they reason from 'their' professional logic.

Structurally increasing professional agency calls for organizing work more strongly according to what public professionals need to deliver good work. The challenge this entails lies not in making an 'absolute' choice but in restoring professional logic to the central place it should occupy when we organize work. The other logics are necessary but need to ultimately serve that professional logic. We have to break away from organizing work in such a way that control, efficiency thinking and an emphasis on 'quantifiable output' are central and from a mode where these have been made an end in themselves rather than a means to an end (Glastra & van Middelkoop, 2018). Return organizational and financial logic back to their right proportions – these are the preconditions that allow public professionals to deliver good work.

NOTES

1. For this chapter, we have drawn on our earlier work. More specifically, the introduction and overview of the literature is largely based on and previously published as the inaugural speech by the first author (van Middelkoop, 2022).

2. Part of the Work Lab of the Amsterdam University of Applied Sciences.
3. The findings and conclusion and discussion chapters draw on three projects which were reported on in a series of earlier Dutch research rapports by the authors (Brouwer et al., 2024; Horsselenberg et al., 2022; van Middelkoop et al., 2023). This findings section draws on parts of the findings of these three reports, giving a more overarching view on the strengthening of the agency of the professionals involved in these projects. More detailed information on the findings and how for instance agency was measured and determined in teams can be found in these publications. Parts of the conclusion and discussion chapter were published earlier in Brouwer et al. (2024) and van Middelkoop (2022).

REFERENCES

Archer, M. (1995). *Realist social theory: The morphogenetic approach*. Cambridge University Press.

Brouwer, P., van Middelkoop, D., van de Mortel, M., Engel, J., Horsselenberg, P., Koeslag-Kreunen, P., Kuijpers, A., Thunnissen, M., & Zitter, I. (2024). *Samen leren rond complexe opgaven in het hbo - een onderzoek naar teamgericht leren en ontwikkelen in zes teams*. Zestor.

Coghlan, D., & Shani, A. B. (2014). Creating action research quality in organization development: Rigorous, reflective and relevant. *Systemic Practice and Action Research*, *27*, 523–536.

Decuyper, S., Dochy, F., & van den Bossche, P. (2010). Grasping the dynamic complexity of team learning: An integrative model for effective team learning in organizations. *Educational Research Review*, *5*, 111–133.

Deglau, D., Ward, P., O'Sullivan, M., & Bush, K. (2006). Professional dialogue as professional development. *Journal of Teaching in Physical Education*, *25*(4), 413–427.

Derksen, K. (2021). *Goed Teamwerk – Hoe teams beter kunnen presteren en floreren*. Boom.

Derksen, K., van Middelkoop, D., van den Berg, L., Bay, N., Horsselenberg, P., & Kaarsemaker, A. (2020). *Samen sterk of nog meer werk? Onderwijsteams in het hbo*. Zestor. Arbeidsmarkt- en opleidingsfonds hbo.

Edmondson, A. (2013). *Teaming to innovate*. Jossey-Bass.

Eteläpelto, A., Vähäsantanen, K., Hökkä, P., & Paloniemi, S. (2013). What is agency? Conceptualizing professional agency at work. *Educational Research Review*, *10*, 45–65.

Evers, J., & Kneyber, R. (2013). *Het Alternatief – weg met de afrekencultuur in het onderwijs*. Boom.

Freidson, E. (1973). Professions and the occupational principle. In E. Freidson (Ed.), *Professions and their prospects* (pp. 19–37). Sage.

Gardner, H., Csikszentmihalyi, M., & Damon, W. (2002). *Good work – When excellence and ethics meet*. Basic Books.

Giddens, A. (1979). *Central problems in social theory: Action, structure, and contradiction in social analysis*. University of California Press.

Glastra, F., & van Middelkoop, D. (2018). *Studiesucces in het hoger onderwijs: Van rendement naar maatschappelijke relevantie*. Eburon.

Hackman, J. (2002). Why teams don't work. In R. S. Tindale, J. Edwards, & E. J. Posavac (Eds.), *Theory and research on small groups* (pp. 245–267). Springer.

Hargreaves, A., & O'Connor, M. (2018). *Collaborative professionalism: When teaching together means learning for all*. Corwin.

Hinostroza, Y. (2020). University teacher educators' professional agency: A literature review. *Professions and Professionalism*, *10*(2), 1–26.

Horsselenberg, P., Hunkar, A., & van Middelkoop, D. (2022). Niet ieder voor zich, maar wij voor ons allen: In dialoog over het functioneren als team. Opleiding & Ontwikkeling. *Tijdschrift voor Human Resource Development*, *2022*(4), 21–25.

Hunkar, A., Zinsmeister, J., & van Middelkoop, D. (2021). *Ongehoord - Een onderzoek naar de arbeidssituatie van groepsleiders in de JeugdzorgPlus. Deelrapport 2 van Werken aan de toekomst van JeugdzorgPlus*. Verwey-Jonker Instituut.

Isaacs, W. (1999). *Dialogue and the art of thinking together*. Doubleday.

Priestley, M., Biesta, G., & Robinson, S. (2015). Teacher agency: Een ecologische kijk op het handelingsvermogen van leraren. In R. Kneyber & J. Evers (Eds.), *Het Alternatief II: de ladder naar autonomie* (pp. 17–32). Uitgeverij Phronese.

Ruijters, M. (2018). *Queeste naar goed werk: Over krachtige professionals in een lerende organisatie*. Vakmedianet.

Schön, D. (1983). *The reflective practitioner – How professionals think in action*. Basic Books.

Tonkens, E. (2008). *Mondige burgers, getemde professionals – Marktwerking en professionaliteit in de publieke sector*. Van Gennep.

van der Krogt, T. (2015). Professionals and their work - Blog book on the tension between professionalization processes and quality. https://profqual.wordpress.com/. Accessed on July 19, 2022.

van Middelkoop, D. (2022). *Professional agency: A plea for revaluing professionals, craftsmen and good work*. Eburon.

van Middelkoop, D., de Jong, A., Bay, N., & Brouwer, P. (2023). *Samenwerken aan effectieve teams in het mbo: Een onderzoek naar het versterken van collectief handelingsvermogen van zes teams*. Amsterdam University of Applied Sciences, The Work Lab.

van Middelkoop, D., Portielje, M., & Horsselenberg, P. (2018). Working apart together: Collectief handelingsvermogen in twee docententeams in het hbo. *Tijdschrift voor HRM*, *2018*(2), 1–20.

van Middelkoop, D., & van den Berg, L. (2020). Afwegingen binnen actieonderzoek. *Sociologie Magazine*, *2020*(3), 20–22. https://sociologiemagazine.nl/magazine/sociologie-magazine-nummer-3-van-2020-0

van Vroonhoven, M. (2024). Kohnstammlezing - wie van leraren uitvoerders maakt, creëert een samenleving zonder toekomst. https://www.uva.nl/content/evenementen/2024/03/merel-van-vroonhoven-houdt-kohnstammlezing-2024.html. Accessed on May 2, 2024.

Vangrieken, K., Dochy, F., & Raes, E. (2016). Team learning in teacher teams: Team entitativity as a bridge between teams-in-theory and teams-in-practice. *European Journal of Psychology of Education*, *31*(3), 275–298.

Vangrieken, K., Dochy, F., Raes, E., & Kyndt, E. (2015). Teacher collaboration: A systematic review. *Educational Research Review*, *15*, 17–40.

West, M., & Hirst, K. (2005). Cooperation and teamwork for innovation. In M. West, D. Tjosvold, & K. Smith (Eds.), *The essentials of team working: International perspectives* (pp. 257–279). Wiley.

Zinsmeister, J., van Middelkoop, D., & van den Berg, L. (2022). Vakmensen over flexwerk: een ondermijnende relatie? *Tijdschrift voor Arbeidsvraagstukken*, *38*(1), 39–58. https://doi.org/10.5117/TVA2022.1.004.ZINS

FROM ASPIRATION TO REALIZATION: HOW THE OUTCOMES STAR SUPPORTS THE DELIVERY AND MANAGEMENT OF RELATIONAL, HOLISTIC, FLEXIBLE, DEVELOPMENTAL AND STRENGTHS-BASED PUBLIC SERVICES

Joy MacKeith

Freelance Writer and Researcher, UK

ABSTRACT

There has been a consensus around the desirability of services that 'do with' rather than 'do to' for some time, with many policy documents setting out this intention. However, this has proved difficult to achieve on a large scale in practice. This chapter describes and evidences how the distinctive design features of the Outcomes Star suite of tools support enabling service delivery, i.e. services that are relational, developmental, motivational, flexible, holistic and contextual. The author recommends their use to bridge the gap between the aspiration and realization of relational, enabling services. However, it is noted that these benefits are not always fully realized due to limitations created by current public administration theory and practice. It is further recommended that, like service delivery, the practice of service management and commissioning also need to follow relational, enabling principles. Without this, the service system puts impossible demands on its workers, asking them to offer relational help while being managed and held accountable in a transactional way. There is evidence that the Outcomes Star tools can also support an enabling approach to service management and

Futures in Public Management
Critical Perspectives on International Public Sector Management, Volume 8, 99–120

ISSN: 2045-7944/doi:10.1108/S2045-794420250000008007

commissioning by (a) providing a shared language and methodology for relational service delivery and (b) providing holistic, relational, developmental data for ongoing learning, service development and learning-based accountability. The piece concludes with a call for further research to explore the role that the Outcomes Star tools can play in supporting an enabling approach to service management and commissioning and to identify how to make the most of this suite of tools in service transformation.

Keywords: Relational public services; transactional; relational public management; enabling; strengths-based; outcomes star; recovery star; trauma-informed; outcomes measurement; person-centred

INTRODUCTION: THE GAP BETWEEN ASPIRATION AND REALIZATION IN PUBLIC SERVICES

What kind of help is most effective when supporting people towards greater well-being and the achievement of goals such as getting into work, recovering from mental illness or finding a settled home? Some writers have focused on the importance of making services strengths-based (Department for Health and Social Care, 2019; McCashen, 2017). Some make their points under the banner of person-centred care (Beresford et al., 2011; The Health Foundation, 2016). Others have made the case for relational service delivery (Bell & Smerdon, 2011; MacKenzie, 2021). There are also calls for service which are trauma-informed (Department for Levelling Up, Housing and Communities, 2023; Knight, 2019) and psychologically informed (Breedvelt, 2016; Johnson, 2023). In practice, while practitioners, policymakers and researchers may have a particular preferred focus, it could be argued that they are all advocating for the provision of services with a similar constellation of coherent and mutually re-enforcing characteristics. These are characteristics that foreground the needs, perspectives, capabilities, goals and agency of the service user – services that 'do with' rather than 'do to'.

There have been a number of attempts to describe what this constellation looks like, including 'Radical Help' (Cottam, 2018) and 'Good Help' (Wilson et al., 2018). My own description 'Enabling Help' (MacKeith, 2021) is summarized in Table 1 and contrasted with 'Prescriptive Help' – which sees the service user as a recipient with a problem that the professional will solve rather than an active and knowledgeable agent with whom they will work in partnership.

Prescriptive help has its place in public services. When we go to the doctor because of a minor health problem, we hope for it to be diagnosed and a treatment prescribed. We don't expect or need to discuss our social networks or how we use our time. When an employment service offers us an IT skills course, we simply want a good course, not a discussion of our diet and sleeping habits. However, when the service is addressing a complex issue that has impacts across many domains of someone's life, there is now a broad consensus that what I am referring to here as Prescriptive Help is not effective (Breedvelt, 2016; Johnson, 2023). However, the reality on the ground is that Prescriptive Help is the norm in most contexts, including those in which the service is helping people with complex

Table 1. The Characteristics of Enabling Help and Prescriptive Help.

Enabling Help Is Help Which Is:	Prescriptive Help Is Help Which Is:
Relational: Emphasizing the importance of a trusting partnership between helper and helped and co-creating goals and actions	*Transactional:* Emphasising the delivery of the intervention by an expert helper who knows the 'right' goals and course of action
Developmental: Helping the person develop perspective, a sense of agency and the skills to address challenges and achieve their goals in a sustainable way	*Quick fix:* Finding the shortest route to achieve pre-determined outcomes without looking at whether deeper changes are needed to sustain them
Motivational/strengths-based: Highlighting achievements and capabilities and how they can be harnessed to achieve goals	*Deficit-based:* Highlighting pathology and diagnosis
Flexible: Tailoring interventions to the particular person and their circumstances. Also known as 'person-centred' or 'bespoke'	*Standardised:* Prescribing standard interventions
Holistic and contextual: Focusing on the whole of someone's life and their wider environment	*Compartmentalised:* Focusing only on the specific issue that has brought the person to the service

and multiple needs (Cottam, 2018; Wilson et al., 2018). The calls for the alternative relational, strengths-based, person-centred approach to working with complex needs grow louder and louder (e.g. Better Way Network, 2021; Fox & Fox, 2023) and yet despite public commitments, policymakers and leaders find it difficult to deliver in practice.

The reasons for this are explored in MacKeith (2021). It is argued that this is the unwelcome legacy of the medical model that has shaped many of the helping professions, which has then been unwittingly sustained through bureaucratic processes and market approaches. However, the focus here is not on the why but on how to change this state of affairs. How do public services go beyond the proclamation of their intention to deliver this kind of help to the realization of those commitments in practice? This chapter presents a suite of tools for delivering and managing services called the Outcomes Star, which may offer part of the answer to that question. Following the literature review, the chapter will describe how the tools are developed and used in practice and then go on to and identify the unique design characteristics that embed relationality, responsiveness and a developmental orientation into their use, both as service delivery and measurement tools. Finally, it explores what can get in the way of the Stars reaching their full potential and makes the case that the service delivery system itself needs to be run on enabling principles. Evidence is presented that the Outcomes Stars can also play a role in supporting enabling, relational management and commissioning. The text will mostly use the term 'Enabling Help' throughout the chapter as a short-hand to refer to the constellation of service characteristics described in this introduction. However, at times it may emphasize one or more particular aspects of Enabling Help, for example, by referring to relational or flexible services.

LITERATURE REVIEW

The first Outcomes Star was developed for use by service providers in the homelessness sector to help them respond in a person-centred way to the growing requirement to evidence outcomes to commissioners and funders resulting from the rise of New Public Management.[1] The tool was found to be helpful not only in measuring change but also supporting that change to happen. It was then developed to enhance these dual roles in services addressing complex and multiple needs in a holistic way. The Outcomes Star was picked up in related service areas outside of the homelessness sector resulting in the development of other versions tailored to different types of service. For example, the Mental Health Recovery Star (MHRS) was developed for use in mental health services, My Star for children and the Family Star Plus for work with vulnerable families. New versions and updated editions of existing Stars have been published every year since 2006, and there is now a suite of over 50 versions of the Outcomes Star. Each version is tailored to a particular need or context and all share in common that they are designed for services: (a) working holistically across many domains of someone's life and (b) working on issues that require a change behaviour on the part of the person being helped or the service, or both. They have been translated into more than 20 languages and are used around the world, particularly in the United Kingdom and Australia. To date, there have been over 1.5 million completions of the Outcomes Stars on the bespoke online app as well as many completions on paper and within in-house and commercial software systems.[2]

There is a substantial body of literature on the measurement of constructs that cannot be directly observed such as well-being, motivation and communication skills (Kaplan & Saccuzzo, 2010). A key tenet of this discipline (known as psychometrics) is that the act of measuring should not impact on the construct being measured (Nunnally & Berstein, 1994). As outlined in the introduction and discussed below, this means that the Outcomes Stars are a paradigm breaking suite of tools as they are designed to both measure and create change. As a result, there is a lack of literature on tools of this kind and indeed a lack of other tools to make comparisons with. However, there is a substantial and growing body of literature on the Outcomes Stars tools themselves, both as tools for supporting service delivery and as tools for measuring outcomes. This is described briefly below.

The Outcomes Stars as Tools for Supporting Direct Service Delivery

The Triangle Research Library lists 52 reports and articles which explore the usefulness of different versions of the Outcomes Stars as tools to support individual change.[3] Of these, 31 are by independent researchers and 21 are written by Triangle staff. Most are in-house reports or external evaluations. All conclude that the version of the Outcomes Star studied brought benefits to keywork practice.

One theme that emerges from these reports is that using the Outcome Star supports client *engagement and empowerment.* For example in an evaluation of the use of three versions of the Outcomes Star in an Australian crisis intervention project, Harris and Andrews (2013) identified a range of benefits to clients including 'the opportunity to define their own reality, identify their own priorities and be accountable for them' (p. 2). York Consulting (2013) reviewed the use of the Family Star in a national UK charity and concluded that 'The Family Star gives service users ownership of the change process, and also helps them develop the skills and resilience to manage the issues they face' (p. 7).

Another theme is that using the Outcomes Stars supports *reflection and understanding*, both on the part of workers and the people they are supporting. For example, Vávrová (2020) describes a quasi-experimental study of the use of the Family Star and My Star (for children) in services for families with children at high risk of abuse and neglect. The study found that in families that had worked with these two versions of the Stars, more of their goals were achieved and there were fewer court removals of children and more voluntary placements than in families where the Stars were not used. A range of benefits were described including that families highly valued the approach because it 'focuses on a wider range of areas of their lives, thus encouraging them to reflect more deeply on their situation, parenting competencies and attitudes' (p. 3). Game (2022) also reports that in an evaluation of a pilot implementation the Parent and Baby Star in South Warwickshire Health Visiting services, 83% of parents felt that the Parent and Baby Star helped them understand what they needed in the way of support. Furthermore, in the report of the development of My Mind Star (the Outcomes Star for mental health in young people), 94% of practitioners reported that they could get a better idea of service users' support needs using My Mind Star and 94% of young people reported that their completed Star was a good summary of their life now (MacKeith et al., 2019). Similar results are reported in the development reports of other versions of the Star.[4]

A third and final theme is that using the Outcomes Stars helps the worker and the person to develop *a positive working partnership*. Joy-Johnson (2016) carried out semi-structured interviews with 10 clients and 4 workers across 3 services to explore the impact on the client: worker relationship of using the Recovery Star. Working with the Star was seen to improve collaborative working between client and worker, to help negotiate new or shared perspectives and support motivation towards improved well-being. York Consulting (2013) reported that using the Family Star 'helped workers reflect on how their relationship with service users impacted on the outcomes achieved' (p. 6).

The Outcomes Stars as Tools for Measuring Outcomes and Supporting Service Development

Most studies of the Stars as measurement tools have focused on their psychometric properties. Many focus on the MHRS, perhaps reflecting a strong research culture in the mental health sector. Nyashanu (2020) carried out a comprehensive literature review, which concluded that the MHRS was an effective outcome measure for determining the functional progress of people living with mental illness due to its established recovery model and characteristics of being client-centred, collaborative and recovery-focused.

Good and MacKeith (2021a) evaluated the psychometric properties of the Family Star Plus and found that it had:

- *good inter-rater reliability*, meaning that the scales were applied in a consistent way by different practitioners;
- *good internal consistency*, meaning that the different outcome domains relate to each other and belong in the same tool;
- *high responsiveness*, meaning that the tool is effective in detecting meaningful change;
- *good predictive validity*, meaning that change measured by the tool predicts future observable outcomes (such as school attendance).

A similar study focusing on the Outcomes Star for homelessness also found high internal consistency, responsiveness and predictive validity (Good & MacKeith, 2021b). Triangle has published information about the psychometric properties of all versions of the Outcomes Star, based on pilot studies of the tools carried out as part of the development process described in the Appendix and also on data collected during routine service delivery (for details, see the Triangle Research Library).[5]

There has been less focus in the published literature on the application of the data in practice, but there are a number of examples. One is an evaluation of the application of the Family Star in a national charity (York Consulting, 2013). It was concluded that in the context of service management 'Family Star data can provide valuable insights into the extent and nature of changes occurring' (p. 3) and that 'Family Star data can be used as a valuable interim indicator of distance travelled towards achieving longer-term outcomes and impact' (p. 7). Game (2022) reported that using Parent and Baby Star data in day-to-day service management helped highlight parents who needed additional support. Similarly, the North Staffordshire Council found that data collected using the Family Star Plus helped to spotlight one district in which parental mental health was a particular issue. This prompted discussions across the council and service providers to identify ways to meet this acute need (case study quoted in Lowe et al., 2022). The Family Star Plus has also been widely used in impact reporting linked to the Supporting Families Programme and in evaluation reports across a wide range of sectors.

METHODOLOGY

Each version of the Outcomes Star is developed in collaboration with service providers with input from people who receive the service. They are piloted to test their usability and effectiveness as keywork tools and to assess their psychometric qualities as holistic measurement tools. The process and pilot findings for each version are documented in development reports (see for example, MacKeith et al., 2018). The overall approach, informed by Participatory Action Research, is described in MacKeith (2011). Appendix 1 provides a brief summary of the four stages of the process.

For the purposes of this chapter, the MHRS has been chosen as an exemplar of how the Outcomes Star works in practice as it is one of the longest-standing and most widely used versions of the tool; now in its fourth edition. It is designed to be used as an integral part of holistic one to one keywork to[6]

- Explain what the service offers and build a working alliance.
- Understand the person's situation.
- Take an overview together.
- Identify priorities, goals and actions.
- Review progress.
- Provide distance travelled outcomes information.

These different elements are described in turn below.

Explaining What the Service Offers and Building a Working Alliance

In the initial stages of building a relationship with someone drawing on support, the worker introduces the person to the version of the Outcomes Star they are working with and explains how it works – something they practice in the one-day training to use the Star. This involves:

- Explaining that the purpose of using the tool is to help them to work together to achieve the service user's goals. The Star is completed together and both worker and person's perspectives are important because the person knows more than anyone else about their situation, needs and priorities, and the worker brings a broader perspective, being outside of the immediate situation and having supported others with similar challenges.
- Introducing the person to the Star graphic, in which each point represents a key domain in that person's life as shown in Fig. 1.
- Introducing the Journey of Change and User Guide. The Journey of Change provides a description of the change process. The User Guide applies that description to each outcome domain, breaking change in beliefs, situation or behaviour in that aspect of the person's life down into a series of steps. The names of the stages of the Journey of Change for the MHRS and an example of the way this is applied to each outcome domain in the User Guide is given in Fig. 2.

Understand the Person's Situation

All of the domains on the Star are discussed in turn, using the User Guide to support the conversation where helpful. Together the worker and person identify where on the scale the person feels they are for each domain (their 'reading' on that scale), and this is plotted on the Star as shown in Fig. 3. If worker and person disagree this is seen as an opportunity for a useful sharing of perspectives.

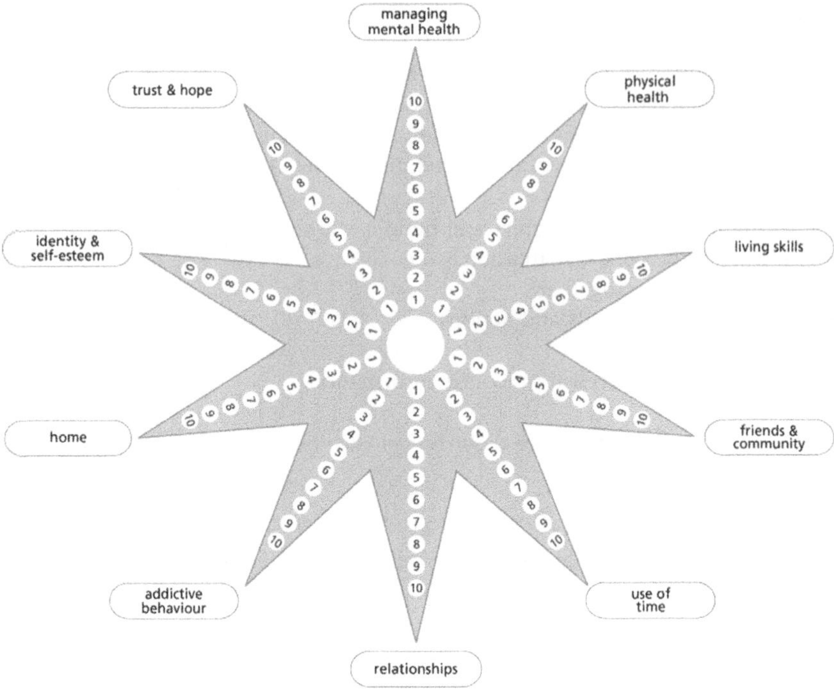

Recovery Star™ (4th Edition) © Triangle Consulting Social Enterprise Ltd
Authors: Sara Burns and Joy MacKeith
www.outcomesstar.org.uk

Fig. 1. The Mental Health Recovery Star (4th Edition).

This can result in the two perspectives coming together. Or if they 'agree to disagree' then both perspectives are recorded.

Taking an Overview Together

The completed Star graphic gives a visual overview of the person's life which is a starting point for reflection and conversation about things that are going well, challenges and connections between domains.

Identifying Priorities, Goals and Actions

This shared reflection naturally leads to a conversation about priorities, goals and the actions required by the worker, the person or others to achieve them. These are then documented in an Action Plan to guide the work going forward.

For each outcome area there is a ten-point scale underpinned by a five-stage Journey of Change:

- Stuck (1-2)
- Accepting help (3-4)
- Believing and trying (5-6)
- Learning (7-8)
- Self-reliance (9-10)

Each point on the scales is clearly defined, for example, the beginning of the 'Believing and trying' stage for the 'Friends and Community' scale is described in the following way:

I'm starting to believe I can have positive supportive social connections

- You want to connect with people and activities beyond mental health groups
- You feel supported enough to move into action

Fig. 2. The Journey of Change and Detailed Scales. Extracts from the Recovery Star. Authors: Joy MacKeith and Sara Burns. Copyright Triangle Consulting Social Enterprise.

Reviewing Progress

After a period of time (often 2–3 months), the Star is completed again. When the two readings are presented on the same Star diagram, this gives a picture of change (see Fig. 4). This again can spark reflection and conversation leading to new goals and actions.

Providing Distance Travelled Outcome Information

Readings can be analyzed across service users to give a service- and organization-level overview of starting needs and outcomes achieved. This is designed to be used alongside other data to support service learning and development. This summarized data can also be used to report outcomes to stakeholders such as commissioners, ideally as part of a learning-based accountability approach. Figs. 5 and 6 provide examples of the kind of reports that are created within the Star Online system.

FINDINGS: THE DISTINCTIVE DESIGN FEATURES THAT SUPPORT ENABLING SERVICE DELIVERY

What is it about the Outcomes Stars that leads to the benefits of improved collaboration, person-centred working and empowerment in keywork and useable management data for service learning and development that were

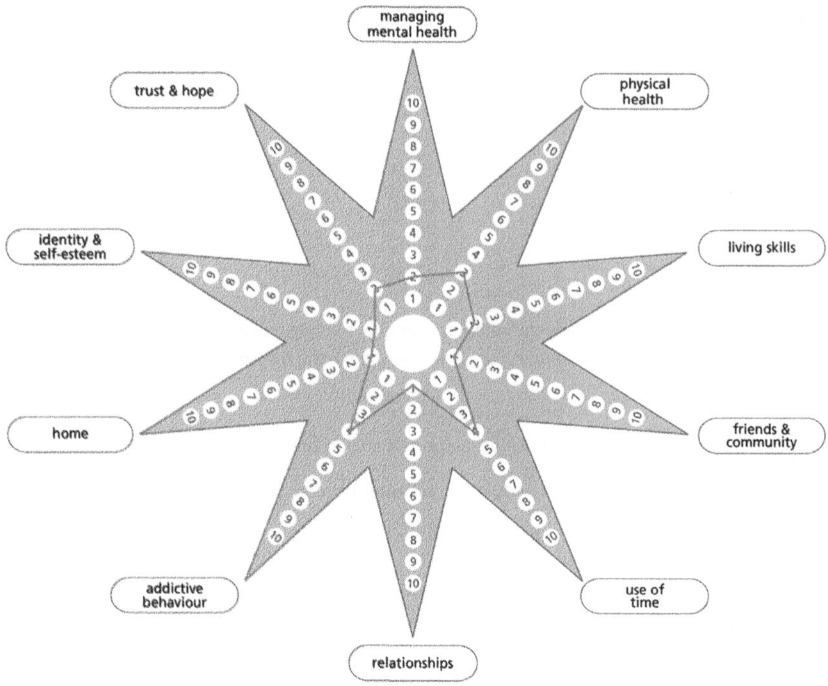

Fig. 3. The Mental Health Recovery Star Completed Once.

described in the Literature Review? In this section, I outline the six distinctive design features of the Outcomes Stars that support an enabling approach to service delivery and how they also bring a relational, holistic and developmental dimension to measurement.

They Are Dual Purpose Tools

As mentioned in the introduction, the Outcomes Stars are intended to both support the process of change towards achieving individual goals and to measure that change. Comparing a Star reading when someone first enters a service with the reading at a later point provides information about distance travelled. In addition, the dialogue between worker and service user to complete a Star can impact on the person's awareness of issues, their beliefs about what is possible and their motivation to try new things. This can then lead to an increased sense of agency, hope and ability to take action. Hence, the tool acts as an intervention in itself and supports a *developmental, motivational* approach to keywork practice.

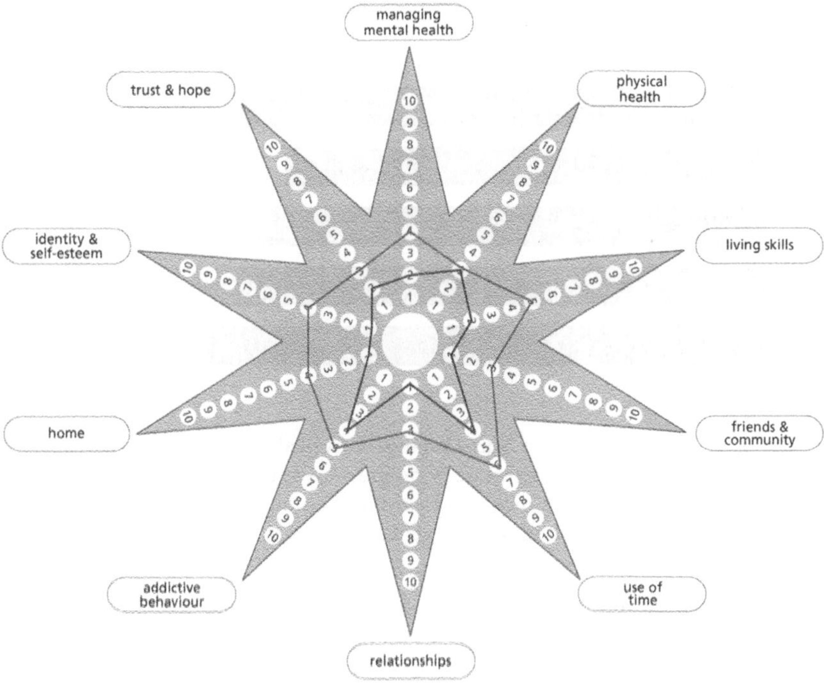

Recovery Star™ (4th Edition) © Triangle Consulting Social Enterprise Ltd
Authors: Sara Burns and Joy MacKeith
www.outcomesstar.org.uk

Fig. 4. The Mental Health Recovery Star Completed Twice.

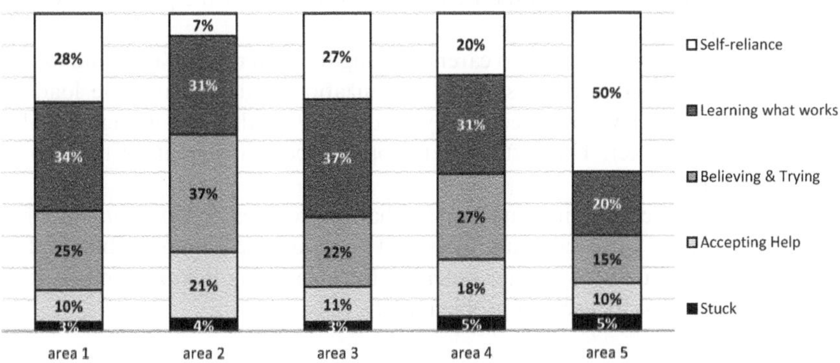

Fig. 5. Generic Outcomes Star Starting Points Report. *Note:* This report is used to provide an overview of needs on entry to the service. It shows the percentage of people at different stages of the Journey of Change for each outcome area. Copyright: Triangle Consulting Social Enterprise Ltd.

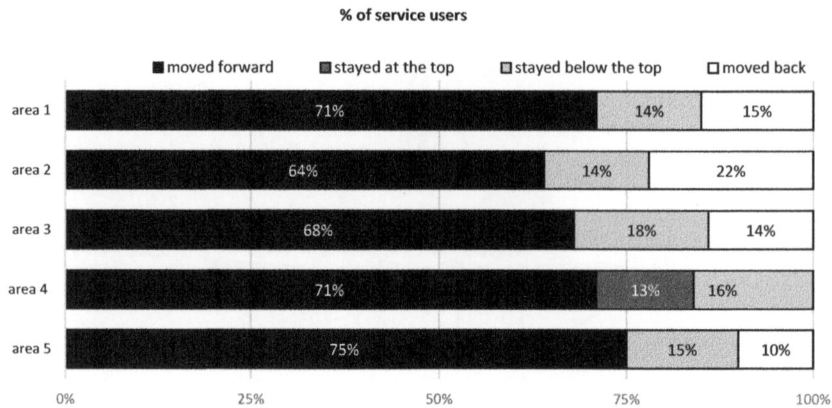

Fig. 6. Generic Outcomes Star Distance Travelled Outcomes Report. *Note:* This report is used to provide a picture of progress made by a group of service users. It shows what percentage have moved forward in each outcome area over a specified period of time. Copyright: Triangle Consulting Social Enterprise Ltd.

The integration of data collection into the keywork process also impacts on the nature and usefulness of the data as is described in the following sections.

They Are Holistic

The outcome areas represented by the points on the Stars cover all key areas of a person's life rather than just focusing on the issue that has brought them into the service. The consequence of this for service delivery is that it becomes *holistic* and *motivational/strengths-based* because it includes all aspects of the person's life and highlights things that are working well, as well as areas of difficulty. It also makes it possible to offer a *flexible* response because every area of the person's life is on the map and in the conversation.

Speaking about the benefits to carers of using the Carers Star, a care advisor at Crossroads Together, a carer support organization said 'Carers have loads of responsibility but they don't necessarily focus on what they are doing or realize how much they matter. They often feel unappreciated so it's great for them to see their strengths.'[7]

The consequence for measurement is that it provides *holistic data* which is broader than data gathered using tools that focus on presenting problems. This gives a richer picture with greater potential for identifying linkages and patterns than when the data focuses on problem areas only.

They Are Completed Collaboratively

Most outcome measures and keywork tools are completed by the service user or the practitioner alone. In contrast to this Outcomes Stars are completed collaboratively. The reading (i.e. where the person is on each scale) is chosen through conversation between the person and the practitioner. This values and recognizes the expertise of both helper and helped. It embeds a *relational* approach which gives importance to both perspectives and the learning that results from the dialogue.

In the words of a keyworker with Pathways to Independence, a small charity working with young asylum seekers 'It gets the young people involved in the process, rather than me just writing a report without the young person there. They can really see what's going on and put their views forward and be part of it.'[8]

It also means that measurement is not an extractive process that is 'done to' the person, it is something that they co-create, so the data collected is co-produced. It could be described as *relational data*. This breaks the normal convention that the act of measuring should aim to avoid altering the thing that is being measured (Morwitz et al., 1993). However complexity theory proposes that the way to increase knowledge within a complex system is to act on the system and observe the impact of that action rather than to stand outside the system and achieve absolute knowledge (Boulton et al., 2015). Thus from this perspective, combining intervention and measurement is entirely appropriate.

They Focus on Engagement Rather Than Severity

The Outcomes Stars put the focus of service delivery on the person's engagement or relationship with the issues they face rather than on the severity of those issues. For example, a scale on 'addictive behaviour' will look at how the person is working with their addiction rather than looking in detail at the frequency of use or the amount they are using. This is *developmental* because it focuses the conversation on the next step for that person rather than the severity of their difficulties.

One person who completed the Star within the criminal justice system described it this way 'I was excited about what the next Outcomes Star would reveal about my progress. It became something to be excited about rather than something to be self-critical about.'[9]

In terms of measurement, this means that the data collected through the Star reflect engagement more than severity. It could be described as *developmental data* because it has direct implications for the style of help that is needed to support the person's progress. For example, someone who is passively engaging with help (Stage 2 on the Journey of Change) needs a different approach from someone who has a fuller sense of agency (Stage 3 and above). In the former instance, the practitioner will need to be quite proactive; in the latter, it is important that the practitioner steps back to some extent and allows the person to take the lead more.

They Are Built on a Developmental Model of Change

The engagement focus is expressed in the 'Journey of Change', a model of personal change that underpins each version of the Outcomes Star (though there are some variations between Stars). The Journey gives service users a picture of what the steps ahead look like, which supports a *developmental* approach in two ways. First, it gives the person receiving help a sense of how they can build new skills and perspectives as they grow into each new stage. Second, as described in above, it helps the worker to identify the kind of help that the person they are working with needs. The model of change is also *contextual* in that it recognizes the impact of external factors on the ability of the person to achieve their goals.

A parent using the Parent and Baby Star with a health visitor in South Warwickshire NHS Trust commented as follows:

> I was struggling with my mental health, and it showed on the Star. The health visitor and I agreed on the help I felt I needed. After a few weeks, she used the Star again, and we could both see the difference the support I had received had made.[10]

In terms of measurement, because this model is applied across each outcome domain to create detailed scales, the data are more precise in its meaning than that created by Likert scales, which are much more broadly defined. It also provides *developmental data at a service level* because its link to the type of help needed makes it very relevant for service learning and development. This means that the data create insights into what is working and not working in service delivery, which can then spur practical changes to improve service effectiveness.[11]

The Visual Display and Shared Sense-Making

The use of a visual graphic to display readings means that results of the Star conversation are immediately shared with the person receiving help in a way that helps them to take an overview together. This makes it possible to take a *relational* approach to setting goals and reflecting on change. It also allows for a very *flexible* and person-centred approach that responds to the unique picture that emerges from the conversation.

The keyworker with Pathways to Independence said:

> It's colourful and attractive and not just another pathway plan they're used to. I've never had a young person disengage with it – they've always been up for doing it. I think it's impossible to introduce it in a boring way because it looks so engaging.[12]

From a measurement perspective, not only the creation of the data, but also *the interpretation of the data is relational* because drawing out links, themes and actions is something that the practitioner and the person do together. Organizations often report that service users feel a strong sense of ownership of their completed Star Chart and are proud of the change that it shows.[13]

POLICY AND PRACTICE RECOMMENDATIONS: THE NEED FOR ENABLING MANAGEMENT AND COMMISSIONING

The material presented in the previous section indicates that the distinctive design features of the Outcomes Star suite of tools have parallel benefits for both the direct work with service users and outcome measurement. This is because of their distinctiveness in relation to:

- Their purpose (both supporting relational keywork and measuring change).
- Their focus (holistic and highlighting engagement rather than severity).
- How they are completed (collaboratively using developmental scales).
- What happens to the data (shared sense-making facilitated by the visual display).

Therefore, one recommendation I would make based on this evidence and analysis is that the Outcomes Stars and other tools based on these design principles should be used as part of wider initiatives to deliver services that are relational, flexible, strengths-based and developmental.

However, there is also evidence that although the design of the tools supports the delivery of Enabling Help, in practice there can be barriers to achieving these benefits (MacKeith, 2021). These include:

- lack of time, training and supervision to support practitioners to use the Star to its full potential;
- lack of management focus on the Star, partly due to accountability processes focusing on other things;
- disruption to the service eco-systems caused by contracting practices which get in the way of continuity and multi-agency collaboration.

In her study of the use of the MHRS, Joy-Johnson (2016) also notes that systemic influences, including lack of skilled supervision and competing demands, are barriers to the kind of long-term alliance that delivers most for clients. Kadir and Fenton (2021) report lack of practitioner time as a constraint when it comes to using the Recovery Star.

What is it that is getting in the way and contributing to these barriers? I believe an important part of the problem is that the current service system is asking workers to take a relational approach to service delivery within a largely transactional paradigm for service management and governance (Dickinson, 2016). I would argue that because there is a disconnect between delivery and management and a lack of appreciation of the way in which approaches to contracting and management impact on direct delivery, the impact of this goes unrecognized. An example of this is the fact that competitive tendering for contracts can get in the way of cooperation between service providers (Lowe et al., 2020). Another example is that attempts to specify outcomes for individuals at contract level can inhibit person-centred work because the provider will be rewarded for a short-term predetermined outcome rather than a long-term sustainable solution (De St Croix, 2018; Lowe & Wilson, 2017) A provider might be rewarded for the person getting into work when addressing debt or mental health are more immediate needs and are essential to enabling the person to stay in work over the long term.

The place where the attempt to offer enabling, relational services meets the prescriptive and transactional service delivery system is often at the level of middle management. The people located here can be pulled in opposite directions by the contradictory demands to deliver responsive relational services while being managed in a top-down procedurally driven way. Needham and Mangen (2016) quote an interviewee who makes this point:

> There is a complicated tension between the desire on the one hand for efficiency and rational processes versus the expectations and needs of customers which is more relational and focused on the personal and the local. Public service workers are expected to find their way through that knot. (p. 271)

I have spoken to service managers who have consciously and deliberately set out to protect the practitioners from the pressure to deliver and evidence certain prescribed outcomes in order to free them to work in a responsive way with service users. They act as a buffer or shock absorber at the place where these contradictory approaches meet. It can work but it exacts a toll on the people who do it.

To be truly effective, there is a need for congruence in the service system. That requires an enabling, relational approach to service management and commissioning as well as to direct service delivery. What then would an enabling service system look like? MacKenzie (2021) describes relational public services as services which not only focus on building strong relationships between the professional helper and service receiver but also between the service provider and local community and between citizens or service users. Writing about services for children with mental or physical health difficulties and their families, King (2009) makes the case for a relational model which involves building strong relationships both between practitioner and family and between practitioner and the wider organization. Broadening this out, I would like to suggest that an enabling management and commissioning would have similar qualities to those of enabling service delivery. These features are as follows:

- *Relational rather than transactional*: This would mean building shared perspectives and goals between different parts of the service delivery system rather than one part telling the other what to do. It also means building trust to support long-term collaboration rather than competition between service providers.
- *Developmental rather than quick fix:* This means taking a learning approach to the achievement of goals rather than trying to implement short-term off-the-shelf solutions. It also implies taking a learning approach to accountability rather than holding services accountable for pre-determined outcomes. This aligns with complexity theory, which states that in a complex environment (which the delivery of human services undoubtedly is), the most effective approach is to take action and learn as you go based on the results in a continuous iteration of action, reflection, learning and further action (Boulton et al., 2015; Greenberg & Bertsch, 2021).

- *Motivational/strengths-based rather than deficit based*: This means harnessing and developing the natural motivation and capacities of the workforce to deliver effective help through training and clinical supervision rather than over-specifying through rigid policies and too great an emphasis on regulating through paperwork.
- *Flexible rather than off the shelf:* Creating a service system that flexes around the citizen rather than expecting them to fit to the service.
- *Holistic and contextual rather than compartmentalized:* This implies looking at the locality and service system as a whole and emphasizing collaboration between services to build a joined up and coherent network of services rather than commissioning individual services in isolation.

This is of course more easily said than done. But it will also be more easily done within an approach to public administration that values these qualities. Many are now articulating what that might look like (e.g. Fox & Fox, 2023; Lowe et al.,2022). There is evidence that the Outcomes Star suite of tools has a part to play at the systems level as well as in direct service delivery. Although there have not been any studies focusing exclusively on the impact of the Outcomes Star across a whole service system, this aspect has been picked up within other studies. For example, Frost et al. (2017) describe a system-wide approach called the 'Integrated Recovery Model' for mental health services and conclude that collaborative measures such as the MHRS can support integrated service delivery by providing a shared language across a range of different service settings. In the evaluation of a pilot implementation of the Work Star across six different services in the London Borough of Hounslow, it was noted that the Work Star created 'a consistent approach within and between organisations in how we describe where particular clients are on their journey towards employment', which supported collaborative working between service providers (London Borough of Hounslow, 2015, p. 2). Harris and Andrews (2013) evaluated the use of 3 versions of the Star in a crisis intervention project in Australia and identified 20 benefits, some of them organization-wide including 'a common approach to case management that is "whole of person" and client centred' (p. 2).

More anecdotally, conversations the author has had with commissioners indicate that one of the features they value about the suite of tools is that there are a range different versions tailored to different groups, which means they can provide a common assessment process across different service providers. One software provider remarked that the Outcomes Star suite of tools was 'the closest the social sector has to a standard set outcome measures'. It has also been reported that as well as supporting collaboration between providers, the shared language can also support dialogue between different professionals (Game, 2022).

Perhaps most importantly, the Outcomes Stars have the potential to bridge the gap between direct delivery and commissioners and senior managers. There can be a lack of understanding among service leaders and commissioners about how the outcomes they are commissioning are achieved on the ground; what supports that and what gets in the way. There can even be a belief that commissioners do not need to know how outcomes are achieved – only whether they have been achieved or not. The Stars can provide a golden thread that can enable those further from direct service delivery to open the 'black box' of service delivery and see what is inside. Through providing reports such as those in Figs. 5 and 6 alongside an explanation of what the Star readings mean in terms of engagement with services and the style of help that is required, the Outcomes Stars can help service providers explain the dynamics of their work. Harris and Andrews (2013) refer to this benefit when they describe the Outcomes Stars as providing 'a common language flowing from client engagement through individual supervision, team practice reflection and program reporting' (p. 2).

These findings indicate that the use of the Outcomes Stars and perhaps other tools with similar design features can support an enabling, relational approach to service management and commissioning as well as service delivery. There is a need for further research to provide more systematic support for this proposition and explore how to maximize the benefits of using the Outcomes Star in this kind of organizational or system change initiative and the necessary conditions that must be in place for these benefits to be realized.

It must always be born in mind that the way a tool is implemented is as important as the quality of the tool (Howlett & Howlett, 2019) and hence the tool on its own can only be part of the answer to the challenge of implementing relational service delivery. The critical role of the context in which the tool is used, as discussed above, must be recognized in further research and in discussions around the potential impact of using the Outcomes Stars or other similar tools. It has been argued here that an enabling approach to management and commissioning is essential to achieving the full benefits to service users of working with an enabling tool.

CONCLUSION

The Outcomes Star is a unique suite of tools with distinctive design features including being holistic, completed collaboratively and being based on a developmental model of change. There is considerable evidence that they can support the delivery of Enabling Help; help which is relational, developmental, motivational (strengths-based), flexible (person-centred), holistic and contextual. There is less research on the impact of the Outcomes Stars at organization and systems level. However, there is some evidence that they can support an enabling approach to public service management through providing (a) a shared language and methodology for relational service delivery and (b) holistic, relational, developmental data for ongoing learning and service development and learning-based accountability. Further research is needed to explore the impact of the tools at organization and systems level and identify how to make the most of the Outcomes Stars in service transformation.

NOTES

1. https://www.outcomesstar.org.uk/wp-content/uploads/Outcomes_Star_Research_Briefing1.pdf. Accessed on November 12, 2024.

2. https://www.outcomesstar.org.uk/about-the-star/what-is-the-outcomes-star/history-of-the-star/#:~:text=The%20Outcomes%20Star%20is%20widely,NHS%20trusts%20in%20the%20UK. Accessed on November 12, 2024.

3. https://www.outcomesstar.org.uk/about-the-star/evidence-and-research/research-library/#tag-link-23

4. https://www.outcomesstar.org.uk/about-the-star/evidence-and-research/research-library/#tag-link-23

5. https://www.outcomesstar.org.uk/about-the-star/evidence-and-research/research-library/#all

6. The term keywork is used throughout this chapter to refer to the activity of providing holistic support to someone over a period of time, including taking an overview of someone's situation, identifying needs, priorities and goals, taking action towards those goals and regularly updating and reviewing progress.

7. https://www.outcomesstar.org.uk/wp-content/uploads/OS-CaseStudy-Carers_Trust_and_the_Star

8. https://www.outcomesstar.org.uk/wp-content/uploads/OS-Case-Study-Planning-Star-PTI.pdf

9. https://www.outcomesstar.org.uk/wp-content/uploads/OS-Case-Study-tyrones-story.pdf

10. https://www.outcomesstar.org.uk/wp-content/uploads/OS-Case-Study-Parent-and-Baby-Star-1.pdf

11. https://www.outcomesstar.org.uk/wp-content/uploads/OS-Case-Study-Staffordshire-Star-Data.pdf

12. https://www.outcomesstar.org.uk/wp-content/uploads/OS-Case-Study-Planning-Star-PTI.pdf

13. https://www.outcomesstar.org.uk/wp-content/uploads/OS-Case-Study-Parent-and-Baby-Star-1.pdf

REFERENCES

Bell, K., & Smerdon, M. (2011). Deep value: A literature review of the role of effective relationships in public services. https://www.community-links.org/policy-learning/publications/page/5/. Accessed on March 6, 2024.

Beresford, P., Flemming, J., Glynn, M., Bewley, C., Croft, S., Branfield, F., & Postle, K. (2011). *Supporting people: Towards a person-centred approach*. Policy Press.

Better Way Network. (2021). Time for a change: A rallying call for a better way. https://www.betterway.network/time-for-a-change. Accessed on March 6, 2024.

Boulton, J., Allen, P., & Bowman, C. (2015). *Embracing complexity: Strategic perspectives for an age of turbulence*. Oxford University Press.

Breedvelt, J. F. (2016). *Psychologically informed environments: A literature review*. Mental Health Foundation.

Cottam, H. (2018). *Radical help: How we can remake the relationships between us and revolutionise the welfare state*. Virago.

De St Croix, T. (2018). Youth work, performativity and the new youth impact agenda: Getting paid for numbers? *Journal of Education Policy*, *33*, 414–438.

Department for Levelling Up, Housing and Communities. (2023). *Trauma-informed approaches to supporting people experiencing multiple disadvantage: A rapid evidence assessment*. Report. Department for Levelling Up, Housing and Communities.

Department of Health and Social Care. (2019). *Strengths-based approach: Practice framework and practice handbook*. Report. HMSO.

Dickinson, H. (2016). From new public management to new public governance: The implications for a 'new public service'. In J. R. Butcher & D. J. Gilchrist (Eds.), *The three sector solution: Delivering public policy in collaboration with not-for-profits and business* (pp. 41–60). ANU Press.

Fox, A., & Fox, C. (2023). How we lost sight of the point of public services: The case for whole system reform moving towards strengths-based and relational services. https://www.newlocal.org.uk/articles/how-we-lost-sight-of-the-point-of-public-services/. Accessed on March 6, 2024.

Frost, B., Turrell, M., Sly, K., Lewin, T., Conrad, A., Johnston, S., Tirupati, S., Petrovic, K., & Rajkuman, S. (2017). Implementation of a recovery-oriented model in a sub-acute intermediate stay mental health unit (ISMHU). *BMC Health Services Research*, *17*(1), 2.

Game, S. (2022). HV tools: Reach for the stars. www.communitypractitioner.co.uk/hv-tools-reach-for-the-stars/. Accessed on March 6, 2024.

Good, A., & MacKeith, J. (2021a). Assessing family functioning: Psychometric evaluation of the family star plus. *Family Relations*, *70*(2), 529–539.

Good, A., & MacKeith, J. (2021b). Psychometric validation of the homelessness star. *Journal of Social Distress and Homelessness*, *31*(2), 1–10.

Greenberg, R., & Bertsch, B. (Eds.). (2021). *Cynefin: Weaving sense-making into the fabric of our world.* Cognitive Edge Pte Ltd.

Harris, L., & Andrews, S. (2013). *Implementing the outcomes star well in a multi-disciplinary environments.* Report. RMIT University, The Salvation Army, Crisis Services Network.

Howlett, M., & Howlett, M. (2019). *Designing public policies: Principles and instruments* (2nd ed.). Routledge. https://doi.org/10.4324/9781315232003

Johnson, R. (2023). *Psychologically informed environments from the ground up: Service design for complex needs.* Fertile Imagination.

Joy-Johnson, L. (2016). *How do clients experience the alliance when working with the mental health recovery star in rehabilitation settings?* Canterbury Christ Church University.

Kadir, S., & Fenton, K. (2021). Staff perspectives on using the recovery star in mental health inpatient rehabilitation services. *Mental Health Practice.* https://journals.rcni.com/mental-health-practice/evidence-and-practice/staff-perspectives-on-using-the-recovery-star-in-mental-health-inpatient-rehabilitation-services-mhp. Accessed on March 6, 2024.

Kaplan, R. M., & Saccuzzo, D. P. (2010). *Psychological testing: Principles, applications, and issues* (8th ed.). Wadsworth, Cengage Learning.

King, G. (2009). A relational goal-oriented model of optimal service delivery to children and families. *Physical and Occupational Therapy in Paediatrics*, *29*(4), 384–408.

Knight, C. (2019). Trauma informed practice and care: Implications for field instruction. *Clinical Social Work Journal*, *47*, 79–89.

London Borough of Hounslow. (2015). Developing a common approach to supporting the progression of young people towards employment pilot project using work star: Evaluation report. https://www.outcomesstar.org.uk/wp-content/uploads/U_WorkStarPilotEvaluationReport2015.pdf

Lowe, T., French, M., Hawkins, M., Hesselgreaves, H., & Wilson, R. (2020). New development: Responding to complexity in public services—The human learning systems approach. *Public Money & Management*, *41*(7), 573–576. https://doi.org/10.1080/09540962.2020.1832738

Lowe, T., Padmanabhan, C., McCart, D., & McNeill, K. (2022). Human learning systems: A practical guide for the curious. https://www.centreforpublicimpact.org/assets/pdfs/hls-practical-guide.pdf. Accessed on March 6, 2024.

Lowe, T., & Wilson, R. (2017). Playing the game of outcomes-based performance management. Is games manship inevitable? Evidence from theory and practice. *Social Policy and Administration*, *51*, 981–1001.

MacKeith, J. (2011). The development of the outcomes star: A participatory approach to assessment and outcomes measurement. *Journal of Housing, Care and Support*, *14*(3), 98–106.

MacKeith, J. (2021). *Enabling help: How social provision can work better for the people it serves.* Report. Triangle Consulting Social Enterprise.

MacKeith, J., Burns, S., Goodbrand, S., & Good, A. (2019). My mind star: The outcomes star for young people's mental health and wellbeing: Development report. www.outcomesstar.org.uk/wp-content/uploads/My-Mind-Star-Development-Report-FINAL_updated.pdf

MacKeith, J., Burns, S., Lamont, E., & Good, A. (2018). *The parent and baby star: Development report*. Triangle Consulting. www.outcomesstar.org.uk/wp-content/uploads/Parent-and-Baby-Star-Development-Report-FINAL.pdf. Accessed on March 6, 2024.

MacKenzie, P. (2021). *The social state: From transactional to relational public services report*. Demos.

McCashen, W. (2017). *The strengths approach: Sharing power, building hope creating change*. St Luke's Innovative Resources.

Morwitz, V., Johnson, E., & Schmittlein, D. (1993). Does measuring intent change behavior? *Journal of Consumer Research, 20*(1), 46–61.

Needham, C., & Mangen, C. (2016). The 21st century public servant: Working at three boundaries of public and private. *Public Money and Management, 36*(4), 265–272.

Nunnally, J., & Berstein, I. H. (1994). *Psychometric theory* (3rd ed.). McGraw-Hill.

Nyashanu, G. M. (2020). Implementation of the mental health recovery star (MHRS) in a community mental health service in aotearoa New Zealand: Review of the evidence and development of an action plan. https://www.outcomesstar.org.uk/about-the-star/evidence-and-research/research-library/#tag-link-12. Accessed on March 6, 2024.

The Health Foundation. (2016). *Person-centred care made simple what everyone should know about person-centred care*. Report. The Health Foundation.

Vávrová, S. (2020). *Improved outcomes in family services following the introduction of the outcomes star*. Evaluation report. https://www.outcomesstar.org.uk/wp-content/uploads/RESEARCHSUMMARY-Strep.pdf. Accessed on March 14th, 2024.

Wilson, R., Cornwell, C., Flanagan, E., Nielsen, N., & Khan, H. (2018). *Good and bad help: How purpose and confidence transform lives*. Report. NESTA.

York Consulting. (2013). *Family star evaluation: Summary report*. Working paper. Family Action.

APPENDIX 1 METHODOLOGY FOR DEVELOPING OUTCOMES STARS

Each version of the Outcomes Star is developed in collaboration with service providers with input from people who receive the service. They are piloted to test their usability and effectiveness as keywork tools and to assess their psychometric qualities as holistic measurement tools. The process and pilot findings for each version are documented in development reports (see for example, MacKeith et al., 2018). The overall approach, informed by Participatory Action Research, is described in MacKeith (2011). The following box provides a brief summary of the four stages of the process.

Stage 1: Exploring the Scope and Need for the Tool

New versions of the Outcomes Star are initiated when at least one service provider (usually many) express a need for the new version. The scoping process involves an exploratory literature review to identify relevant research and policy and establish whether a new version of the Outcomes Star is needed or whether an existing version or other tools exist that could meet the need. It also involves exploring the appropriate scope of the proposed new version of the Star, for example, what is the appropriate age range for a Star being developed for young people? If it is concluded that a new Star is needed and there is funding and collaborators to support the development, then the development process proceeds.

(Continued)

Stage 2: Creating the Pilot Version of the New Star in Consultation With the Working Group

A working group is established comprising keyworkers and managers from the collaborating services. Where possible, service users are also part of the working group. If this is not possible, then they participate through focus groups and one-to-one interviews. The working group's input is organized around three one day workshops.

Workshop One comprises a variety of exercises and discussions to draw out the expertise and experience of those present around the intended outcomes of the service and steps towards these end goals. Following the workshop, the material and literature review are analyzed to create a provisional Journey of Change and identify the outcome domains for the new Star. These form a 'skeleton' which is then fleshed out with the detailed descriptions of change provided by participants to create the Star Chart and User Guide for the first draft of the Star. The draft tool is presented to *Workshop Two* and detailed feedback is received which is then used to create the pilot version of the tool.

Stage 3: The Pilot

Keyworkers from collaborating services receive a one-day training course and they then try out the pilot Star with the people they are working with. Pilots usually last between 6 and 12 months and at the end of the pilot period keyworkers and the people they are working with complete questionnaires about their experience of working with the Star. In addition, the Star readings collected during the pilot are analyzed to establish the psychometric properties of the pilot tool.

Stage 4: Finalizing the Tool

At *Workshop Three*, these findings are shared. The people who have been using the tool also provide in depth feedback in person, not only on the content of the tool but also on its scope, format and guidance for its use. On the basis of the post-pilot questionnaires, psychometric analyses and Workshop 3 feedback, the pilot version is revised to create the final version including Guidance for Workers and, for some Stars, flashcards.

'MINESTRA RISCALDATA?' USING EXISTING TRANSACTIONAL DATA TO PROVIDE INSIGHT INTO RELATIONAL ACTIVITY IN ACTIVE LABOUR MARKET PROGRAMMES (ALMPS)?[1]

Giampaolo Montaletti

Northumbria University, UK

ABSTRACT

This chapter aims to show how existing 'transactional' administrative data ('minestra riscaldata' – literally translated as 'reheated soup' meaning same old story) can be used to 'uncover' hidden relational aspects of outcome-based policy programmes. A mixed statistical–qualitative methodology is outlined and illustrated in the context of a case study of active labour market programmes (ALMPs) in Lombardy, Italy. The analysis makes use of administrative data reshaped using network diagrams to identify temporal change points in the evolution of relationships. The results including the graphical artefacts produced were then used in dialogue with experts and people involved in the programmes to provide new interpretations. From the discussion of the case emerges an understanding of relational dynamics, innovations in services and paths for future evaluation. Finally, the possibility of a new form of accountability, as the analysis of network dynamics, provides more granular insight into how outcomes are produced via interactions among actors.

Keywords: Administrative data; relational public services; relational public administration; network diagrams; labour market statistics; labour activation; active labour market programmes

---

Futures in Public Management
Critical Perspectives on International Public Sector Management, Volume 8, 121–136

ISSN: 2045-7944/doi:10.1108/S2045-794420250000008008

INTRODUCTION

Highly relational services are appearing as an answer to the increasing complexity of today's social and economic environments where delineation of boundaries and linearity of results given the input of the public actions are no more describing the reality. Some active labour markets programmes (ALMPs) started with a significant relational orientation and customization of personal support, but 'the political drive moved from a relational services stance to more a transactional basis' (Montaletti et al., 2022) with more emphasis on 'standardization of costs which is presented as a "simplification", resulting in commodification of actions so that personalization is really no more in place' (Montaletti et al., 2022). ALMPs are mainly deployed with 'payment by results'-based payments systems. Many scholars pointed on the emerging of cherry picking (Lowe & Wilson, 2017; Pastore, 2020) and gaming (Scarano, 2023).

Different statistical methods have been used to evaluate this class of ALMPs: propensity score matching (Colombo et al., 2015; Scarano, 2023), counterfactual evaluation (Colombo et al., 2015) and logit estimates of relative risk ratios (Pastore, 2020). All these approaches have been able to find advantages and shortcomings of the programmes, but they were mainly aimed to 'investigate the extent to which such approaches are able to make service providers accountable for client outcomes' (Scarano, 2023).

When ALPMs programmes are organized as result-based services, accountability is designed as a function of the results of the procedures. The evolution to relational services makes the above-mentioned evaluative approaches difficult to adapt at the definition of outcome as a systemic, emergent property: 'outcomes are shaped by interdependent, dynamically interacting factors far beyond the individual or organisational boundary that cannot be wholly separated into component parts' (French et al., 2023). This definition of outcome as an emergent across boundaries property opens (more than) one research question 'How can we make sure that engaging with complexity does not lead to a de-emphasis, or worse still, a deficit of accountability? . . . A pragmatic goal therefore might be to determine a model of accountability which is a workable compromise in both democratic and functional terms' (French et al., 2023). Responding to this challenge, the following is the aim of this chapter: can dynamic graph analytics be used to represent the evolution of relationships between actors involved in a policy programme on labour activation, using administrative datasets? And can we use dynamic graph analytics in an evaluation process?

The next section will explore the use of graphs analytics in sociology to describe networks of human relationships and anomaly detection to explore the graphs dynamics as a tool. This is followed by methods section outlining a six-step method and then the outputs of the application of the approach using existing transactional data from ALMPs in Italy. The chapter ends by outlining the lessons for policy and practice and conclusions.

LITERATURE REVIEW

Along with a diffusion of the theories of complexity in the last 20 years, a great deal of effort has been devoted in many disciplines to give a representation and when possible 'modelling of the real world ... to help inform our actions' (Mowles, 2021). In social sciences, different modelling exercises have developed to describe complex systems showing adaptability and dynamic evolution: 'Those collective wholes that do not evolve and learn are complex systems; those that do are complex adaptive systems (CAS)' (Youngman et al., 2014). Diffusion of information systems and social networks have made the use of graph-based representations (Arnaboldi et al., 2015) and as a method to explore networks (Kingan, 2022) increasingly possible and relevant. Yet, the policy and practices of the learning and evaluation of policy instruments such as ALMPs remains moribund (Montaletti et al., 2022).

The discipline of sociology has adopted graphs to explore the dynamic evolution of relationships: 'Relationships emerge, evolve, decline, come to an end, start up again, change, and take on different qualities' (Bidart et al., 2020, p. 29). Many statistical tools, often based on exponential regression graph models (ERGMs), have been developed to describe network dynamics (Krivitsky, 2023). Applying the innovative use of network dynamic graph analytics to understand the evolution of events during the lives of people involved in welfare support programs adopting the following definition 'a dynamic network is one whose entire structure varies with respect to time' (Crane, 2018). This definition is often applied to networks of conversations in social networks or via other media involving roles and rules giving shape to the interactions (the edges of the network) among the participants (the nodes). Dynamic networks are often used to show represent the evolution (in terms of formation and dissolution) of structural changes in relationships. It is important to stress the difference from the evolving networks, where new relationships are added to already existing networks without any change in their existing structures, as it often happens in social networks.

Egocentric sampled networks have been used to reduce the computational burden related to the size of networks exploring the role of racial disparity in HIV diffusion in the USA (Krivitsky & Morris, 2017). The relevant event framework has been used to modelling communication behaviour within emergency settings (Butts, 2008). All these methods are used to infer the importance of roles and rules in social settings using structural characteristics of the relationships to forecast the evolution of the network. The temporal exponential random graph model (TERGM) has been widely adopted to model dynamic networks. Due to its limits, TERGM have been used for networks with a limited number of nodes, like in small communities, schools or companies (see Krivitsky, 2023 for case discussions) while some networks of relationships are too wide to make them computable and require sampling. Sampling implies that some properties of the full graphs are kept in the subsamples, and these had deep implications on the adequacy of sampling procedures and validity of the conclusions. Even more challenging is the design of a TERGM model, where a selection process of variables is usually driven by the evaluation of statistical parameters, so that for each case or network to be modelled a specific process of exploration and evaluation needs to be planned. The existing literature recommends that this class of models needs to be well-fitted as a single set of ERGM covariates cannot explain networks from different contexts (Kandanaarachchi & Hyndman, 2022).

A varying-coefficient exponential random graph models (VCERGMs) has been used to monitor the evolution of the co-voting networks at the US Senate (Lee et al, 2020). In this study, the emergence of anomalies in the evolution of political alliances (as part of the opposition voting for the government) is detected using a VCERGM. In recent times, a wide variety of deep learning methods have been developed to capture anomalies, and it has been suggested that anomaly detection, which aims to identify rare observations, is among the most vital tasks in the world and has shown its power in preventing detrimental events, such as financial fraud, network intrusion and social spam (Ma, 2021). Anomaly detection is also widely used as a tool to identify change points in the structure of dynamic networks (Kandanaarachchi & Hyndman, 2024).

Nevertheless, there is a diffused consensus on the limits of modelling (any kind of) in social science and in complexity as one academic observes: 'it is impossible to have a perfect model of a complex system. This is not because of some inadequacy in our modelling techniques, but a result of the meaning of the notions 'model' and 'complex'. There will always be a gap between the two. This gap should serve as a creative impulse that continually challenges us to transform our models, not as a reason to give up' (Cilliers, 2001). While this chapter shares and seeks to offer a new application of this vision, the author also shares the qualification that 'there is feedback from the world that tells us something about the appropriateness of our models.' (Cilliers, 2001).

METHODOLOGY

This section offers an overview of the process of the use of a specific class of statistical algorithms to represent the evolution and identify change points of a network of relationships. The suggested methodology proposes a six-step path with three nodes, represented in Fig. 1 and outlined in Table 1.

Extracting Relationships

Transaction processing systems (TPS) are information systems used to manage payments, issuing of invoices, the control of warehouse movements and the keeping of general accounts. As they present basically the first generation of workflow-oriented systems, they are widely diffused in public administrations to manage welfare support programmes. TPS store their information in databases, where the transaction between the public administration and the persons are usually formally described. A single transaction record contains information about the person, a date of the transaction, a description of the transaction and

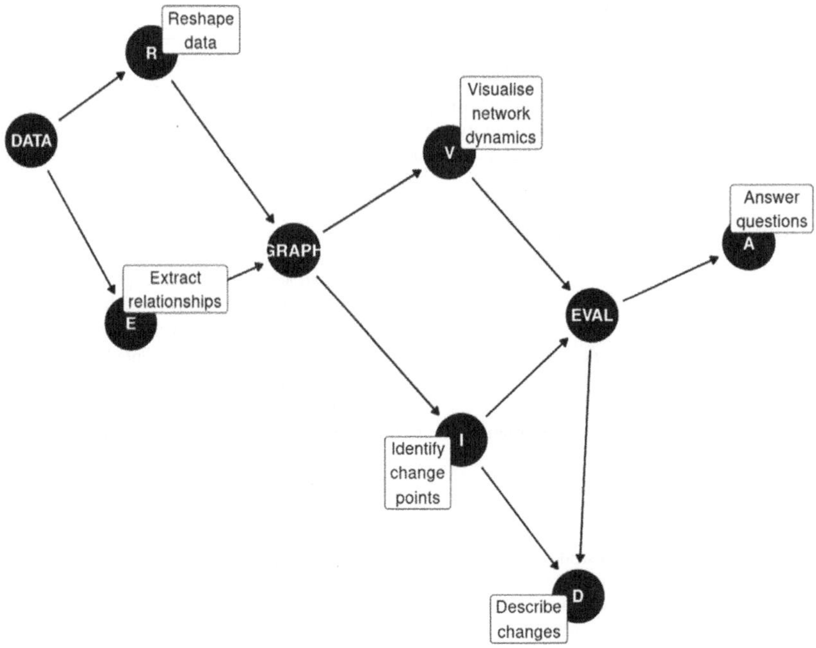

Fig. 1. From Data to Evaluation Using the Proposed Methodology.

other relevant data. We can have TPS storing information about bank accounts, training events (an attendance ledger is set of transactions), ambulance interventions, labour contracts, visits at the public employment services (PESs), nights spent in a hotel, telephone calls, benefit payments and many other different events. We can read these transactions as relationships among the person and the institution/entity or person owning the records. Extracting records from different databases makes possible to build succession of events/relationships of one or more persons with other persons/institutions/entities and pass this succession to a graph representation.

Data Reshaping

The datasets have been collected and imported in R (R Core Team, 2024) and further processed with the TSNA library to rearrange the data as dynamic networks with edge formation and dissolution (Bender-deMoll & Morris 2021). The graphs can be represented as a contiguity matrix, as to say a matrix with all nodes are presented in rows and in columns, and the crossing cell holds a 1 when there is a link and a '0' when there are no links. A dynamic graph can be represented as a time series of contiguity matrices.

Table 1. Outline of Stages in the Method.

Stage	Action	Notes
Extract relationships	Extract information from existing datasets: user_id, entity_id, type of_link (e.g. contract, assistance_programme), start_date, end_date.	Every row in the table represents a relationship between the user/person/ beneficiary and an entity (employer, public employment service, private employment service. . .)
Reshape data	All the collected events (rows) are collected in one file as a sequence.	The events table is passed to a procedure that reshapes it in temporally ordered series of adjacency matrices, expressing the existence of a relation as a binary relationship, with weights 1 and 0.
Visualise network dynamics	Using network dynamic tools	The matrices are represented as graphs in a movie like succession, make evident how relationships are formed and dissolved.
Identify change points	Use the Oddnet algorithm to identify changing points	The same series of matrices are passed to the Oddnet algorithm that provides signalling at the point the graph has reached significant changes in structure (points in time)
Describe changes	Show the illustrations to experts/service providers and ask them to freely describe the changing points	Due to the potential ambiguity the changing point should be described openly: e.g. could be labelled as 'start of operation', or 'change of intensity of the meetings with the user' or 'end of the programme' or 'discharged'.
Answer questions	Respond to the question: What is happening? Why it happens as this time? Is this positive? Is this in line with the scope of the programme?	A range of answers/interpretations are collected and used to describe what origins of the dynamic may be.

Visualizing Network Dynamic Processes

Network dynamics have been represented using the NDTV library to produce animations of the graphs used during the discussion of the cases (Bender-deMoll, 2022).

Identifying Change Points

The R library Oddnet has been used for the detection of changing points in graph structures (Kandanaarachchi & Hyndman, 2024). The R library igraph (Csardi & Nepusz, 2006) has been for the computation of the metrics used by the Oddnet library. The structural characteristics of the graphs above can be summarized with a set of indicators computed on their contiguity matrix. A very often used indicator is called density and presents the percentage of cells with value = 1 in the matrix; as the nodes presented more connections along the times, the density increases. When the relationships are dissolved, the density decreases. Other indicators can be computed to evaluate the centrality of some nodes (proportional to the number of connections they have and the distance between them and the other nodes in terms of connection) or the marginality. Without making a complete list of all the metrics, what is important for us is that the evolution of the relational structure can be described along the time with a collection of time series, without the need to print and manage all the graphs, especially when the dimension of the nodes and of the links increases. For a full list of the features computed on a time series of graphs, please refer to the study of Kandanaarachchi and Hyndman (2024).

Describing Changes

The output (movies, graphs representation at the changing points) is presented to expert and/or policy designer. In later discussions with domain experts, the meaning of the time points has been explored and expressed. The decision about the meaning of observation and discoveries are left to those working in on the matter. Using a feature based, time series modelling technique we should make it possible to compare quite different policy measures and different datasets (Kandanaarachchi & Hyndman, 2024). This consultation process follows the suggestion from the American Statistical Association (ASA) (Wasserstein & Lazar, 2016) about the use of statistical tests: 'Scientific conclusions and business or policy decisions should not be based only on whether a p-value passes a specific threshold' (ASA, 2016). In a wider interpretation of the ASA statement, policy decisions can't be based only on model parameters, but they need to be based on domain knowledge as well.

Answering Questions

Having drafted an explanation of the change points, we used it to pose some evaluative questions to the stakeholders in face-to-face sessions.

- What is happening here?
- Why it happens as this time?
- Is this positive or negative?
- Is this in line with the scope of the programme?
- Who is responsible for the final status of the people involved?

At this stage of the process, we abandon statistical modelling, simulation or forecasts, all possibilities that are not precluded by graphs representations. In fact, the changes in relational structure can be used as a signalling system with no pre-defined polarity in the evaluation process: the evaluation is left in the hands of the domain experts and/or in the hands of an 'interpretative community' involving those who are involved in the programmes (Cornford et al., 2013). For this purpose, it was crucial in the sessions to underline that change points shown in the material had no singular interpretation. For instance, a less intense use of resources and relationships could be interpreted negatively as disengagement with ALMP or as a positive change due to improved autonomy on the part of the client or equally that they have taken on a caring responsibility. It is the duty of the community to render a qualitative evaluation to give explanations of meanings and directions of the signal.

APPLYING THE METHOD: ALMPS IN ITALY

In this section, we use data from administrative datasets on ALMP to describe the network dynamics of labour market policy in Italy to demonstrate the application of this method. The data are used to describe the evolution of networks of relationships among individuals and their links with employers and public and private employment services involved in a jobseeker's support programme.

Extracting Relationships

We collected information about careers and jobseekers involved in support programs for unemployed people in a region in the north of Italy. The programme is a national one but is managed at regional level 'to introduce a comprehensive reform of active policies and vocational training, by improving employment services and providing personalized labour market activation plans' (Italian Government, 2021). The Recovery and Resilience Facility finances the programme with EUR 4.4 billion and the final goal is to reach at least 3 million people in 4 years from 2021 to 2025.

The administrative data were extracted from two main sources:

- The electronic declaration of employment contracts to the regional information CO electronic service, where every single public and private employer must notify any employee team variation (Strano et al., 2008) including information about start and duration, the profession, the employer and his activity sector. This communication includes temporary agency mediated work contracts, including the same information as per contracts and the information about the intermediary (represented as triangles in the graph).
- The enrolment in the support programme with a PES and, when present, a private employment service (PRES) that takes care of tutoring the jobseeker and managing his personal programme on behalf of the PES.

The programme is managed in Italy with the coordination of the PESs. The dataset has been collected from about 14,000 jobseekers supported for a 6 months' time providing training and contacts with employers. For these job seekers, all the records of their past contracts with employers were collected from an administrative database managed by PES network. In the proposed method, all the persons and institutions are described as categories and roles, all the links among the nodes are described as belonging to general classes (contracts, agreements, interventions and so on) with no personal information showed or saved for any other purpose. For the functioning of the analysis, no information about the characteristics of individuals have been used. All the times of start and end of contracts and programme participations are reported as relative times, with no reference to calendar dates that should make the clients and the organizations identifiable. To simplify the illustration of the case, we use a limited number of clients (the first 50 enroled in the programme).

Data Reshaping

The data were collected for different scopes, other than describing networks and they come by transactional services. This poses some limits, but not an existential one, as transitional services live embedded in complex systems of relationships anyway, and they carry signals of their relational complexity; these signals are what we try to extract and use. Graphs of interconnected nodes mimic relationality, and they can be used to be rigid or flexible organizational assets without the need to change the data structures we use. But, as we use already existing data, we did a choice of the information, and we cannot really stand for everything.

Fig. 2 is the graph of workers (the triangular nodes), the employers they have been working for (the squared nodes), the temporary agency (grey-circular nodes) that mediated their contracts with the employers and the PES (the black-circular nodes) that enroled them in the programme. The edges stand for different records: the edges from the job seekers to the employer represent a contract, the link between the triangular and the grey node represent a contract mediated by an agency and the link between the triangular and the black nodes stand for the participation in the support programme. The temporary agencies are also entitled to take part in the programme as mediators to ease people back to employment by signing an agreement with the PES for the duration of the programme.

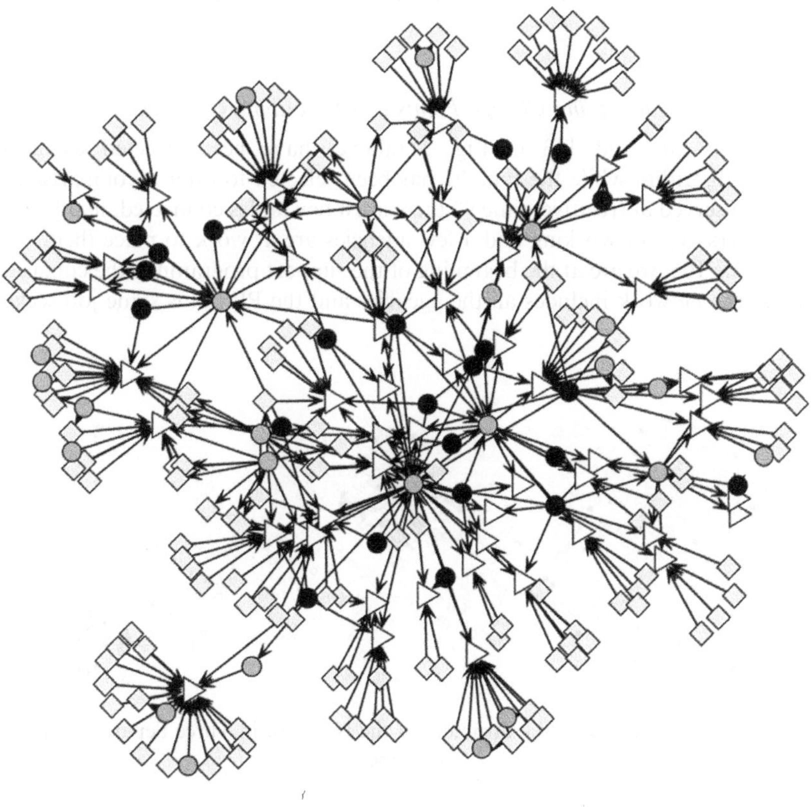

Fig. 2. ALMP Sample Graph.

Visualizing Network Dynamics

The graph presented above is not a dynamic one, as to say all the nodes and links are presented together, while some links were active in the past only.

We limited the representation of the graph to a sample of 50 people only because a wider graph is too big to be presented in this form. From this representation, it can be seen that

- There are more employers the jobseekers, as the career of the jobseekers taking part in the programme is very often a fragmented one, with many brief times close-ended contracts.
- Some employers have links with more than one jobseeker and 'contribute' people to the programme.
- Some agencies have a significant presence as they link with all the other actors, tending to cluster together and being central nodes in some regions of the representation.

Networks evolutions through time were animated using the NDTV package (Bender-deMoll & Morris, 2021). For the purposes of this chapter, we three 'snapshot' pictures (in Fig. 3) representing the status of the network at different time points or indexes (for the purposes of graphic rendition the full elapsed time of the dynamic graph has been divided in 122 time periods of 30 days, approximately 10 years).

Identifying Change Points and Describing Changes

The points 106 and 113 in Fig. 3 (above) have been selected using the Oddnet algorithm while the time 92 has been selected to offer a comparison. It can be observed at (relative) time 92 there are a few nodes connected: many of the job seekers are not working and a few agencies are at work to place them.

At time 106, we are at the beginning of the support programme: the connected part of the network includes all the agencies and the PES plus some job seekers

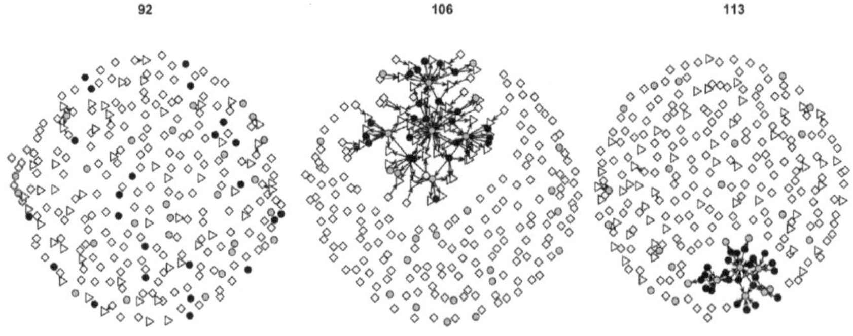

Fig. 3. ALMPs Case, the Structure of the Network in Three Separate Points in Time.

and a few employers. All the job seekers, the PES and the agencies will be involved later, but the denser part of the graph shows a structural jump in comparison with the sparse graph at time 92.

At time 113, the job seekers in the sample have concluded their participation in the programme. The network among agencies and PES is still connected, waiting for the enrolment of another group. Some people are still at work, connected with employers, but the density of graphs is visibly reduced from time 113, signalling another structural change in the network.

Presenting these changing points to experts of the policy under analysis generated a variety of insights on the reasons for the changes over time.

- PES and agencies coalition are due to the financials of the programme that will incentivize the placement results obtained by the private sector.
- PES role makes them central to the network during the financial life of the programme.
- Some of the employers are same the workers had contracts in the past so that the results are accounted for a returning contract or the renewal of an existing relationships, posing questions about the any change induced by the programme.
- The end of the maximum time defined for the help at the jobseeker decides the dissolution of a big percentage of links with the PES while some relationships are supported by the private agencies.

Answering Questions

The monitoring of the change in the relational structure proved to be fruitful in terms of reflection on the development of the policy programme. It could be seen that short-term programme durations show a sudden increase in interactions among service providers and clients, usually bringing short term results, while the intensity of the contacts drops at the end of the programme, leaving people with problems and with their results (in terms of new contracts) to manage.

Responsibility (in terms of active relationships) is left to employers that will handle integration and for the next round of unemployment. No follow up and co-operation with employers potentially leaving clients alone, with no substantial change in the level of their interaction trends before the beginning of the support programme.

One group participant noted that the responsibility of the PES can't be extended to the past when the instability in the life of the jobseeker was generated by a succession of short-term contracts. On the other hand, the way accountability is designed in these sorts of programmes ends with the direct support programme. A 'window of responsibility' should not leave the client nor the employers alone in the same situation where they were before.

So, an open question is posed to the idea of programme duration and co-operation among nodes of the network to share accountability and outcomes.

POLICY RECOMMENDATIONS FOR RELATIONAL SERVICES

In terms of lessons learnt from case study, it is possible to argue that the use of administrative data to manage performance leads programmes to foreground quantitative events and variables causes. The relative lack of (or minor) qualitative elements fails to support the interpretations of change in user behaviours nor to describe meanings or guide the direction of the interventions. Using the steps described here however shows that it is possible to use administrative data to check when the structure of relationships reaches 'meaningful' change points, potentially signalling to the caseworkers and managers; it is time to improve their understanding what is happening. The learning here is that this kind of analytic approach is closer to a description of complexity (or 'complexity aware'), and relationships are the objects used to describe the evolution and the effect of the programs and could also be used for evaluation in future relational services.

Such representation of network dynamics could be used to:

- understand the present impact of different type of welfare interventions;
- support the dialogue in a network of caseworkers/managers/contractors about the intensity and outcomes of interventions;
- redefine concepts as accountability as a shared process of ongoing mutual learning.

The use of change points detected by an algorithm looking for anomalies gave us the possibility to focus on structural change. In the case structural change sends a signal about the evolution of the relationships generated by the introduction of policy measures and support programs. While usually we tend to evaluate programs by short-term results (whether the unemployed finds a job, the ability to reduce the use in drugs and other metrics according to the different programs), very seldom we can reflect on the persistence of results along the time. Is the programme generating a change in people's lives? Is it a persistent change? Is it going to last? In many social and economic development programs the effect of the programme ends with the programme's termination or within a predefined duration time.

The relational 'thickness' experienced by clients fades out before the results is met, so that the end of the programme decides the end of the benefits or intended results.

Embrace Methods to Check Relationships in Functional Terms

> How can we make sure that engaging with complexity does not lead to a de-emphasis, or worse still, a deficit of accountability? ... A pragmatic goal therefore might be to determine a model of accountability which is a workable compromise in both democratic and functional terms. (French et al., 2023)

The proposed method uses the relationships among the networks of care and their clients as an object that can be formally described and further processed and computed as many other accountability tools. This method represents accountability as a shared responsibility descending from the cooperation among the actors and changing patterns of contacts with the clients. When the complexity of needs keeps growing along with a decreasing agency of the clients, then the relational approaches need to be embraced in a cooperation space that defines the levels of accountability along with levels of cooperation. The network aware representations are also putting evidence on the de-facto emergence of hierarchical functions as a process of discovery in the evolution of the networks, and this is something that is left to the reflections of the actors of the network.

The 'evidence' presented by the statistical tools we have experimented are a part of 'functional terms' mentioned above while they are leaving space to a democratic discussion of the meaning of the evidence, their interpretation, use and consequences on the subsequent actions the communities of practice, the welfare networks and the managerial political levels of the administrations will decide to implement.

Analyze Adaptation to Assess Accountability

Functional accountability appears from a shared flow of adaptations. As it is shared, accountability is shareable or fractional so that even in a dynamic space, it can be attributed to actors and made partially computable while what to do with the results of flowing accountability (rewards or punishments) is left to the democratic exercise. The attribution of a shared responsibility is proportional to the frequency of contacts with the clients and is balanced by the strength of cooperation with other entities and services providers.

So, what does this look from the perspective of the various stakeholder. For instance, *from the view of providers the more they are in contact with the client, the more they are responsible (and accountable) for the trends in somebody's life; the more they share knowledge and cooperate with other providers, belonging to a network of practice, the more they share accountability with others.*

This does not make a provider unable to engage in misbehaviour such as 'gaming' the data, but it does put the emphasis on the management and collaborative networks to constantly refine what they intend for clients as 'a better life' or a 'positive outcome' or at least to engage in a process continual re-definition at given signals from the monitoring activities thereby making accountability a community activity. This also allows a much more engaged discussion on what is going on in the network by pooling intelligence and responding to changes in circumstances (see Montaletti et al., 2022).

Keep the Interpretative Community Connected to the Formative Evaluation Toolbox

The main changes in relationality detected by algorithms are a point for reflection about the evolution of shared responsibility and should be part of a learning circle where impact on groups of clients and their lives and systemic change induced by cooperative practices are under a qualitative and quantitative evaluation dialogue.

The monitoring experiments have been conducted using already existing datasets, collected for distinct reasons from transactional services managed by public institutions. The availability of data coming from already existing procedures and information systems has a cost but reduces the costs for further data collection. The use of open-source tools ensures that no added licence costs are needed to set up a proper evaluation workflow. The code used to explore the datasets is open and can be inspected; open-source tools also allow replicability of the experiments and the embedding of the procedures in already existing information systems.

Monitor the Fairness of the Proposed Algorithms

The proposed method is not using or consuming information about the calendar dates of the facts that are reported as relative times from a conventional date of beginning. All the conclusions expressed are opinions of experts at various levels involved in the programs described, and as a matter of policy, their conclusions should not be drawn automatically from the statistical processes used to analyze the data but be transparently open to community interpretations.

CONCLUSION

From this evidence, the use of network dynamics analytics is a promising emerging tool for the evaluation of relational services. It has the potential to enable the use of open methodologies to explore the complexity of existing or emerging relational services cooperating in networks with traditional transactional services and welfare institutions in a multi-agency environment. The method could be used with few or no adaptations to compare programs having quite different structures and characteristics, different scales of implementation and with different institutional and time constraints.

According to the limits imposed by the national and international regulation about personal data protection, it is worth collecting information and describing the stories of those who oversee the service and of the programme. This will help those case loading and public managers in understanding what came before they started doing their work and give an answer to the question: who is accountable for what?

The answer will include the client of the service: his orientation and willingness to change is a key to the quality of the relationship and the individual outcome in a medium to long run.

The future research activities in this field will regard

- scalability of the method on larger graphs and identification of sub-graph clusters within larger collections of data;

- make the algorithm explainable to better explain to non-technical users how the change point is identified and described;
- use of the method with data collected by relational programmes.

(Smith et al., 2025)

Although this chapter has outlined and demonstrated a method for achieving relational insight from transactional data for the practices to spread and scale a change in the ways in which initiatives such a ALMPs are governed and operationalized is probably necessary, much work is left to do to allow an implementation on a new generation of information systems and platforms to support the accelerated development of relational services and those services required to evaluate them.

NOTE

1. Italian motto for 'same old story', literally 'reheated soup'.

REFERENCES

American Statistical Association. (2016, March). Principles to improve the conduct and interpretation of quantitative science. *ASA News*. https://www.amstat.org/asa/files/pdfs/p-valuestatement.pdf. Accessed on February 20, 2024.

Arnaboldi, V., Passarella, A., Conti, M., & Dunbar, R. I. M. (2015). *Online social networks* [edition unavailable]. Elsevier. https://www.perlego.com/book/1809311. Accessed on May 20, 2024.

Bender-deMoll, S. (2022). Ndtv: Network dynamic temporal visualizations. *R package version 0.13.3*. https://CRAN.R-project.org/package=ndtv. Accessed on February 19, 2024.

Bender-deMoll, S., & Morris, M. (2021). TSNA: Tools for temporal social network analysis. *R package version 0.3.5*. https://CRAN.R-project.org/package=tsna. Accessed on February 19, 2024.

Bidart, C., Degenne, A., & Grossetti, M. (2020). *Living in networks*. Cambridge University Press. https://www.perlego.com/book/4223678. Accessed on May 20, 2024.

Butts, C. T. (2008). (Vol. 38, pp. 155–200). A relational event Framework for social action. *Sociological Methodology*. http://www.jstor.org/stable/20451153. Accessed June 3, 2024.

Cilliers, P. (2001, June). Hierarchies and networks in complex systems. *International Journal of Innovation Management*, *5*(2), 135–147.

Colombo, E., Mezzanzanica, M., Montaletti, G., & Ronzoni, G. (2015). Counterfactual model for labour market evaluation policies. In *55th Congress of the European regional science Association: "World renaissance: Changing roles for people and places"*. 25-28 August 2015, Lisbon, Portugal, European Regional Science Association (ERSA), Louvain-la-Neuve. https://www.econstor.eu/bitstream/10419/124850/1/ERSA2015_01719.pdf. Accessed on May 30, 2024.

Cornford, J., Wilson, R., Baines, S., & Richardson, R. (2013). Local governance in the new information ecology: The challenge of building interpretative communities. *Public Money and Management*, *33*(3), 201–208.

Crane, H. (2018). *Probabilistic foundations of statistical network analysis* (1st ed.). CRC Press. https://www.perlego.com/book/1575300/probabilistic-foundations-of-statistical-network-analysis-pdf. Accessed on May 2, 2024.

Csardi, G., & Nepusz, T. (2006). The igraph software package for complex network research. *Inter Journal, Complex Systems*, *1695*. https://igraph.org. Accessed on February 19, 2024.

French, M., Hesselgreaves, H., Wilson, R., Hawkins, M., & Lowe, T. (2023). Ch 7: Harnessing complexity for better social outcomes: A reform and research agenda. In M. French, H. Hesselgreaves, R. Wilson, M. Hawkins, & T. Lowe (Eds.), *Harnessing complexity for better outcomes in public and non-profit services*. Policy Press. https://doi.org/10.51952/9781447364139.ch007. Accessed on February 19, 2024.

Italian Government. (2021). Active labour market policies and vocational training. https://commission.europa.eu/projects/active-labour-market-policies-and-vocational-training_en. Accessed on March 28, 2024.

Kandanaarachchi, S., & Hyndman, R. (2022). Anomaly detection in dynamic networks. https://arxiv.org/abs/2210.07407v1

Kandanaarachchi, S., & Hyndman, R. (2024). Oddnet: Anomaly detection in temporal networks. *R package version 0.1.1*. https://CRAN.R-project.org/package=oddnet. Accessed on February 19, 2024.

Kingan, S. (2022). *Graphs and networks* (1st ed.). Wiley. https://www.perlego.com/book/3476008. Accessed on May 20, 2024.

Krivitsky, P. N. (2023). Statnet development team "temporal exponential random graph models (TERGMs) for dynamic network modelling in Statnet". https://statnet.org/workshop-tergm/tergm_tutorial.html. Accessed on March 28, 2020.

Krivitsky, P. N., & Morris, M. (2017, March). Inference for social network models from egocentrically sampled data, with application to understanding persistent racial disparities in HIV prevalence in the US. *Annals of Applied Statistics 11* (1) 427–455. https://doi.org/10.1214/16-AOAS1010

Lee, J., Li, G., & Wilson, J. D. (2020). Varying-coefficient models for dynamic networks. *Computational Statistics & Data Analysis*, *152*, 107052. https://doi.org/10.1016/j.csda.2020.107052

Lowe, T., & Wilson, R. (2017). Playing the game of outcome-based performance management: Is gamesmanship inevitable? Evidence from theory and practice. *Social Policy and Administration*, *51*(7), 981–1001.

Ma, X. (2021). A Comprehensive survey on graph anomaly detection with deep learning. *arXiv:2106.07178*. https://doi.org/10.48550/arXiv.2106.07178

Montaletti, G., Martin, M., Wilson, R., & Jamieson, D. (2022). Trovarsi Fra L'Incudine E Il Martello? Platform Infrastructures and the work of place-based policy entrepreneurs: A multiple stream approach (MSA) analysis of the regional labor market Planning processes in Lombardy, Italy. In *Entrepreneurial place leadership negotiating the entrepreneurial landscape* (pp. 111–134). Emerald Publishing Limited. https://doi.org/10.1108/S2040-724620220000015007

Mowles, C. (2021). *Complexity* (1st ed.). Routledge. https://www.perlego.com/book/2991545. Accessed on May 20, 2024.

Pastore, F. (2020, November–December). The quasi-market of employment services in Italy. *Journal of Policy Modelling*, *42*(6), 1248–1269. https://doi.org/10.1016/j.jpolmod.2019.06.008

R Core Team. (2024). *R: A language and environment for statistical computing*. R Foundation for Statistical Computing. https://www.R-project.org/. Accessed on February 19, 2024.

Scarano, G. (2023). Outcome-based contracting and gaming practices in marketized public employment services. Dilemmas from the Italian case. *Journal of Social Policy*. https://doi.org/10.1017/S0047279422001003

Smith, M., Hesselgreaves, H., Charlton, R., & Wilson, R. (2025). The 'liberated method'—A transcendent public service innovation in polycrisis. *Public Money and Management*. https://doi.org/10.1080/09540962.2025.2456120

Strano, G., Lunetta, D., Torri, L., Genta, G., & Verreschi, G. (2008). CO e-Service: The Italian eGovernment revolution for the compulsory communication of the employment status. *European Journal of ePractice*, *4*, 1–14.

Wasserstein, R. L., & Lazar, N. A. (2016). The ASA statement on p-values: Context, process, and purpose. *The American Statistician*, *70*(2), 129–133. https://doi.org/10.1080/00031305.2016.1154108

Youngman, P. (2014). *Complexity and the human experience* (1st ed.). Jenny Stanford Publishing. https://www.perlego.com/book/1662886. Accessed on May 20, 2024.

THE PUBLIC SERVICES BURNING PLATFORM: USING EXISTING TRANSACTIONAL DATA TO MAKE A CASE FOR RELATIONAL PUBLIC SERVICE APPROACHES

Ron Charlton

Gateshead Council, UK

ABSTRACT

There are believed to be 363,000 people across England experiencing multiple disadvantages. The ecosystem of services and organizations need reform to support people with multiple complex needs (MCN) as it is failing people and not providing the holistic support desperately needed, failing to understand context and concentrating on efficiency instead of efficacy and resulting in repeated failure demand with no discernible impact on outcomes.

The aim of the 'Burning Platform' (BP) is to use existing transactional data to make a case for relational public services. It provides a comprehensive picture of people's journey through the system and the cost across services. Additionally, to evidence what happens when using a relational model of public service based on person-centred case work and contextualized inter-agency working, with people that are high demand, high cost and who are having a rough time. The BP allows us to demonstrate the change in trajectory of costs and stability of service interactions historically when compared to this approach. Without this approach, government ministers will not have a basis for comparison and will default to their perception of the current system, stifling change.

The BP method not only looks through a service lens but also through the experience of clients, obtaining detailed narratives. It then combines the quantitative and qualitative data in equally measure and then presents the information in an innovative and visually impactful way.

Futures in Public Management
Critical Perspectives on International Public Sector Management, Volume 8, 137–155

ISSN: 2045-7944/doi:10.1108/S2045-794420250000008009

Keywords: Multiple complex needs; burning platform; public services; new public management; relational; metrics; failure demand; waste; outcomes; costs

INTRODUCTION

In 2020, it was estimated that 363,000 adults were experiencing multiple disadvantage across England, including a combination of homelessness, substance misuse, mental health issues, domestic abuse and contact with the criminal justice system, and are among the most vulnerable in our society (Ministry of Housing, Communities and Local Government, 2020). As a retired police communities chief inspector, the author has witnessed first-hand the challenges posed by existing New Public Management (NPM) frameworks. Designed to improve efficiency and accountability, the consequences are that it often fails to address the nuanced needs of individuals, amplified even further when suffering complex needs. Also, as a carer for a sibling with complex needs, they understand the difficulties of navigating support across fragmented services that operates within metrics that don't reflect realities. This provided unique insights when developing the burning platform (BP) and what follows is their account from within the work of the challenges and opportunities of a relational approach to public service.

Changing Futures was funded by central government and the National Lottery Community Fund financed for 4 years, at a cost of £77 million to improve outcomes for adults experiencing multiple disadvantage. The aim was to test new sustainable ways of bringing the public and community sector partners together at a national, regional and local level to help people change their lives for the better. Changing Futures Northumbria (CFN) is one of the 15 local partnerships across England. Central to the work of CFN was the concept of the 'Liberated Method' (LM) and before we explain the rationale and process by which the BP was developed, it's important to provide contextualization of the LM to gain the understanding of what we are comparing the current system of services to.

The LM provides a structured consistent approach to casework across different contexts and settings that allows for bespoke relational approaches. CFN caseworkers *were* trained in applying the '2 Rule, 5 Principle' model of practice (Smith et al., 2025). There *were* two overarching rules, 'do no harm' and 'stay legal', with five principles that underpin this (Smith et al., 2025):

- *Understand, not assess* (caseworkers build trusting relationships and deep contextual understanding with citizens that avoid standardized assessments that fail to understand 'what matters').
- *The relationship between the caseworker and citizen sets the scope* (caseworkers provide creative solutions to meet citizen's needs, avoiding missing nuances that unlock engagement and progress which are not pre-specified).
- *Decisions are made in the work* (caseworkers are empowered to make decisions and have access to a budget, avoiding referrals to managers who have no knowledge of context).

- *Pull for help or refer and hold* (caseworkers pull in specialisms when needed, avoiding doing our bit and passing the citizen on).
- *No time limits* (avoiding restricting support to arbitrary timescales).

Learning is central to the LM, and this was key to the creation of a third rule of 'agree purpose'. The rules are sacrosanct while the principles provide wriggle room to absorb the complexities going on in people's lives. Coining a phrase used by the SRO of CFN, 'If you start with systems you end up with systems, if you start with people you end up with solutions'. So that is where we started, with the people we were trying to help.

This LM provides a contrast to the status quo existing within the context of a public service delivery landscape entrenched in the NPM paradigm. From the outset of CFN, there was a desire to make lasting change, and it was recognized this was only the first step of the journey to public service reform. Over the years, the UK Government has made significant financial investments in addressing MCN and system change across the national landscape. Changing Futures is one such investment; however, despite these substantial expenditures, the issue continues to exist as a significant challenge for services, '...generating significant costs to the public purse without seeing improved life outcomes' (Ministry of Housing Communities & Local Government, 2020, p. 4). Coxon (2024) points out the frailties of continuing to invest in bad situations that will only deteriorate further and that '...Quantifying the cost of inaction often presents the strongest business case for investing in a social innovation approach that builds trust and collaboration for long-term change'. To scaffold the programme's legacy, it was necessary to provide an argument for change that resonated at all levels, especially in central government, to influence long term change. The programme team wanted to change mindsets, so they recognized the harsh and harrowing realities going on in people's lives; otherwise, they may not have a basis for comparison and will default to their perception of the current system, stifling change. One way of drawing attention to create a space for conversations was to demonstrate the impact on people and the reality and extend of the costs across the whole service landscape.

Meeting this aspiration was the aim of the 'BP', which was the use of existing transactional data to make a case for relational public services. This is achieved by evidencing a comprehensive picture of people's journey through the system and the cost across services. Additionally, to evidence what happens when you strip back the system constraints and work in a way that is bespoke, comprehensive with multi-agency support using the LM, with people that are high demand, high cost and having a rough time. The BP demonstrates the change in trajectory of costs and stability of service interactions historically when compared to the LM approach. The BP not only looks through a service lens but combines this extensively (and uniquely perhaps in this context) with the lens of citizens to understand the impact of services in their lives by obtaining detailed narratives through building trusting relationships, each taking several months. It then combines the quantitative and qualitative data in equal measure and presents the information in an innovative and visually impactful way using swim lanes.

The rules, regulations and expectations placed on individuals working across services shape their behaviours, actions and decision-making, ultimately influencing the system's normal operation and these are what we call key logics. The BP has enabled the development of a comprehensive understanding of what the key logics are across public services and how they impact on individuals and the system in terms of both cost and impact and how they need to change going forward. The ultimate goal was to provide compelling evidence to inform commissioners, central government and delivery partners in their efforts to plan and design future service provision for individuals facing MCN to have better outcomes (for more detail see Smith et al., 2025).

LITERATURE AND HISTORICAL LESSONS FROM WORKING WITH CITIZENS WITH MCN

> Public services are currently based on the 'New Public Management' (NPM) paradigm that has prevailed since the 1980s. "Despite being described as flawed..." (Osborne et al., 2014), NPM still persists.

NPM was introduced in the United Kingdom primarily during the 1980s and 1990s as part of broader reforms aimed at modernizing public services by the Conservative government under Prime Minister Margaret Thatcher. The United Kingdom had faced significant economic challenges during the 1970s and early 1980s, including high inflation and unemployment. There was a widespread criticism of perceived inefficiencies and ineffectiveness within traditional public services. NPM was, and continues to be, seen as a way to cut costs, improve productivity and provide better value for money in public expenditure through the introduction of market mechanisms, competition and the use of contracts. Of particular interest for this chapter is the focus on public accountability for performance by setting clear objectives and measuring outcomes (French et al., 2023).

NPM still persists despite a myriad of evidence calling for change. The United Kingdom still adopts a top-down approach to governance and public administration, with target-driven incentivization of performance frameworks and short-term commissioning of predefined determinates of outcomes. These fail to deliver holistic positive change in people's lives while designing out complexity. Lowe et al. (2016) argue that social intervention outcomes are reduced to what is easily measurable, and this simplification does not capture the complexity going on in people's lives as they fail to factor that '...outcomes are a product of multiple factors interacting in emergent ways.' Wilson et al. (2024) describe how NPM has a legacy of transactionalism which '...has denatured waves of public service reforms, making them unfit for contemporary governance'. They also point out that NPM's transactional legacy limits the scope of potential solutions because of '...marketization, contracts and extrinsic incentives.'

The negative impact of NPM for people with MCN is acknowledged in the Changing Futures prospectus when the government minister with responsibility for rough sleeping and housing in England explains that people with MCN have been entrenched in a cycle of disadvantage, trauma and ill health for years resulting in a repeated cycle of crisis demand within public services, '...generating significant costs to the public purse, yet failing to improve people's lives' (Ministry of Housing Communities & Local Government, 2020, p. 4).[1]

Individuals with MCN, '...often struggle to engage with everyday life, experience very poor quality of life, and feel socially isolated and on the margins of society' and regularly fail to get the support they need or end up in siloed and inappropriate services (Neale et al., 2019), making understanding the core issues faced by individuals dealing with MCN unfeasible.

Fulfilling Lives (an 8-year government funded programme) estimated that beneficiaries with MCN were consuming on average £28,800 per annum (Welford et al., 2022, p. 11) of public services and by the end of the programme, each service user was using £700 less of public services (Welford et al., 2022, p. 21). Hold on to this fact, the relevance will become clear.

It is widely acknowledged that better measurement of societal outcomes can drive a more informed approach to statecraft (French et al., 2023). However, research of intervention models for MCN found 'limited evidence (...) which meets generally accepted standards of evidence quality' (French & Hesselgreaves, 2023). Attempts to work in a more relational way with people with MCN have failed to endure partly due to a lack of 'evidence' to demonstrate efficacy and therefore sustain such programmes large and small, such as the Framework for Multi-Agency Environments (FAME), Every Child Matters, Sure Start, Troubled Families and Fulfilling Lives as examples of a litany of 'failed' policy initiatives.

French et al. (2023, p. 9) argue for radical change so that public services deliver human and relational services by '...investing in the capability of public service systems to engage meaningfully with the complexity of people's lives.' To change the paradigm to relational services, we also need to understand and respond to the true realities of people's lives, of equal importance, is the evidence supporting the argument for change. Extensive and persuasive evidence that NPM is failing, is yet to realize a move away from this paradigm.

In this chapter, we will explore the process, iterations, challenges and learning involved in developing a method that provides the evidence for change to public relational services. We will utilize a case study to illustrate the development of this method, which uses a relational approach to showcase the journey of individuals interacting with public services. By incorporating historical service data and personal narratives, we will highlight the impact that the current paradigm of NPM had on trying to address needs without context and uncover an alarming extent of failure demand (circa £2 million in this one case study) and missed opportunities across public services. Such was the extent of the waste, the implications for future consumption are stark, presenting an urgent need to reduce waste and tackle inequality leading us to conclude a 'BP' exists in public services, hence the name of the method. Using the BP, we further evidence how people experiencing MCN lives can be transformed by the 'LM,' through bespoke relational support, while reducing costs to the public purse.[2]

METHODOLOGY: THE CASE HISTORIES APPROACH: WHERE TO BEGIN?

When reflecting on the initial exploration of the BP, the initial brief from the Senior Responsible Officer (SRO) for CFN was something like, 'Can you look at what it is like for people who experience MCN using public services and what it has cost the public purse and compare it with the change in trajectory to costs and outcomes for people using the LM.' To the point, but where on earth do you start with that?

To provide some context, although as the lead and in the main, the sole person working on this, the author possessed a wealth of experience within public services, seeing first-hand the consequences of failing to understand the context of people's lives. However, there was no data analytical or data governance experience to inform what followed, which was a steep learning curve. An external agency was brought in to support the development of the BP for a short period.

There was an impressive looking working plan developed against a tight timeline covering 'Case File Foundation Setting'; 'Client's Narrative Build'; 'Case File Build & Review'; 'Final Analysis & Case File Build'; 'Implement system change' (the last one was so far removed from reality!) and so on. This was doomed to fail from the beginning, although not known at the time, and proved impractical and unworkable on a number of fronts and needed flexibility and time, like the LM, based around relationships. First, if we were going to deep dive into the lives and histories of people who are at the far chasm of need, possibly traumatized, who have a deep-seated mistrust of services and had been let down time and again, why should they be prepared to share their real stories? You need to earn that trust, and the only way to do that, is through building an equitable relationship which takes time. Second, data sharing and governance arrangements and more importantly relationships and partnerships for the parties to agree and release data proved to be a long process with some services.

The aim of the work was to uncover the deepest truths and emotions hidden within the citizens experiences and their interactions with services. There was a desire to understand every aspect of our case histories stories, knowing that each citizen possessed a unique story to tell about themselves but also the story of 'system's' encounters with them so what they knew and what the various organizations knew about those encounters. We also recognized the vulnerabilities of the citizens and that their participation must be of their own volition, fully informed of the implications and without any coercion.

The beneficiaries within CFN BP case studies were in the early stages of their recovery and still leading chaotic lifestyles but supported by the caseworkers with intensive engagement, had transitioned from extrinsic high support to a level of stability and intrinsic agency which was essential to obtaining true explicit consent. The caseworkers were heavily involved in the selection as they had built trusting relationships and knew if they were ready, there were other factors involved to ensure all ethical considerations had been considered with the appropriate governance arrangements in place. Three case studies were selected to provide the basis of the 'BP'. We present one of them in Appendix 1 below whom we will call 'Brian'.

To fully grasp the depth and volume of the themes conveyed in Brian's story, it would require much more than just a chapter (or an Appendix in a Chapter). The point here is to emphasize that by establishing a relationship based on mutual respect and trust, citizens are more inclined to share their true realities of their lives, their context. Equally, humanizing services and understanding a citizen's context would allow more informed decisions about the right support and who/what is needed to provide it that will make the citizens lives better, reducing failure demand and building capacity back into services.

Accessing Historical Service Interaction Data

As we set out at the start of this section Brian's narrative, as well as informing about the impact services had on him and some of the key logics at play, also allowed an understanding of which services we needed to source data from. In this case, it comprised two police forces, four local authorities, five healthcare trusts, the regional ambulance service, the prison service and probation. The voluntary and charity sector were not featured heavily in the narrative but undoubtedly would form part of the story and would have added greater depth to the findings.

Services were asked five basic questions regarding the complete sum of interactions with Brian from the age of 18 to get what we needed from the historical service data:

- When was the interaction?
- What was it for?
- What happened?
- What was the outcome?
- Were any other services involved?

Working closely with the Data Protection Officer within a local authority, 14 Data Sharing Agreements (DSA) were created. That is the relatively easy part, getting all the agencies to agree to release personal data was very challenging and time consuming and needed determined perseverance. The author found an inherent reluctance from some services to share personal sensitive data with concerns surrounding General Data Protection Regulation (GDPR) and the Data Protection Act. Key to success was building relationships with services, particularly with the strategic leads and Information Governance Teams (IGT), ensuring a shared understanding of purpose and potential benefits for citizens and their service. A summary of lessons learnt from this process are presented below:

It is crucial to start this process as soon as possible, as overcoming internal processes and concerns within certain services can be lengthy and difficult, as evidenced by one service failure to respond to the request well into the second year from the initial contact, at the time of writing now finally providing data. There were many refusals and concerns on the way and obstacles to overcome that requires negotiation and establishing common ground.

Flexibility to absorb each organization's internal policies and requirements for data release via IGT is necessary to minimize resistance. Be mindful that the request is adding to workload. The key is to show how this will benefit their organization going forward.

Strategic buy-in at the beginning is vital with some services to facilitate constructive conversations with IGT that are likely to have concerns about sharing sensitive personal data. Even with strategic buy-in, it is necessary to persuade IGT of the merits of the project.

Where there is no strategic link within an organization, a bottom-up approach ought to be taken, persistently going through the normal data request channels to reach the right people to start conversations with.

Keeping track of conversations and agreements is key to maintain momentum with organizations that otherwise could fall into the 'too hard to do' list and disappear. There always will be omissions, but tracking to date shows 538 emails, 34 face-to-face meetings and 25 telephone conversations.

This undertaking is challenging and highlights an often overlooked aspect of service delivery, namely the necessity of sharing data more extensively, particularly with interdependent services. Challenges across public services include 'cultural and skills barriers; poor data quality; a lack of public trust; and security and privacy concerns'. Many services, including central government, have highlighted that data are not shared widely or effectively enough and is failing to gain the best value from it (UK Parliament, 2022).

The absence of a comprehensive understanding of individuals across services hinders the ability to offer effective solutions that enhance people's lives. However, this is not enough in itself, how organizations deliver services and understand people's context and how they use data is vital. The BP argues for the need to look at data differently and building contextual agile evaluation measures that iterate with the work. Empirical evidence shows that rationalist approaches of measuring outcomes to set social interventions on an objective basis and aligning incentivization across divergent interests of services such as commissioners, employees and users have been weak (French et al., 2023). Other than precise measures such as mortality or disease incidence, it fails to understand the complexities of MCN. It must also be acknowledged that if the shift of cultural mindsets across public services that is clearly required is to materialize the data and measures by themselves are not enough in isolation. As well as culture, a number of things must align that includes commissioning, leadership and evaluation.

Looking at Data Differently

Using a relational lens means an approach that collects and analyses data differently (see Cornford et al., 2013; Wilson et al., 2024). In the context of BP, this involved a bottom-up approach, understanding the transactional historical data, connecting events across services and overlaying the context from Brian's story to understand the impact on him and the consumption of public services it had taken and at what cost. Conversely, the same principles are applied once Brian became a beneficiary of CFN so that we could compare if there was any change in the trajectory of impact, effectiveness of the LM, public service consumption and cost.

This holistic approach allows for a comprehensive understanding of Brian's experience and the effectiveness of public services applied across the whole place-based service landscape. It is likely that the historical costings obtained are a significant underestimation of the real costs to the public purse for various reasons ranging from information systems upgrades/changes over time which made retrieving data from outdated systems daunting and in some cases was unachievable. Also, siloed service data capture without the ability to connect events in a proportion of service interventions led to lost/obscured service interactions and thereby related costs. There was also the fact that services for a range of reasons sometimes fail to capture data that would have been valuable to the work. Additionally, when covering timespans of several decades, data retention requirements under GDPR rules led to the (appropriate) deletion of data by some agencies.

In contrast, due to the strong trust established between the caseworkers and the citizens, along with the intensive nature of the engagement, we have a high level of confidence in understanding the events in the lives of the case studies. Therefore, the post-costings for the LM provide a more accurate depiction of the actual costs of public service consumption.

The United Kingdom has well-established national level unit cost programmes with publicly available lists (Mayer et al., 2022), and as such these were used where possible, despite varying views on unit costings, this demonstrated the orders of magnitude we are seeing across public services.

FINDINGS

There have been in excess of 3,500 interactions with public services captured. Brian's historical costs to the public purse currently stands at £1,910,398. *Some* of the public service interactions he was involved in over 14 years are as follows:

- 389 police call outs.
- 207 arrests.
- 115 nights in police custody.
- Spending 5 years in prison (sentencing was twice this amount).
- 797 presentations to Accident and Emergency Departments.

- 261 ambulance call outs.
- 78 mental health assessments.
- 434 nights in supported accommodation.
- 80 adult concern notifications to adult social care.

Table 1 breaks down the historical costs of Brian's consumption of services segregated into service categories. It then shows the costs to the same service categories for the periods of 0–12 months and 12–24 months when deploying the LM.

Table 1. Historical Costs Per Service Category v 0–12 Months and 12–24 Months Costings Post CFN.

Service Type	Brian's Historical Public Consumption Costs per Service Type (£)	Liberated Method Public Consumption Costs 0–12 Months (£)	Liberated Method Public Consumption Costs 12–24 Months (£)
Criminal justice	£915,105	£660	£0
Health	£857,713	£71,084	£1,454
Mental health	£60,562	£1,211	£0
Housing	£62,889	£6,378	£478
Social care	£940	£282	£0
Drug/Alcohol services	£5,332	£1,733	£0
Benefits	£0	£6,746	£122
BETEL (Christian faith-based charity)	£7,857	£873	£0
CFN	Not applicable	£35,590	£11,004 (expenses not included)
Total	£1,910,398	£125,557	£13,058

The criminal justice system stands out, with 1,315 historic interactions (not including probation) compared to only 12 post CFN (with no arrests). Post CFN intervention, service interactions are targeted in delivering 'what matters', resulting in a significant reduction in failure demand and service 'bounce'. Fewer services were needed to actively contribute to Brian's recovery, through 'pulling' for specialisms when needed because the caseworkers understood his needs and had context, thus, interventions with quality outcomes.

In terms of costs, health services as well as criminal justice absorb much of the failure demand, as indicated in the cost summaries above in Fig. 1. The total cost for 1 year after CFN is higher than expected. However, there are a few factors that can explain this. First, we have a much better understanding of the details of what has happened, so the costing is more accurate compared to historical data. Second, there is an increase in support, which comes at a cost. Also, the system on many occasions failed to deliver what was needed to help him to thrive, so countermeasures were deployed, such as placing him in hotels, otherwise there would have been no stability in his life to unlock his intrinsic capabilities. There is also what we are calling 'service lag', things that happened prior to becoming a beneficiary where the consequences play out within the 12 months of data, such as court appearances. Let's not forget, Brian was really struggling when he came to CFN and had 14 years of alcohol dependency, which takes time to support him to deal with his trauma and addiction.

In the 5 years and 7 months leading up to CFN, the average annual cost was £202k in stark contrast to the £28k fulfilling lives estimated. The costs were increasing until it peaked the year prior to becoming a CFN beneficiary. Even for 7 months of 2022 (Brian joined CFN in July), the costs totalled £274,110, and if the consumption was maintained for the remainder of the year, this would have cost £469,903. So clearly significant costs have still be made while achieving quality outcomes for Brian. Taking the average of £202k, this still represents a 38% cost saving to the public purse in the first year. A review of the costs of the post CFN costs between 12-24 months has shown £13,058 a 93.6% reduction of the 5-year average before joining CFN (*note this does not include expenses costs which will have reduced from the previous year)*, and we know significant improvement of Brian's outcomes have been achieved. At the time of writing, using the LM, Brian has now built his community through his intrinsic development and has been abstinent for over a year, he is employed part-time in a university educating NHS professionals on the harsh realities of the life he experienced with MCN. He has maintained a tenancy and now chairs AA meetings and is giving back to his community, and this has all been achieved at a reduced cost to the public purse. So massive tangible outcomes at reduced cost.

It is expected that the cost will peak before decreasing year after year. Additionally, the reduction in failure demand is significant while most importantly, the client is experiencing a recovery and improvement in their quality-of-life outcomes. Across the three case studies, the historical public resource consumption was £4 million. The average cost to public services in the year preceding becoming beneficiaries across the three case studies was £193,659. If you multiply this figure by 363,000, the number of people across England believed to be experiencing MCN, then this is eye watering sums of money, arguably a large proportion of which will not impact on better outcomes for people. It is clear that a BP exists in public services, the extent of which is worse than anticipated. Mackenzie (2021) argues that almost all of the debate around public service is predicated on the fact that people should have actions done to them. As demand increases, the need for more actions is prevalent against a backdrop of political narratives focused on doing more things, not making a difference; this is called 'inputism'. This feeds into theories of public service improvement focusing on public services as a '. . .transactional moment between the state and individual citizens. . .', which is fundamentally misguided (Mackenzie, 2021).

Presenting the Findings and Analysis Using Swim Lanes

We present the client's journey in the form of 'swim lanes' – a type of flowchart that delineates between service area interactions (see Figs. 1 and 2) in a way that visually displays both quantitative and qualitative data over time. Crucially, this visualization allows us to show the complexity in the system for people experiencing multiple disadvantages by highlighting the number of services involved in each person's life. The swim lanes show the services that the client interacted with from the data sources we had and highlight connections, communication and handoffs between these lanes (i.e., service interconnectivity per event).

CONCLUSION: THE 'SO WHAT' QUESTION?

This chapter makes the case to move from the NPM paradigm to relational public services through the evidence that transactional data have provided. The use of transactional data has confirmed a myriad of existing evidence that the entrenched approaches within public services are failing to improve outcomes for people experiencing MCN (Ministry of Housing, Communities & Local Government, 2020, p. 4l; Neale et al., 2019; Osborne et al., 2014). However, what is remarkable, even shocking, is the way that the three case studies demonstrate the extent of the waste and missed opportunities, leading us to conclude there is an existing 'BP'. Current rhetoric from across the political spectrum argues that public services are currently unsustainable, need urgent reform and are failing people with MCN. Past attempts to reform have tended to either focus on addressing urgent 'need' or to reduce 'waste'. The contribution outlined here shows that it possible do both and further to achieve this sustainably. Public service reform is critically needed to deliver relational public services The BP evidences this need by demonstrating, working relationally, in this case the application of the LM, as a means to provide a structured approach that absorbs human complexity and improves outcomes while saving the cost to the public purse, thus rebuilding capacity back within services.

There are significant lessons to be drawn from this work, we need to rethink the way data are currently collected and used and move to a person centric 'outside in' approach, so there is an informed understanding of the impact public service decisions and interventions have on people. Currently, data are interpreted by categorizing people in separate boxes defined by single issues, producing different labels within different public services (Bramley et al., 2015). As Brian's case demonstrates, there were a lot of disconnected labels. As a consequence, the fragmented nature of public services meant that there was no capacity for (or even the possibility of) routine systematic data analysis of individual service users' journeys across even a small local public service landscape. This chapter has demonstrated that the BP provides a methodology to combine costing service-level interaction data across public services within a geographical footprint, enabling analysis of public consumption by service users and how public services collectively impact people's lives.

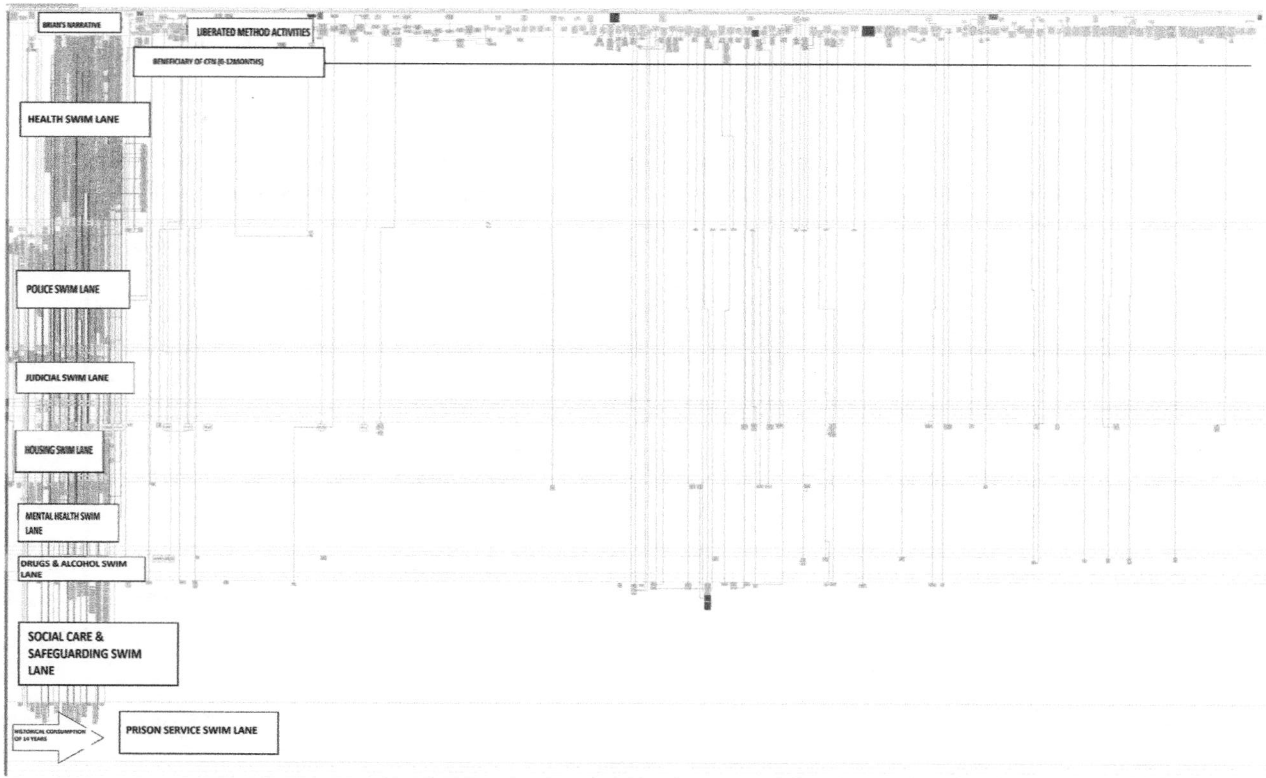

Fig. 1. Zoomed Out Version of Swim Lanes for Brian's Public Consumption History and 12 Months as CFN Beneficiary. *Note:* You will notice how failure demand and the amount of service bounce are significantly reduced post CFN involvement into quality demand.

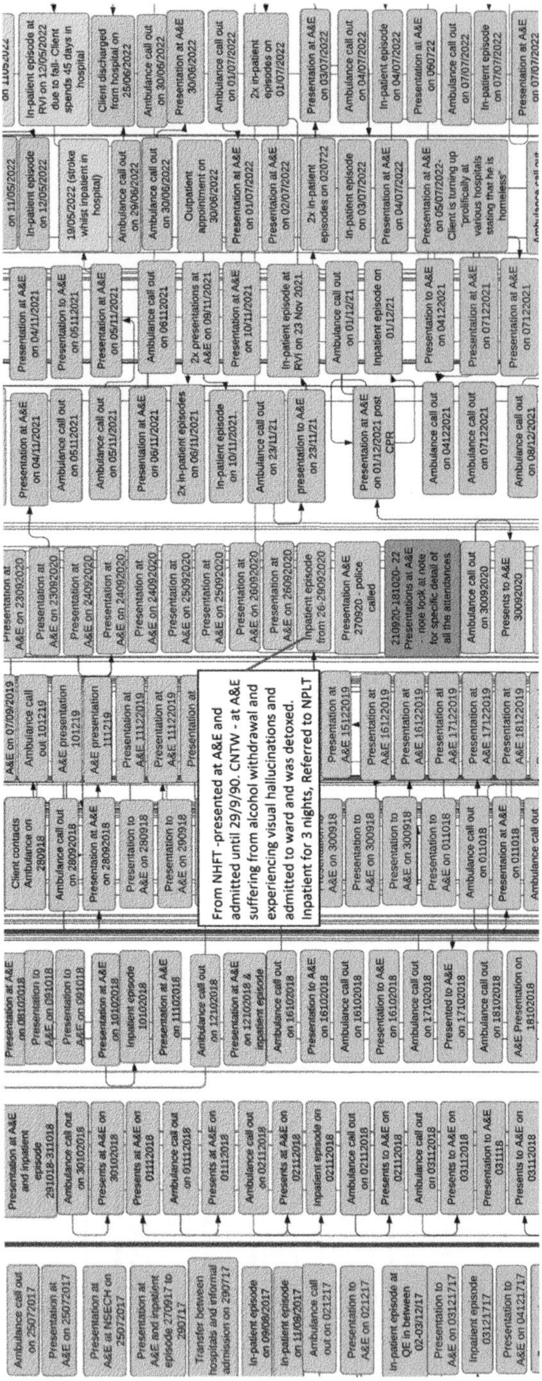

Fig. 2. Zoomed in View of Small Section of Historic Data for Brian (Each Individual Box Allows a Dive Into the Context of the Intervention and Each Event Connects the Services Involved With the Black Arrows). *Note:* Area highlighted in Fig. 2.

To use data in this way, public services must be emboldened to effectively share data more widely (UK Parliament, 2022) as no single service can provide the solution to the complexity that surrounds people. This requires a collaborative approach and a shared understanding of context that cuts across interdependent services to make informed decisions that help people to thrive while informing preventative strategies at the primary, secondary and tertiary levels. For this method to be sustainable and designed into services, hard yards were put in developing this method, gaining access to data, working with individuals to understand their stories, developing agreements and policies for data use across agencies. This may suggest practical barriers in mainstreaming this approach. But opportunities to provide more focus in the method exist, achieving similar effects with less data. The BP shows that when needs are not met for people experiencing MCN, the result is significant crisis presentations in the health and criminal justice settings, the exception may involve domestic violence, where victims may avoid engagement. The BP shows that the trajectory of public consumption is increasing before citizens became beneficiaries of CFN. Concentrating in health and the criminal justice settings for a year prior to starting the method for public consumption could yield an effective baseline to understand the before/after trajectory of public service consumption and outcomes achieved.

Additionally, the individual narratives took several months but are crucial to understanding historical impact and can provide case workers context to what support citizens need. Similar results can be achieved if case workers are upskilled to elicit historic events that has led to the MCN as the trusting relationship develops, bespoke to the individual in a trauma informed way. Case worker interventions and journaling provides accurate detail of public consumption when using the LM, this also includes time capture of interventions providing an accurate costing model. The BP analysis allowed the swim lanes to delineate the extent of the waste across services and enables the key logics driving service delivery to emerge, which otherwise may not have been detectable. There is emergence across public services of the influence of BP in how data are viewed and used. For example, Changing Futures Sussex are working with the local authority to understand suicide prevention, developing the method to operationalize analysis in swim lanes to understand what is happening across services. Calderdale Council have commissioned a BP for local context called ‘Costing of our Mistakes’.

The BP work has provided startling evidence of the waste in public services for people with MCN and in the case studies, have shown that their situation has been made worse. It provides persuasive evidence to call for relational delivery of public services while highlighting the urgency to rethink what data we collect and how we use it to commission services and understand the effectiveness of improving outcomes for people. Coxon (2024) argues that ‘...social innovation approaches *may* not lend themselves to traditional measurement approaches, which can be uncomfortable for government’. He could have been even more direct as they do not align with social innovation. Public services must reconsider their approach to evaluating performance and shift towards an ‘outside in’ perspective that starts with people and not the system itself. This requires a fundamental shift in mindset, placing people at the centre of the evaluation process.

Finally, data and measures on their own are not enough to move to relational services, what is also needed simultaneously is changes to the way the system actors lead, evaluate, commission and a shift in cultural mindsets that require further research and insight.

NOTES

1. Changing Futures is a 4 year £77 million programme funded by the Department for Levelling Up, Housing and Communities and the National Lottery Community Fund, aiming to improve outcomes for adults experiencing multiple disadvantage, including combinations of homelessness, substance misuse, mental health issues, domestic abuse and contact with the criminal justice system.
2. The liberated method is a way of delivering public relation services, see Smith et al. (2025).
3. Anti-Social Behaviour Order (ASBO).

REFERENCES

Bramley, G., Fitzpatrick, S., Edwards, J., Ford, D., Johnsen, S., Sosenko, S., & Watkins, D. (2015). Hard edges: Mapping severe and multiple disadvantage in England. https://pure.hw.ac.uk/ws/portalfiles/portal/7906947/Hard_Edges_Mapping_SMD_FINAL_VERSION_Web.pdf. Accessed on July 2, 2024.

Coxon, N. (2024). Churchill fellowship to explore how governments can promote social service integration for people with complex needs. https://www.churchilltrust.com.au/fellow/nick-coxon-vic-2022/. Accessed on March 20, 2024.

French, & Hesselgreaves (2023). *Reducing health inequalities for people experiencing severe and multiple disadvantage: An evaluation of the 'Liberated Method'*. Unpublished funding application. Northumbria University.

French, M., Hesselgreaves, H., Wilson, R., Hawkins, M., & Lowe, T. (2023). *Harnessing complexity for better outcomes in public and non-profit services*. Policy Press.

Lowe, T., Wilson, R., & Boobis, S. (2016). The performance management of complex systems – Enabling adaption. https://www.humanlearning.systems/uploads/TobyLowe-PMAconferencepaper-FINAL.pdf. Accessed on June 17, 2024.

Mackenzie, P. (2021). The social state: From transactional to relational public services. https://demos.co.uk/wp-content/uploads/2023/02/The-Social-State-Report.pdf. Accessed on February 27, 2024.

Mayer, S., Laszewska, A., & Simon, J. (2022). Unit costs in health economic evaluations: Quo Vadis, Austria? https://www.mdpi.com/1660-4601/20/1/117. Accessed on March 19, 2024.

Ministry of Housing, Communities and Local Government. (2020). Changing futures: Changing systems to support adults experiencing multiple disadvantage. https://assets.publishing.service.gov.uk/media/5fd35420d3bf7f30641aa2fc/Changing_Futures_Programme_-_Propectus_for_local_EOIs.pdf. Accessed on January 25, 2024.

Neale, J., Parkman, T., & Strang, J. (2019). Challenges in delivering personalised support to people with multiple and complex needs: Quality study. *Journal of Interprofessional Care*, *33*(6), 734–743. https://doi.org/10.1080/13561820.2018.1553869

Osborne, S. P., Radnor, Z., Kinder, T., & Vidal, I. (2014). Sustainable public service organisations: A public service-dominant approach. *Society and Economy*, *36*, 313–338.

Smith, M., Hesselgreaves, H., Charlton, R., & Wilson, R. (2025). New development: The 'liberated method'—A transcendent public service innovation in polycrisis. *Public Money & Management*, 1–9. https://doi.org/10.1080/09540962.2025.2456120

UK Parliament. (2022). Sharing public sector data. https://researchbriefings.files.parliament.uk/documents/POST-PN-0664.pdf. Accessed on February 26, 2024.

Welford, J., Moreton, R., Keast, M., Milner, C., & Roberts, J. (2022). The fulfilling lives programme: Supporting people experiencing multiple disadvantage. https://www.tnlcommunityfund.org.uk/media/insights/documents/Summary-of-programme-achievements-evaluation-findings-learning-and-resources-2022.pdf?mtime=20221128143121&focal=none. Accessed on June 17, 2024.

Wilson, R., French, M., Hesselgreaves, H., Lowe, T., & Smith, M. (2024). New development: Relational public services—Reform and research agenda. *Public Money & Management*, 1–6. https://doi.org/10.1080/09540962.2024.2344902

APPENDIX

Brian's Story

Brian was a train driver, married and owned his own property and in his early 30's. When driving a train, someone jumped intentionally onto the tracks, giving him insufficient time to stop and was unfortunately killed. He was traumatized; a subsequent coroner's inquest apportioned no blame. While all of this was going on, his marriage broke down and he lost his family home, further compounding his mental health and he was now consuming 3–4 litres of vodka a day. He lost his job and initially had funds to pay for hotels and purchase alcohol.

Inevitably, his money ran out, and now being alcohol dependent, he used to turn up at family addresses for funds; they helped at first, but due to the amount of anti-social events in their localities, the police became involved that resulted in restraining orders and an ASBO.[3] He then spiralled into a repeated cycle of street homelessness and prison sentences for the next 14 years, suffering strokes, a heart attack and a severe brain injury due to a fall while intoxicated. He had given up on life and was not engaging with services.

Brian's Narrative

Brian's story shed light on the deep and unsettling realities in his life, as he struggled with MCN. Through his narrative, we gain an understanding into the profound effect of being misunderstood by services that often deal with the presenting issues, without knowing the holistic context to their predicament.

Before starting with Brian's narrative, building a relationship had already started through getting his explicit consent. When first meeting him with his case worker to seek consent, this was 3 hours of Brian just wanting to talk to somebody. We met again and another 2 hours of him talking about his life and a further meeting before gaining his consent. This was crucial part of the process which occurred naturally with the other case studies, wanting to be heard when they had been so used to not being.

(Continued)

(Continued)

Over several months, this relationship grew where the author would fit around Brains life rather than making appointments for him to meet at predetermined times, working closely with him and his caseworkers. There were many occasions when he didn't show, but this was anticipated; we needed to show Brian, we are going nowhere, mirroring the liberated case work. He had been so used to being rejected and services closing his case for non-engagement. We knew the difficulties he was experiencing and his context. This perseverance cannot be underestimated in building a trusting relationship while unpeeling the onion layers to understand the root causes of his addiction.

When we met, rather than having prepared questions, conversations flowed naturally from gentle probing and steering the conversations in the right direction. They could be erratic at times, with inevitable memory recall issues, only to be expected having spent most of his time intoxicated when not in prison. With his consent, the conversations were recorded and transcribed later.

When Brian's journey is viewed through a relational lens, it gives you a whole bunch of different answers but importantly, better questions.

Brian recalled when he was referred for help in terms of accommodation that all services referred him to hostels. He said, 'this is a constant problem, and I cannot get well'. The problem with the hostels is that there is no support provided and the other occupants have similar issues. When put together in one place, this exasperates existing behaviours as well as exposing to others and stated his alcohol consumption got worse. He stated that he has been placed in several sheltered accommodations that are supposed to be 'dry' and staffed 24/7, yet there is open use of drugs in the rooms, drinking alcohol in shared spaces such as the lounge. He has been robbed, had possessions stolen and been beaten up on numerous occasions. He can't handle being in these establishments and feels safer on the streets, so then the local authority deems him as being intentionally homeless, when he seeks support. This compounds his mistrust of services and results in non-engagement and consequently a staggering amount of crisis presentations to services such as A&E.

This demonstrates a compounding effect, amplifying the challenges faced by citizens and other services, leading to a cycle of repeated failure demand that rarely improves their outcomes concerning complex needs.

Brian recalled numerous medical episodes when street homeless including a bad fall when he received a severe head injury that required three operations on his brain and the time he suffered a cardiac arrest. He recalled being found unconscious and a police officer administering Cardiopulmonary Resuscitation (CPR) that broke 5–6 ribs but kept him alive until an ambulance arrived, ending up in a special trauma ward for 4 weeks. He remembers withdrawing from the alcohol as he awoke and suffering delirium and fits with not consuming alcohol. Upon release from hospital, there was no continuity of

(Continued)

support, and he was told to report as homeless to the local authority, which he did, but they maintained the stance of him being intentionally homeless, as a result he continued sleeping rough on the streets, not only potentially life threatening but another missed opportunity.

His story also provided insights into how he was not understood. Many services, if you are alcohol dependent require the citizen to reduce their consumption before certain services can be provided. He said, when seeking support from recovery services for a detox,

> ...if you go into there, say look I need some help, and they say to you, what help do you need? and I say I'm an alcoholic and I need a detox, they'll say you will have to show us that you want one by reducing your alcohol use, you tell that to an alcoholic, an alcoholic that is on the streets is even worse, what I'm saying is, they are somebody who can't stop drinking, so how can you tell an alcoholic to reduce?...that's what you always get.

He further stated, '...I mean to tell an alcoholic just to stop, it's a choice, they shouldn't even be working in the field of alcohol'.

Brian frequently breached his ASBO trying to feed his addiction, leading to custodial sentences. Upon release from prison with no support, he wanted to move himself out of the area, for his and his family's benefit, to prevent further breaches so presented in another local authority area as homeless. Having no local connection, he ended up as street homeless, his addictions worsened and resulted in crisis presentation failure demand.

His experiences with services highlight a further common theme across the case studies; they are set up for failure. When he has been released from prison he is told to report to the local authority for housing. Upon his release, he finds himself without any support or accommodation, ultimately ending up on the streets. In addition, he is required to adhere to certain conditions outlined in his licence. However, with no stability or somewhere to live or means of contact he struggled to comply with his licence conditions, leading to his arrest, another court appearance and ultimately returning to prison. This cycle further demonstrates the failure demand at play.

A NEW METHOD FOR CONCEPTUALIZING AND MODELLING FOR RELATIONALITY AND RELATIONAL ENTERPRISE

Mike Martin

Northumbria University, UK

ABSTRACT

The following chapter examines the wider epistemic framing required to understand relationality, which is ultimately a lived shared experience which may be represented and recounted in stories and may be evidenced in observations and data but cannot be reduced to such hermeneutic interpretations or to calculation and predication. Taking this into account, the chapter proceeds to present a model of relational enterprise in terms of conversational relationships, which makes clear the distinction between relational governance and transactional governance. In order to achieve this, the purposefulness and goal-directed nature of relationality is analyzed from a cybernetic perspective, using Krippendorff's concepts of systems determination applying this framing to consider the concepts of a relational service in the context of wider service environments. Based on this, a model of relational enterprise as a map of conversational processes linked by information generation and interpretation processes is presented.

Keywords: Relationality; governance; platforms; communications; trust; public service management; digital government; information systems

INTRODUCTION

That care and welfare is relational, in a way, would be a truism, requiring no further discussion, were it not for the systems and processes we have observed and experienced over the last few decades, which have been involved in the policy

Futures in Public Management
Critical Perspectives on International Public Sector Management, Volume 8, 157–168

Published under exclusive licence by Emerald Publishing Limited
ISSN: 2045-7944/doi:10.1108/S2045-794420250000008010

formation, procurement, delivery, management and evaluation of public services and support systems in the health, care and welfare sectors (see Bartels & Turnbull, 2020; Wilson et al., 2024). These have been consistently 'irrelational', and the resulting irrelationality has become systemic, thereby creating perverse behaviours (for instance see French et al., 2023; Lowe & Wilson, 2017). We use the term not merely to indicate an absence of relationality but a propensity to create barriers and render relationality more difficult to generate or experience. In most areas of public care and well-being services, relationality, where it has been experienced, has been an epiphenomenon, occurring despite the systems, and being the outcome of a sense of vocation and commitment among carers.

It is not simply that the dominant New Public Management (NPM) paradigm (Chandler, 2017; French et al., 2023) reduces all systems behaviours to measurable transactions, but the information architectures and methods, which are mandated in procurement and embedded in commercial information systems supply, demand that care relationship processes must be reduced to clearly defined use-cases and business logics, recorded in pre-designed forms and data structures that are fixed and immutable in use and in practice (see Martin & Wilson, 2020 for a deeper analysis of the history of digital government). There is no concept of relationality that can be articulated and inscribed in management or information systems that are constructed within this paradigm. In this chapter and the following one, we will explore how relationality could be inscribed in information infrastructures and reflected in the management and governance systems they support. To do this, we must examine how relationality can be appropriately conceptualized and the nature of the information systems in which these conceptualizations could be inscribed and could evolve.

LITERATURE

The notion that an information system to support relationality must exhibit evolving structures and behaviours is an important one: any relationship of care and well-being, whatever its starting point or domains of action, must involve change and learning. Any relational system must, therefore, be in a constant state of re-determination, capturing and inscribing these developmental changes in its structure and operation, not just in the content that it records and communications. As we will see, later in this discussion, relational learning is not merely the accumulation of information; it involves both the purposeful creation and spontaneous emergence, acceptance and an incorporation of new relationships and in the pragma, praxa and doctrines of the relational enterprise in which it is embedded.

The essentially experiential aspect of relationality is underlined in the objectives of this volume; it is concerned with peoples' experience not just their interactions. Krippendorff links the concept of experience, from within, to the that of the 'constitutive determination' of a system:

> Systems that can be [fully] understood [only] by participating in them are constitutively determinable. The latter especially applies to social systems, constitutively involving knowledgeable human participants. They also include what second-order cybeneticians do. (Krippendorff, 2009)

We would elaborate Krippendorf's attribution of this form of determination to be not simply social but socio-cultural because human knowledge is always grounded in, and relative to, a cultural milieu. Using Krippendorf's concept of constitutive determination, we are able to link key aspects of the social scientific notions of relationality to those of cybernetics, which is the observation and study of the informational and behavioural aspects of purposeful, goal-directed systems. This disciplinary cross-over represents a core aspect of the approach adopted here to establish linkages and correspondences across epistemic registers (Martin & Wilson, 2020).

In this chapter, we will be developing the following cybernetics-oriented argument: relationships entail conversation, and relationality, as the term is used in this volume, implies a certain quality of conversation that is captured in the Habermasian notion of communicative action (Habermas, 1984). Here, the participants have, or strive for, an authentic commitment to mutual understanding and to shared objectives of care and development. We will further argue that the associated notions of relational enterprise, and relational service, entail what Krippendorf refers to as 'second order cybernetics' (Martin et al., 2009), they entail both conversations of care and conversations *about* these conversations. It is through second-order conversations about conversations that relational governance and human learning can be (re)-institutionalized and sustained.

METHODOLOGY: THE SOCIO-TECHNICAL AND THE SOCIO-CULTURAL

Krippendorf's characterization of constitutive determination is the fourth and highest level of what we are taking to be a stack of determinations of the nature of what we will refer to as techno-socio-cultural complexes. In this discussion, we will characterize socio-technical systems, as sense-making projections of such complexes, which can be determined at all three of the lower levels. These must be defined both in terms of their extensional structures and behaviours and their intentional purposes and objectives, and we observe that the wider and inclusive view, needed to account for relationality, requires the consideration of these socio-technical systems in their socio-cultural contexts.

The three lower levels of systems determination, which, when taken together, as a set of projections, providing the architectural framing for the definition of a socio-technical systems, are as follows:

> Systems whose behaviour is deducible from a finite history of examination and measurement are observationally determinable. This reflects the epistemological stance of detached observers who seek to discover systems properties by testing all possible hypotheses about that systems structure against the data it produces. (Krippendorff, 2009)

This corresponds to the transactional and functional definition of those aspects of a system that can be defined appropriately in terms of mechanisms. We will take traffic lights as a simple and accessible example of a socio-technical system embedded in its wider techno-socio-cultural context. These are observationally determined in a model which is a finite state machine, made of timers, actuators, indicators, sensors and power sources, deployed in street furniture. This is designed to perform a repeating pattern of behaviours, and this can be modelled in Forrester's Systems Dynamics (Forrester, 1961) terms of:

- buffers – the roads and sidewalks;
- stocks – stationary, waiting vehicles and pedestrians;
- flows – moving vehicles and pedestrians.

The next level concerns synthetic determination as an informatic or semiotic process. It involves the identification and naming of the parts of the system and the establishment of the relationships that hold between them. In relation to the lower, engineering projection, the informatic projection identifies the processes, which are engaged in handling data and the denotation of the entities and relationships represented in that data. This provides the terminology and taxonomy required to articulate the design or programme of the system. Krippendorff characterizes this as follows:

> Systems that can be built and set in motion are synthetically determinable. This reflects the epistemological stance of designers who have access to the structure of a system having determined its makeup. (Krippendorff, 2009)

In the case of traffic lights, we have the (symbolic) meanings of combinations of red, amber and green and the (iconic) meanings of the upheld palm or the walking or standing figure appearing in specific (indexical) positioning of street furniture components at the intersection. These have the denotations for the users of stop, get ready to go, go, get ready to stop, cross or wait. They are observed and decoded by drivers and pedestrians. At this level, all the terms that have meaning in the system are defined.

The architectural discourse of NPM is limited to the observational and data denotational determinations where the only things that count in the system are, in fact, physically observable and countable; concepts such as responsibilities, accountabilities or purposes are non-functional requirements that cannot be represented in these technical system definitions or be part of the contractual acceptance criteria of their procurement.

In the case of socio-technical systems, as opposed to merely technical systems, the terminology and taxonomy of the informatics projection not only refers downwards, to the functional processes of the system, but also upwards to provide the terms and agreed meanings associated with the intentional aspects of the system, which are determined at the next level corresponding to the conversational projection of the socio-technical system.

> Systems that can be lived with or utilized by interacting or communicating with them competently are hermeneutically determinable, for example [some] computers as well as people. (Krippendorff, 2009)

We might question the term 'interacting' here as being too weak and narrow: hermeneutic determination, in a relational, socio-technical system, relates to the conversational discourse between parties who have shared intentions and who are also engaged in its constitutive determination.

'Do not jump the lights, and do not treat them as the starting signal of a race' adopting the role of the racer or 'Do not dawdle and delay on green' are assertions of the norms and expectations of behaviours of road users. The traffic engineers who designed the system and set the timing parameters are also discharging the responsibilities of roles pursuing the principles and intentions of safety, efficiency and fairness for road users and pedestrians who engage with the intentions of courtesy, responsibility and mutuality expected of them. This is the description of the socio-technical system at the *conversational-hermeneutic* level. What actually counts as dawdling, racing or fairness is a situated interpretation.

Finally, out with the socio-technical system and within the socio-cultural context, we have the experience of the vagaries of urban and sub-urban road use and the styles and habits of different communities and national populations. This reflects the fourth level associated with concepts of the identity and histories of societies. Anyone who has driven in many places around the world will have experienced these differences. In Tokyo, we observe pedestrians patiently and obediently waiting for the walk sign even though there are no vehicles to be seen; in Florence, the traffic lights seem to represent the 'field of play' in a rivalry between scooters, cars and pedestrians. In some parts of Africa, they appear to be interpreted as vague suggestions to road users. This is the *socio-cultural* level of the experience of being part of, and participating in, a socio-technical system.

Martin and Wilson (2020) use Krippendorf's framework and a number of other approaches from different philosophical and disciplinary contexts, to develop the concept of epistemic registers and systemic projections, in the development of an approach to an architectural discourse of socio-technical systems. This work underlines the challenge of combining reasoning within and between discourses at the different epistemic registers of (a) empirical realism, (b) semiotic constructivism and (c) hermeneutic interpretivism, but without this architectonic, they claim, the overall coherence of socio-technical systems cannot be established or maintained. The description of traffic lights, as a socio-technical system, is taken from that work.

Against this background, the core argument of this chapter can now be re-articulated: A relational socio-technical complex (RSTC) is one that is in a state of co-evolution with its socio-cultural context. Here, the constitutive determination is a determination of the outcomes and consequences of the operations within and between hermeneutic, synthetic and observational determinations. A consequence of this definition is the fact that an RSTC cannot be pre-designed but must emerge and grow from the appropriation of a relatively simple primordial system of basic or generic conversations about what sort of conversations are required to formulate shared ethos and objectives and to operationalize and deliver them. This corresponds to the emergence, operation and governance of a community of shared interest and practice. At its most abstract definition, the core functionality of an RSTC is the support of:

- The negotiation of goals, norms and expectations as a mesh of conversational relationships in which rights and responsibilities have been allocated to roles and the roles distributed to, and accepted by, participants.
- The participation in these conversations and the generation and curation of their contents and progress.
- The subsequent evaluation of their outcomes, consequences and the experience of participating in them leading to their reformulation and evolution.

ANALYSIS

So, our task is to build an appropriate and requisite conceptual model of relationality, in terms of the relational enterprise and of relational service. We must identify the nature of the conversations they entail. This will allow us to define the sort of service platform that could be specified to support their reification and governance in specific contexts.

The epistemic framing that has been established in this first section of the chapter is summarized in Fig. 1.

We refer to four 'views' as ways of conceiving of and representing aspects of complex realities in terms of (a) that which is countable and can be measured, (b) that which can be represented and interpreted, which includes the counts and the measurements but also includes the stories and conversations and finally (c) there is the phenomenal realm of participation and experience. It is in the final and inclusive realm that relationality occurs; it is essentially, something to be experienced. Instances of its occurrence correspond and are correlated to events and behaviours within the three views but cannot be reduced to them.

These correspondences and correlations, at the conversational, informatic and engineering levels, correspond to 'relational work', and in the next section, we will discuss how such work is essentially conversational in nature.

Fig. 1. The Epistemic Registers of a Techno-Socio-Cultural Complex.

The Relational Work

The question 'what is the work here?' is a fundamental one. From the cybernetic perspective, purposefulness is at the core of the notions of enterprise and of service and purposefulness implies doing work. In what we can now call the 'Relational Service Enterprise', there are three sorts of work being undertaken and all three types are fundamentally conversational in nature, i.e. they are concerned with both actions that have effect in the world, including in hearts and minds of participants, and also with the generation, capture and communication of information.

The notion of 'conversation' we are adopting here is both rich and inclusive, and we will be elaborating a 'conversation theory' to support representation and reasoning about conversational systems in the next chapter. At this stage, we make the following observations:

- As we have asserted, a relational service is, at its core, conversational in nature: there can be no relationship without conversation, and real relationships involve authentic conversation. We have further noted that this corresponds to Habermas' concept of communicative action, which is contrasted with strategic, dramaturgical or institutionalized action in Habermas (1984). It cannot, in principle, be pre-scripted and can only, ultimately, be defined in terms of shared intentions of mutual communication and understanding. So, the first sort of work is associated with the conversations of care. These involve carer conversations with clients and carer conversations with each other and with themselves, i.e. the creation and curation of records for the purposes of continued care and development and, as we shall see, also for the purposes of management, learning and governance.
- The conversations of care have side effects which cost some entities money and save expense for others; they represent the discharge of duties and the execution of plans. There is a need to account for this, so the second sort of conversational work that is undertaken in the relational service enterprise comprises management conversations about capacities, capabilities, budgets and accounts. A requirement of platforms to support relational care is that the information associated with these conversations, in which management information is generated and shared, should, as far as possible, be produced as a side effect of the conversions of care themselves, and not as an overhead and additional demand on practice, even less, the information dealt with, and controlled by, the technology.
- The third type of work associate with the relational enterprise is associated with conversations about the conversations of care; these are the conversations of governance. Here, three questions are addressed on the basis of evidence which includes both experiential accounts (stories) and empirical data: (a) Is this what we intended? (b) Do we still intend this? (c) How could this be improved at both the level of the individual case and at the levels of the wider enterprise and its environment?

The Service Environment

A consequence of the inclusivity of the notion of relationality is that any consideration of a relational service must be considered in the context of a wider service environment which is represented in Fig. 2 below.

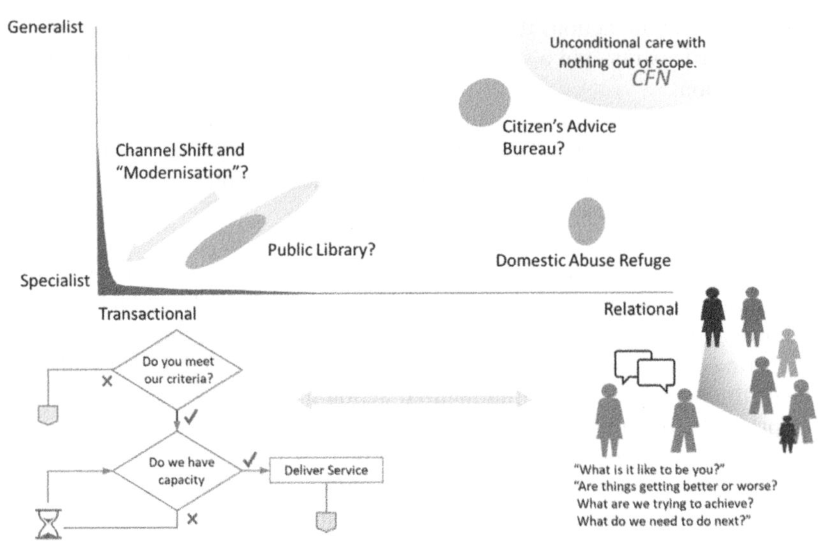

Fig. 2. The Service Environment.

The *y* axis of our 'service space' denotes the spectrum from highly specialized services to generalist services while the *x* axis spans from the narrowly transactional to the highly relational. We characterize these extremes of the *x* axis in terms of a deterministic flow chart on the one hand to an open-ended conversation between parties where the client may be embedded in a complex of both supportive and also damaging entanglements and relationships on the other hand. We (tentatively and for illustration purposes) position a number of existing services in this space noting that public libraries have, in recent years, striven to extend their basic book and media lending services to more generalist and relational services as a community hub and that initiatives to 'channel shift' (NHS, 2014) in reality, drive services downward and to the left in the effort to reduce the 'transaction costs of care'.

An important observation to be made here is that there are many public services, extending even to areas of care and well-being, which can be appropriately transactional. For most of us, for most of our lives, need is specific and episodic: simple transaction is the preferred and efficient option. However, for some individuals for extended periods of their lives and for most of us at some points in our lives, particularly towards their close, there is an urgent need for the transactional components of complex multi-agency care plans to be intermediated and brokered relationally. As has been evidenced in a number of chapters of this book, the absence of appropriate relational capacity in the service environment produces failure demand, prodigious cost and much suffering: the *Changing Futures Northumbria* project's experience is producing clear evidence of the needs and benefits of the deployment of relational capacity as an essential aspect of any efficient and effective service environment (Charlton et al., 2025; Smith et al., 2025).

The Relational Enterprise

We will now consider our first stage in conceptual systematization, which attempts to represent the logically interrelated conversational processes of a relational enterprise together with their informational drivers and products.

In this model, principles and values drive the process of articulating and maintaining the mission of the enterprise which, in turn, drives the articulation and maintenance of programmes, which identify objectives and set targets. Management processes generate plans and deploy resources on the basis of these and ensures that appropriate records and accounts are maintained. Delivery involves the interpretation and execution of plans, the use of resources and the maintenance of the record in the generation of outputs that can be observed and measured and outcomes which must be captured in conversations and discourses.

Finally, plans and resources, records, output data and stories and accounts, the evidence of what has taken place, are all drivers of governance and missioning processes which maintains, refines and evolves the principles and values of relational practice both in terms of the relational service and in terms of the relationships between the enterprise and other members of the service community and environment.

We are considering the functional processes represented here as being conversational in nature and, therefore, as defined in terms of the sorts of information they interpret and the sorts of information they generate and communicate.

The model of Fig. 2 has been labelled with the RSVP terminology of Lawrence Halprin (Halprin, 1970). Equating the delivery of a relational service to the 'performance' of a 'score' recognizes the characteristics of uniqueness or bespoke-ness of each instance, on the one hand, but also that previous composition and orchestration were also involved, on the other hand, and it is not simply a question of improvisation. We use the term 'resorting' rather than Halprin's resourcing, in this version of the RSVP cycle, to stress the idea that what is needed is an arsenal of infrastructural tools, facilities and capacities which are organized and to hand and can be flexibly adapted and reconfigured in the face of presenting need; think of a skiing resort and all the different sorts of provision and paraphernalia that it implies. Since, as we have observed, the work of the relational service enterprise is conversational, a significant proportion of the informational aspects of the infrastructural arsenal are concerned with processes of communication as opposed to data collection and processing.

The term 'valuacting', which Halprin coined, recognizes that, in this sort of creative, relational context, adding value, extracting value and evaluation cannot be alienated from each other and associated with different actors: they are all part and parcel of shared conversational work. While valuaction is associated with our concept of relational governance, all the conversational activities of, and in, the relational enterprise are valuactions, which is equivalent to the normative assertion that all roles should participate, in some way, in governance, and the relational enterprise is necessarily co-creative and co-productive.

In normal parlance, the term 'governance' is associated with the responsibilities and deliberations of a board of directors. In Fig. 3, we elaborate the model to show that this concept of the directorial governance of an enterprise is not the same as the concept of relational governance we have been discussing. Note that the dividends of a relational enterprise are more usually considered to be social or political rather than financial and the concept of directorial governance represented here relates primarily to the external contexts, environments and relationships of the relational enterprise.

Fig. 3 implies that commercial enterprise is not incompatible with relationality and the principles of non-profit distribution, social enterprise and cooperatives are entirely consonant with the possibility of a relational approach. Fig. 4,

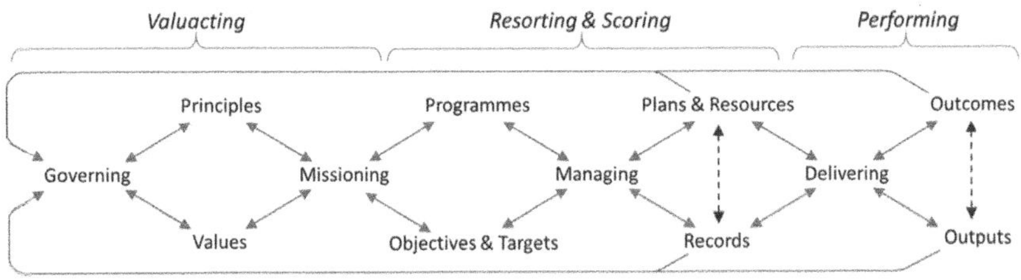

Fig. 3. The Relational Enterprise.

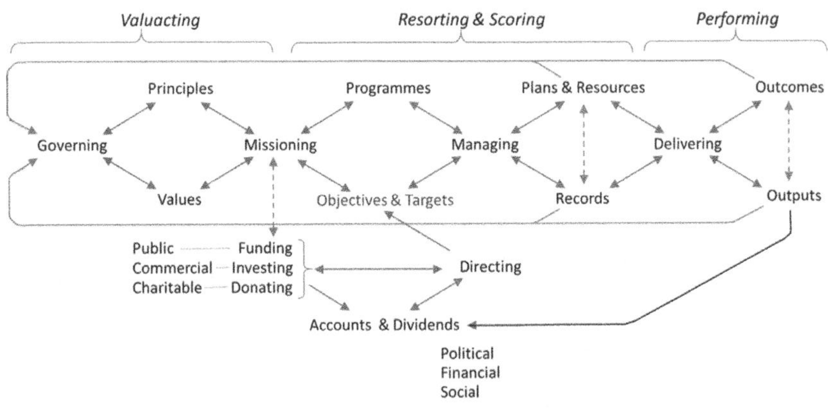

Fig. 4. Directing the Relational Enterprise.

Fig. 5. Commercial Enterprise.

however, represents the narrowly commercial venture as a degeneration of the relational enterprise where the mission is a foregone conclusion and remains fixed, simply being concerned with return on financial investment and management of risk, while externalities, i.e. non-financial outcomes and products or emissions, weather positive or negative and irrespective of beneficiaries or victims, are disregarded.

In the NPM version of Fig. 4, the directorial conversations are concerned with targets and budgets and are evaluated in public political discourses, the whole process being driven in first-order linearity, on the basis of legislative and policy programmes (Fig. 5).

CONCLUSION

This chapter has explored two aspects of a rigorous conceptualization of relationality. The first concerns the recognition of the multiple levels of epistemic commitment that must be accommodated in the architectural discourse of relational enterprise and the second explored the structure of relational enterprise itself and the nature of its governance. Together, these discussions indicate a fundamental link between the concept of relationality and that of conversation.

These concepts and models are prerequisites for the consideration of any technical infrastructure or platform to support relational enterprise and service and provide a starting position for the exploration of the requirements and architecture for any such development. Martin and Jacucci [this work, p. 166] build on this models to outline such an architecture and define its key features, which involves a shift from the data processing and distribution systems paradigm (Martin et al., 2024; Martin & Wilson, 2020), based on the empirical engineering view of that which can be counted and measured to a communications paradigm, which also considers that which can be represented and interpreted.

REFERENCES

Bartels, K., & Turnbull, N. (2020). Relational public administration: A synthesis and heuristic classification of relational approaches. *Public Management Review*, *22*(9), 1324–1346.

Chandler, J. (2017). *Questioning the new public management*. Routledge.

Charlton, R. (2025). The public services burning platform: Using existing transactional data to make a case for relational public service approaches. In R. Wilson, H. Hesselgreaves, M. French, M. Hawkins, D. Jamieson, M. King, & J. Kimmitt (Eds.), *Futures in public management: The emerging relational approach to public*. Emerald Publishing Limited. (in this volume).

Forrester, J. (1961). *Industrial dynamics*. MIT Press.

French, M., Hesselgreaves, H., Wilson, R., Hawkins, M., & Lowe, T. (2023). *Harnessing complexity for better outcomes in public and non-profit services*. Policy Press.

Habermas, J. (1984). *The theory of communicative action* (Vol. I). Beacon.

Halprin, L. (1970). *The RSVP cycles: Creative processes in the human environment*. George Braziller.

Krippendorff, K. (2009). Ross Ashby's information theory: A bit of history, some solutions to problems, and what we face today. *International Journal of General Systems*, *38*(2), 189–212.

Lowe, T., & Wilson, R. (2017). Playing the game of outcomes-based performance management. Is gamesmanship inevitable? Evidence from theory and practice. *Social Policy and Administration*, *51*(7), 981–1001.

Martin, M., Walsh, S., & Wilson, R. (2009). A social informatics intervention: Theory, method and practice. *KITE Research Group. Newcastle University*. http://www.woa.sistemacongressi.com/web/woa2009/papers/Martin_Walsh_Wilson.pdf

Martin, M., & Wilson, R. (2020). Inter-organisational systems: A neo-socio-technical perspective. https://aisel.aisnet.org/ukais2020/22

Martin, M., Wilson, R., & Jamieson, D. (2024). Moving towards relational services: The role of digital service environments and platforms. In S. Baines, R. Wilson, C. Fox, I. Narbutaite Aflaki, A. Bassi, H. Aramo-Immonen, & R. Prandini (Eds.), *Co-creation in public services for innovation and social justice* (pp. 162–178). Policy Press.

NHS. (2014). NHS channel shift strategies survey report. https://www.gossinteractive.com/media/4282/NHS-Channel-Shift-Strategies-Survey-2014/pdf/GOSS_channelshift_survey_NHS_FINAL_2.pdf

Smith, M., Hesselgreaves, H., Charlton, R., & Wilson, R. (2025). The 'liberated method'—A transcendent public service innovation in polycrisis. *Public Money and Management*. https://doi.org/10.1080/09540962.2025.2456120

Wilson, R., French, M., Hesselgreaves, H., Lowe, T., & Smith, M. (2024). New development: Relational public services—Reform and research agenda. *Public Money and Management*, *44*(6), 553–558.

MODELLING, REASONING ABOUT AND PROVIDING PLATFORMS TO ENABLE RELATIONAL CONVERSATIONS

Mike Martin[a] and Gianni Jacucci[b]

[a]*Northumbria University, UK*
[b]*University of Trento, Italy*

ABSTRACT

In this chapter, we build upon the previous work to demonstrate the purposefulness and goal-directed nature of relationality is analyzed using a conversation analytic approach. The chapter sets out the case that current information system practice, based on the data processing and distribution (DPD) paradigm, which is limited to observational and synthetic determination, that is to say, definition in terms of functions and capacities that are the consequence of designed structures, is expressively inadequate to address the requirements of relationality. Hermeneutic interpretation and the constitutive determination of lived experience are essential aspects of any complete conceptualization of relationality. On this basis, we apply the modelling process as a map of conversational processes linked by information generation and interpretation processes to create a definition and specification of a future Trusted Governable Platform fit for relational public service.

Keywords: Relationality; governance; platforms; communications; trust; public service management; digital government; information systems

INTRODUCTION

The concepts of relational enterprise and relational service [Martin, this work] demand a fundamental shift in information systems paradigm from the data processing and distribution (DPD) approach to that of information communications

Futures in Public Management
Critical Perspectives on International Public Sector Management, Volume 8, 169–181

Published under exclusive licence by Emerald Publishing Limited
ISSN: 2045-7944/doi:10.1108/S2045-794420250000008011

(IC) (Martin & Wilson, 2020). This is a consequence of the essentially conversational nature of relationality itself. Further, relationality implies second orderliness (Krippendorff, 2009): that is to say, there must be conversations about conversations in pursuit and maintenance of communicative action (Habermas) and shared purpose, that is to say, governance as well as operational use must be relational. Martin also observes that all the conversational activities in the relational enterprise are valuactions (Halprin): they inalienably combine value adding, value extraction and evaluation, in relation to the whole range of human and social capitals.

If relationality is to be supported by appropriate technical infrastructure, then the ongoing, second-order conversations of governance must be open to the participation of any and, indeed all, first-order roles in a co-creative and co-productive approach. The actual scope and inclusion in these governance conversations is, however, entirely a matter of local policy in any particular instance of a Trustworthy Governable Platform. As we shall see in this chapter, the technical design and affordances of an *environment* which supports the emergence and operation of Trustworthy, Governable Platforms must be strictly policy neutral. It is a requirement on such an environment that it provides the tools and language to model, and explicitly inscribe, *any* policy or moral ordering in the platforms it enables. This is in stark contrast to the 'hard wiring' of policy and power structures of current platform approaches which involve requirements modelling and design phases that are distinct and strictly separated from those of operational use and management.

In this chapter, the notion of conversation is analyzed, an approach to a conversation theory developed and a conversation modelling language and notation presented. The objective of this work is to create an architectural framework for structured communication service definition and to identify the high level requirements on, and affordances of, any technical service platform, which claims to be able to support and sustain relational enterprise and services.

LITERATURE: DEVELOPING THE CONCEPT OF CONVERSATION

The model of relational enterprise considered in Martin (In Press previous chapter) represents an attempt at a systematic conceptualization which has the purpose of identifying and characterizing the structure of the conversational processes that constitute a relational enterprise, Fig. 1. Each of the processes is named with a term that carries a connotation – a set of meanings and associations in normal discourse. Within the formalism of the model, however, the denotation of each activity term is associated with the nature and identities of the sets of information objects that represent its drivers and its products. For example, the informational aspects of the term 'delivery' is defined as accounting for the consumption of 'resources' in the execution of 'plans' and the generation of data about 'outputs' and testimonies about 'outcomes'. These are all informational in nature, so the last of these is associated with discourses and texts about states of affairs in peoples' hearts and minds: relational delivery involves the subsequent *telling and responding to stories*, not simply the filling of forms and the collection of data; the being together, virtually and really, implied by the etymology of the term quoted at the beginning of this section. All of the activities of the relational enterprise are conversational in the sense that, whatever real-world actions they involve, such as travelling, buying furniture or food, comforting or encouraging, they also involve generating and interpreting, recording and sharing information, i.e. an engagement in conversations and, as we discussed in the last chapter, in conversations about those conversations.

Because this is the case, the next level in the consideration of the relational enterprise, and the service it delivers, involves a more detailed analysis of the concept of conversation, and if we are to be systematic about this, then we must establish a requisite, that is to say, expressively and analytically adequate, conversation theory. So, what is a conversation? The extract below gives us a starting point.

> conversation 1340, from O.Fr. conversation, from L. conversationem (nom. conversatio) "act of living with," prp. of conversari "to live with, keep company with," lit. "turn about with," from L. com- intens. prefix + vertare, freq. of vertere (see versus). Originally "having dealings with others," also "manner of conducting oneself in the world;" specific sense of "talk" is 1580. (Online Etymology Dictionary)

We have already identified the challenge this represents: any notion of 'conversation' must encompass both what is detected, measured and counted but also include the norms and expectations of the participants and an interpretation of what they intend to happen. The last of these is necessarily a matter of the enquiry, sense-making and deliberations of governance. The representation or model of a conversation has a normative aspect, which captures institutional intentions and expectations, and a descriptive aspect, which captures the relationship between the expected protocols and sequences of exchange and what actually occurred in any given instance of a type of conversation. The evaluation of the comparisons between these representations, in the context of the story telling and testimony of participants, is relational governance as we have defined it. This involves conversations between role holders about whether an account of what happened, and the supporting evidence, corresponds to what was hoped for, expected and intended. It also involved the assessment of whether those intentions and expectations have evolved. And, as we have asserted, relationality, which, itself, is a normative term, further implies that all the parties with a stake, have a right to be represented and to participate in these conversations of governance. This is an example of the narrative perspective of complexity explored by Tsoukas and Hatch (2001).

It should be noted that the purpose of conversation modelling approach developed here is to create architype models of future conversations in terms of the distribution of roles and responsibilities and the structures and orchestrations of the messages they publish to each other, that is to say, meta-data type and process definitions. They provide the basis for the negotiation and record of shared expectations and commitments to the way participants intend to act together.

Any particular instance of a TGP will generate its own set of specific conversation forms and contents, under its own policies, by editing and republishing and promulgating its own elaborations of a basic set of primordial conversational architypes or adopt and adapt others that have been shown to be effective in similar circumstances in other communities. This work of renegotiation conversational relationships and, as a consequence, deploying new or modified structured communications services (SCS), is administrative work supported by administration and governance sessions on TGP community hubs.

The first consequence of this potential for systemic autopoiesis is that initial or seed community platform, that is being defined here, is a primordial meta-platform, a seed from which instance TGP platforms can emerge and evolve. The second is that the normal processes of requirements capture, implementation and deployment are disrupted, and we have the potential for inter-agency and community evolution 'one conversation at a time' obviating the need for 'big bang' system procurement and organizational change.

However, we repeat the important observation that while this approach enables, and we would say, positively nurtures inclusive participation in the co-construction and governance of the platform, each community will adopt the degree of emancipation it wishes or it can afford. This represents a new approach to critical system thinking in the information systems field.

Communication Services

In the approach we are proposing here, technical platforms intended to support conversational processes must take the form of communications service systems (CSS). This is in contrast to conventional DPD platforms, which reduce the concept of communication to the flow of data into and out of databases according to pre-defined data models, reporting structures and queries. Communications infrastructure has had a long history. In a basic CSS, such as the (plane old) telephone or email, there are only two explicit structural roles: the sender, or originator, and the receiver(s); the purposes, norms and expectations of the relationships between them remain implicit in the content of the exchange. We will here introduce the concept of a structured communications services where the parties have explicit institutional roles that have been committed to, prior to any instance of the conversation and which generate the norms and expectations associated with relationships and interactions between them. We will consider the conversation of care between a practitioner key-worker, a lived experience key worker and a client as an example of an institutional conversation (of care) context. In such relationships, protection, accountability, governance and learning necessitate the need for record, and in the approach being developed here, this record is treated as a by-product of the ongoing conversation between the parties rather than a data object to be maintained and queried in its own right. First, we note that this conversation takes place over an extended period of time and is split up into a series of encounters or sessions. In order to be completely inclusive, these 'encounters' may involve any single, any pair or all three parties: we are including the 'notes to self' as well as exchanges between parties as part of this conversation/relationship. We are also including face-to-face, remote synchronous and remote asynchronous encounters or exchanges as parts of the conversation.

All of the things we have identified as part of the conversation, so far, belong to the category of events happening in time and space; they are, or can be, part of the descriptive representation of the conversation. But, as we have observed, we need the ability to represent the normative, prescriptive aspect of the conversation, and relationality dictates that this cannot take the form of a script or procedure to be followed: the modern call centre is the antithesis of relational service!

METHODOLOGY: A CONVERSATION THEORY

The conversation theory and notational approach presented here has evolved over many years and has been applied to the negotiation and analysis of many complex socio-technical situations. It defines intended conversations between role holders in a declarative part which specifies the expected distribution of the following parameters among the parties:

- *Significance*: what is at stake for each of the role-holder parties, what each gain from a successful conversation and loses or suffers if the conversation fails in its objectives. This includes their respective responsibilities, that is to say the distribution of credit or blame with respect to the outcome, and accountabilities, which are the duties to inform relevant third parties about aspects of the conduct of the conversation.
- *Mutuality*: the responsibility each of the parties should take for the well-being and successful outcome of the other. This includes rights and expectations of privacy, needs and duties to inform and rights to know, which may involve third parties.
- *Resource*: the distribution of capabilities and capacities normatively required for each of the role-holding parties to fulfil their role.
- *Initiative*: Is the agency or distribution of rights and abilities to control the course and conduct of the conversation.

Note that each of these facets of the conversation may be symmetrically or asymmetrically distributed, and we must stress that these are normative in the sense that, in any institutionalized setting, they represent the norms and expectations of interactional behaviour.

A very accessible and powerful illustration of the expressive power of this conceptual parameterization of human relationships is to apply it to the long-term dynamics of familial relations from infancy, childhood, adolescence, young adulthood, maturity, seniority to dotage: our relationships with our off-spring is the epitome of relationality. They are protracted, sometimes agonistic, involving the continuing re-negotiation and rebalancing of the relational factors in conversations that are reflexive, i.e. both first and second order at the same time. These constant shifts and adjustments in the balance of the conversational parameters represents a key factor in the characterization of the relationality of a conversation in contrast to transactional situations that are pre-defined and fixed in terms of prerequisite conditions, transactional events and consequent redistributions of rights and resources.

We have noted that, in addition to this declarative specification, and as part of its implementation, institutionalized conversations also have a protocol which not only defines the norms and expectations of initiation, turn taking and closures of any conversational encounter but also identifies a set of 'instruments' associated with them. All of the connotations of the term apply: we have seen in the last chapter, Halprin's terminology of delivery (Halprin, 1970) being the performance of a score and the connotation of musical instrument applies, but there is also the suggestion of a tool to do particular sort of work or make a type of observation or experiment and also of 'legal instrument', such as a contract, signalling the existence of commitments to a set of rights, obligations and responsibilities between parties. These meanings are all relevant to our use of the term in this conversation theory. An instrument, in the abstract protocol definition of a conversation theory, denotes an information object that is, in intentional terms, the trace of the performance, and the information content, of an act. In extensional terms, it is an observed, and usually recorded, contribution to an ongoing conversation.

Since instruments are information objects that are generated and interpreted (written on an occasion and subsequently read on other occasions), they impose a temporal or ordering logic in the sense that an information item must have already been generated in order to be capable of interpretation. In the approach we are developing here, the definition of an instrument in terms of a set of communicational functions and purposes is translated into the structure of a 'datagram', which is a specific set of data, within a coding system, which, in the architectural language we are developing, is referred to as a 'publication'. So, in the platform, a conversation is a growing sequence of (sequences of) publications.

The logical entailments between sequences of contributions by specific role-holders to a conversation define a conversational protocol and a set of conventions. As an example, the strong asymmetries of significance and mutuality mean that in the early stages of the relationship between key workers and chaotic clients, in the context of crisis or emergency care, nearly all the responsibilities for initiating encounters and for their content will be with the key workers, and the instrumental responsibilities are associated with maintaining the journal and participating in case conferences. The protocol is extremely flexible, and there is considerable key worker agency. In subsequent stages of relational care, it has been a well-established social work principle to use progressive goal setting as a way to nurture progress (Locke, 1996). In conversational terms, this involves the generation and maintenance of an instrument, which could be called 'our current objectives and priorities'. This is an abstract intentional concept; to be made real and to implemented it, it must be embodied in one or more information objects, for example, a more or less structured note on paper, a laminated printed summary on a card that the client holds and a 'sticky' entry in the case journal. The content of this instrument will then figure as inputs to other conversations such as a case conference. Notice that, in this example, laminating the current objectives note makes it both physically and psychologically more durable: the modality of an instrument is associated not only with its information content but also with the intentional and emotional associations. Making the entry 'sticky' means that it is only one click away, wherever you are in the journal.

ANALYSIS: USING CONVERSATIONAL INSTRUMENTS

As explored in the previous chapter and reproduced here Martin's model of relational enterprise, represented in Fig. 1 below, there is an ongoing relationship between governance and missioning conversations, and this involves the maintenance of an articulation of the principles and values of the enterprise as the explicit criteria, which will be applied to the interpretation and evaluation of records, accounts and testimonies.

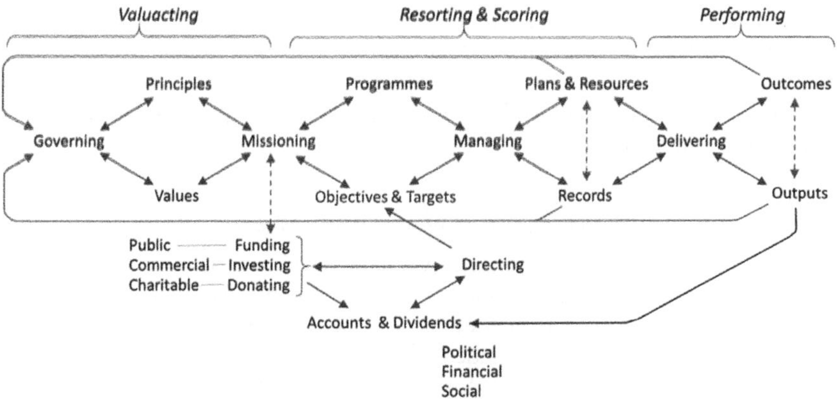

Fig. 1. The Relational Enterprise. *Source:* From Martin, This Work p. 166.

In practical terms, we have clear example of how the criteria of relational governance can be made explicit in the liberated method (Smith et al., 2025), which is based on three rules and six principles. Rules are mandates, and any evaluation of rule-based behaviour is a prediction: ultimately, the rules have either been followed or have been broken; statements of fact are either true or false. Now a rule may be high level and encompassing such as 'Remain Legal' and 'Do no harm' in the case of a programme seeking to create relational public services and the predication here can be complex and contended, but ultimately, recourse is to legal process that produces a verdict. Alternatively, rules may be quite specific such as 'At all stages, agree objectives.' Here, the predication is based on the existence of an artefact such as the one we have discussed: an item in the record. Whether the objectives committed to were appropriate, effective or even feasible are matters of the application of doctrine, pragmatics and practice and are associated with the second aspect of governance criteria concerning principles.

The application of a principle is situated and necessarily involves initiative and discretion: the outcome can only be a matter of subsequent interpretation. So, rules control, and principles guide; behaviours and relational governance involve making the former as constructive as possible, in the face of unavoidable boundary constraints, and the latter as helpful, supportive and encompassing as possible. This is in sharp contrast to the motivations of new public management (NPM) which has the objective of maximizing certainty of outcome and control while minimizing risk.

In the approach being developed here, we are not rejecting the maximization of the certainty of outcome and of control but are stressing that in the complex, emergent contexts of relational care and development, there is also a need for a narrative approach to the governance of relational enterprise (Tsoukas and Hatch, 2001). And, as we have observed, this entails the challenging process of communications both within and between the empirical and the hermeneutic registers, between predication on data and the shared sense-making and interpretation of narratives. In the next section, we will explore an approach to more formal aspects of modelling and analyzing conversational processes in support of these relational governance conversations.

Representing Conversational Models

The concept of relational governance we have developed here implies the comparison between what was intended, in terms of conversational processes and what the conversational outcomes actually turned out to be. This implies that we can capture and represent intended conversational structures. We will now consider a notational framework for the representation of such conversational models. The motivation is to maintain the required formal structuring while emphazising the accessibility and relevance of the process.

The model of Fig. 1 identifies conversational processes and their informational inputs and outputs. In our discussion of conversation theory, however, we have focused on participants as role holders. We must now make this distinction explicit in our notational framework. The objective here is to create a modelling language, which is expressively adequate to define any prospective or observed conversational situation and the normative distribution of rights interests and responsibilities that its authors intend. This is of the utmost importance because the purpose of the modelling approach is to define and configure structured communications platforms that are configurable to evolving local policy. If such a modelling framework can be established, in a context where the consequent SCS can be more or less automatically configured and deployed, then the policy, moral ordering and control aspects of the platform have been rendered independent of technical support, which is external to the relational enterprise itself.

The iconography which is presented here, particularly the use of little figures to signify conversational roles, is designed to provoke responses such as 'who has that responsibility round here?' or 'an individual who has that role should not also have that one'. In this discussion, an ostensive semantic applies, meaning you can point at what you are referring to. As we have indicated, the objective of the notation is to create boundary objects, in the form of conversational webs and graphs, around which the discussions, negotiations and commitments of relational enterprise can be conducted and captured effectively.

The Conversation Graph

In the approach suggested here, a conversational model has two distinct types of nodes corresponding to (a) roles and (b) instruments. In the first stages of a normative conversational modelling process, which will define some aspect of the operation of an intended human institution, a graph of role nodes is connected by edges which represent conversational relationships. Note that the roles, at this level of abstraction, represent a set of allocable responsibilities, a number of which could be combined into the role of a single individual or could be allocated to different individuals. Thus, an abstract, role-based conversational model can be composed and distributed onto the real roles for individuals, and these composition processes can be analyzed for conflicts and synergies of interest because it is conversational relationships that are being composed.

An example of the management of conflicts of interest is the operation of a research hospital where the doctor–patient relationship gets composed with that of the experimenter–subject relationship. This creates a first-party conflict of interest because of the particular combination of significances and mutualities it entails. This is managed through the introduction of a set of additional conversations involving an ethics committee and creates the context for a new set of instruments, taking the form of the approved protocol, the explanation and the consent forms. Another example of a conflict of interest would be that of referee in relation to contestants in a zero sum-game and that of sponsorship of one of the contestants. This would be an unresolvable, third-party conflict of interest: the ref. must be neutral.

There are many examples of conversations that take the form of multi-party deliberations, i.e. meetings. The case conference is an example of this, and we represent it as the distribution of the role nodes around an edge-circle, implying that each participant is in conversation with all the others. Examples of these conversation model/maps are represented in Fig. 2.

The second stage in conversational modelling involves the identification of the instruments as a set of additional nodes, each of which is associated with a conversational edge between role nodes. The new edges that link instruments into the role graph link the generator(s) of each instrument with all the roles that interpret it. These links correspond to acts and are represented as arrows in Fig. 2, indicating their directedness.

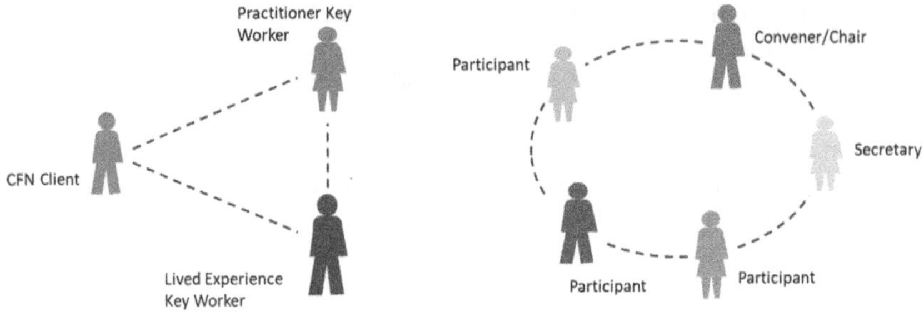

Fig. 2. A Three-Way Conversation and a Deliberation.

In the case of a meeting conversation, the instruments that are placed within the circle are all interpretable by all the participants but may be generated only by certain roles or may be taken to be the joint publication of the meeting; the secretary, however, might be the only role that can perform the write actions on them. There may be instruments accessible to only one or more of the meeting participant roles. These are represented outside the circle. For example, it could be the case that the whole case journal is not part of the internal information of each case conference of that case but is available to the case workers and the case manager. A report for the conference could be generated by the case workers and made internal to the case conference, which might include participants being consulted about some particular aspect of the case relevant to that conference. Examples of the 'instrumentalisation' of a conversation graph and a deliberation conversation are presented in Fig. 3.

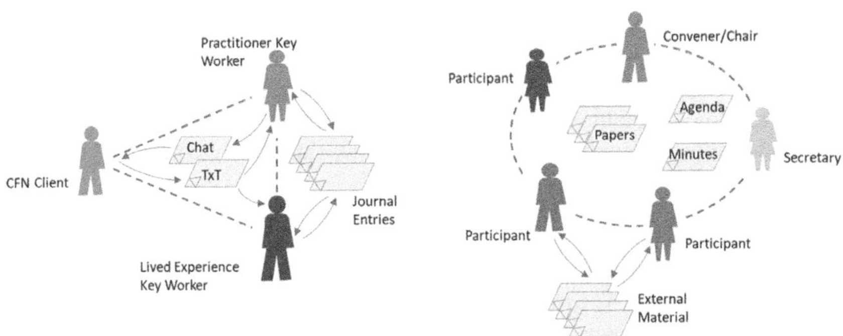

Fig. 3. The Instruments of a Conversation and a Deliberation.

IMPLICATIONS FOR POLICY AND PRACTICE

However, as we have shown in the previous chapter and previously, the current problems of information systems paradigms mean that such facilities for the delivery of relational approaches to public services remain largely unavailable or unachievable within the current context (see Jamieson et al., 2020, Martin & Wilson, 2020; Martin et al., 2024). This reductionism is the unavoidable underpinning and assumption of conventional approaches to information infrastructure and falls significantly short of the informatic requirements of relational operation, whether in the context of the notionally singular relational enterprise or, even more acutely, in the case of multiple peer agency interaction and collaboration. In conventional approaches, roles, responsibilities and relationships must be either implicit and therefore managed and governed as epiphenomena of generic documents and messages or be fixed in pre-defined workflows and data models which are only modifiable through external technical support and re-design.

On the basis of the discussion here, any alternative architecture, claiming to be capable of supporting and sustaining relationality, must address the following key functional requirements:

- It must support instances of conversations of care between role holding individuals under explicit sets of rules, principles, norms and expectations, i.e. provide a structured conversation service capacity.
- It must curate the content and provenance of all the exchanges in these conversations to support further conversations of governance and learning.
- It must enable the outcomes of governance and learning conversations to be re-inscribed and incorporated in the rules, principles, norms and expectations of the conversation services it offers.

The Trustworthy Governable Platform

The detailed consideration of these core functional requirements leads to the following architectural principles of design and implementation:

- All content generated, interpreted and curated in the platform takes the form of publications.
- A publication has two parts: a content part and a provenance part.
- All publications are instances of archetype definitions, which define their structure and any orchestrations associated with them.
- Architypes are also publications.
- Publications can only be accessed or generated in well-formed sessions associated with a conversational context represented in a conversational model that has been designed, negotiated and committed by participants. For example, a meeting will involve several preparatory sessions, involving individuals or groups, where the shared instrument/publications will be published, and deliberation session which is the meeting itself.
- The provenance of any publication consists of the data associated with the particular session instance in which it was generated. It is this that captures and preserves the original context and purpose of the content.

(Continued)

(Continued)

- All sessions are associated with a particular conversation which is associated with the activities and relationships between a set of participating roles. Examples of this would be a case, in a relational case management platform, or a project, involving multi-party procurement, construction and hand over or a production run in a manufacturing setting.
- There are administration sessions in which certain acts of publication have side effect of extending or modifying the topology of the network. Thus, a community hub can 'spawn' branches which correspond to the domains of a set of peer community member organizations which are able to enrol their respective affiliates.
- Other administrative sessions support the modification and republication of architypes in response to the negotiation of new roles and communications as part of the relational enterprise governance process.

A consequence of this approach is to make all aspects of the evolving coverage and operation of the platform matters of internal decision and (re)publication incremental and dynamic, removing the need for separate, external technical support.

CONCLUSION

The argument of this chapter has been that because relationality involves the personal and collective experience of participants, subjective experience is part of the definition and identity of a relational service and of the enterprise that has the mission to deliver it. This further implies that a relational enterprise is an example of a techno-socio-cultural complex (TSCC). Now, if the technical system, which is to be part of and to support the operation of a TSCC, is defined in terms of DPD, i.e. exclusively in terms of pre-defined use cases and functions operating on data, then the operation and performance of the resulting overall organizational system can only be evidenced and evaluated in terms of these processes. Thus, we claim, the DPD architecture is expressively inadequate for the support of relational service and enterprise and has the strong propensity to reduce them to transactionality, a process which is re-enforced by NPM theory and practice.

We have outlined a proposal for an alternative approach to the architecture of technical information systems, which is based on a communications paradigm and the concept of the SCS. The technical system can now be specified in terms of capacity and quality of delivery of conversation support services; while this is still entirely functional in nature, it retains a clear link to, and implication of, intentionality within the concept of a 'conversation support service'. An SCS supports instances of ongoing conversational interactions, not simply as basic 'chats' of social media but as structured exchanges between role holders who have negotiated and committed to particular rights and responsibilities in relation to shared norms, expectations and objectives. This is to say, the SCS definition can capture the purposes and contexts associated with any of its instances and of all the information that is generated and exchanged within them.

But this definition of the technical part of a relational TSCS in not yet sufficient. The conversational intentions and the roles and exchanges that represent the commitments to engage in them must themselves be the outcomes of governance conversations, and these conversations must be ongoing, representing the inscription of evolving values and principles and learnings within relational enterprise as a TSCS.

An instance of a conversation then becomes a growing sequence of publications generated by a set of role-holding participants with shared responsibilities and purposes. The conversation service sessions have appropriate access to previous contributions (publications) and are capable of generating new contributions according to the role of the initiator of the session and the logics and protocols of the current state of the conversational exchange. Each of these publications has a provenance associated with the session in which it originated, and this provides comprehensive traceability of the context and purpose of all the content mediated by the platform.

As stated in the Introduction, the TGP we are proposing is a meta-platform. Each specific instance of TGP evolves in the conversation fabric of the community from archetype germ elements. The moral ordering, emancipations and distributions of power, initiative and control emerge and evolve independently in each social community according to its local conditions, histories and culture.

REFERENCES

Halprin, L. (1970). *The RSVP cycles: Creative processes in the human environment*. George Braziller.

Jamieson, D., Wilson, R., Martin, M., Lowe, T., Kimmitt, J., Gibbon, J., & French, M. (2020). Data for outcome payments or information for care? A sociotechnical analysis of the management information system in the implementation of a social impact bond. *Public Money and Management*, *40*(3), 213–224.

Krippendorff, K. (2009). Ross Ashby's information theory: A bit of history, some solutions to problems, and what we face today. *International Journal of General Systems*, *38*(2), 189–212.

Locke, E. A. (1996). Motivation through conscious goal setting. *Applied & Preventive Psychology*, *5*, 117–124.

Martin, M., & Wilson, R. (2020). Inter-organisational systems: A neo-socio-technical perspective. https://aisel.aisnet.org/ukais2020/22

Martin, M., Wilson, R., & Jamieson, D. (2024). Moving towards relational services: The role of digital service environments and platforms. In S. Baines, R. Wilson, C. Fox, I. Narbutaite Aflaki, A. Bassi, H. Aramo-Immonen, & R. Prandini (Eds.), *Co-creation in public services for innovation and social justice* (pp. 162–178). Policy Press.

Smith, M., Hesselgreaves, H., Charlton, R., & Wilson, R. (2025). The 'liberated method'—A transcendent public service innovation in polycrisis. *Public Money and Management*. https://doi.org/10.1080/09540962.2025.2456120

Tsoukas, H., & Hatch, M. J. (2001). Complex thinking, complex practice: The case for a narrative approach to organizational complexity. *Human Relations*, *54*(8), 979–1013, 018452.

I'VE GOT THE POWER! A SOCIAL PEDAGOGICAL EXPLORATION OF POWER DYNAMICS IN RELATIONAL LEADERSHIP AND PRACTICE WITHIN PUBLIC SERVICES

Lowis Charfe

University of Central Lancashire, UK

ABSTRACT

In response to the impact of New Public Management (NPM), there is a growing awareness of the importance of relational leadership and practice in public services, with organizations looking for guidance and support in developing this. The expanding human learning system (HLS) network of people and organizations is an example of the breath of interest and commitment to service reform that places human flourish at its heart. To effectively develop relational leadership the uncomfortable issue of power must be surfaced and explored if ethical relational leadership is to be truly established. To aid this, I have developed a framework that expands the Danish social pedagogy model of the 3 Ps to assist relational leaders to address and challenge issues of power within relational working. This chapter sets out to explain how to apply this to the organizational context and direct work of public services so that there is more transparency around the inherent power that we navigate within our human relationships that are at the heart of all public services.

Keywords: Social pedagogy; relational public services; human learning systems; disempowerment; leadership; power dynamics; 3 Ps framework; professional self; personal self; private self

Futures in Public Management
Critical Perspectives on International Public Sector Management, Volume 8, 183–196

Published under exclusive licence by Emerald Publishing Limited
ISSN: 2045-7944/doi:10.1108/S2045-794420250000008012

INTRODUCTION

> One of the great problems of history is that the concepts of love and power have usually been contrasted as opposites - polar opposites - so that love is identified with a resignation of power, and power with a denial of love... We've got to get this thing right. What is needed is a realisation that power without love is reckless and abusive, and love without power is sentimental and anemic. Power at its best is love implementing the demands of justice, and justice at its best is power correcting everything that stands against love. Martin Luther King Junior (1967, cited in Leadbeater, 2020)

Over the last few years, there has been a refocusing on and reclaiming of relational practice and how it can be embedded within public services, from direct practice, organizational systems to organizational culture. The growing human learning systems (HLS) (Lowe & Pilmmer, 2019) network demonstrates the wide range of individuals, organizations, institutions and professional bodies looking for guidance and support on how to place relationships at the heart of what they do. This has been coupled with a growing awareness and discussions around the limited impact of New Public Management (NPM) to provide real service reform and improved outcomes for people receiving services within the public service sector (Worsley & Wylie, 2020). As Evans (2016) has rightly highlighted, poorly designed systems and processes have impacted and overshadowed any well-meaning and ethically based practice within the public sector. It is clear that there is a growing appetite to redesign and transform organizational systems and culture, as well as the day-to-day practice, within public services so that it is ethically rooted in supporting humans to flourish and helping people live a good life (Cottam, 2021; Diener & Biswas-Diener, 2019).

This focus on how public services can become more 'human' (Lowe & Eichsteller, 2021) is fundamentally about reconnecting public services with their moral purpose and in doing so recognizing the importance of relationships. A part of the complex nature of this work is the inherent power dynamics contained within relational practice, which are often over-looked. This chapter's objective is to offer a contextual exploration of this issue while also answering the question of how the use of social pedagogy can assist in the development of relational leadership and practice, based on the HLS ethos of supporting human flourishing (Lowe et al., 2021). The HLS approach helps explain 'why' relational practice is important, and it is argued here that social pedagogy offers guidance on 'how' to develop this (Charfe & Eichsteller, 2021).

The contextual argument set out in this chapter concentrates on the use of the social pedagogical 3 Ps model. With the help of my colleague Gabriel Eichsteller, we have developed it to support critical exploration and a deeper understanding of how issues of power within relational leadership and practice can be addressed. Due to the relational element of power (Foucault, 2002; Reitz & Higgins, 2020), which is discussed further in this chapter, the application of this framework can be applied, not just to the everyday practice of public sector workers but also to the management structures and multi-agency work that takes place within these organizations.

As this chapter puts forward an argument for the use of a Danish social pedagogical method, a brief explanation of social pedagogy and the synergies with the relational developments happening with public services is needed. Before I offer an explanation, I think it's important to highlight the point that, due to the manualized approach (Harbo & Kemp, 2020) embedded in NPM, people desire a clear, concise and defined explanation. The danger with defining social pedagogy and HLS in these terms often risks them being used in an 'instrumental' manner, which in turn continues the status quo and does not lead to challenging systems or supporting the radical change desired in these complex environments. To reflect the complexity of relational leadership and practice within the environment public services operate in, social pedagogy is also complex and multi-layered. In response to questions of how social pedagogy can address any given issue or circumstance the social pedagogues will often say 'it depends' (Charfe & Gardner, 2019).

To be clear from the start, social pedagogy is not a method or approach. It is an ethical, theoretical and practice orientation that embeds reflexivity, all of which shapes the way we understand and respond to the world around us (Charfe & Gardner, 2020; Eichsteller & Holthoff, 2011). It differs from a paradigm (Lowe & McIntosh, 2023), even though it shares many of the same elements, as it is not a new shift in thinking but rather something that already has a long historical tradition in many European and Latin American cultures and societies (Charfe & Gardner, 2019). A more apt description is offered by Hämäläinen (1989) who states that social pedagogy is a meta-theory that can assist us to understand social issues through a relational and educational lens. Education here is understood in its broadest sense, and to use relational leadership and HLS (Lowe et al., 2021) terminology, we would see this as *learning*. Building on Hämäläinen's (1989) definition, Stephens (2013) offers the analogy of a lens, describing the social pedagogue as someone who views the world through the lens of social pedagogical values, thoughts and actions. It is therefore not a method that can be picked up and used in certain situations and disregarded in others but, rather, an approach that centres on deeply held beliefs, ethical, relational and theoretical practices. To return to Hämäläinen's (1989) assertion that social pedagogy is a meta-theory, he writes that within it, it also contains social pedagogical theories, concepts and methods that people who are not social pedagogues can utilize. For example, the 3 Ps model focused on in this chapter can be used in addressing power dynamics in relational practice even though someone using it may not fully understand social pedagogy or in fact be a social pedagogue.

In explaining social pedagogy further, we should understand two core elements. The first is the ability to work alongside and 'be with' people through relational practice. The second is the application of 'pedagogical solutions to social problems' (Stephens, 2013, p. 27), using educational (learning) approaches to develop individual, organizational and social change while promoting social justice. We can see here the synergies between social pedagogy and the arguments being put forward for relational working and reform within the public sector (Wilson et al., 2024). And it is because of these and the focus of social pedagogy on 'the deeper purpose of supporting wellbeing, learning and social inclusion and selecting or developing methods that contribute to these aims and seem meaningful within a given practice situation' (Charfe & Eichsteller, 2021, p. 376): that I would argue social pedagogy has a lot to offer to the growing debate around relational leadership. The use of it in both theory and practice, alongside the HLS approach, can greatly enhance leadership and practice and assist in the cultivation of true relational leadership within public services.

LITERATURE REVIEW

There is already a wide range of published texts and research findings around the issue of power and relational leadership and practice, as well as organizational change. One of the first and most notable is the work of social psychologists French and Raven (1959), who identified five bases of power and argued that leadership and power are inextricably linked. They stated that the success of leadership can be linked to the different bases of power which influence leadership behaviour and communication (French & Raven, 1959). As a seminal piece of research, their work has formed the basis for further research developments in the field of organizational management and leadership studies. More contemporary studies include the work of Zhao et al. (2016), who explored the relation power base, which was added by Raven (1996 cited in Zhao et al., 2016) to the original five bases. Their research found evidence of direct and indirect relational power, and that leaders and managers that lacked positional power were often able to use relational power to deal with complex issues. They stated that 'the ability to develop good interpersonal relationships with others becomes the most essential quality a leader needs' (Zhao et al., 2016, p. 526). They also stressed that more research was needed to assist in understanding how relational power operates in different settings, countries and cultures. 'Speaking Truth to Power', the 5-year study by Megan Reitz and John Higgins (2017, 2019) looked at power dynamics within organizations and found that power is very much alive in public service organizations and that it continues to silence staff at the cost of 'relationships, creativity, engagement and performance' (Reitz & Higgins, 2020, p. 270). As a result of this lack of performance, and, as argued for by Wilson et al. (2024), there is a growing case for the need to move from the *transactional* nature of public services to the *relational*. Within the current research, the discussions and developments around relational public service reform focus on the issue of shared power and decision-making (Cottam, 2021; Glover, 2023; Lent & Studdert, 2021; Lowe et al., 2021a; New Public Alliance, 2020). While this continues to be highlighted as important, it overlooks the issue of power dynamics and how to address these within the more direct and relational aspects of public service leadership and practice.

For clarity, when the term 'power' is used in this chapter, I will be using the theory put forward by Foucault's (2002). His theory is useful in critically analyzing, exploring and understanding power in the context of relational leadership within public services. There is a varied field of academic discussion and competing theories around power (Karim, 2023). These include such postmodern theorists like Lukes (2005) who conjectures that it is importance to understand the source of power, which he claims comes from three key elements: decision-making, agenda setting and thought control. In contrast, 'Foucault (1982) regards power as relational and fluid in its manifestation rather than something which is possessed and exercised' (Karim, 2023, p. 1062). Foucault (2002) maintains that power is a core element of all human relationships and that it is ever present in all relationships no matter a person's position within a social structure (Gilbert & Powell, 2010; Taylor, 2014). For Foucault (2002), certain groups or socioeconomic classes within society do not hold all the power. He argues that this belief is a misconception and that in actual fact 'power circulates via a myriad of social networks penetrating deep into the far corners of social life playing out its effects through the everyday interactions of autonomous individuals' (Gilbert & Powell, 2010, p. 6). This can be clearly seen in the *systems* element (Lowe & Pilmmer, 2019) within the HLS paradigm. This element of HLS also acknowledges the complex web of relationships that form the systems that we operate within and that it is these relationships that shape the outcomes sought (Lowe et al., 2021). It is this acknowledgement of the centrality of relationships within Foucault's theoretical perspective of power that underpins the contextualized standpoint of the extension to the 3 Ps model we have developed (Charfe & Eichsteller, 2024) to assist in exploring power (Charfe & Eichsteller, 2024).

METHODOLOGY

Using a social pedagogical methodology, the connection between theory and practice is of utmost significance when working with complexity and social change. As Freire (1970) highlighted, knowledge, dialogue and action inform critical reflection that pushes forward transformational change in society. He termed this as *praxis* (Freire, 1970) and the 3 Ps model is a reflexive praxis model aimed at expanding knowledge through open dialogue that assists in evolving an individual's direct practice.

The 3 Ps Model Explained

The 3 Ps (Jappe, 2010) is a Danish social pedagogical model that is widely used by social pedagogues to consider and develop appropriate boundaries within their relational practice. The concept has three aspects: the *professional*, *personal* and *private* (Charfe & Gardner, 2019; Charfe & Eichsteller, 2024; Jappe, 2010). The *professional* relates to the role and remit we have within the relationship; while the *personal* aspect assists critical self-reflection about what parts of ourselves, we bring into relational practice; finally, the *private* sets out what aspects of ourselves we are not going to share as we navigate complex and ethical relational practice. The 3 Ps model supports the development of authentic relationships by exploring the nuances and boundaries between our professional self and the *use of self*; which parts of the our personality and private life do we share to help form authentic, genuine, supportive and caring relationships (Charfe & Eichsteller, 2024). For a more detailed explanation, you can read more about the 3 Ps model ThemPra's website (https://www.thempra.org.uk/social-pedagogy/key-concepts-in-social-pedagogy/the-3-ps/).

From a social pedagogical perspective, the centrality of relational practice is key, but for me, this starts with the mindset and value base of the individual – what we call Haltung in social pedagogy (Charfe & Gardner, 2019; Eichsteller & Holthoff, 2011). To read more about Haltung, go to the ThemPra webiste (https://www.thempra.org.uk/social-pedagogy/key-concepts-in-social-pedagogy/haltung-in-social-pedagogy/). As can be seen from the literature written about relational leadership and practice, when it comes to power, the focus is often on the structures and *how* power operates. To take the public sector field of social work as an example, there have been several models and frameworks (Karim 2023; Tedam, 2021; Tew, 2006; Thompson, 2006) aimed at assisting individuals to understand power dynamics. These all focus on how power operates either broadly within society or the systems professionals work within. In contrast and to return to the importance of mindset, we (Charfe & Eichsteller, 2024) have expanded the 3 Ps model to focus on critically reflecting on positionality and power (Jacobson & Mustafa, 2019). Underpinned by standpoint theory (Hall, 2020), the expansion of the 3 Ps model we've created explores and delves deeper with a more distinctively personal understanding of how our own social and political experiences have shaped our views and use of power. The framework facilitates more reflexive thinking which England (1994, p. 244) describes as 'self-critical sympathetic introspection and the self-conscious analytical scrutiny of the self'.

Using the methodology of reflective conversations (Reason & Bradbury, 2001), the 3 Ps framework has been used as a teaching method in lectures and training sessions. Creating a space and offering navigation point (Jensen, 2018) to guide the discussions around an individual's understanding of power. Again, reflecting the key point within social pedagogy and HLS that relational leadership and practice operate within complexity and therefore a manualized (Harbo & Kemp, 2020) and instrumental approach limits the ability to radically change practice, systems and organizational culture. The 3 Ps is a contextualized framework that is not based on normative or prescriptive decision-making, but rather hermeneutic understanding (Keane & Lawn, 2015). The discussions and reflective conversations have helped students and participants to think about their understanding of power but also how they are going to adapt their practice to address power imbalances and work in more equitable ways within their relational leadership and practice.

DISCUSSION

The 3 Ps Framework in Practice

Reitz and Higgins (2020, p. 271) state: 'To be interested in others is more than a technical skill, it involves a specific life philosophy – a fundamental curiosity and humility. A commitment to "power with or for" rather than "power over".

Utilizing Gadamer's hermeneutics theory (Keane & Lawn, 2015) supports the curiosity and understanding that Reitz and Higgins (2020) state is important to move beyond the technical. We have kept the three headings of *professional, personal and private* as these are an important part of exploring our understanding of power through a relational lens. We often have power and authority within our *professional* roles which at times is certainly linked to our position within an organization. We have authority to enact and enforce laws and policies, to assess people and their situations, to command actions and determine outcomes. Within the *personal* aspect of the 3 Ps, we also have our own views on the role and remit of the job we do and the way that we apply the power and authority we have to certain situations. I would argue that the *private* domain is the most important when it comes to relational leadership and practice. As human beings, our first reaction to a situation often stems from the *private* feelings we have, and they will cloud or direct the *professional* response we give. It is this domain along with the *personal* that helps us to develop the conscious application of relational leadership and the positive direct use of power that we have (Zhao et al., 2016).

Let's now look in more detail at each of the sections outlined in the Table 1 (translated by Harbo, 2010, adapted and expanded from Jappe, 2010 and cited in Charfe & Eichsteller, 2024) below:

Approach to Public Service Work

In the top row is the title approach. Here, practitioners are asked to reflect on their attitude and beliefs in the purpose of their *professional* role and the work they do. What do they think are the important aspects of their job? Why do they come to work? This critical self-reflection assists us to understand how our beliefs shape the manner in which we approach our work. If you believe your *professional* purpose is to support human flourishing, to help people live a good life then that will influence the view of the work you do and how you interpret and

Table 1. The 3 Ps (Professional, Personal and Private) of Self.

	Professional Self	Personal Self	Private Self
Approach (To public service work)	Rights based Human rights Multi-disciplinary Relational	Eagerness to collaborate and work in partnership with. Understanding the need to walk alongside somebody.	Pursuing our own agenda. Thinking that we know best due to our professional position.
Needs	Others	Others/Own	Own
Power	Formal authority. Critical self-reflection and awareness of power dynamics and structures. Empowerment, co-production, and advocacy as professional methods.	Informal authority and self-awareness/role modelling. Ability to connect equality as human-to human. Humility, owning human flaws.	Unconscious and uncritical uses of power and privilege. Advantage blindness (Fuchs et al., 2019) Wanting to rescue people – drama triangle. Incongruence

understand your remit and role. A positive example of this can be seen in the work of Changing Futures Northumbria and the liberated method they use (see Example of Practice, HLS, 2024). Their two Rules and five Principles (Smith et al., 2025) sets out the very clear purpose of the work they do, which has been translated into direct relational leadership within all aspects of the team and their direct practice. There is a commitment to relational practice, and as an organization, they provide all staff with support to meaningfully embed this *professional* approach into their direct practice, moving from the transactional and bureaucratic, to a relational way of working. With regards to staff recruitment, they focus on the knowledge and skills a person has and not on how well a person may fill the caseworker role (Example of Practice, HLS, 2024). This links clearly to the *personal* element of the 3 Ps; a willingness and ability to genuinely work collaboratively and alongside the individual, which is key to a building, maintaining and sustaining trusting relationships. We need to reflect on our ability to work in partnership and check out our understanding of this and how that might change depending on circumstances and with different relationship we have. With regards to relational leadership, as Reitz and Higgins (2020) highlight that this also requires an awareness of how others interpret our role and the expectations they might have of us. How these expectations might affect openness to collaboration and work in partnership with others who might see leadership in hierarchical terms. The *private* domain prompts us to reflect and check that we are not pushing forward our own ideas or agenda or believing that we know what best to do in answer to the situation and needs of the person we are supporting (Charfe & Eichsteller, 2024). This is key in being open to work in truly relational ways and can be challenging for relational leaders who may have outcomes and deadlines to meet as well as organizational and external pressures.

Needs

The second row emphasizes the necessity to reflect on *needs*, requiring practitioners and relational leaders to ask *whose needs are being met?* Within the *professional* element, the purpose of public services is to be public servants and meet the needs of the people we support. In a very honest account, Mike Crowther the CEO of Empowerment (an advocacy project based in Blackpool) highlights the negative impact of not reflecting on this question with regards to the *professional* aspect of the work (Crowther, 2021). He emphasizes the limited impact and lack of positive change made to the lives of the people he and his organization were supporting, as well as the unhappiness of working in ways that were incongruent to what the perceived approach and focus of the work was. As Laloux (2016) highlights in his research around self-managed teams and TEAL organizations, the focus of command and control in NPM does not lend itself to towards helping the staff to flourish, knowing that they are not meeting the moral purpose of their work.

This links to relational leaders and practitioners being able to reflect and have an awareness of their own needs in relation to their work which is focused on in the *personal* domain of the framework. There will be legal and organizational expectations and requirements placed on them depending on which area of the public service they work within. This will include things such as assessment and legal timescales, organizational aims and remits. Being open and transparent about these is important. But there will also be much more personal needs that a relational leader will have, such as being in a position to find solutions and answers to problems, being on time for meetings, etc. This section asks questions such as how do they manage their needs with a relational way of working while also meeting the needs they have in adhering to the statutory and organizational requirements that are placed on them? This requires a high level of openness and transparency and the skills to build a supportive relationship with clear boundaries where each person is aware of their role and position within the relationship, and there is an equitable balance of each other's needs (Charfe & Eichsteller, 2024). Using the *private* domain of the framework will assist practitioners to make sure that they are not pursuing their own needs. This is not always done in a malicious or controlling way but out of a desire to help or assist people.

Power

The final row of the framework has a specific focus on power. Within this section, relational leaders and practitioners are prompted to consider the formal power dynamics that are present in their *professional* role. What is their own understanding of these, and how does it influence their practice? This column asks that they consider the power contained within the formal authority they have such as enacting and enforcing laws and policies, assessing people (including staff) and their situations, to command actions and determine outcomes (Charfe & Eichsteller, 2024). Being able to have high levels of legal and ethical literacy that then inform their understanding of the power and authority they have linked to a leadership position and role is vital. Relational leaders and practitioners need to be able to use legal powers to build equitable relationships and promote positive life changes and increase well-being for the person/people being supported, as well as their own staff team. Relational leaders and practitioners can be incredibly powerful and have high levels of formal authority and power. It is therefore apposite that they critically reflect and 'examine how they conduct themselves when they hold greater power and how they can exercise their power without making the other person feel humiliated or at their mercy' (Charfe & Eichsteller, 2024, p. 137).

It is also important to acknowledge within this domain, the powerlessness public sector workers and leaders can feel, and the narrow perspective often attributed to power; seeing it 'as a zero-sum game, in which one party only has power when the other party doesn't' and that 'gaining power requires taking someone else's power, and the only way to share power is by giving it up' (Charfe & Eichsteller, 2024, p. 137). The impact of this way of thinking can be that an individual practitioner may try and hold on to the limited power they feel they have, thus negatively impacting further on their ability to build an equitable relationship. Having a more in depth understanding of the ways in which power operates can shape power 'as a generative force that can spread in the same way that a candle's flame can light another candle without getting extinguished' (Charfe & Eichsteller, 2024, p. 137). An excellent example of how this can become a reality can be seen in the Brent Care Journeys Example of Practice (HLS, 2024). This was a 'pioneering strategic alliance between Barnardo's and the local authority of Brent (London)' aimed to develop a systemic change within the children looked after and leaving care system (Brent Care Journeys, HLS, 2024). The power structures alive within the care system in England is complex and multi-dimensional; from the tension between statutory services within local authorities and the third sector; commissioning of services to multi-agency working. Finally, and most importantly, the disempowerment of children and young people within the looked after system (Wood & Selwyn, 2017). To challenge these inherent power differences, Brent Care Journeys first recognized that systemic change only happens when people with lived experience have more power and agency. They created situations and environments where there were flatter power structures to help share power and authority and did this by using the focus of 'learning' and the conscious use of empowering language. All expertise and knowledge were seen as equal when developing systemic change. There was also total transparency about who was/is powerful, and they were brave enough to 'disrupt and redress this' (Brent Care Journeys, HLS, 2024). They did this by making conscious efforts to place lived experience at the core of their team, so they could shape the direction of the work.

Moving on to the *personal* domain, relational leaders and practitioners need to be critically aware of the informal power they may bring and how they use these to develop positive relational practice based on anti-oppressive and human rights (Charfe & Eichsteller, 2024). Critical self-reflection is required here as well as being able to work alongside (Petrie, 2020) and in partnership while also being open to showing our flaws and limits to our knowledge and abilities (Charfe & Eichsteller, 2024). We need to be able to sit comfortably with the fact that as public sector workers, we do not need or have the solutions or answers to every problem. Sometimes, the most important thing a practitioner can do is be present, listen and offer recognition to the person they are working alongside. Again, referring back to Brent Care Journeys (HLS, 2024), we can see this action and the positive systemic changes that happened as a result. A relational approach to address issues of relational power that helped them redefined boundaries as 'care' that meant the project team used their personal skills to develop clear, fair, safe, warm, trustworthy and accountable relationships. But the most important part was the *personal* ability and awareness of each team member to 'place themselves in situations that are uncertain' and be able to 'own this characteristic' (Brent Care Journeys, HLS, 2024). This requires individuals to understand and return to the shared purpose of the work focusing on their understanding of the 'why' (Sinek, 2019) they are doing what they are doing while avoiding reverting to hierarchical positions and using their power to make decisions when situations become difficult. Also paying attention to unity and well-being was important and being able to acknowledge this on a personal level, which then was supported by the relational leaders and relational activism (Brent Care Journeys, HLS, 2024). As previously mentioned with regards to the *private* domain of the 3 Ps, this often shapes the instant reactions or thoughts we have to a situation or person. Constant self-refection on the feelings we have with regards to power and our responses to it is important in relational leadership. This aspect of the 3 Ps supports us to become more aware of any previous unconscious or uncritical use of power and privilege. Being aware and understanding the biases that we hold, but also the advantages and privileges that have assisted us in getting to the professional positions we hold, is key. As with *Needs*, this lack of awareness or acceptance does not always come from a desire to misuse the power advantage gives us. However, we do need to be much more aware of these privileges and make sure that we do not continue to allow entrenched power dynamics to carry on existing.

RECOMMENDATIONS FOR POLICY AND PRACTICE

To move from the transactional approach in public services to a relational one that supports not only the people who receive services, but also the staff that work within these, is complex, uncertain but also exciting. And, I would argue, morally justified. As I've discussed in this chapter, power dynamics within relational leadership and practice must be surfaced and addressed if there is to be lasting positive change within the public sector. Where do we start and what have we learnt from organizations and relational leaders so far? What do relational leaders need to do to address power? It's challenging and complex, but here are what I believe are the two most important starting points.

First is the importance of mindset and an awareness of the values that support the moral purpose of public services. As discussed in the *professional* domain of the 3 Ps, we have to be able to reflect and be transparent and open about what we understand the moral purpose of our work to be, or, as Sinek (2019) states, 'the why'. There must be a wiliness to keep returning to this as our navigation point, the stake in the ground that tethers us to our moral purpose. There should be an understanding of and a commitment to the need for transparency and openness about the power and authority we have. This understanding should be used when trying to shape positive systemic change and create real meaningful opportunities for collaboration with people who have lived expertise of public services. Therefore, from a *personal* perspective, our own mindset matters, and how we understand what is meant by relational leadership, relationship-based practice, collaboration and power will all shape how we enact these in our practice.

One of the risks and dangers is that relational leadership becomes the newest fad and trend and a phrase that is used without real relational action. The incongruence between positive mission statements and aims with the reality of what is experienced by somebody using a public service is a well-known frustration. Therefore, the moral purpose and ethics of relational practice have to be felt and experienced in the way relational leaders support their staff to embed this into their everyday direct work and organizational structures. Having an open mindset and a belief in being able to work in collaboration with people, sharing power and using power for positive means, is a fundamental starting point. The ethics and values of relational practice have to be felt in the direct work at every level. Therefore, the recruitment of people who not only have this value base and mindset but also are able to embed this into their work is essential. The 3 Ps framework has been designed to assist reflective conversations to begin this process.

The second and final recommendation recognizes the different and complex nature of public services and that, because the *context* of the work matters, it is difficult to highlight certain infrastructures, resources and approaches without it becoming yet another tool kit or manual. Therefore, what needs to happen is much more reflexive thought and actions, relational leaders need to pay attention to the relational and power dynamics (good and bad) throughout every aspect of an organization and system. Focusing on relational spaces where the use of relational practice can be supported and nurtured while addressing issues of power and authority. Relational leaders need to be aware of the everyday examples of power that are inherent within organizations, examples such as seating, the language used and where the work takes place (in communities), and how to flatten these power structures.

CONCLUSION

As this chapter argues the key to change is making sure that any organizational system, policy and procedure is viewed through a relational lens asking the following questions:

- How does this support and nurture relational practice and who's needs are being met?
- Who is missing from the conversation and being part of the organizational changes and how do we make sure they are genuinely included?

Finally, an important aspect of this that has been highlighted by some of the HLS Examples of Practice is the importance of coaching and/or supervision at all levels to protect and foster relational practice. Having spaces where open dialogue and learning can happen that then shapes the direct practice and system changes is key and this needs to happen at all levels of an organization. To support both of these key recommendations, this chapter has expanded and developed Jappe's (2010) 3 Ps model to help people not only begin discussions but also address the importance of power in shaping their own relational leadership and practice. Because as we know, with power comes great responsibility.

REFERENCES

Charfe, L., & Eichsteller, G. (2021). Human learning systems meets social pedagogy: How a social pedagogical perspective can bring HLS to life. In A. Brogan, G. Eichsteller, M. Hawkins, H. Hesselgreaves, B. N. Jennions, T. Lowe, D. Plimmer, V. Terry, & G. Williams (Eds.), *Human learning systems: Public service for the real world*. ThemPra Social Pedagogy.

Charfe, L., & Eichsteller, G. (2024). Making sense of power and politics in everyday practice through the 3 Ps. In J. Przeperski, M. Rezaul Islam, R. Baikady, & S. M. Sajid (Eds.), *The Oxford handbook of power, politics and social work*. Oxford University Press.

Charfe, L., & Gardner, A. (2019). *Social pedagogy and social work.* SAGE.

Charfe, L., & Gardner, A. (2020). 'Does my Haltung look big in this?': The use of social pedagogical theory for the development of ethical and value-led practice. *IJSP, 9*(1). https://doi.org/10.14324/111.444.ijsp.2020.v9.x.011

Cottam, H. (2021). The radical way: Shifting the social paradigm. https://www.hilarycottam.com/the-radical-way_shifting-the-social-paradigm/. Accessed on September 7, 2023.

Crowther, M. (2021). Empowerment case study, human learning systems. https://www.humanlearning.systems/case-studies/. Accessed on October 20, 2024.

Diener, E., & Biswas-Diener, R. (2019). Well-being interventions to improve societies. In *The 2019 global happiness and wellbeing policy report 2019*. Sustainable Development Solutions Network. Global Council for Happiness and Well-being.

Eichsteller, G., & Holthoff, S. (2011). Conceptual foundations of social pedagogy: A transnational perspective from Germany. In C. Cameron & P. Moss (Eds.), *Social pedagogy and working with children and young people*. Jessica Kingsley Publication.

England, K. (1994). Getting personal: Reflexivity, positionality, and feminist research. *The Professional Geographer, 46*(1), 80–89.

Evans, K. (2016). Public service markets aren't working for the public good … or as markets. In C. Pell, R. Wilson, & T. Lowe (Eds.), *Kittens are evil: Little heresies in public policy*. Triarchy Press.

Foucault, M. (1982). The subject and power. *Critical Inquiry, 8*(4), 777–795. https://doi.org/10.1086/448181

Foucault, M. (2002). *Power: Essential works of Foucault 1954-1984*. Penguin.

Freire, P. (1970). *Pedagogy of the oppressed.* Penguin Books.

French, J., & Raven, B. (1959). The bases of social power. In D. Cartwright (Ed.), *Studies in social power* (pp. 150–167). Institute for Social Research.

Fuchs, B., Reitz, M., & Higgins, J. (2019). Do you have advantage blindness? *Harvard Business Review*. https://hbr.org/2018/04/do-you-haveadvantage-blindness

Gilbert, T., & Powell, J. L. (2010). Power and social work in the United Kingdom: A Foucauldian excursion. *Journal of Social Work, 10*(1), 3–22. https://doi.org/10.1177/1468017309347237

Glover, B. (2023). Recovery through reform: Launch paper of the future public services taskforce. *Demos*. https://demos.co.uk/research/recoverythrough-reform-launch-paper-of-the-future-public-services-taskforce/

Hall, J. N. (2020). The other side of inequality: Using standpoint theories to examine the privilege of the evaluation profession and individual evaluators. *American Journal of Evaluation, 41*(1), 20–33. https://doi.org/10.1177/1098214019828485

Hämäläinen, J. (1989). Social pedagogy as a meta-theory of social work education. *International Journal of Social Work, 32*(2), 117–128.

Harbo, L. J. (2010). *The 3 Ps in Danish social pedagogy*. Personal communication.

Harbo, L. J., & Kemp, R. (2020). Social pedagogical perspectives on fidelity to a manual: Professional principles and dilemmas in everyday expertise. *International Journal of Social Pedagogy, 9*(1), 12. https://doi.org/10.14324/111.444.ijsp.2020.v9.x.012

Human Learning System (HLS). (2024). *Human Learning System: Insights 2024, HLS insights – Findings from our 2024 action research*. Human Learning Systems. https://www.humanlearning.systems/hls-insights-findings-from-our-research-2024/. Accessed on April 24, 2025.

Jacobson, D., & Mustafa, N. (2019). Social identity map: A reflexivity tool for practicing explicit positionality in critical qualitative research. *International Journal of Qualitative Methods, 18*. https://doi.org/10.1177/1609406919870075

Jappe, E. (2010). *Håndbog for pædagogstuderende*. Frydenlund.

Jensen, M. (2018). Fellowship as social-pedagogical treatment. *Scottish Journal of Residential Child Care, 17*(3), 1–21.

Karim, S. (2023). Power-informed practice in social work. *Journal of Social Work, 23*(6), 1062–1079.

Keane, N., & Lawn, C. (2015). *Hans-Georg Gadamer, the blackwell companion to hermeneutics*. Wiley Blackwell. https://doi.org/10.1002/9781118529812

Laloux, F. (2016). *Reinventing organisations: An illustrated invitation to join the conversation on next-stage organisations*. Nelson Parker.

Leadbeater, C. (2020). *Love meets power*. The Australian Centre for Social Innovation.

Lent, A., & Studdert, J. (2021). The community paradigm: Why public services need radical change and how it can be achieved. *New Local*. https://www.newlocal.org.uk/publications/the-communityparadigm/

Lowe, T., Brogan, A., Eichsteller, G., Hawkins, M., Hesselgreaves, H., Plimmer, D., Terry, V., Sharfe, L., Cox, J., French, M., Hill, B., Masters, J., Norman, R., Sanderson, H., Smith, M., & Wilson, R. (2021). *Human learning systems: Public service for the real world*. ThemPra Social Pedagogy. https://realworld.report/

Lowe, T., & Eichsteller, G. (2021). Being Human: Public services for real life. In A. Brogan, G. Eichsteller, M. Hawkins, H. Hesselgreaves, B. N. Jennions, T. Lowe, D. Plimmer, V. Terry, & G. Williams (Eds.), *Public services for the real world*. ThemPra Social Pedagogy.

Lowe, T., & McIntosh, R. (2023). *What on earth is a paradigm anyway?* Centre For Public Impact (CPI). https://www.centreforpublicimpact.org/insights/what-on-earth-is-a-paradigm-anyway. Accessed on October 19, 2024.

Lowe, T., & Plimmer, D. (2019). *Exploring the new world: Practical insights for funding, commissioning and managing in complexity*. Collaborate CIC; Northumbria University; Community Fund; The Tudor Trust.

Lukes, S. (2005). *Power: A radical view* (2nd ed.). Palgrave.

New Public Alliance. (2020). Wisdom-from-the-System.pdf. https://newsystemalliance.org/wp-content/uploads/2020/12/Wisdom-from-the-System.pdf

Petrie, P. (2020). Taking social pedagogy forward: Its fit with official UK statements on promoting wellbeing. *IJSP*, *9*(1). https://doi.org/10.14324/111.444.ijsp.2020.v9.x.017

Raven, B. (2008). The bases of power and the power/interaction model of interpersonal influence. *Analyses of Social Issues and Public Policy*, *8*(1), 1–22.

Reason, P., & Bradbury, H. (2001). *The SAGE handbook of action research: Participative inquiry and practice*. SAGE.

Reitz, M., & Higgins, J. (2017). *Being silenced and silencing others: Developing the capacity to speak truth to power*. Hult Research. https://www.meganreitz.com/s/Being-silenced-and-silencing-others-Developing-the-capacity-to-speak-truth-to-power-report_Final_low-3frr.pdf

Reitz, M., & Higgins, J. (2019). Managers, you're more intimidating than you think. *Harvard Business Review*. https://hbr.org/2019/07/managers-youre-more-intimidating-than-you-think

Reitz, M., & Higgins, J. (2020). *Speaking truth to power*: Why leaders cannot hear what they need to hear. *British Medical Journal*, *5*, 270–273.

Sinek, S. (2019). *Start with why : How great leaders inspire everyone to take action*. Penguin Business.

Smith, M., Hesselgreaves, H., Charlton, R., & Wilson, R. (2025). The 'liberated method'—A transcendent public service innovation in polycrisis. *Public Money and Management*. https://doi.org/10.1080/09540962.2025.2456120

Stephens, P. (2013). Social pedagogy: Heart and head. In P. Hermann (Ed.), *Studies in comparative social pedagogies and international social work* (Vol. XXIV). EVH Publishing.

Taylor, D. (2014). *Michel Foucault: Key concepts*. Taylor & Francis Group.

Tedam, P. (2021). *Anti-oppressive social work practice*. Learning Matters.

Tew, J. (2006). Understanding power and powerlessness: Towards a framework for emancipatory practice in social work. *Journal of Social Work*, *6*(1), 33–51. https://doi.org/10.1177/1468017306062222

Thompson, N. (2006). *Anti-discriminatory practice*. Palgrave McMillian.

Wilson, R., French, M., Hesselgreaves, H., Lowe, T., & Smith, M. (2024). New development: Relational public services—reform and research agenda. *Public Money & Management*, 1–6. https://doi.org/10.1080/09540962.2024.2344902

Wood, M., & Selwyn, J. (2017). Looked after children and young people's views on what matters to their subjective well-being. *Adoption & Fostering*, *41*(1), 20–34. https://doi.org/10.1177/0308575916686034

Worsley, A., & Wylie, R. (2020). Public value management and social justice. In R. Wylie (Ed.), *Public value management: Institutional design and decision for the common good*. Rowman and Littlefield.

Zhao, X., Shang, Y., Lin, J., Tan, J., Li, H., & Lui, T. (2016). Leader's relational power: Concept, measurement and validation. *European Management Journal*, *34*(5), 517–529.

HOW CAN ECOSYSTEMS HELP US TO MAKE SENSE OF COMPLEXITY IN SOCIAL CARE?

Emily Burn and Catherine Needham

University of Birmingham, UK

ABSTRACT

The social care sector is facing a wide range of challenges after years of underfunding and growing demand. Attempts to reform social care have had limited success. Multiple actors are involved in the commissioning and delivery of social care. However, it can be difficult to characterize this complexity in an accessible way that encourages a focus on improved outcomes for people accessing care and support.

The ecosystem concept offers a route for policymakers and practitioners to engage with complexity. An ecosystem is framed as an ecological metaphor where the well-being of the whole depends on how well the constituent parts of the ecosystem interact with one another. The ecosystem encompasses multiple groups of intersecting actors which directs us to think about the associations and relationships in the ecosystem and to appreciate the importance of relational approaches that span institutional boundaries.

Applying the metaphor to the social care system draws out discussions on emergence and the role of ecosystem architects whose relational approaches can influence how the ecosystem functions. We discuss how policymakers and practitioners can apply the ecosystem concept and establish that this frame can promote whole system thinking. The metaphor emphasizes the connections between actors and organizations without leading to a sense of overwhelm and fatalism.

Keywords: Ecosystem; social care; unpaid care; public services; complexity; commissioning; outcomes

Futures in Public Management
Critical Perspectives on International Public Sector Management, Volume 8, 197–209

ISSN: 2045-7944/doi:10.1108/S2045-794420250000008013

INTRODUCTION

Public services operate in a complex landscape. In an increasingly connected world, outcomes are dependent on other actors' behaviour. Policy initiatives developed over many months of consultation and engagement can still miss the mark and not achieve their intended aims. Implementation challenges likely tell only part of the story of intervention failure, and it is difficult to predict with precision the results of public service reform. Policymakers and practitioners are enmeshed in complexity and need to steer services towards improvement and better outcomes.

We propose that the metaphor, or heuristic, of an ecosystem can assist policymakers and practitioners in making sense of the complexity of public service delivery. Over the past two decades, it is increasingly common for groups of social organizations to be described as an ecosystem (Adner, 2017). Central to the concept of an ecosystem are the interactions between actors, organizations and resources. Ecosystems are 'networked social structures in which units are linked by loose or tight ties that enable or enhance the interactions and exchanges among diverse organizations and actors' (Mars & Bronstein, 2018, p. 382). Sometimes, the language of ecosystem is deployed in ways which recognize its complex adaptive implications although the term is sometimes also used to describe the range of actors and organizations without reference to their complex interplay.

In this chapter, we draw out the features of an ecosystem that can help us to respond to complexity and develop relational public services. The ecosystem metaphor directs us to think about the adaptive connections between actors alongside their capacities and assets. First, we provide a brief introduction of the social care system and apply French et al.'s (2023) four types of complexity to draw out the difficulties the system faces. Following this, we outline the key attributes of an ecosystem and establish how this metaphor helps us to think relationally. Finally, we apply the ecosystem metaphor to social care and explore how the heuristic can be used by practitioners and policymakers. We close the chapter by making a series of recommendations about how ecosystem thinking can be embedded to progress relational public services.

LITERATURE REVIEW: COMPLEXITY IN THE SOCIAL CARE SYSTEM

The social care system provides support to older and disabled people, people with a long-term mental health condition and unpaid carers. In many countries, these services are labelled long-term care although in England (our empirical focus here) the language of social care is used (Needham et al., 2024). The design of social care policy is shared between central government and 153 local authorities (Needham & Hall, 2023). At a local level, the planning and delivery of social care involves a range of organizations and resourcing arrangements. People may contribute in part or in full to the costs of their care and local authorities may not have direct commissioning relationships with providers who work with self-funders. Local authorities are expected to work with the community to understand local needs to ensure these are met by the mix of services. The formal social care system could not function without the contribution of unpaid carers – family, friends and neighbours – who provide a huge amount of support, alongside the broader community (Petrillo & Bennett, 2023). There have been efforts to move social care away from a focus on tasks towards a focus on outcomes, well-being and quality of life (GOV.UK, 2022). Despite these intentions, concerns remain about the quality and sustainability of care services and the strains facing those providing and receiving care (House of Lords Adult Social Care Committee, 2022).

A number of challenges have affected the functioning of the social care system, making it difficult to secure high quality support that enhances well-being. Demographic changes mean that demand for services is growing (Bottery & Mallorie, 2024) while local authority funding is constrained (Foster, 2024). The recruitment and retention of the care workforce continues to be difficult in many areas and threatens the sustainability of the social care system (Foster, 2023). In England, the Care Act 2014 placed a duty on local authorities to ensure a wide variety of good quality social care services were available. Additional duties included investing in prevention to support the well-being of the local population, providing support to unpaid carers and supporting the uptake of personal budgets. However, the objectives of this legislation remain largely unmet (Burn et al., 2024). Furthermore, plans to reshape social care funding have stalled after decades of discussion and delay (Foster, 2022). There is wide agreement that the social care system is in need of reform; however, there is no coherent long-term plan for how the Government will achieve its vision for social care (House of Commons Committee of Public Accounts, 2024; National Audit Office, 2023).

Two dynamics have added to the difficulties of effective reform in social care. The first is that care is inherently relational. While contracting has attempted to reduce care to a set of standardized tasks, effective social care relies on interpersonal relationships. These relationships enable the care that an older or disabled person receives from paid or unpaid carers although it is important to note that care relationships are often reciprocal: 'the world is not divided into carers and cared-for as if they are separate and permanent classes' (Noddings, 2013, p. xxi). Relationality may also be about the ways that commissioners, providers and families engage with one another outside of formal contractual terms. There is increased awareness that all public services, including social care, are based on effective relational working – between public servants and with the public. Increased awareness of this is part of what Bartels and Turnbull (2019) characterize as a 'relational turn' within public administration (see also Wilson et al., 2024).

The second dynamic is that social care is a complex system. Like other public services, it is an open system, intersecting in nonlinear ways with other services: housing, education, employment and immigration. The interplay of public, for profit and not for profit providers, the overlapping jurisdictions of national and local government, and the strong presence of the family as a supplier of care alongside state and market make it a particularly complex system. This has implications for how it can be described and studied. Munro and Hubbard (2011), writing in the context of children's social care, note that we need a 'wide-angled lens' to capture the interplay of system features. We need ways to help practitioners understand how to work within complexity (Hood, 2014).

There are two ways to make complexity more manageable, both for scholars and for practitioners. The first is to recognize that there are different types of complexity, and these can be separated out as conceptually distinct. French et al.'s (2023) four types of complexity are useful here, and we discuss these in detail. The second is to develop a more intuitive and integrative model – this is what we do in the next section when we look at social care as an ecosystem.

Looking first at the four types of complexity in public services, French et al. (2023) separate out compositional complexity, experiential complexity, dynamic complexity and governance complexity. The first form, *compositional complexity*, captures the interdependencies between and within public services that influence the outcomes people achieve. This moves us away from thinking about public services as discreet units of action towards recognizing the wider connections affecting how services function. The design and delivery of social care services depends on a range of organizations working together. The commissioning relationship between local authorities and providers is just one example of these connections. People's experience of services is dependent on wider processes affecting referrals, eligibility criteria and assessment. There are strong connections between the social care system and other public services, such as the housing system, healthcare, the local labour market and the benefits system. Decisions in these areas will have intended and unintended effects on the social care system. Furthermore, the availability of social care services relies on the interdependencies between local authorities and providers. However, local authorities do not have oversight of all service provision in an area. While local authorities hold responsibility for social care provision, they have limited control over the factors that influence the functioning of the system.

Central to positive public service outcomes is the quality of interactions between individuals and services. The second form, *experiential complexity* (French et al., 2023), acknowledges that people may have different ideas about what makes a good service for them. People do not arrive at services as a blank slate but bring with them their own life histories and wider social connections across time and geography. These individualized factors will influence people's perceptions and interactions with services. Social care is no different. Local authorities are dependent on the strength of their relationships with local communities to design appropriate services. Co-production is promoted through the Care Act 2014 statutory guidance (GOV.UK, 2023). Co-productive processes recognize experiential complexity and the knowledge and expertise that people who draw on care and support hold (Social Care Institute for Excellence, 2022). Quality services can only be delivered when providers understand the people they work with as individuals who bring with them their own experiences and strengths. Appropriate support that meets people's needs is dependent on the relationship forged between the social care workforce and people drawing on care and support. Experiential complexity cautions us away from thinking that everybody's encounters with social care services will be the same. What works for some will not work for others and the individual needs to be placed at the centre of care planning.

The third type, *dynamic complexity*, highlights the fluidity of the wider factors that influence public services. The interactions that affect outcomes cannot be assumed and are subject to change. A wide range of policies and conditions affect the social care system. Delivering social care services depends on wider conditions such as the local labour market, migration policies, inflation and wage rates to name a few. Unforeseen disrupters, such as the COVID-19 pandemic, technological developments (such as tracker and sensor devices to monitor activity) and economic shocks (for example the cost of living crisis), have reshaped relationships between organizations in the social care system. Organizations involved in the design and delivery of social care have had to adapt to these changing conditions. Although providers are encouraged to be outcomes-focused – and indeed may be financially incentivized to be so – these outcomes are contingent and uncertain.

French et al. (2023, p. 31) position the final form, *governance complexity*, as arising from 'the task of mobilising and coordinating' the relationships and flows of resources that make up public services. Past behaviours and decisions affect how public services operate, and this path dependency can mean that it is difficult to bring about change in a predictable way. Governance structures formalize the relationships between public service organizations and may facilitate or inhibit actions. In social care, governance complexity can arise through internal local authority policies relating to eligibility, care and support assessments, contract monitoring and the assessment and measurement of service quality. The integration of social care with the National Health Service (NHS) and related governance structures, such as integrated care systems (ICS) and boards (ICBs), represent another form of governance complexity, built on the legacy of previous attempts to bring services together. Governance structures may establish the criteria of 'acceptable' service provision and outcomes which practitioners need to navigate. This form of complexity is about knowing how to get things done in a public service system and managing the constraints or the facilitators in the system.

Separating out these four types is a helpful way to make complexity manageable and to understand the different conceptual strands within it. However for practitioners seeking to work within complexity, there may be a need to find more intuitive ways to talk about complex systems. We propose that the ecosystem metaphor encourages a whole-system approach without leading to defeatism and overload and we discuss this in the next section.

Describing Relational Public Services as an Ecosystem

The idea of ecosystems was popularized by Tansley (1935) and has subsequently been used in various ways to describe interactions in the natural world using models and as a metaphor (Pickett & Cadenasso, 2002). The ecological metaphor has been used in the management and organizational development fields and has been applied to the study of public services (Osborne, 2021). Ecosystems are made up of groups of interacting organizations arranged on multiple levels (Mars & Bronstein, 2018). These nested levels can be thought of as being at the macro- (national agencies), meso- (regional or local agencies) and micro-levels (provider and user interactions) (Chandler & Vargo, 2011). Howard and Hyland-Wood (2024, p. 111) position ecosystem approaches as 'opening policy processes to new actors and practices, leading to a radically "decentred" policymaking'. They identify two key features at the foundation of ecosystem functioning. The first is that ecosystems are emergent, and there is 'mutual adjustment' (p. 112) and adaption without requiring overt control and direction from a central actor. Information and resources continually flow within an ecosystem and actors will have only imperfect knowledge of how the different parts of the ecosystem relate to each other (Levin, 1998). It is difficult to accurately predict change and actors' navigation of the ecosystem is assisted by positive and negative feedback loops (Lips & Eppel, 2022). Ecosystems tend towards equilibrium, or balance, but ecosystems may resist attempts to create change (Mars et al., 2012). They may be vulnerable to external shocks and disruption which can lead to the reorganization of actors and flows of resources. Ecosystems' emergent properties reflect dynamic and experiential complexity and the uncertainty of public service outcomes.

The second cornerstone of an ecosystem is the 'heightened or *radical interdependencies* between their components' (Howard & Hyland-Wood, 2024, p. 113) and reflects the compositional and governance forms of complexity. The decisions and behaviour of each actor influences all others in the ecosystem whether intended or not. This wider influence means that some actors' entry or exit into the ecosystem can lead to the breakdown or foundational change of the ecosystem (Howard & Hyland-Wood, 2024). Actors with this level of influence are referred to as 'keystone actors' (Mars et al., 2012), denoting their importance to the ecosystem as a whole. Interdependencies and processes of emergence mean that keystone actors do not have direct control and can only hope to influence the functioning of the ecosystem. The decentred leadership of an ecosystem discourages viewing policy and service interventions as a simple relationship between inputs and outputs.

Keystone actors have a mobilizing role, described as 'seeding and feeding' the ecosystem (Howard & Hyland-Wood, 2024). Seeding refers to actions 'providing fertile material to start the organic growth process, upon which an ecosystem grows and adapts' (p. 113). Feeding the ecosystem encompasses actions to maintain the quality of relationships between actors. The flow of resources throughout the ecosystem is key to initiating and maintaining connections between actors. Actors who have this mobilizing function have also been given the title of 'ecosystem architects' and work to influence interactions between the component parts (Snihur et al., 2018). Ecosystem architects may be proactive and steer the ecosystem towards internal aims or reactive and respond to external factors that may be experienced as shocks and disruption. Daymond et al. (2023) identify that ecosystems can emerge as new associations form or evolve as relationships between actors change, including their entry and exit from the ecosystem. In an emerging ecosystem, the architect works to create the conditions necessary to bring together new actors. The emphasis within an emerging

Table 1. Ecosystem Characteristics and Complexity in Social Care.

Type of Complexity (French et al., 2023)	Ecosystem Characteristics	Social Care Example
Compositional	The ecosystem has nested levels – macro, meso and micro.	The range of organizations involved in the design and delivery of social care, including care providers, people drawing on services and local authorities. Decisions in other areas of public services, such as health and housing, will influence the effectiveness of social care services.
Dynamic	Outcomes in an ecosystem are emergent and difficult to predict.	Organizations delivering social care have to adapt to changing conditions. Providers may be encouraged to be outcome-focused, but outcomes are never guaranteed. Technological developments and economic shocks can affect how care is delivered.
Experiential	Actors in an ecosystem are interdependent. Each actor will bring their own resources to an interaction.	People will experience social care services in different ways. A one-size-fits-all approach should be avoided and services should be focused on individuals' needs. Quality services depend on the relationships developed between the social care workforce and people drawing on care.
Governance	Keystone actors working to establish and maintain the relationships between actors within an ecosystem.	The rules and regulations that inform how resources flow through the social care system. This can include local authorities' policies on eligibility to access services, care and support assessments, direct payments and contract monitoring.

ecosystem is the coalescence of actors. In an evolving ecosystem, architects establish the conditions for co-operation, directing resources towards joint working. In Table 1, we link the four types of complexity to ecosystem characteristics and give an example of how they are present within social care.

DISCUSSION: MOVING TOWARDS A FLOURISHING SOCIAL CARE ECOSYSTEM

We need a way to make complexity manageable for those working in public services. One option is to disaggregate types of complexity as French et al. (2023)

have done, and we see this as having a value in separating out conceptually distinct elements of care. However, the other approach is to take a more holistic metaphor – that of an ecosystem – and work with people's intuitive understandings about the interrelated nature of ecosystems and the components of ecosystem well-being.

Thinking about the well-being of the care ecosystem and whether it is flourishing offers a way to work towards improving outcomes for people who draw on care and support. Ecosystem well-being depends on how well its component parts interact and whether institutional arrangements promote alignment between the different levels of an ecosystem (Frow et al., 2019, p. 2667). In a flourishing ecosystem, the component parts have aligned goals, and there is mutual support between organizations to achieve the aims and objectives of public services. A flourishing ecosystem adapts to crisis and strain (Brodie et al., 2021).

Using the ecosystem metaphor in the context of social care enables us to consider the elements of flourishing (Burn & Needham, 2023). An ecological ecosystem – a natural landscape – has above ground parts which are visible to the eye and those which are not (below ground). Similarly, we can think of the social care ecosystem as having both visible and invisible elements. The visible elements capture formal services such as residential care homes and domiciliary care, along with links to NHS services. The invisible parts include community activities and associations which are an important part of people's support network. These activities could include sports and hobby clubs, faith organizations and neighbourhood networks that can give life meaning, enhance emotional well-being and delay people's entry into formal services (see Needham (2023) for a visual representation of the care ecosystem).

The visible and invisible parts of the social care ecosystem are interdependent, and relationships are central to both. Quality of life depends on being able to participate and make the most of social connections. The outcomes derived from formal services will depend on the availability of opportunities in the local community. Similarly, appropriate and high-quality formal services can give people the daily support they need to engage and develop stronger associations in their local area. A flourishing social care ecosystem requires both the visible and the invisible parts to be functioning well. If either part breaks down then pressures can be transferred, either to formal services or the more informal community ties. Ecosystem degradation may result from this imbalance, leading to a long-term loss of the capacity to support people to achieve positive outcomes and have thriving relationships.

The ecosystem lens allows policymakers and practitioners to think and talk about the interconnectedness of different elements and to chart a course for intervention. They can zoom in and out to locate the most appropriate level to support relational working. By zooming into the micro-level, the focus is on the individual citizen and any support received through unpaid care or social care services. The emphasis is on relationships between the individual and service providers and how this interacts with relationships with family, friends and communities. At the meso-level, the local authority is the focus. This draws policymakers and practitioners to consider commissioning processes and local authorities' relationships with providers and understanding local needs. Care needs assessments and mechanisms to facilitate choice and control, such as direct payments are also embedded within this level. Zooming out to the macro-level reveals the wider associations with other systems that affect social care, for example the labour market and the implications of migration policies on the recruitment and retention of the care workforce. Although at this level there is a tendency to focus on structures rather than relationships, it is clear that structural interventions – e.g. closer working between health and social care – continue to rely on relationships brokered by 'boundary spanners' and 'brokers' (Neal et al., 2022).

POLICY AND PRACTICE RECOMMENDATIONS FOR RELATIONAL PUBLIC MANAGEMENT

The ecosystem metaphor shifts thinking from assumptions of a clear link between intervention and outcome towards appreciating emergence and uncertainty. Policymakers and practitioners may consider themselves to be ecosystem architects and are encouraged to be broader in their thinking, moving away from the idea of discrete interventions towards reflecting on the system holistically. Relationships are foregrounded at the micro-, meso- and macro-levels.

There are a number of recommendations of how the ecosystem metaphor can be introduced and used:

Understanding the Role of Ecosystem Architects

Working with the ecosystem metaphor requires practitioners to abandon the perception of linear relationships between interventions and outcomes. For many this involves shaking off the legacy of new public management with its emphasis on assessing performance via measuring outputs (Pollitt, 2016). Practitioners' reflections on their position within the ecosystem metaphor acknowledges compositional and governance complexity. Moves should be made towards embedding forms of leadership that emphasize leadership as socially situated rather than residing in one 'heroic' figure (e.g. the distributed leadership model (Spillane, 2005)). There may be multiple ecosystem architects and a key role for leaders is in understanding and sustaining the relationships between them. New approaches to accountability may also be required which may necessitate a rethink of how we use data and information to learn about the impact of services on people's lives. For example, the organization 'Matter of Focus' uses the concept of *contribution* rather than *attribution* when seeking to establish how a particular intervention has made a difference in a complex system (Morton & Cook, 2023).

Depicting a Flourishing Ecosystem

Mapping the connections between organizations can surface compositional and dynamic complexity within public services. However, system maps risk being overly complicated and overwhelming, plus they only present a snapshot at one time (French et al., 2023). Their utility can be lost without also developing the vision of how the system should function. An ecosystem metaphor derived from the natural world maintains a whole-system approach with a dual-focus of promoting understanding of the dynamics between actors and organizations and also emphasizing ecosystem well-being. It is easier to talk about and map what it might mean to move the ecosystem from a degraded system towards flourishing. Policymakers and practitioners, working with people who draw on services, can work together to develop a local vision of a flourishing ecosystem. Social care includes a diverse range of services and local authorities develop multiple strategies to inform the design and delivery of care. Mapping these strategies using the ecosystem concept surfaces interdependencies and may reveal how the choices and trade-offs made in one part of the system affect other areas.

Foreground Relationality in the Ecosystem

Flourishing public services are built on developing trusted connections. Across all levels of the ecosystem, actors should acknowledge mutual reliance and interdependencies and seek to strengthen relationships. Experiential complexity recognizes that people comprehend and interpret these interdependencies in different ways. People drawing on services may have different ideas about what makes a good service compared to practitioners. The barriers inhibiting an ecosystem from flourishing may include blockages in the flow of information and resources or actors' conflicting values or incentives, all of which limit dialogue and trust-building. Ecosystem architects will not have perfect knowledge, and moves towards a flourishing ecosystem should encompass incrementalism and experimentation (Lindblom, 1979), which requires trust between parties. There will always be trade-offs in any decision and thinking about whose well-being is being enhanced by the ecosystem can reveal tensions and compromises. In the same vein, recognizing areas of potential conflict can also lead to open discussions that have the potential to strengthen the ecosystem.

At the macro-level of the ecosystem, local authorities and other governance bodies need to be consulted early when developing new policy proposals. Constructing partnerships at the local level can work to address logjams that may arise. At the micro-level, strengths-based approaches to commissioning facilitates working in partnership with communities and individuals (Social Care Institute for Excellence, n.d.). Co-production has gained wide-spread support as a means to develop appropriate social care services. However, the Social Care Institute for Excellence (2023) found that co-production often occurred in small pockets of best practice, rather than being integrated throughout the whole system. System pressures, such as lack of resource and time, prevented true co-productive relationships being formed. These pressures have wider ramifications for service quality and the outcomes achieved by people who draw on care. The ecosystem metaphor guides us to think about the dynamics between the multiple levels in public service design and delivery, without losing sight of complexity and emergence.

CONCLUSION

The term ecosystem is often used to describe the range of actors and organizations involved in a sector or public services. This can be done in an overly simplistic or optimistic way that ignores the features of complex adaptive systems. Alternatively, it can be done in an overly complicated way, getting lost in efforts to produce definitive flow diagrams of the whole system. Finding a way to talk about the ecosystem drawing on metaphors from the natural world can offer a path between heroic assumptions of system control and paralyzing fears of fatalism. The design and delivery of social care encapsulates the four forms of complexity. The configuration and ramification of these forms of complexity will be experienced in different ways according to how stakeholders are positioned in the ecosystem.

Integral to the ecosystem metaphor is the quality of relationships and interdependencies on which public services are built. The emphasis on adaptation and emergence means that no single agent can control the ecosystem. A flourishing ecosystem is one in which incrementalism and experimentation is supported by rapid communication and high-trust relationships. This kind of flourishing calls for a leadership approach in which practitioners are empowered to forge connections across partners and develop strengths-based approaches to working with citizens. It requires an understanding that the well-being of an ecosystem depends on the balance between its component parts, some of which are not controlled by or even visible to the state. Through humility, trust and adaptivity, relational public managers can foster a context in which citizens can flourish.

ACKNOWLEDGEMENTS

This chapter draws on research funded as part of the Centre for Care. The Centre for Care is funded by the Economic and Social Research Council (ESRC, award ES/W002302/1), with contributions from the Department of Health and Social Care's National Institute for Health and Care Research (NIHR) and partner universities. The views expressed are those of the author(s) and are not necessarily those of the ESRC, UKRI, NHS or NIHR.

REFERENCES

Adner, R. (2017). Ecosystem as structure: An actionable construct for strategy. *Journal of Management*, *43*(1), 39–58. https//doi.org/10.1177/0149206316678451

Bartels, K., & Turnbull, N. (2019). Relational public administration: A synthesis and heuristic classification of relational approaches. *Public Management Review*, *22*(9), 1324–1346. https//doi.org/10.1080/14719037.2019.1632921

Bottery, S. and Mallorie, S. (2024) Social care 360. *The King's Fund*. https://www.kingsfund.org.uk/insight-and-analysis/long-reads/social-care-360. Accessed on March 15, 2024.

Brodie, R. J., Ranjan, K. R., Verreynne, M.-l., Jiang, Y., & Previte, J. (2021). Coronavirus crisis and health care: Learning from a service ecosystem perspective. *Journal of Service Theory and Practice*, *31*(2), 225–246. https//doi.org/10.1108/JSTP-07-2020-0178

Burn, E., & Needham, C. (2023). *What does it mean to describe social care as an ecosystem?* Centre for Care. https://centreforcare.ac.uk/commentary/2023/06/social-care-as-an-ecosystem/. Accessed on April 29, 2024.

Burn, E., Redgate, S., Needham, C., & Peckham, S. (2024). Implementing England's Care Act 2014: Was the Act a success and when will we know? *International Journal of Care and Caring*, *8*(1), 47–63. https//doi.org/10.1332/239788221X16916503736939

Chandler, J. D., & Vargo, S. L. (2011). Contextualization and value-in-context: How context frames exchange. *Marketing Theory*, *11*(1), 35–49. https//doi.org/10.1177/1470593110393713

Daymond, J., Knight, E., Rumyantseva, M., & Maguire, S. (2023). Managing ecosystem emergence and evolution: Strategies for ecosystem architects. *Strategic Management Journal*, *44*(4), 1–27. https//doi.org/10.1002/smj.3449

Foster, D. (2022). *Proposed adult social care charging reforms (including cap on care costs)*. House of Commons Library. https://researchbriefings.files.parliament.uk/documents/CBP-9315/CBP-9315.pdf. Accessed on March 15, 2024.

Foster, D. (2023). *Adult social care workforce in England.* https://commonslibrary.parliament.uk/research-briefings/cbp-9615/. Accessed on December 4, 2023.

Foster, D. (2024). *Funding for adult social care in England.* House of Commons Library. https://researchbriefings.files.parliament.uk/documents/CBP-7903/CBP-7903.pdf. Accessed on March 15, 2024.

French, M., Hesselgreaves, H., Wilson, R., Hawkins, M., & Lowe, T. (2023). *Harnessing complexity for better outcomes in public and non-profit services.* Policy Press. https://policy.bristoluniversitypress.co.uk/harnessing-complexity-for-better-outcomes-in-public-and-non-profit-services. Accessed on March 8, 2024.

Frow, P., McColl-Kennedy, J. R., Payne, A., & Govind, R. (2019). Service ecosystem well-being: Conceptualization and implications for theory and practice. *European Journal of Marketing*, *53*(12), 2657–2691. https//doi.org/10.1108/EJM-07-2018-0465

GOV.UK. (2022). *People at the heart of care: Adult social care reform.* https://www.gov.uk/government/publications/people-at-the-heart-of-care-adult-social-care-reform-white-paper/people-at-the-heart-of-care-adult-social-care-reform. Accessed on December 3, 2024.

GOV.UK. (2023). *Care and support statutory guidance.* https://www.gov.uk/government/publications/care-act-statutory-guidance/care-and-support-statutory-guidance. Accessed on March 15, 2024.

Hood, R. (2014). How professionals experience complexity: An interpretative phenomenological analysis. *Child Abuse Review*, *24*(2), 140–152. https//doi.org/10.1002/car.2359

House of Commons Committee of Public Accounts. (2024). *Reforming adult social care in England. Twenty-second report of session 2023–24.* https://committees.parliament.uk/publications/43918/documents/217743/default/. Accessed on March 15, 2024.

House of Lords Adult Social Care Committee. (2022). *A "gloriously ordinary life": Spotlight on adult social care. Report of Session 2022–23.* https://committees.parliament.uk/publications/31917/documents/193737/default/. Accessed on March 15, 2024.

Howard, C., & Hyland-Wood, B. (2024). The promise and performance of data ecosystems: Australia's COVID-19 response. *Policy & Politics*, *52*(1), 108–130. https//doi.org/10.1332/03055736Y2023D000000001

Levin, S. A. (1998). Ecosystems and the biosphere as complex adaptive systems. *Ecosystems*, *1*(5), 431–436. https//doi.org/10.1007/s100219900037

Lindblom, C. E. (1979). Still muddling, not yet through. *Public Administration Review*, *39*(6), 517–526. https//doi.org/10.2307/976178

Lips, M., & Eppel, E. (2022). Understanding public service provision using digital technologies during COVID-19 lockdowns in New Zealand through a complexity theory lens. *Global Public Policy and Governance*, *2*(4), 498–517. https//doi.org/10.1007/s43508-022-00057-8

Mars, M. M., & Bronstein, J. L. (2018). The promise of the organizational ecosystem metaphor: An argument for biological rigor. *Journal of Management Inquiry*, *27*(4), 382–391. https//doi.org/10.1177/1056492617706546

Mars, M. M., Bronstein, J. L., & Lusch, R. F. (2012). The value of a metaphor: Organizations and ecosystems. *Organizational Dynamics*, *41*(4), 271–280. https//doi.org/10.1016/j.orgdyn.2012.08.002

Morton, S., & Cook, A. (2023). *How do you know if you are making a difference? A practical handbook for public service organisations*. Policy Press.

Munro, E., & Hubbard, A. (2011). A systems approach to evaluating organisational change in children's social care. *British Journal of Social Work*, *41*(4), 726–743. https//doi.org/10.1093/bjsw/bcr074

National Audit Office. (2023). Reforming adult social care in England. https://www.nao.org.uk/wp-content/uploads/2023/11/Report-reforming-adult-social-care-in-England.pdf. Accessed on April 29, 2024.

Neal, J. W., Neal, Z. P., & Brutzman, B. (2022). Defining brokers, intermediaries, and boundary spanners: A systematic review. *Evidence & Policy*, *18*(1), 7–24. https//doi.org/10.1332/174426420X16083745764324

Needham, C. (2023). *A flourishing social care ecosystem*. Centre for Care. https://centreforcare.ac.uk/care-ecosystem/2023/11/flourishing-social-care-ecosystem-lbrodrick/. Accessed on April 29, 2024.

Needham, C., & Hall, P. (2023). *Social care in the UK's four nations: Between two paradigms*. Policy Press. https://bristoluniversitypress.co.uk/care-in-the-uks-four-nations. Accessed on February 24, 2024.

Needham, C., Morris, H., Miller, R., Ayton, D., O'Connor, M., Hall, K., & Skouteris, H. (2024). Social care: Time for a name change? *International Journal of Care and Caring*. (published online ahead of print 2024). https://doi.org/10.1332/23978821Y2024D000000023. Accessed on April 26, 2024.

Noddings, N. (2013) *Caring: A relational approach to ethics and moral education*. University of California Press.

Osborne, S. P. (2021). *Public service logic: Creating value for public service users, citizens, and society through public service delivery*. Routledge. https://www.routledge.com/Public-Service-Logic-Creating-Value-for-Public-Service-Users-Citizens/Osborne/p/book/9780367539337. Accessed on November 15, 2023.

Petrillo, M., & Bennett, M. (2023). *Valuing carers 2021: England and Wales*. Carers UK. https://www.carersuk.org/media/2d5le03c/valuing-carers-report.pdf. Accessed on March 8, 2024.

Pickett, S. T. A., & Cadenasso, M. L. (2002). The ecosystem as a multidimensional concept: Meaning, model, and metaphor. *Ecosystems*, *5*(1), 1–10. https//doi.org/10.1007/s10021-001-0051-y

Pollitt, C. (2016). Managerialism redux? *Financial Accountability & Management*, *32*(4), 429–447. https//doi.org/10.1111/faam.12094

Snihur, Y., Thomas, L. D. W., & Burgelman, R. A. (2018). An ecosystem-level process model of business model disruption: The disruptor's gambit. *Journal of Management Studies*, *55*(7), 1278–1316. https//doi.org/10.1111/joms.12343

Social Care Institute for Excellence. (2022). *Co-production: What it is and how to do it*. https://www.scie.org.uk/co-production/what-how/. Accessed on March 15, 2024.

Social Care Institute for Excellence. (2023). *Experiences and understandings of co-production in adult social care. Findings from SCIE's co-production survey 2023*. https://www.scie.org.uk/co-production/supporting/breaking-down-barriers/. Accessed on December 3, 2024.

Social Care Institute for Excellence. (n.d.). *Critical review tool for social care leaders*. https://www.scie.org.uk/strengths-based-approaches/leadership/review-tool/. Accessed on March 15, 2024.

Spillane, J. P. (2005). Distributed leadership. *The Educational Forum*, *69*(2), 143–150. https//doi.org/10.1080/00131720508984678

Tansley, A. G. (1935). The use and abuse of vegetational concepts and terms. *Ecology*, *16*(3), 284–307. https//doi.org/10.2307/1930070

Wilson, R., French, M., Hesselgreaves, H., Lowe, T., & Smith, M. (2024). New development: Relational public services—Reform and research agenda. *Public Money & Management*, *44*(6), 553–558. https//doi.org/10.1080/09540962.2024.2344902

RELATIONAL SERVICE DESIGN AND NEW PUBLIC MANAGEMENT: NAVIGATING A PARADOX?[1]

Marlieke Kieboom[a] and Mieke van der Bijl-Brouwer[b]

[a]*Public Service of British Columbia, Canada*
[b]*University of Sydney, Australia*

ABSTRACT

Relational public services require a relational service design approach, yet the complexity of this approach is rarely acknowledged, and examples of its application in public administration literature are few and far between. This issue challenges the design of relational public services: designing with the status quo leads to designs for and of the status quo. To bridge the gap, this book chapter develops a new typology and practice of relational public service design. The typology distinguishes between designing for relational services and service designing as relating. The former emphasizes the role of relationships in the service outcome of public service design processes while the latter focuses on the role of relating in the role and practices of designers who are service designing. An auto-ethnographic case study from British Columbia (Canada – Turtle Island) illustrates this typology and depicts the challenge of designing relationally in a complex, non-relational public administration context, in this case a dominant New Public Management (NPM) paradigm. We demonstrate that public relational service design practice cannot take hold as long as designers and public managers are not aware of NPM's dominance, precisely because NPM promotes and requires 'unrelationality', creating a paradox. To transcend this paradox, we propose expanding the concept of relationality in public service design in multiple dimensions: within the mindset of the public service designer and their practice. This involves integrating systemic design to address contextual complexity and reflexive relational design to counteract non-relational tendencies in their work environment. We conclude by suggesting future research directions.

Futures in Public Management
Critical Perspectives on International Public Sector Management, Volume 8, 211–237

ISSN: 2045-7944/doi:10.1108/S2045-794420250000008014

Keywords: Relational public services; relational design; service design; public design; public service; system design; contextual complexity; reflexivity

INTRODUCTION

> Nobody lives everywhere; everybody lives somewhere. Nothing is connected to everything; everything is connected to something. Donna Haraway - Staying with the Trouble: Making Kin in the Chthulucene (2016, p. 31)

Relational services require relational service designing. Service design is a human-centred design approach, aimed at investigating 'people's experiences, interactions and practices as a main source of inspiration for redesigning or imagining new services' (Meroni & Sangiorgi, 2011, p. 203). The service design literature has undergone a significant shift from viewing service design as the design *of* services performed by two main actors: service providers (representing an organization providing a service) and customers (users of a service) to a perspective of designing *for* service that is deeply linked to the quality of interpersonal relationships between humans as 'relational beings' (Cipolla & Manzini, 2009; Kimbell, 2011). This shift emphasizes the creation of new relations within a socio-material context rather than designing services as static objects. Designing for service, or what we refer to in this chapter as relational service design, focuses on facilitating and nurturing interactions among various actors rather than simply designing a service blueprint for a standard, transactional service.

Cipolla and Manzini argue that relational services cannot be designed in a traditional sense; they can 'only be "enabled,"' i.e. they need to be designed in such a way as to 'start up, support, and continuously sustain interpersonal encounters between the participants' (2009, p. 50). On this particular topic however exists a research-practice gap, particularly when considering the application of relational service design in public administration. Public administration is here defined as the study and implementation of government policies and programs. It involves the management of public resources to achieve the goals of the government and serve the needs of the public. Public administration finds expression in areas such as budgeting, planning, personnel management, policy analysis and service delivery. Its organizational model has evolved from the traditional bureaucratic compliance model in the 1950s to New Public Management (NPM) in 'Western' anglophone countries from the 1980s onwards. In the NPM paradigm 'attempts to improve the performance of the state have relied on command and control from above and choice and competition from outside' and are ruled by a 'targets and markets management technique' (Cooke & Muir, 2012, p. 7). It is characterized by measurement and competitiveness to generate cost-efficiency, effectiveness and fiscal accountability, reducing public service interactions between governments and citizens to a 'strategic transaction' (Wilson et al., 2024).

Some academics claim that NPM has transitioned into newer public administration paradigms such as New Public Governance (NPG) that emphasize service effectiveness and outcomes, design of inter-organizational relationships and where trust, relational capital and relational contracts act as the core governance mechanisms (Hollstein et al., 2017; Osborne, 2006; Torfing & Sørensen, 2014). However, this view is contested. In public administrations in the United Kingdom, United States, Canada and New Zealand, it has been proven that NPM has 'zombified' staying power (Wilson et al., 2024), in which 'citizen-centred design for the social good' is both used as a response to and as a measure of neoliberal austerity, or the obscuring thereof (Story, 2020, p. 205).

The objective of our study is to explore and discuss the application of relational service design in public administration. We focus on two particular aspects: the context in which relational service design is practised – in this case, the dominant organizational paradigm of NPM – and the design practices applied within. Through a case study, we demonstrate that public relational service design practices cannot fully take root unless the influence of NPM practices is recognized and openly challenged, as NPM inherently fosters 'unrelationality', leading to a paradox. We propose enabling public service designers and managers to become more aware of – and intentional about – the types of public relational design they are practicing and the contextual constraints at play, in order to make way for more relational public service outcomes. We introduce two essential elements of a bi-directional (inward-outward) practice to address the paradox: first, a systemic design practice that considers the complexity and layers of the challenge at hand and second, a reflexive relational design practice. This practice requires public managers and service designers to reflect both on their context and their own thought and position when relating to people in need of public services.

This chapter unfolds in four sections. The first section discusses the current literature on relational service design and public administration. The second section presents an auto-ethnographic case study of the application of relational service design in a public administration in British Columbia, Canada. In discussing the case and the entangled role of the public relational service designer in the third section, we identify the paradox between the need for relational service design and the anti-relational nature of public administration that is embedded within an NPM paradigm. We discuss what it requires from the relational public service designer to overcome this paradox. The fourth section contains our conclusion: although relational service design sits uncomfortably along an organizational paradigm like NPM, there are systemic and reflexive design practices that actively transcend the status quo; however, more practical examples and future research are needed. We close out with suggesting future research directions.

LITERATURE REVIEW

Design is a field of practice with a connected academic discipline of design studies. While design practice originated in architecture and product design, it is increasingly used as a process that leads to the creation of any type of intervention that – as Herbert Simon (1996) stated – changes existing situations into preferred ones, including services, procedures, strategies and policies. Designing is both a way of reasoning or 'thinking' and a way of 'doing' supported by a set of practices. Design reasoning is distinct from scientific reasoning and has been described using terms such as 'abductive reasoning' and 'framing' (Dorst, 2011), 'co-evolution of problem and solution' (Dorst & Cross, 2001) and 'synthesis' (Nelson & Stolterman, 2012). This reasoning process is supported by a wide variety of principles and practices. The most well-known and applied principles and practices in the context of the public sector include human-centred design, iterative design and co-design. Human-centred design is a group of methods and principles aimed at supporting the design of useful, useable, pleasurable and meaningful product or services for people, by gaining and applying knowledge about human beings to design products or services that meet their needs (van der Bijl-Brouwer & Dorst, 2017). Iterative design is the incremental improvement of designed interventions and the generation of knowledge about the problem domain by developing and testing prototypes (van der Bijl-Brouwer, 2019). Co-design or 'participatory design' is the involvement of citizens, end-users and other relevant stakeholders in the design process (Blomkamp, 2018).

While design reasoning requires a certain level of expertise, it is also acknowledged by various scholars that 'everybody is a designer'. Manzini refers to this natural human ability to adopt a design approach as 'diffuse design' (Manzini, 2016). In the context of the application of design in the public sector, Junginger (2015) argues that design is already present in everyday organizational life and part of the organizational DNA, 'long before any service designer or other design professional enters the scene'. Beyond the organizational context, Vink et al. (2021) recognize the agency of all actors, highlighting that many actors are involved in an ongoing process of collective designing.

Over the past two decades, design has been increasingly adopted within governments and public institutions as a way to improve policy and service innovation and create value for society (Bason, 2014; Junginger, 2013, 2015). Designers are embedded within innovation labs working alongside government organizations (McGann et al., 2018) but also increasingly hired and embedded as design professionals within government agencies (Kim et al., 2022). Design is used both to improve public services and to address more open and complex or 'wicked' challenges (Rittel & Webber, 1973). A growing body of literature speaks to design as politics. Design is a matter of choices – of what will be and thus what will not be (Fry, 2010). From this perspective, it is important to note that 'design tends to express itself from the point of view of the people involved' (Manzini, 2015, p. 93).

Relational Views in Service Design Research

One of the sub-disciplines of design studies is 'service design'. Sangiorgi and Prendiville (2017) explain how the term service design originates in service marketing literature from the 1980s (Shostack, 1984) and later appears as a phase in new service development (Edvardsson & Olsson, 1996). In this book chapter, we draw on a more recent literature that views service design as a human-centred design approach, aimed at investigating 'people's experiences, interactions and practices as a main source of inspiration for redesigning or imagining new services' (Meroni & Sangiorgi, 2011, p. 203).

An important shift in the service design literature is the move from seeing service design as being about design *of* services to design *for* service (Kimbell, 2011). Rather than seeing services as objects that can be prescribed and controlled through for example the design of a service blueprint, Kimbell describes how designing for service is aimed at the creation and development of 'proposals for new kinds of value relation within a socio-material world' (Kimbell, 2011, p. 49) and sees 'service as enacted in the relations between diverse actors, rather than as a specific kind of object to be designed' (Kimbell, 2011, p. 42).

This relational view on service design has also been promoted by Cipolla and Manzini (2009), who proposed a framework to reinforce the ability of the service design discipline to deal with the interpersonal relational qualities in services, which they refer to as a relational service. They suggest that relational services cannot be designed; they can only be enabled, i.e. 'they need to be designed in such a way as to support, and continuously sustain interpersonal encounters between the participants' (p. 50).

Human relationships have been considered in service staff–consumer relationships but also relationships between service users (see for example Postma & Stappers, 2006; Snelders et al., 2014); between staff in collaborative services (see for example Baek et al., 2017) and between heterogeneous actors in service networks (Carvalho & Goodyear, 2017). The personal characteristics of such relationships are highlighted by Cipolla and Manzini (2009). The explicit value proposition of relational design lies in prioritizing relationship building as an outcome *of* design, with a deep focus on the relationship of the designer to what is designed (Manzini, 2015). Relational design thus challenges the perceived duality between the design expert and the design*ed* (Nielsen & Bjerck, 2022). Awareness of positions of power of the designer in relation to the design*ed* is of special importance in service design (Goodwill et al., 2021; Escobar, 2018). 'In any service there will always be someone with a need and someone with the capacity to help with fulfilling this need', write Akama and Tonkinwise (in Blomkvist et al., 2023, p. 46). Awareness of these interactions is thus an essential 'service design material' (Blomkvist et al., 2023).

While the relational view on service design has been widely adopted in the literature (see e.g. van der Bijl-Brouwer, 2022), there remains a gap between academic conceptualizations of relational services and its application in practice, both in the public and private sectors.

Practising Relational Service Design in Public Administration

The emergence of relational public services is increasingly explored, i.e. in the context of social innovation (Barbalho & Engler, 2022), relational welfare states (Cottam, 2018; Mackenzie, 2021; Mendoza & Vernis, 2008; Mulgan, 2012), public administration and non-profit services (Bartels & Turnbull, 2020; French et al., 2023; Wilson et al., 2024) and healthcare innovation (Neuhoff et al., 2022). However, a typology and a description of relational service design practice in a public administration context is specifically lacking while patterning different types of relations (Story, 2020, p. 211) and design practices (Bjerk & Nielsen, 2022, p. 1068) could benefit the field. To generate greater conceptual clarity and celebrate diversity in approaches, we introduce an original typology for relational public service design practice and describe design practices and outcomes within. We make a distinction between two types of relational public service design: (1) design *for* relational public service (building on Cipolla and Manzini's framework) and (2) public service design*ing* as relating. The former focuses on how relationships impact public service outcomes, like increased trust or citizen agency. The latter focuses on the designer's relationality (role, positionality and practices) and how the public service design process affects people involved, such as changes in power dynamics or cultural beliefs.

Design for Relational Public Service

Design *for* relational public service focuses on design for the delivery of relationships *as the public service*. There are several different relational design dimensions in this type of design. First, there is design that enables human-to-human relationships in public services, e.g. more personal interactions between service users and service providers, or between communities and public service actors in a public service system. These interactions are aimed at creating resonance, openness, trust and connection reflective of the complexity, ambiguity and entanglement of human lives and are aimed towards creating conditions for people to access their own capability to thrive. This perspective draws on Cipolla and Mazini's Buberian understanding of 'interpersonal relational qualities' in which people are seen neither as users or clients nor as theoretical 'humans' but as 'relational' beings (2009). Such a viewpoint draws our intention to the whole social system of related humans and the effect that positive relationships can have on the knowledge flows, creativity, collective care and resilience of communities, organizations, families and other social systems (van der Bijl-Brouwer, 2022). A relational design approach thus marks a clear departure from the transactional nature of traditionally designed services. An example of this type of relational public service design in practice is the 'Liberated Method', a change methodology that was developed in a series of prototypes and which focused upon freeing up the creativity and compassion of front-line case-workers to address citizen needs in Northumbria (United Kingdom).

The second dimension enables improved human–service ecosystem relationships aimed at reducing system complexity, e.g. an integrated instead of a fragmented service experience based on a life experience, such as child birth, retirement or injury. Also described as 'life event design' or 'government-wide customer experience design', the relational service designer reasons from a citizen's significant 'life experience-event' and designs for a series of connected service experiences across silos: within and across (government and non-government) agencies, even across levels of government (federal, provincial, city) – rather than reasoning from within bureaucratic silos and pre-conceived, individual solutions. In this type of relational service design, there is an opportunity to enable the redesign of institutions from within and eco-systemically. An example of this type of public ecosystem design is found in The Office of Management and Budget's 'Customer Experience' design team in the United States and in New Zealand around a life-journey based design called 'SmartStart' for parents with young children. A recent study emphasizes the importance of self-organizing 'communities of service' in this work to connect capabilities of service-providing organizations and allow them to build relationships across 'life event service ecosystems' (Gros, 2020, p. 95).

A third dimension covers human–planet relationships. This type of relational public service design takes into account and strengthens a 'do no harm' relationship between people and other living and non-living beings (Shafafi & Bazoli, 2023). More-than-human design, life-centred design or regenerative design approaches have emerged in response to the pressing issues of climate change, species extinction and the rise of autonomous technologies (Thackara, 2006). These challenges invite designers to account for the needs of all living and non-living beings (i.e. animals, rivers, plants) and their interactions with humans, aiming to develop climate-resilient and life-generating environments for the future. One example of a public service design is a 'more-than-human' exhibition, a collaboration between the Town of Victoria Park and students of the University of Western Australia's School of Design. In the exhibition, citizens were invited to think about their role in creating a town where both humans and 'more than human' inhabitants can co-exist and thrive.

Service Designing as Relating

The outcomes of design processes depend on how the designer sees the world and what their position is in relation to the people, communities and places they design with and for (Manzini, 2015). The second type, service designing *as relating,* is concerned with whom or what designers are relating to in their design processes. There are several characteristics of service designing as relating.

The first characteristic concerns the consideration of power relationships within the design process (Goodwill et al., 2021). Relational public service design can be a facilitated process led by an expert designer who is mindful of their privilege, empathetic to the challenges through lived experience and committed to divesting power with the community. Yet, they are aware that power within civil society communities is not homogeneously distributed: ambiguous filters such as privilege and chance shape which ideas are emphasized. The 'Relationship Project' in the United Kingdom aims to design an infrastructure to support a thriving field of relationship-centred practice with policymakers, academics and community action groups. Within a case study in the Barking and Dagenham borough of East-London describes how 'hopeful disruption' has been a helpful relational practice for public servants (i.e. social workers) to connect to people. Hopeful disruption is 'the willingness to take risks and disrupt norms in order to create possibilities for meaningful connection, such as lowering formality in a conversation with youth.' The project acknowledges that 'the service manager, policy maker, commissioner, political leader invariably is, or has been, a patient, a service user, a carer, a parent.' (Lloyd-Rose et al., 2024, p. 63). Alternatively, relational public service design may be performed *by* community members instead of 'expert' public service designers in order to further challenge existing power imbalances. In this type of relational design, there is attention for reducing the use of extractivist, transactional and non-relational research methodologies, such as surveys, observations and interviews, as they could reinforce and perpetuate patterns of division and oppression (Udoewa & Gress, 2023, p. 101).

The second consideration is concerned with pluriversal design or the inclusion of other ways of being and thinking (Escobar, 2018). In pluriversal design the designer is aware of and applies different worldviews within design processes, i.e. colonial, western, deductive, objective worldviews and decolonial, indigenous, subjective, generative worldviews. An example of this growing body of work is presented by design practitioner–academic Manuhuia Barcham. Manuhuia, who was raised on a marae and speaks Maori, shares a case study focused on the restoration of a riverine system in Aotearoa | New Zealand. He demonstrates how different ways of being influence our ways of designing. He advocates for a pluriversal, culturally diverse design approach where 'worlds – Māori and non-Māori – can come together to create new ways of governing our relationships with ourselves and the natural world' (2022, p. 16).

A third element is relating to place and strengths. In place-based services for-with whole communities, the designer does away with the idea of individual service 'consumers' in need of separate services but instead reasons from 'place' (i.e. a neighbourhood, a river estuary) in connection to the whole community in terms of their strengths and needs. An example is a design project involving sport and physical activities teams in the borough of Camden (United Kingdom) to understand the barriers to physical activity. Instead of looking at 'the needs' of the community in relation to leisure centre services, the designers mapped 'assets' and identified what the system of physical activity is across the entire borough, asking themselves, 'how can we strengthen it?' By stimulating what is already working, they encouraged a system-wide approach to increasing physical activity in the borough that has designed itself to be unique to the individual needs of the diverse community it serves (Drummond, 2019).

Introducing a relational service design typology (see Table 1) offers public service designers conceptual clarity on which type of relational design they are applying and why in order to become more explicit in what kind of outcome they intend to achieve. This typology is not meant to be exhaustive, and other dimensions and characteristics could be added in the future. We also acknowledge that one could question whether all parts of a public administration within the concept of a nation-state should become relational in the same ways. In 'The Relational State' (2012, p. 23), Geoff Mulgan points out that some services (i.e. defence, foreign policy, tax) might require less engagement and commitment from citizens while other services require 'co-production' with citizens (i.e. health, housing, education, environment, family services).

Design for relational public service in which human-to-human relationships are centralized currently appears to be the most common focus in public relational service design. We believe that practising both types in tandem and in a non-dualistic manner, which ultimately expands our understanding of

Table 1. Typology and Description of Design Practice in Relational Public Service Design, by Kieboom and van der Bijl-Brouwer.

Type 1: Design for Relational Public Service	Dimension 1: Human-To-Human Relationships	Dimension 2: Human–Service Ecosystem Relationships	Dimension 3: Human–Planet Relationships
Designer action	Designer enables interactive, personal, relational relationships	Designer connects service experiences based on people's life events	Designer includes all living beings
Space	Between service users and service providers as 'relational human beings', between communities and public service actors	Across and within government and non-government agencies, across levels of government (Federal, Provincial, City)	Between humans and other living and non-living beings
Design outcome	To resemble the relational complexity at hand so that people can access their own capability to thrive	To reduce system complexity	To develop climate-resilient and life-generating environments for future generations
Type 2: Service Designing as Relating	**Dimension 1: Relating to Power**	**Dimension 2: Relating to Different Worldviews**	**Dimension 3: Relating to Place, Strengths**
Designer action	Designer relates to community and divests power	Designer relates to different worldviews within design processes	Designer applies place and strength-based approaches tied to a geographical area
Space	Between their own power/privilege/lived experience and that of the people they are designing with-for	Between their own worldviews and the worldviews of people they are designing with-for	Between their own histories tied to place and the place of communities in need of relational designing
Design outcome	In order to challenge existing power imbalances, address oppression, increase trust and agency	To generate and respect diverse outcomes	To lift up a whole community tied to a place

relationality, can offer better opportunities for positive and innovative outcomes for humans, communities and public service institutions. This approach mirrors the entanglement and complexity of the socio-economic, ecological or organizational context in relation to the designer and what should be designed. However, the application of relational service design practice of any type remains rare in public administration.

While the role of relationality is being explored and different types of relational design practice are being developed, there remains a significant knowledge gap on relational service design in a public administration context. What is the practice challenged by? In the next section, we introduce an auto-ethnographic case study by the first author of this chapter, Marlieke, about an attempt to design relationally in a complex service design challenge faced by a team of service designers in the Public Service of British Columbia in regard of the opioid overdose public health emergency in British Columbia, Canada | Turtle Island. The objective of the study is to further explore the application of relational service design in public design practice and demonstrate how the practice of design for relational service is intimately tied to service designing as relating while being fundamentally challenged by (elements of) its NPM context.

METHODOLOGY AND AUTO-ETHNOGRAPHIC CASE STUDY

> Relationality requires that you know about me before you can begin to understand my work. (Writes AnishinaabeKwe (Ojibway woman) Melanie Goodchild, 2021, p. 54)

To adhere to our continuing practice of reflexive relationality in this chapter, we, the Dutch authors Marlieke Kieboom and Mieke van der Bijl-Brouwer, think it is important at this stage to introduce ourselves and our position in society prior to introducing our own work on public relational service design.

We both hail from the same geographical area in the Netherlands – Zeeland; however, a sea arm splits the land apart. This sea arm explains why Marlieke speaks Dutch with a Flemish accent while Mieke grew up speaking a Zeeuws dialect. We both live or have lived in countries with a colonial past and acknowledge how colonization continues to affect the present and future. We self-identify as cis-gender women and our skin colour is white. We acknowledge our privileged position in society without erasing our own experiences with the adversarial effects of misogyny, socio-economic inequality and other late-stage capitalism ills. Our names being very similar is pure coincidence.

For the past decade, we have focused on writing, teaching and researching about how systemic thinking and design practice is applied in practical settings in society, academia and government, albeit Mieke in the context of academia and Marlieke with(in) governments. Our slight differences in how we view the world and perceive our work were respectfully explored in dialogue and through writing in the past few years. This chapter is a result of our coming together on our views and experiences on applying relational service design in our respective fields of expertise. Within this chapter, Marlieke's contribution lies in unearthing the paradox of practising relational service design within a NPM paradigm and bringing in the case study while Mieke structured our thoughts and further embedded the paradox within design literature. Our discussion and collaboration over relational public service design and its typologies has strengthened both our work and our thoughts on the field.

The following case study is chosen to expose the high levels of plurality and complexity present in the practice of designing relationally in a public service context. The three anecdotes that follow are auto-ethnographic, *post scriptum,* personal reflections of Marlieke, from her in-depth experience as a public service designer tasked with a complex service design project. Auto-ethnography is a type of ethnographic representation that consists of a blend of autobiographical and ethnographical data formed into a text which is produced by an author who has been the subject of ethnographic writing (Besio, 2009). Marlieke's relational practice to a public service design project thus includes her own personal, biassed, subjective view and is constrained by her own positionality, and as such is illustrative of the required reflexivity for relational public service designers as argued for later in this chapter. Reflexivity is here defined as 'a dynamic process of cultivating an awareness of the multiplicity of social structures internalised by oneself and others' (Vink & Koskela-Huotari, 2022, p. 6) to generate 'ongoing scrutiny of the choices that are made when identifying and integrating diverse values, priorities, worldviews, expertise, and knowledge' (Polk, 2015).

In addressing the potential critique regarding bias, it is important to draw on Lincoln and Guba's perspective on the trustworthiness of data in naturalistic settings (Schwandt et al., 2007). To uphold qualitative standards of rigour, this study emphasizes trustworthiness, richness of data and transparency. Recognizing that an unbiased account is not the objective nor is it possible, this research leverages personal experience as a source of rich, hard-won data and insight. By acknowledging and reflecting on the researcher's positionality, the study aims to enhance the depth and credibility of its findings and provide richer and more contextualized insight than a standard, detached study could achieve.

This account does not represent the views of the Government of British Columbia or the British Columbia Public Service (BCPS). However, efforts were made to ensure alignment with the BCPS Code of Conduct – particularly in regard to confidentiality and public comments – as well as the Oath of Employment, specifically in terms of impartiality. Furthermore, the account reflects the corporate values of integrity, service and courage, which public servants in British Columbia are required to uphold. Advice from an ethics inquiry was also sought and implemented in the preparation of this account.

The collection of auto-ethnographic, 'voice from the field' type anecdotes are aimed at learning from, rather than critiquing government approaches, individual government officials or current government policy. Part of the material for the anecdotes stems from reflective conversations with design colleagues. Consent was sought to publish the reflections where lived experiences of others were involved, yet to adhere to a practice of auto-ethnography further cross-validation of data was not pursued. We acknowledge that applying a relational research approach would further strengthen argumentation towards a relational public service design approach. Due to several constraints, this approach was not in the realm of possibility for this study.

FINDINGS AND DISCUSSION

This case study discusses stories that touch on sensitive topics such as drug use, death and intergenerational trauma related to the drug poisoning and overdose emergency in British Columbia, Canada | Turtle Island. The situation described is ongoing: since the Province of British Columbia declared a provincial health emergency in 2016, over 14,400 people lost their lives to a drug overdose.[2] In March 2024, unregulated drug toxicity is the leading cause of death in British

Columbia for persons aged 10–59, accounting for more deaths than homicides, suicides, accidents and natural disease combined.[3]

In 2017, the Ministry of Mental Health and Addictions was established. Soon after, a small team (two service designers, a co-op student and a service design manager) was tasked to perform a 6-month service design project, which spanned into 2018. Their initial design brief was to inform the design and development of a digital application to lower the number of overdose deaths, specifically of people who were using drugs at home alone. At the time, the statistics showed that over 90% of the overdoses occurred indoors, of which more than 50% in private homes. People who were most at risk were men, aged 30–59 and Indigenous (in Canada Turtle Island: First Nations, Métis and Inuit) people. What follows are Marlieke's anecdotes, in which we signal relational and relating practices [in brackets] to aid the reader in recognizing different types of relational service design in outcomes and processes. If there were contextual constraints at play, we indicate them with [non-]. These indicators were subjectively assigned by the authors to provoke a discussion about relationality, further underlining how the perspectives and positions of public service designers influence the process of relationally designing public services. In reality the level of relationality might be more of a sliding scale rather than a binary setting. At the time of the events, the designer was applying standard service design principles and systemic design but was not yet familiar with the concepts of relationality or NPM.

Anecdote 1 – Expanding the Design Brief and Collaboration

I – Marlieke – was tasked by a senior executive at the time to investigate how to build a digital application that could monitor if someone was overdosing and alert emergency services if needed [relational]. Not strange, given our Ministry's department was concerned with creating 'good digital service experiences' for citizens to encourage 'self-service' [non-relational]. After some initial consultations, my colleague and I questioned if a product-driven service was the right approach. What was behind the overdose statistics? With support of the senior executive we gathered our project team at the partnering Ministry. During the meeting we proposed to expand our design brief towards better understanding why people are overdosing alone, what are their (or their surviving relatives, friends) ideas for change, and if an app should be built, what would be the considerations for such an app? We framed our request as a risk-lowering approach, by not putting all our service design eggs in one basket. The partnering Ministry somewhat reluctantly agreed but was worried we wouldn't find people to talk to. After all, personal possession and use of drugs was illegal at the time and we were 'government workers'. 'I think we should outsource this work to a consultancy' [non-relating], said a public manager during the meeting. I looked over to my leadership, who in return looked at me and asked: 'can we do this?'. 'We can do this', I said, 'if the Ministry can trust and support taking a new approach, an approach that will involve all of us' [relating].

(Continued)

We named our project 'Behind the Numbers', in which we took a systemic and trauma-informed service design approach in which we intentionally looked across organizational boundaries [relational]. We first prototyped research insights with new relationships (i.e. between people, academics, policy analysts, community organizations, emergency service providers, health authorities). Second, we prototyped our services taking a co-design, trauma-informed approach [relating]. In Fig. 1 (below), we demonstrate how this approach resulted in a spiral-shaped research and design methodology.

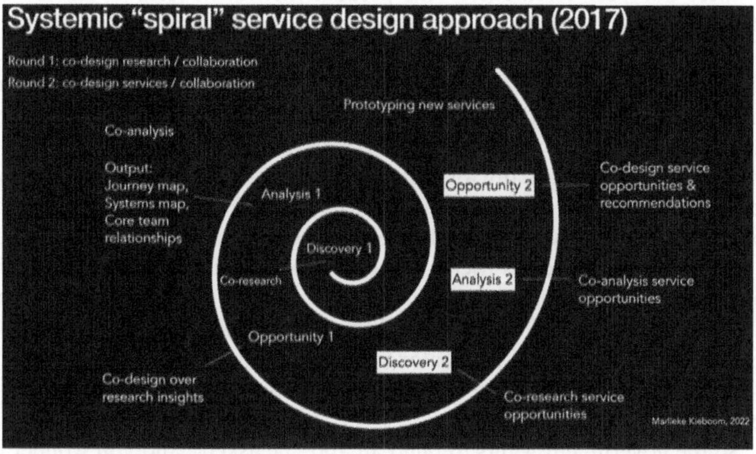

Fig. 1. Spiral-Shaped Research and Design Methodology in the Behind the Numbers Service Design Project in 2017. *Source:* Image by: Marlieke Kieboom.

The service design team ended up having over 100 conversations people with lived experience (people who use illicit substances like cocaine, crack or heroin alone, their family and friends) and with service providers across 30 different organizations (health authorities, first responders, policymakers, community action groups, academia) to better understand their experiences and the challenges they face [relational]. We also gained permission to work with a (paid) peer researcher with lived experience using drugs, a first in the history of the BC Public Service [relating]. A significant, organizational design challenge remained: the brief and funding came from just one team (Communications & Public Engagement) in one Ministry [non-relational] while the social challenge at hand crossed, and continues to cross, many policy areas (housing, income inequality, public safety, health), Ministries and even jurisdictions if we consider criminal law or the origins of the drugs [relational].

(Continued)

(Continued)

The brief was severely time constrained and thus bounded: while the drug poisoning and overdose emergency had decades to emerge, our service design*ing* budget reached as far as six months. This was in part due to the cost-recovery obligation the service design was subject to. In this 'fee for service', model a government unit charges another government unit internally for a service delivered in order to encourage cost effectiveness through competition [non-relational].

Anecdote 2 – Relating to Each Other

To meet our peer researcher – his pseudonym was 'Voices' – for his 'job interview', I had to drive 40 kilometres out of town with my service design colleague and our manager. I double-checked the address. It looked like there was just an abandoned shack with a broken front door and a trailer. Out came Voices though: in his 50s, stubble beard, hoarse voice. He reluctantly shook hands with us, 'the government ladies', as he would call us for the first little while. I had dressed casually for the occasion [relating] while my manager was wearing office attire [non-relating]. Voices showed us around his squatted home, which to him was 'a safe place to use drugs' – heroin about twice a day, in his case. Voices and his friend ran a clandestine 'safe injection service' for approximately 15 friends [relational]. They would use drugs in their presence to lower the chances of dying alone from an overdose of deadly fentanyl. In case it went wrong, they had naloxone (opioid reversal medication) kits in every room, provided by the local harm reduction community organization [relational].

'So the government wants to build an app', he asked, 'and you wonder if I would use it?'. He peered through his eyes and scuffed: 'you really think I would think about an app when I take my shot [of heroin]? Or that I trust the government?'. An awkward silence ensued. 'I get it', I said, 'it's fair to think that' [relating]. We decided to move to a cafe and continue our conversation while our manager stayed outside to take some calls. We hear about Voices' great uncle, who was a premier of BC in the 1910s. 'He'd be proud of me if he knew you wanted to hire me!', he joked. 'So, have you ever used drugs?' [relating] while looking in all seriousness at us, service designers. Was this a test, I wondered, a job interview in reverse? Reluctantly one of us admitted to having some experiences with [.] [relating]. Voices looked up, folded his hands on the table and said: 'Alright, I'll work with you. How much are you going to pay me?' [relating].

Our team ended up working with Voices for the duration of the project. His lived experience in using substances alone was invaluable to better understanding the complexity of the toxic drug emergency. He co-designed questions, hosted and facilitated conversations, connected the design team to folks with lived experience, accompanied us at meetings, and held us accountable throughout with both his knowledge and his undeniable wit and candour [relational].

(Continued)

Voices and I maintained a connection after the project ended [relational], however his work ties to the Ministry abruptly ended with the project [non-relational]. Voices often expressed jokingly how disappointed he was in the eventual outcomes of 'service design' but also stressed how proud he was of building relationships 'with the government' and for bringing stories 'deeper into government'.

Anecdote 3 – Designing With(in) Ourselves and With Each Other

Our way of researching, through forming deep relationships with service providers across organizations and through deeply relating with people with lived experience using drugs, became reflected in our relational service designs, such as 'design safe, supervised, open spaces [at work places, in hospitals, beyond shelters for unhomed people] to use drugs', 'design anti-stigma training for-with all hospital staff, from doctors to security staff' and 'design an awareness campaign to open up a Province-wide dialogue in families, workplaces'. These relational service designs in turn required creating and maintaining deep(er) relationships within ourselves, as well as within public service managers and executives. In this regard, I had to reckon with my own assumptions and knowledge gaps. I learnt to shift to 'people-first language' (i.e. from saying 'drug users' to 'people who use drugs') [relating]. One time, we co-hosted a prototyping workshop about designing safe places to use drugs with people who use drugs, but our design team failed to provide such a place – not in the least because illicit drug possession was illegal. Luckily, we found out later that our peer researcher Voices had provided his 'clandestine services' once again [relational], this time for our workshop participants behind the workshop space in the garage. We remained 'government workers', after all, he shared.

Relational design practice seemed far outside of the comfort zone of my 'higher-ups'. For instance, my leadership at the time, who although very supportive of our work, told me much later that one time I came close to 'being fired' because my comments had been 'out of line' in a meeting with a senior Ministry executive [non-relating]. It happened at a pivotal decision-making moment in which the executive appeared to lean towards prototyping a few low-hanging fruit-type service designs. In an attempt to redirect attention back towards evidence that more complex, long-term service opportunities could yield higher impacts, I decided to speak up about 'social stigma' from a personal point of view and invited people in the room to also come forward and speak to their own experiences [relational, relating]. My point being: if we, in this room, can't talk about our own personal views and problems on pain, trauma and drug use, then how could we relate or connect to and thus impact the entangled problems we are trying to work with? But the response to my action – dead silence in the room and later the threat of expulsion from the public service [non-relational] – indicated that I had

(Continued)

(Continued)

crossed an invisible but firmly drawn boundary, either between cultural and organizational hierarchies or between being a designing public service innovator focused and being an 'entangled', compassionate human.

The invisible line was far more visible for our peer researcher, for whom we didn't find a formal way of paying him a salary and who wasn't invited to meetings with executives, potentially out of fear that he could be 'disruptive' [non-relational]. Within my position of privilege and power, I found relational ways to design *with* Voices [relating], by paying him with VISA gift cards, by pre-recording a speech he wrote or by writing down his life story in our research material [relational]. While I, as a service designer, was accommodating for and committed to building (personal and professional) relationships and relations between people, between organizations through care, empathy, trust and connection, our public service managers, executives and organizational cultures and structures acted from a contradicting frame – a paradox I had yet to understand and explore.

The design project surfaced new yet more standard (transactional) service opportunities for government services (i.e. better access to healthcare, stable housing and employment) and recommendations for new laws and policy, such as the decriminalization of drugs for personal use and the safe supply of uncontaminated drugs. Here, we focus on the relational and non-relational service outcomes that could be attributed to the relational service design approach that was taken.

Relational Public Service Outcomes

Our project resulted in a 'reframe' of a province-wide media campaign that is ongoing to date. Originally set to promote abstinence from using drugs, it was redirected towards reducing social stigma by encouraging open conversations about mental health and drug use within social circles. The project cautioned against the design of a digital app. Our research found it could promote further social isolation and deepen inequality. Second, working with paid peer researchers and providing safe places to use drugs at gatherings became a more established practice for the Ministry of Mental Health and Addiction. Third, a relational service design model of co-designing collaborations across organizations prior to co-designing services enabled for a set of service opportunities that could be adopted *by* the collaborations, instead of executed by and owned by the Province. For example, a few years later a set of support services was set up for construction workers by their workers union in collaboration with harm reduction organizations. Fourth, openly published, relational service design learning materials, such as a visualization of the problem landscape (journey map, systems map), a story booklet with 25 stories from people with lived experience and service providers, an opportunity booklet, a case study and a blog, continues to enable engagement with other public service designers and public service providers over learning about the complexity of (designing in) the toxic drug emergencies.

Non-relational Public Service Outcomes

First, the cost-recovery 'consultancy' model we worked in and the position of this work within a communications team led to actioning on the anti-stigma awareness communications campaign service design *only* while the opportunities pointed at a multitude of cross-organizational service designs, also in the policy realm at a Provincial and Federal public administration level (i.e. decriminalization). These remained unactioned. Second, carefully built community advocacy organization–government relationships, which required ongoing deep attention and trust from the Ministry(ies) post-service design, waned and soured over time as deeply wished for policy changes weren't actioned on. Third, since the project heavily focused on understanding how to lower overdose *deaths* through designing new services, it may have missed an opportunity to investigate the deeper, underlying, interconnected elements of the problem: pain and trauma as long standing effects of industrialization and colonization on society (Escobar et al., 2024), a perspective that was also mentioned by research participants themselves via a systems mapping exercise. Could a design research question that was more conscious of the complexity and relationality of the challenge at hand have generated different service design outcomes? Fourth, within myself, as a human, the project resulted in experiencing cognitive dissonance after the project ended. While the situation was ongoing in public life, my professional 'relating' and relational knowledge in this public service design project ended together with the end of the project budget.

LESSONS FOR POLICY AND PRACTICE

This case study illustrates how several elements of our relational service design typology were practised in tandem. While the designers introduced relational practices and networked ways of working, the study depicts the challenge of designing relationally in a complex public administration context that portrays elements of non-relationality. Cottam (2011) points at the 'dilemma of the welfare state' as a possible cause: a service provider–recipient design frame leads to putting the onus on the individual to figure out a complex maze of discrete, disconnected services available to them, instead of making it the responsibility of the many service institutions involved who help the individual improve their situation. Yet we suspect that another factor might be at play: designers and public managers may act either unaware or unknowingly under the 'shadows' cast by dominant, non-relational management paradigms that influence their design practices.

In this case the dominant organizational paradigm portrays apparent characteristics of 'New Public Management' (NPM). NPM is 'concerned with a disaggregated state, where policy making and implementation are at least partially articulated and disengaged, and where implementation is through a collection of independent service units, ideally in competition with each other.' (Osborne, 2006, p. 5). While the service design project itself signals a shift towards a willingness to work in new, un-siloed NPG ways, the case study portrays a dominant mixture of traditional, bureaucratic public administration and NPM characteristics at play at the expense of trust, relational capital and relational contracts. This was prominently visible in the working relationship with peer researcher Voices, who was welcomed in some spaces (i.e. co-design, prototyping), yet was not fully invited in others (i.e. paid salary, executive meetings). This dynamic was also noticed in the working relationships with partners: they were strengthened during the project, then expelled after. See Table 2 for further data points to support this observation.

Table 2. Characteristics of New Public Management and New Public Governance in Relation to Service Design Practice, Including Data Points From Anecdotes, by Kieboom and van der Bijl-Brouwer.

	Characteristics of New Public Management (NPM) Work Context	Characteristics of New Public Governance (NPG) Work Context
Policy type	*Public policy and service delivery steered by hierarchy and competition*	*Public policy and service delivery steered by networks*
	Cost-recovery ('fee for service') model with strict lines and budget, threat of disciplinary measures for designer, top-down tasking and decision-making, distinction between ruler (e.g. decision-maker, service provider) and actor subjective to the ruler (e.g. citizen, peer researcher)	Temporary systemic design project 'Behind the Numbers' brought together a network of organizations
Organizational structure	*Disaggregate, separate entities*	*Cross-boundary collaborative activities and multi-organizational arrangements*
	Ministries each have their area of expertise, policy team and service delivery teams are separate	Temporary relationships and collaborations formed in systemic design project 'Behind the Numbers'
Approach	*Generate trust through contractual control*	*Generate trust through care: people as partners, co-producers of public policies and services*
	6-month contract, small budget, professional team and deadline, peer researcher not trusted to come to executive meetings.	Work with people with lived experience using drugs, peer researcher to provide coherence, central value: care. Requires a longer time frame.
Focus	*Product*	*Network*
	Focus on digital application as solution to scale care anonymously	Focus on forming relationships as service outcome to improve care in people's relations

Table 2. *(Continued)*

	Characteristics of New Public Management (NPM) Work Context	Characteristics of New Public Governance (NPG) Work Context
Service type	*Transactional service focused on cost effectiveness, performance indicators, measurement*	*Relational service focused on creating public 'good'*
	Lower overdose deaths, provide objective evidence for solutions, provide care through 'self-serve' digital option	Human relationships and relating form core design material for new services to understand pain, trauma, care
Conceptual framework	*Imports business concepts, techniques and values*	*Uses concepts from complexity sciences and systems thinking*
	Use of service design, talk of service user-service provider dichotomy	Use of system design as a way to design services
Design role and engagement	*Designer-as-public-servant (neutral)*	*Designer-as-human-public-servant (reflexive)*
	Designer acts as neutral facilitator of service design process	Designer relates to service providers, people with lived experience, different worldviews, themselves

We argue that NPM in its essence promotes and requires a certain 'unrelationality', creating a paradox for the relational public designer. On the one hand, they have to adhere to the non-relational requirements of NPM to not be met with marginalization or career limitations within the public administration they work for. On the other hand, the designer has to meet the complexity of the problem with relationality and relating in order to work with it and design services for it.

The paradox is further complicated by the unique, entangled role of the relational public service designer. First, they are a public (or civil) servant who is bound by a work contract (i.e. an oath promising impartiality and providing objective evidence to elected officials, a salary paid by public taxes in exchange for work) within the jurisdiction (i.e. a city, a country) in which the public administration resides (Altshuler & Behn, 1997). Within this role exists a myriad of roles: service provider, service designer, service manager, decision-maker, etc. Second, they are a designer who is tasked with innovating services within this jurisdiction, or the facilitation thereof, while being constrained by the public services, policies and laws that already exist (Bason, 2014, 2017; Junginger, 2013). Third, as citizens of a state they agree to form a 'collective care contract': in return for paying taxes and giving up freedom to state surveillance, constituents can vote and have access to public services when needed, i.e. public healthcare, education, the justice system, border protection and infrastructure (Wimmer, 2002). Fourth, they are a relational human being, who are part of and connected to places, communities, families, ancestors and more-than-human beings and as such hold their own beliefs and views of the world they design in (Goodchild, 2021; Haraway, 2016).

As such the performance of this entangled, quadruplet role play (public servant, designer-innovator, citizen, human) poses constraints on the practice of relational public service design and faces the public service designer with a number of dilemmas. First, public servants-as-humans are governed by the views of the ruling government at the time while public-servant-as-designers may receive feedback from humans-as-citizens about the services that need innovating, creating tensions. As such, public designer-as-citizens may even be (positively or negatively) affected by their own designs (of policy, of services) in their personal lives. In addition, the views of humans-as-citizens that public servants-as-designers design with constitute of their own designer-as-human view on the world and their position in society, which in turn forms their designs. Furthermore, public service designs by public servants-as-designers are bounded by its jurisdiction, while complex, deeply relational design challenges such as climate change and international migration often permeate geographical, judicial boundaries or even bodily boundaries of designers-as-humans (i.e. inhaling smoke from human-induced wildfires, micro-plastic in blood streams). Fourth, when public service is framed as 'collective care optimization', it aims to design the need for relationships *out* of service provision in order to scale (i.e. 'self-service', transactional service). This results in conflicting accountabilities in the workplace. While the public servant-as-designer requires intense relationship building (co-design, participatory design) and relating (to differences in power, positionality, worldview) with humans-as-citizens in order to enable a good (relational or transactional or otherwise) service, the public service manager and executive decision-maker are held accountable in non-relational, less designer areas, i.e. cost-efficiency, service delivery in a timely manner, competition and risk management.

Not designing for this paradox or the entangled, inherently relational role of the designer might explain why public relational service design attempts are met with a certain level of institutional inertia: the system reverts back to its old state once the pulse for change disappears as described in the service design outcomes of the case study. To transcend the paradox and the dilemmas it poses, we propose to expand the conceptual notion of relationality: relational public service design ought to go *beyond* the pursuit of building mere relationships and view public designers themselves as inherently complex and entangled and thus relational. Arturo Escobar (2020, p. xiii) conceptualizes 'radical relationality': 'the fact that all entities that make up the world are so deeply interrelated that they have no intrinsic, separate existence by themselves'. In this expanded view, one can only attempt to understand a person, an animal, the land and a public service in relation to oneself, to each other and to its context. Yet, we acknowledge that this view could pose philosophical or ethical dilemmas to the designing public servant: how to deliver objective evidence for decision-making?

Adjacent to the conceptual expansion, we argue that to achieve relational outcomes, public service designers themselves must become more aware of the role of relationality in their work and the complexities (i.e. non-relationality, power dynamics) their work context brings in order to design for both relational and non-relational tendencies in tandem. To aid the designer in navigating this effort we introduce two essential, bi-directional (inward-outward) elements of design practice to address the paradox and dilemmas encountered: first, a systemic design practice that considers the complexity and layers of the challenge at hand and second, a reflexive–relational design practice that promotes relating in different ways and acknowledges the choices made – and thus potential trade-offs – in a relational design practice (i.e. elevating the voice of peer researcher 'Voices' over others).

A systemic design approach raises awareness to the context in which services are designed and takes it into account as something to design with. Systemic design is concerned with design for human and more-than-human connections to enable systemic change, also referred to as system-shifting design (Drew et al., 2021). It is a design approach which combines design practice with systems thinking theory in practice, drawing on theories such as complexity science, cybernetics, ecology and design studies (van der Bijl-Brouwer, 2022). The need to integrate service design with systems thinking approaches has been argued for by various service design scholars (Blomkamp, 2022; Sangiorgi et al., forthcoming; Vink et al., 2021). Public relational service design that is integrated with such systemic approaches is an emergent approach in practice. Kim (2023), for example, identified such a practice in local government that aimed for systemic change through intentional acts of building relational infrastructures. Kim identified this practice in the case of the Southern Initiative (TSI) established in 2012 by Auckland city council, 'a place-based innovation hub focused on local and system-level transformation to improve social, economic, cultural and environmental wellbeing for current and future generations of South and West Auckland' (Burkett & Boorman, 2020). TSI is linked to a relational type of service designing through the integration of The Auckland Co-design lab. In their design training, the Co-Design Lab taught 'Whānau-centric co-design principles' that emphasize the indigenous community's decision-making power and autonomy in design processes. In addition to this relational service design approach, a systems change approach is enacted through infrastructural elements such as a networked structure, facilitating a diverse portfolio of strength-based, community-led initiatives, and a comprehensive and culturally grounded learning framework named Niho Taniwha (Burkett & Boorman, 2020). The infrastructure shows characteristics of networked governance as explained in Table 2, and as such suggests that the relational service designing practice of the Co-Design lab and the relational, systemic and networked governance structure of TSI mutually reinforce each other towards achieving relational outcomes.

A relational systemic 'outward looking' approach, as described above, needs to be complemented with a personal 'inward looking' approach. In relational systems thinking, stemming from Indigenous knowledge paradigms, the act of *relating* is included as an active component of critical systems thinking (Goodchild, 2021). Here, the designer is *part of, not separate from* what ought to be designed and is cognizant of the ontological aspects of design: what we think is what we design, and in return designs us. The focus on the act of relating requires us to take a reflexive approach in public service design contexts. In reflexive practice, designers, citizen-humans and public managers are invited to reflect together. Within this model, the designer could reflect on the choices made in the relational design process: for example, in our case study, peer researcher 'Voices' receives significant power and attention in the design process while other community voices might have been more subdued.

Reflexivity can be defined as 'a dynamic process of cultivating an awareness of the multiplicity of social structures internalised by oneself and others' (Vink & Koskela-Huotari, 2022, p. 6) to generate 'ongoing scrutiny of the choices that are made when identifying and integrating diverse values, priorities, worldviews, expertise, and knowledge' (Polk, 2015). Reflexive practice reduces chances of 'reproducing existing inequities by keeping power concentrated in the hands of those that are already privileged – be it more influential stakeholders or the designers themselves' (Goodwill et al., 2021, p. 45). The practice of structured, reoccurring reflexive personal and group practices, such as journaling, storytelling and evaluative dialogue during innovation processes can support liberating social constructs in innovation processes. It may also reduce the chances of experiencing disciplinary measures, especially if practised collectively across power hierarchies with people in leadership roles.

Reflexivity has a role to play at the institutional level, such as in public administration. Josina Vink and Kaisa Koskela-Huotari (2022) demonstrate how service design methods such as journey mapping and systems mapping in itself are reflexive tools that increase people's awareness of how institutional structures influence and shape both people's actions as well as the institutions they inhibit. Vink and Koskela-Huotari mention three core processes in which service design can play a 'reflexive' role beyond merely producing an 'end-to-end-service': revealing hidden (social) structures, noticing structural conflict and appreciating the possibility of structural change. Feminist scholar and theorist Donna Haraway offers a way to practise reflexive-relationality through 'tentacular' thinking (2016, p. 51). Tentacular thinking embraces complexity, interconnectedness and ambiguity, much like the movements of an animal's tentacles. It emphasizes the importance of staying open to multiple perspectives and being willing to engage with the messy realities of life.

CONCLUSION: NAVIGATING THE PARADOX OF PUBLIC RELATIONAL DESIGN

> For the master's tools will never dismantle the master's house. (Audre Lorde, 1984)

Public relational service design practice is complex, lacking definition and fraught with dilemmas. Practising relationality in service design within public administration thus requires careful consideration to remain true to the intention and core values of relational design. Yet a knowledge and practice gap exists in relational service design approaches in public administration. This chapter aimed to contribute to its development by introducing a public relational service design typology and by analyzing a case study on designing in a drug poisoning public health emergency in British Columbia, Canada | Turtle Island. This practical example illustrated the paradox and constraints of relational public service design in an NPM-dominant context. The performance of the public service designer, who navigates multiple roles as a public servant, designer-innovator, citizen and human, is particularly constrained. The designer must navigate the paradox between the demands of hierarchical, non-relational systems with the need for relational, participatory design practices. Furthermore, NPM creates a system in which public service managers remain far removed (no relationships) from the service delivery and design domain. They are not required to relate to the problem and not required to build relationships with people or parties experiencing the problem.

Our research suggests a deeper awareness is needed of the inherent tension between the need for relational approaches to address complex societal issues and non-relational, organizational-managerial paradigms (i.e. NPM) in which design functions. Additionally, there must be a deeper awareness of how public leaders and designers relate to the people they design with and the relationships they create. As designers, we can create conditions for relationships to be shaped and shape our own relationship to the design context. As public leaders, we can allow for designers and human-citizens to reside in a temporary place of ambiguity and uncertainty to generate space for a collective design act for humanity and be involved in the process of creating knowledge and wisdom for our collective future.

To stay true to complexity, or 'close to the trouble' in Donna Haraways' words, we propose acknowledging and intentionally designing for the dilemmas that relationality poses in a public administration context. Expanding the conceptual notion of relationality in public administration design – not only as the pursuit of building relationships but as seeing ourselves as radically relational, as 'service design material' (Blomkwist et al., 2024) – is a way to explore this. Furthermore, we examined two other practices: expanding our awareness outwards (to systems, places, contexts) and inwards (our notions of ourselves and how we relate to the world). By integrating systemic design approaches and reflexive practices, designers can better navigate the paradoxes and dilemmas they face, even within the constraints of existing public administration paradigms. Yet, the role of power makes a relational design process imminently more complex and ambiguous: there are both oppressive and liberatory dynamics to be found within civil society communities, designers and government. It is important that designers are aware of their privilege and power with regard to shaping the design process, providing access to the design process, decision-making within the design process and setting the rules of designing (Goodwill et al., 2021). In addition, a non-binary view on the complexity of power relations is required, overcoming a tendency to recreate binary dynamics: the professional experts vs experts by experience, the powerful government vs the powerless community.

We recommend further research to better understand how failure to recognize, acknowledge and consequently not design for, the complex paradox of relational public service design, may be related to incremental public service innovations that tend to maintain, not transform the status quo. Exploring the boundaries imposed by nation-states through a lens that is imaginative, cosmopolitical and radically open could also invite new ways of seeing and thus designing (see Meyer, 2019; Wimmer, 2021). In addition, further research is required to explore how relational service design practice may contribute to efforts for systemic change and shaping infrastructure that is embedded within an NPG paradigm, for example by case studies of emerging practices such as the above-mentioned Southern Initiative in Auckland, New Zealand | Aotearoa.

NOTES

1. This chapter is written on personal title and in personal time and does not represent the views or positions of the organizations the authors are affiliated with.
2. Source: https://www.cbc.ca/news/canada/british-columbia/toxic-drug-deaths-march-2024-1.7196617#:~:text=More%20than%2014%2C400%20people%20in,first%20declared%20in%20April%202016.
3. Source: https://news.gov.bc.ca/releases/2024PSSG0001-000069#:~:text=Unregulated%20drug%20toxicity%20is%20the,accidents%20and%20natural%20disease%20combined.

REFERENCES

Altshuler, A. A., & Behn, R. D. (Eds.). (1997). *Innovation in American government: Challenges, opportunities, and dilemmas*. Brookings Institution Press.

Baek, J., Sojung, K., Pahk, Y., & Manzini, E. (2017). A sociotechnical framework for the design of collaborative services. *Design Studies*, *55*, 54–78.

Barbalho, T., & Engler, R. (2022). Concepts and analysis of a relational service from the design perspective. *MIX Sustentável*, *8*(2), 31–44. https://doi.org/10.29183/2447-3073.MIX2022.v8.n2.31-44

Barcham, M. (2022). Weaving together a decolonial imaginary through design for effective river management: Pluriversal ontological design in practice. *Design Issues*, *38*(1), 5–16. https://doi.org/10.1162/desi_a_00666

Bartels, K., & Turnbull, N. (2020). Relational public administration: A synthesis and heuristic classification of relational approaches. *Public Management Review*, *22*(9), 1324–1346.

Bason, C. (2014). Introduction: The design for policy nexus. In C. Bason (Ed.), *Design for policy* (pp. 1–8). Gower Publishing Limited.

Bason, C. (2017). *Leading public design: Discovering human-centered governance*. Policy Press.

Blomkamp, E. (2018). The promise of co-design for public policy. *Australian Journal of Public Administration*, *77*, 729–743. https://doi.org/10.1111/1467-8500.12310

Blomkamp, E. (2022). Systemic design practice for participatory policymaking. *Policy Design and Practice*, *5*(1), 12–31. https://doi.org/10.1080/25741292.2021.1887576

Blomkvist, J., Clatworthy, S., & Holmlid, S. (2023). *The materials of service design*. Edward Elgar Publishing.

Burkett, I., & Boorman, C. (2020). *Review of TSI 2020 – Strengths and opportunity*. Griffith University.

Butz, D., & Besio, K. (2009). Autoethnography. *Geography Compass*, *3*, 1660–1674.

Carvalho, L., & Goodyear, P. (2017). Design, learning networks and service innovation. *Design Studies*, *55*. https://doi.org/10.1016/j.destud.2017.09.003

Cipolla, C., & Manzini, E. (2009). Relational services. *Knowledge, Technology & Policy*, *22*, 45–50. https://doi.org/10.1007/s12130-009-9066-z

Cooke, G., & Muir, R. (2012). *The possibilities and politics of the relational state (essay)*. https://www.ippr.org/articles/the-relational-state-how-recognising-the-importance-of-human-relationships-could-revolutionise-the-role-of-the-state

Cottam, H. (2011). Relational welfare. *Soundings*, *48*, 134–144.

Cottam, H. (2018). *Radical help: How we can remake the relationships between us and revolutionise the welfare state*. Hachette.

Dorst, K. (2011). The core of 'design thinking' and its application. *Design Studies*, *32*(6), 521–532.

Dorst, K., & Cross, N. (2001). Creativity in the design process: Co-evolution of problem-solution. *Design Studies*, *22*(5), 425–437.

Drew, C., Robinson, C., & Winhall, J. (2021). *System-shifting design: An emerging practice explored.* UK Design Council. https://www.designcouncil.org.uk/fileadmin/uploads/dc/Documents/Systemic%2520Design%2520Report.pdf

Drummond, S. (2019). Service design: Creating a relational state. https://sarah-drummond.com/2019/06/service-design-creating-a-relational-state/. Accessed on November 14, 2023.

Edvardsson, B., & Olsson, J. (1996). Key concepts in new service development. *Service Industries Journal*, *16*, 140–164.

Englert Corrêa Meyer, G. (2019). Strategic design, cosmopolitics and obscure situations. *Strategic Design Research Journal*, *12*(3), 417–426. https://doi.org/10.4013/sdrj.2019.123.08

Escobar, A. (2018). *Designs for the pluriverse: Radical interdependence, autonomy, and the making of worlds.* Duke University Press.

Escobar, A. (2020). *Pluriversal politics: The real and the possible.* Duke University Press.

Escobar, A., Osterweil, M., & Sharma, K. (2024). *Relationality: An emergent politics of life beyond the human.* Bloomsbury Publishing.

French, M., Hesselgreaves, H., Wilson, R., Hawkins, M., & Lowe, T. (2023). *Harnessing complexity for better outcomes in public and non-profit services* (1st ed.). Policy Press. https://doi.org/10.51952/9781447364139

Fry, T. (2010). *Design as politics.* Bloomsbury Publishing.

Goodchild, M. (2021). Relational systems thinking: That's how change is going to come, from our earth mother. *Journal of Awareness-Based Systems Change*, *1*(1), 75–103.

Goodwill, M., van der Bijl-Brouwer, M., & Bendor, R. (2021). Beyond good intentions: Towards a power literacy framework for service designers. *International Journal of Design*, *15*(3), 45–59.

Gros, C. (2020). *Life events in the design of public services: Creating communities of service in the Finnish National Aurora AI program.* MA thesis. Aalto University.

Haraway, D. J. (2016). *Staying with the trouble: Making kin in the Chthulucene.* Duke University Press.

Hollstein, B., Matiaske, W., Schnapp, K., & Schnegg, M. (2017). Networked governance: A new research perspective. https://doi.org/10.1007/978-3-319-50386-8_13

Junginger, S. (2013). Public foundations of service design. In S. Miettinen & A. Valtonen (Eds.), *Service design with theory: Discussions on change, value and methods* (2nd ed., pp. 57–69). Lapland University Press.

Junginger, S. (2015). Organizational design legacies and service design. *The Design Journal*, *18*(2), 209–226.

Kim, A. (2023). *Embedding design practices in local government: A case study analysis.* Dissertation (TU Delft). Delft University of Technology. https://doi.org/10.4233/uuid:0be72865-8064-4120-8103-c57b1321a3f0

Kim, A., van der Bijl-Brouwer, M., Mulder, I., & Lloyd, P. (2022, 25 June–3 July). *A study on strategic activities to foster design practices in a local government organization.* DRS2022, Bilbao. https://doi.org/10.21606/drs.2022.528

Kimbell, L. (2011). Designing for service as one way of designing services. *International Journal of Design*, *5*(2), 41–52.

Lloyd-Rose, M., Robinson, D., & Robinson, I. (2024). *Putting relationships first. The case for relationship-centred communities, organisations and systems.* The Relationships Project.

Mackenzie, P. (2021). *The social state: From transactional to relational public services.* https://demos.co.uk/research/the-socialstate-fromtransactional-torelational-publicservices/. Accessed on November 15, 2023.

Manzini, E. (2015). *Design, when everybody designs: An introduction to design for social innovation.* MIT.

Manzini, E. (2016). Design culture and dialogic design. *Design Issues*, *32*(1), 52–59.

McGann, M., Blomkamp, E., & Lewis, J. M. (2018). The rise of public sector innovation labs: Experiments in design thinking for policy. *Policy Sciences*, *51*(3), 249–267. https://doi.org/10.1007/s11077-018-9315-7

Mendoza, X., & Vernis, A. (2008). The changing role of governments and the emergence of the relational state. *Corporate Governance*, *8*(4). https://doi.org/10.1108/14720700810899130

Meroni, A., & Sangiorgi, D. (2011). *Design for services*. Routledge.

Mulgan, G. (2012). *Government with the people: The outlines of a relational state (essay)*. https://www.ippr.org/articles/the-relational-state-how-recognising-the-importance-of-human-relationships-could-revolutionise-the-role-of-the-state

Nelson, H. G., & Stolterman, E. (2012). *The design way – Intentional change in an unpredictable world* (2nd ed.). The MIT Press.

Neuhoff, R., Johansen, N. D., & Simeone, L. (2022). Story-centered co-creative methods: A means for relational service design and healthcare innovation. In M. A. Pfannstiel, N. Brehmer, & C. Rasche (Eds.), *Service design practices for healthcare innovation*. Springer. https://doi.org/10.1007/978-3-030-87273-1_25

Nielsen, B., & Bjerck, M. (2022). Relational design. *Proceedings of the Design Society*, *2*, 1061–1070. https://doi.org/10.1017/pds.2022.108

Osborne, S. P. (2006). The New public governance? *Public Management Review*, *8*(3), 377–387. https://doi.org/10.1080/14719030600853022

Polk, M. (2015, January). Transdisciplinary co-production: Designing and testing a transdisciplinary research framework for societal problem solving. *Futures*, *65*, 110–122.

Rittel, H. W. J., & Webber, M. M. (1973). Dilemmas in a general theory of planning. *Policy Sciences*, *4*(1973), 155–169.

Sanders, E., & Stappers, P. (2008). Co-creation and the new landscapes of design. *CoDesign*, *4*, 5–18.

Sangiorgi, D., van der Bijl-Brouwer, M., Patricio, L., & Winhall, J. (Forthcoming). A systemic perspective on service design. In L. Penin, A. Prendiville, & D. Sangiorgi (Eds.), The Bloomsbury handbook of service design: Plural perspectives and a critical contemporary agenda. Bloomsbury Visual Arts.

Sangiorgi, D., & Prendiville, A. (2017). *Designing for service: Key issues and new directions*. Bloomsbury Publishing.

Schwandt, T. A., Lincoln, Y. S., & Guba, E. G. (2007). Judging interpretations: But is it rigorous? Trustworthiness and authenticity in naturalistic evaluation. *New Directions for Evaluation*, *114*, 11–25.

Shafafi, P., & Bazoli, G. (2023). *Do no harm framework in design: A valuable business consideration. Point of view*. Designit. https://www.designit.com/stories/point-of-view/do-no-harm-in-design-part-one

Shostack, G. L. (1984). Designing services that deliver. *Harvard Business Review*, *62*, 133–139.

Simon, H. A. (1996). *The sciences of the artificial* (3rd ed.). The MIT Press.

Snelders, H., van de Garde-Perik, E., & Secomandi, F. (2014). Design strategies for human relations in services. In *Proceedings of the Fourth ServDes Conference: Service Futures*, 09–11 April 2014, Lancaster, UK. https://research.tue.nl/en/publications/design-strategies-for-human-relations-in-services

Story, C. (2020). *Obscuring austerity: The politics and practice of 'Citizen-centred' design*. PhD dissertation. York University.

Thackara, J. (2006). *In the bubble: Designing in a complex world*. The MIT Press.

Torfing, J., & Sørensen, E. (2014). The European debate on governance networks: Towards a new and viable paradigm? *Policy and Society*, *33*(4), 329–344. https://doi.org/10.1016/j.polsoc.2014.10.003

Udoewa, V., & Gress, S. (2023). Relational design. *Journal of Awareness-Based Systems Change*, *3*(1), 101–128.

van der Bijl-Brouwer, M. (2022). Service designing for human relationships to positively enable social systemic change. *International Journal of Design*, *16*(1), 23–34. https://doi.org/10.57698/v16i1.02

van der Bijl-Brouwer, M. (2019). Problem framing expertise in public and social innovation. *She ji: The Journal of Design, Economics and Innovation*, *5*(1), 29–43.

van der Bijl-Brouwer, M., & Dorst, K. (2017). Advancing the strategic impact of human-centred design. *Design Studies*, *53*, 1–23.

Vink, J., & Koskela-Huotari, K. (2022). Buliding reflexivity using service design methods. *Journal of Service Research*, *25*(3), 371–389.

Vink, J., Koskela-Huotori, K., Tronvoli, B., Edvardsson, B., & Wetter-Edman, K. (2021). Service ecosystem design: Propositions, process model, and future research agenda. *Journal of Service Research*, *24*(2), 168–186.

Wilson, R., French, M., Hesselgreaves, H., Lowe, T., & Smith, M. (2024). New development: Relational public services—Reform and research agenda. *Public Money & Management*, 1–6. https://doi.org/10.1080/09540962.2024.2344902

Wimmer, A. (2002). *Nationalist exclusion and ethnic conflict: Shadows of modernity*. Cambridge University Press.

Wimmer, A. (2021). Worlds without nation-states. Five scenarios for the very long run. *Nations and Nationalism*, *26*, 1–16.

CONCLUSION: FUTURES IN RELATIONAL PUBLIC MANAGEMENT APPROACHES

Rob Wilson[a], Hannah Hesselgreaves[a], Max French[b], Melissa Hawkins[b], David Jamieson[b], Martin King[b] and Jonathan Kimmitt[c]

[a]*Manchester Metropolitan University, UK*
[b]*Northumbria University, UK*
[c]*Durham University, UK*

> People who pronounce themselves in favour of the method of legislative reform in place of and in contradistinction to the conquest of political power and social revolution, do not really choose a more tranquil, calmer and slower road to the same goal, but a different goal. Instead of taking a stand for the establishment of a new society they take a stand for surface modifications of the old society. (Rosa Luxemburg, Reform or Revolution (1899) in 2006 – p. 58)

As we can see, there is nothing new in the idea that our experiences of the public realm can be better. Indeed, the idea of a relational approach itself is in a way re-emerging from the previous decade when it was initially proposed (Cooke & Muir, 2012; Muir & Parker, 2014; Wilson et al., 2024). The idea for this edited collection was born in the warm glow of a successful inaugural Relational Public Services Conference in the summer of 2023 and fed by stoking the coals of the fire at the subsequent 2024 event. What does this collection of chapters from around the world have to tell us about the ways and means of making relational public services part of the future ways that governments, societies, communities and members of the public achieve 'good lives'?

The intention of this concluding section is to reflect the collection's central proposal considering the conceptual and empirical contributions of the 13 chapters in the context of the emerging relational public management area. We consider what the future holds for embracing relational approaches to public

Futures in Public Management
Critical Perspectives on International Public Sector Management, Volume 8, 239–246

ISSN: 2045-7944/doi:10.1108/S2045-794420250000008015

services and public management and how the experiences and approaches described scale or apply in a meaningful way. It should help us locate some pertinent theoretical gaps and research questions, which might guide future action inquiry.

We seek to achieve this by addressing the five organizing questions we set out at the beginning of the book for public management scholars, leaders and practitioners that we consider most fundamental in moving this approach into operational reality:

- How do we now understand the potential trajectories, risks and opportunities in taking relational approaches?
- How can we address the new governance and management requirements of organizations and practice of relational public services?
- What requirements does relational management and public service reform have of new roles and responsibilities for stakeholders?
- What development and capacity building resources, including leadership, organizations and infrastructures, do we need to create to support relational management approaches?
- What is the new agenda for education, research and practice in the coming years?

HOW DO WE NOW UNDERSTAND THE POTENTIAL TRAJECTORIES, RISKS AND OPPORTUNITIES IN TAKING RELATIONAL APPROACHES?

A recent and important contribution to the debates in the area defines relational as 'the complex interconnectedness of people, socio-political contexts and governance systems' (Bartels et al., 2024). This edited collection attests to the importance of networks, collaborations and coalitions as the basis of the approach, particularly represented in Chapters 1–7. The problem for those promoting a relational stance has not been from a lack of efforts or sheer persistence of initiating these innovations. Rather, it is the sheer scale of the task of growing, implementing, and sustaining these efforts appropriately (Baines et al., 2024). The debates about 'personalisation' and 'personal budgets' from the previous decade demonstrate how a relational attempt to 'universalise' the approach at a national level can lose the community absorption and emergent properties of relationality required for personalization to work (see the work of Simon Duffy on Personal Budgets in Pell et al., 2016). The interpretation of the evidence of these as 'failed' innovations is part of the problem as everyone who has read the first half of the volume will recognize if they did not know it already from their own endeavours (Baines et al., 2024; Wilson et al., 2024).

The problem of scalability in this sphere is one of the normative linear innovation models which we are working to emphasize the sharing and spreading of new ways of working like it were jam, assuming every context is the same despite the evidence of the failure of this widespread assumption (Baines et al., 2024). The commonly assumed conventions of evidence-based policy has become a brake on the sort of systemic innovation long overdue in public management and the service environments in which public and civic life happens. Change is inevitable as the current logics and models are failing everyone: citizens, communities and the workers (professionals, staff and volunteers) and the institutions and politicians who seek to serve. So, to paraphrase previous political leaders, 'It's the emergence stupid!' The idea that we can plan and design process didactically from the centre(s), except perhaps around narrow specific issues such as taxation, is clearly increasingly limited. Evidence shows that some transactional things can be, need to be and should be done, but the limits to the effectiveness of such approaches (and the mechanisms for evidencing them) are increasingly falling short of what is needed both in terms of social outcomes but also crucially how people feel about them.

Chapters 1–5 show us at a variety of scales that people, communities and places really matter and relating with them and helping them relate to each other is fundamental for change. Nease et al. (Chapter 1), McCabe and McCabe (Chapter 2), Ormston and Macaulay (Chapter 3), James et al. (Chapter 4) and Middlekoop and Horsselenberg (Chapter 5) show that the motivation to work in a relational way is both agnostic and challenging in context for staff as well citizens and communities. Chapters 6–8 demonstrate how local public and civic organizations can be 'liberated' to enable improvements in relating to those who they are working with to set out on a mutually beneficial and generative journey. Liberation in and of itself is not enough – those seeking to make these changes whether at place, organization or practice levels require method(s). However, this calls for the additional work of civil servants determining their own motivations, purposes, capacities and capabilities after decades of having their goals, processes and performance defined for them (French et al., 2023). The opportunities are therefore significant as we can see in Chapters 9–13, which offer inspiration for starting points anywhere in the landscape (whether a leader, manager, academic, service provider, worker, volunteer or in all likelihood some combination of these). So, the trajectories, opportunities and risks of relational approaches are inherently interconnected across scales, roles, and sectors. Chapters 1 (Nease et al.), 4 (James et al.) and 5 (Middelkoop & Horsselenberg) illuminate the ways in which the worlds of practitioners and practice can be enhanced by adopting relational approaches through action learning and reflexive practices. Burn and Needham's contribution (Chapter 12), in particular, offers an ecosystems perspective to help piece together some of these actors and factors that may offer ways forward to 'steer' or 'cultivate' more constructive dialogues.

HOW CAN WE ADDRESS THE NEW GOVERNANCE AND MANAGEMENT REQUIREMENTS OF ORGANIZATIONS AND PRACTICE OF RELATIONAL PUBLIC SERVICES?

The pull of the relational comes from the repeated failure and subsequent demand generated by the current means of operating public services. Forty years of marketization has not delivered the promised efficiencies least of all the effectiveness promised and has potentially made things worse (see for instance Bevan & Hood, 2006; Hood & Dixon, 2016) Relations between citizens and the state matter from co-production (Ostrom, 1996) to street level bureaucrats (Lipsky, 1980) to public service encounters (Bartels, 2013) whether in contexts of the lives of our children, our families or our communities well-being, education, welfare, environment or health. The spaces and occasions where these interactions occur have become increasingly pressured as the contradictory pressures to channel shift, ration and streamline have come into conflict with ideas that citizens have a role in the shaping of their experiences in interactions whether it be from the results of consultation, insights from co-creation or wider forms of deliberative democracy.

Chapters 1–4 show how this sort of work can be achieved albeit always under conditions of varying precarity where inevitable shifts in the wider landscape mean that the energies of the protagonists can become subverted into sustaining programmes by whatever means possible. Bridging this apparent paradox means that we bring these things together as any approach to relationality is often underpinned by transactional elements and vice versa. Doing the work within the existing structures and logics but also working on the system is key to sustaining these approaches. The chapters from MacKeith (Chapter 6) demonstrates the different tools which support the adoption of a relational lens. Montaletti (Chapter 7) and Charlton (Chapter 8) demonstrate the power that data generated for performance management purposes can bring to the producing insight to learn as opposed to merely being managed from afar. Kieboom's work (Chapter 13) shows how design processes can be deployed in ways that are sensitive to the context of citizens and reflective of the (sometimes) challenging historical relationships between communities and the state.

This leads us to think that there is a need to open the meaning of governance and management in public service organizations and networks in these spaces. Co-production cannot just be at the point where communities and citizens encounter the state as this places an inordinate pressure on those relationships. A relational approach ought to be all the way up and all the way across and that learning in and about those spaces is the key to unlocking the insights about the ways in which we might move forward (Bartels, 2020; Hesselgreaves et al., 2021; Lowe et al., 2021; Smith et al., 2025).

WHAT DOES A RELATIONAL APPROACH TO PUBLIC SERVICE REFORM MEAN FOR NEW ROLES AND RESPONSIBILITES FOR STAKEHOLDERS?

Where the public encounter public services are potentially important points of exchange and learning – these can culminate in positive/open experiences and/or closed experiences and/or negative ones. Relationality does not preclude poor experiences of these sort of encounters but can begin to sensitize parties to an overarching aim of better exchanges and improvement through relations both of the subject at hand and more broadly. This aim in turn has implications for the ways and means in which things can be shared with the idea that supporting the exchange of resources and ideas is part of the requirements of public service infrastructure(s) (as seen in Chapters 8–12), leadership, management, governance as well as the spaces of practice. Adopting what Bartels et al. (2024) have recently called a 'relational mindset' could be the route to opening up the potential for emergent mutuality and reciprocity in the public realm. The role of stakeholders (including academics and universities) then is to move beyond the rhetorics of fairness and social injustice to take mutual responsibility for these co-productions and shape the methods and spaces in which the 'commons' can be enacted, re-enacted and governed (Heimburg et al., 2022, Heimburg & Ness, 2021). Included in these responsibilities are the adoption of learning practices, emergent learning relations and relatedly, the recording of data to inform these processes. Action learning is a practical framing for co-production – it's collective, productive and dynamic.

WHAT DEVELOPMENT AND CAPACITY BUILDING RESOURCES, INCLUDING LEADERSHIP, ORGANIZATIONS AND INFRASTRUCTURES, DO WE NEED TO CREATE TO SUPPORT RELATIONAL MANAGEMENT APPROACHES?

In our view, outcomes are improved not by a rationalistic optimization of service efficiency but by strategic investment in the dynamic capabilities of public service systems. Our own work on outcomes and complexity recently developed a working model (French et al., 2023, p. 95) of Complexity Outcomes combines three Dynamic Capabilities (Adaption; Coordinative and Stewardship) and four Complexities (Governance, Dynamic, Experiential and Compositional).

Using Teece et al.'s (1997) dynamic capabilities theory, we outlined three capabilities essential to enabling public services to respond to the emergent demands – stewardship, adaption and coordination (French et al., 2023). This framework of capabilities offers an alternative architecture to the current industrial approaches to an outcome creation process, which can in reality only ever be emergent (Lowe & Wilson 2017). Again, this is not to devalue the importance of taking a transactional approach but to recognize that not every problem can be solved in an explicit process-driven frame by efficiency alone. Re-engaging with the idea that public service organizations and the networks they operate in need to be able to deliver both incremental and radical responses to improvement and service delivery in contexts where 'market failure' is morally, ethically and politically unacceptable (for an example of this in the Children's arena Kathy Evans in Pell et al., 2016).

This points to ideas of organizational ambidexterity: a collective response that has the capacity to deploy resources in both an exploitative and exploratory way (Tushman & O'Reilly, 1996). For organizations to operate in this way requires a more loosely coupled approach to assets and resources where the meanings of data are open to interpretation and changes in interpretation. Making meaning then leads us to examine the prevailing assumptions in the leadership framings, infrastructures and platforms we are using. It also points to a change in the nature of what it is to be a civil servant and leader in this context (Hobbs, 2019; Needham & Mangan, 2014). In terms of leadership, James et al. (Chapter 5), in working in new ways, Ormston and Macaulay (Chapter 4) and in particular, Charfe's contribution (Chapter 11) encourage to reflect on the utility of social pedagogy as an enabling device to surface the issue of power in relational working. Chapters 9 (Martin) and 10 (from Martin & Jacucci) first point to the need to expand our thinking about our enterprises' (organizations and networks) resources and services to meet these new relational demands and then the means by which these might be enacted through new forms of platform as the means to support changes in practice and insight.

WHAT IS THE NEW AGENDA FOR EDUCATION, RESEARCH AND PRACTICE IN THE COMING YEARS?

What is promising from this collection is the international efforts towards building an understanding of relationality in public management. This momentum is to be captured and harnessed both as a record of shift (knowing there is movement) and of learning (knowing there is utility and value in the movement). Equally striking is the common sense of endeavour and struggle across the continents. From the macro-perspective of the United Kingdom (in parallel with other states) as the state has fragmented (Elliott et al., 2022), there has been a parallel decline of public management and administration courses (for evidence in the United Kingdom, see Bottom et al., 2022). Wider questions about the 'relevance gap' of academic Public Administration and Public Management research (including Bouckaert & Massey, 2018; Drechsler, 2019) prevail. Even eminent academics such as the late Christopher Hood and Christopher Pollitt documented the multiplicity and intersectionality of these problems over many years yet found the 'system' ground on regardless. All of this points to a fracture between public administration research and practice (Pollitt, 2017, 2020).

One of the things we have come to realize on our journeys to this point is that relational working is a 'team sport'. As our friend and colleague Mark Smith put it in the Foreword: 'the simple and profound truth (is) that if you're not learning alongside somebody then you're not working relationally with them, and the second is that a focus upon learning is more productive that a focus upon productivity.' He also is often heard rehearsing the aphorism 'we can start to do lots of this on Monday!' Those in the policymaking space will continue to agonize about the specifics of 'legislation' and 'evidence-based' approaches to 'one size fits all' intervention, but direct change is increasingly out of their hands as people in places, communities and organizations are increasingly driven to collectively act in context rather than await instruction. Our coming together is a recognition that mutuality and learning alongside from each other's action is fundamental to our success and our ability to learn from the failure. However, relational journeying is also inherently a 'contact sport'. By necessity, relationships are struggles and rewards. Education, research and practice will themselves need to adopt a relational character – education will be work-based and inquiry-driven, research and evaluation will seek relational outcomes and co-develop relational measures and practices, and parts of public service will evolve roles to occupy the spaces between service remits that ensure interactions are meaningful.

Over recent years, we have been making our own progress, and systems thinking and complexity theory have been a source of learning and inspiration for us and those who have attended the Towards Relational Public Services conference (including the contemporary work of Chris Mowles, Jean Boulton, John Seddon, Dave Byrne, Diane Finegood, Mike Jackson, David Snowden, Ralph Stacey and Robert Geyer among others). The theorizing around complexity which registers with the experiences like those written about by our contributors in this book is an important ongoing endeavour for social science.

There is a sense of optimism around the approach of slow, incremental movement building as an alternative to the deliverology 'lever-pull' mentality, which draws attention to policymaking authorities and agencies and away from policymaking. A classic dilemma in change work -–engineer it or let it emerge? – can be partially discharged by engaging with the notion of planned emergence. Our chapters offer some hope that an oscillation, and indeed complementarity (Palus et al., 2020) between inherent dualities of top down/bottom up, abstraction/concrete, open/closed system perspectives and insiderness/outsiderness, is possible as a means of absorbing relational working across practice, policy, policymaking, management and governance. Perhaps then Relational Public Mangag-ING should be regarded as an active process of engagement with and in the work not the structure or end point 'management' as such – this means perhaps that relational public services are in essence participative and reflexive. This may then be the point that cultivating the the capacity for emergence that may the aim rather than defining it. Reader you are not alone!

REFERENCES

Baines, S., Wilson, R., Fox, C., Aflaki, I. N., Bassi, A., Aramo-Immonen, H., & Prandini, R. (Eds.). (2024). *Co-creation in public services for innovation and social justice*. Policy Press.

Bartels, K. (2013). Public encounters: The history and future of face-to-face contact between public professionals and citizens. *Public Administration, 91*(2), 469–483.

Bartels, K. (2020). Transforming the relational dynamics of urban governance: How social innovation research can create a trajectory for learning and change. *Urban Studies, 57*(14), 2868–2884.

Bartels, K., Heimburg, D. V., Jordan, G., & Ness, O. (2024). Debate: A relational agenda for changing public administration research and practice. *Public Money & Management*. https://doi.org/10.1080/09540962.2024.2402873

Bevan, G., & Hood, C. (2006). What's measured is what matters: Targets and gaming in the English public health care system. *Public Administration, 84*(3), 517–538.

Bottom, K., Diamond, J., Dunning, P. T., & Elliott, I. (2022). *Handbook of teaching public administration*. Edward Elgar Publishing.

Bouckaert, G., & Massey, A. (2018). In memoriam of Christopher Pollitt. *International Review of Administrative Sciences, 84*(3), 427–429.

Cooke, G., & Muir, R. (2012). *The relational state: How recognising the importance of human relationships could revolutionise the role of the state*. Institute for Public Policy Research. https://ippr-org.files.svdcdn.com/production/Downloads/relational-state_Nov2012_9888.pdf

Drechsler, W. (2019). After public administration scholarship. In A. Massey (Ed.), *A research agenda for public administration* (pp. 220–234). Edward Elgar Publishing.

Elliott, I. C., Bottom, K. A., Carmichael, P., Liddle, J., Martin, S., & Pyper, R. (2022). The fragmentation of public administration: Differentiated and decentered governance in the (dis) United Kingdom. *Public Administration*, *100*(1), 98–115. https://doi.org/10.1111/padm.12803

French, M., Hesselgreaves, H., Wilson, R., Hawkins, M., & Lowe, T. (2023). *Harnessing complexity for better outcomes in public and non-profit services* (p. 144). Policy Press.

Heimburg, D., & Ness, O. (2021). Relational welfare: A socially just response to co-creating health and wellbeing for all. *Scandinavian Journal of Public Health*, *49*(6), 639–652.

Heimburg, D. V., Prilleltensky, I., Ness, O., & Ytterhus, B. (2022). From public health to public good: Towards universal well-being. *Scandinavian Journal of Public Health*, *50*(7), 1062–1070. https://doi.org/10.1177/14034948221124670

Hesselgreaves, H., French, M., Hawkins, M., Lowe, T., Wheatman, A., Martin, M., & Wilson, R. (2021). New development: The emerging role of a 'learning partner' relationship in supporting public service reform. *Public Money & Management*, *41*(8), 672–675.

Hobbs, C. (2019). *Systemic leadership for local governance: Tapping the resource within*. Palgrave Macmillan Cham.

Hood, C., & Dixon, R. (2016). Not what it said on the tin? Reflections on three decades of UK public management reform. *Financial Accountability & Management*, *32*(4), 383–491.

Lipsky, M. (1980). *Street-level bureaucracy: Dilemmas of the individual in public services*. Russell Sage Foundation.

Lowe, T., French, M., Hawkins, M., Hesselgreaves, H., & Wilson, R. (2021). New development: Responding to complexity in public services—The human learning systems approach. *Public Money & Management*, *41*(7), 573–576.

Lowe, T., & Wilson, R. (2017). Playing the game of outcomes based performance management. Is gamesmanship inevitable? Evidence from theory and practice. *Social Policy & Administration*, *51*(7), 981–1001.

Luxemburg, R. (2006). *Reform or revolution*. Dover Edition.

Muir, R., & Parker, I. (2014). Many to many: How the relational state will transform public services Institute for public policy reform. https://www.ippr.org/files/images/media/files/publication/2014/02/Many-to-many_Feb2014_11865.pdf

Needham, C., & Mangan, C. (2014). *The 21st century public servant*. University of Birmingham.

Ostrom, E. (1996). Crossing the great divide: Coproduction, synergy, and development. *World Development*, *24*(6), 1073–1087.

Palus, C. J., McGuire, J. B., Stawiski, S., & Torbert, W. R. (2020). The art and science of vertical development. In *Maturing leadership: How adult development impacts leadership* (pp. 59–81). Emerald Publishing Limited.

Pell, C., Wilson, R., & Lowe, T. (Eds.). (2016). *Kittens are evil: Heresies in public policy*. Triarchy Press.

Pollitt, C. (2017). Public administration research since 1980: Slipping away from the real world? *International Journal of Public Sector Management*, *30*(6–7), 555–565.

Pollitt, C. (2020). Shadowland: The poorly mapped, underdiscussed yet vital interface between public administration research and practice. In G. Bouckaert & J. Werner (Eds.), *European perspectives for public administration: The way forward* (pp. 249–271). Leuven University Press.

Smith, M., Hesselgreaves, H., Charlton, R., & Wilson, R. (2025). The 'liberated method' – A transcendent public service innovation in polycrisis. *Public Money and Management*, 1–9. https://doi.org/10.1080/09540962.2025.2456120

Teece, D. J., Pisano, G., & Shuen, A. (1997). Dynamic capabilities and strategic management. *Strategic Management Journal*, *18*(7), 509–533.

Tushman, M. L., & O'Reilly, C. A. (1996). Ambidextrous organizations: Managing evolutionary and revolutionary change. *California Management Review*, *38*(4), 8–29. https://doi.org/10.2307/41165852

Wilson, R., French, M., Hesselgreaves, H., Lowe, T., & Smith, M. (2024). New development: Relational public services—Reform and research agenda. *Public Money & Management*, *44*(6), 553–558.

INDEX

Printed and bound by CPI Group (UK) Ltd, Croydon, CR0 4YY

30/07/2026

14932632-0003